THE URBAN SCHOOL

Buildings for Education in London 1870-1980

Ron Ringshall
Dame Margaret Miles
Frank Kelsall

Greater London Council
The Architectural Press: London

First published in Great Britain by the
Greater London Council in association
with the Architectural Press Ltd.

© Department of Architecture and
Civic Design, Greater London Council
1983.

ISBN 0 85139 695 X

Typeset, printed and bound in Great Britain
for GLC Supplies Department (CRS)
Typesetting: MS Filmsetting of Frome
Printed by Page (Brothers) Ltd
of Norwich (53414) 6/83

THE URBAN SCHOOL

Buildings for Education in London 1870-1980

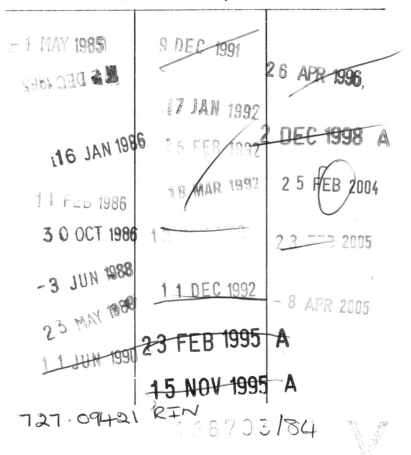

Contents

Colour illustration on front cover:
Frank Barnes Primary School,
Harley Road, London, NW3

Anyone familiar with the London education scene can instantly identify the age and nature of most of our educational buildings — Robson and Bailey School Board elementary schools, the 1902–1914 county grammar schools, the early polytechnics, the standard pattern of inter-war elementary schools, the purpose built comprehensive schools of the '50s and '60s, the primary schools of the late '40s and early '50s with their 'utility' exteriors but splendidly equipped interiors, and the cost-limited primary schools of the '70s.

What is not, perhaps, sufficiently realised, and what is strongly brought out in this valuable work, is the relationship between the various forms of construction and the related educational philosophies and economic constraints of the time.

One of the many strands in the fabric which has made the London Education Service what it is, is the close relationship between the Education Department and the architects of the Board, Council or Authority. This book, opening as it does with a penetrating analysis by Dame Margaret Miles of the development of London's education, sets architectural and technical developments firmly in their educational context.

It has been a matter for great regret that falling school rolls and increasing financial pressures have made the last thirteen years, during most of which I was Leader of the Authority, lean years for school buildings. In 1970 Pimlico, for all its adventurous design, represented the last traditional secondary school building, and the new ideas, prepared so hopefully for a 'community school' at Thomas Calton, have had few opportunities to be put into practice. Only in further education have the architects had some scope, culminating in the fine new buildings of Hammersmith and West London College, and even here financial constraints have resulted in the disappointment of still-births of the new designs for the City and Thames Polytechnics.

I am happy to be associated with this review of a great architectural tradition, which has provided successive generations of educational administrators and politicians with appropriate and memorable buildings in which to carry out their educational policies. We should not forget that we have still got hundreds of buildings which are a century old or more; one looks forward to the day when it may be possible for our architects once more to take up the task of replacing them with buildings fully adapted to modern educational and architectural idioms.

Ashley Bramall

Leader of the ILEA 1970–81

Introduction by
Peter Jones

This is an appropriate moment to publish a book about education building in London. The last few years of falling rolls, new educational initiatives and a curtailment of capital spending have combined to change the whole character of our work. 1980 witnessed the completion of the large building programmes and the big individual schools and colleges, many of which had been started on the drawing board as long ago as 1971 or 1972. For the time being very few major new buildings have appeared in the building programmes. Nearly all the work we do is for the adaptation, alteration and extension of existing premises. In fact, much more is spent annually at present on the maintenance of buildings than on capital projects.

The book marks the end of an era of school building in London which began after the last war and intensified during the fifties, sixties and early seventies. Half the floor space in the Authority's 1,500 or so schools and colleges was built during this period. It also describes the beginning of education building activity in London. The period between the setting up of the London School Board and the start of the first world war, which also included the early years of the London County Council, matched this more recent period in the intensity of its building activity. The schools from that period are nearly all still intact and continue to dominate benevolently their localities. They have many years of useful life in them yet.

Nearly all the buildings in this book are *urban* schools and colleges in the sense that they are part of the fabric of London. They have been formed by its constraints and, in turn, have contributed to its character.

For over 100 years the people who helped to commission, design and build the schools have found great personal satisfaction and a sense of achievement from direct participation in such a vital and worthwhile service. These buildings are the testimony.

Director of Architecture

3

THE BACKGROUND TO EDUCATION IN INNER LONDON

A Hundred Years of English Education

An analysis by Dame Margaret Miles

There is no English Educational System, as lecturers on educational matters delight in telling their audiences, particularly if they come from overseas. There are various sub-systems which run sometimes in harmony with and sometimes not only independently of, but in ignorance of each other. The overall pattern has grown almost haphazardly, and though the separate parts may have been planned there is no overall plan. Scotland has its own more centralized system, but English education is a complicated piece of 'ad hocery', or a palimpsest in which new patterns do not replace the old but have been imposed on them. It is therefore difficult for the would-be historian to decide which of the many lines of development to use as a framework; for example the changes in the delicate balance of power between central government and the local authorities, the diminishing influence of the churches, the development of educational ideas and their influence on school practice, social and economic changes and their effect on education, the growth of the teaching profession and many other possibilities. However, one way of getting a broad view of at least the last hundred years is by examining the great educational documents, including Acts of Parliament, administrative memoranda, and the reports of commissioned inquiries which seem to have appeared at roughly ten year intervals.

Each great legislative step forward resulted in practical activity which in turn raised many new and unforeseen issues. Thus between the Acts of Parliament committees and commissions were set up to examine what was happening and to recommend action. For example, after the 1870 Act the Cross and Bryce commissions prepared the way for the Act of 1902, and the two Hadow reports and the Spens report provided background thinking for the 1944 Act. After 1944 the pattern is less clear and though the Crowther, Newsom, and Plowden reports did a great deal of useful analysis and alerted the public to current problems, they did not open a clear way to the next stage.

Although public money was first put into education by the Liberal government of 1832 (£20,000) it was the Act of 1870 which founded public education in England and Wales.

In one of the debates which led up to the passing of the 1870 Education Act, Robert Lowe warned the House that it was possible to plan a pattern of schools which was either cheap or efficient; if it was to be efficient it would not be cheap, and if it was cheap it would not be efficient. Britain in the latter half of the 19th century needed an efficient means of instructing the children of the working classes so that her industry and commerce could keep pace with that of her rivals, particularly the new Prussian-dominated Germany which had already established an elementary school system. Government thinking, however, was quite in line with public opinion in wanting to do this as cheaply as possible; thus there were strains within the system of public education from the beginning. Support for the proposals to provide minimal instruction for the children of the poor (it is revealing how often the poor is used to define the working classes) came from varied sources; philanthropists who saw schooling as part of the general amelioration of the lot of the labouring classes, politicians who were responsible for the franchise act of 1867 (Representation of the People Act) which gave all males living in towns the vote and who now declared that 'we must educate our masters,' and others among the rich and powerful who thought a small injection of schooling might be an antidote to the spread of revolutionary ideas rooted in discontent. (Others of course thought just the opposite, that such a process would cause the masses to get above themselves.) In any event on 17th February 1870 W E Forster, son-in-law of Arnold of Rugby, and brother-in-law of Matthew, introduced his Elementary Education Bill in the House of Commons. In a clear and forthright speech he reminded the House that only two fifths of them attended some kind of school and only one third of them were still there between the ages of ten and twelve. The Bill recommended grants to existing voluntary (church and nonconformist) schools and the establishment of School Boards, with power to raise a rate, in areas not served by a voluntary school. Non-denominational religious instruction was to be given in the new schools but parents had the right to withdraw their children on conscientious grounds. Hence the elementary school pattern was to have scripture first thing every morning. 'Our subject,' said Forster 'is to complete the voluntary system, to fill up the gaps sparing public money where it can be done without.'

The Act was a great step forward and is a landmark in educational history but it contained the seeds of many future problems because, by spending as little money as possible and retaining the existing schools, the awkward dual system of voluntary and maintained schools was set up and uneasy requirements for non-denominational religious instruction were imposed on the state schools.

It was not surprising at the time that the reformers and philanthropists, who came from the public school educated upper classes, never thought of the new schools as national schools to which their own children might go. They were, as their successors have continued to do, planning schools for other people's children.

The heritage of 1870 has continued to affect succeeding generations as they try to balance the national utilitarian need for schools with the needs of the children to be educated and to spend as little as possible without losing sight of the practicalities. As they grapple with the problems of denominational and voluntary schools and the place of religion in the others, those administering the public system continue, though perhaps decreasingly so, to send their own children to private schools.

The enormous increase in the numbers of pupils attending schools after 1870 raised important questions of what next? One effect of the new Board schools had been to increase, as a result of competition, the numbers of voluntary schools and their pupils. There were many children attending the new schools who showed by their application and achievement that they needed and could profit by a longer education.

As these children stayed on at school in ever increasing numbers the schools found themselves growing what came to be known as 'higher tops', and as Britain was again slipping behind in the industrial and commercial world it became necessary to look for a public system of secondary education to produce clerks and technicians for Britain's expanding trade and growing imperial responsibilities. Already the Board of Trade's Science and Art Department was making grants to senior classes in elementary schools for Science and Art teaching and the new counties and county boroughs were empowered to spend a penny rate on technical or manual instruction, but the law made no provision for publicly maintained education beyond the age of twelve.

These developments were examined by the Cross and Bryce Reports in which there is much vigorous writing and clear analysis, and which prepared the way for the Act of 1902. A J Balfour, outlining the main provision of this Bill, emphasised the need for technical, secondary and primary education to be administered by the same authorities which were to be the new County Councils and he called for support for the Bill 'to enable us to close for ever these barren controversies which for too long have occupied our time, and in the interests alike of parental liberty and educational efficiency to terminate the present system of costly confusion'.

Unfortunately it didn't happen like that because, instead of establishing the new secondary schools on different lines including a strong technical element, the influence of the Wykhamist Sir Robert Morant was stronger than that of Michael Sadler at the Science and Art Department who had visited and admired the German technical schools. Thus the new secondary schools were modelled in curriculum, content and style on the English Public Schools, just as a generation later the secondary modern schools too often looked back to these same secondary grammar schools instead of forward to new styles and curricula. The new local authorities which were given responsibility for education by the Act were usually generous in the ways they established the new schools, not least London which was certainly prepared to spend money, and whose new secondary schools were, and are, a monument to Edwardian solidity and wealth. But, as elsewhere, their model was the already established public school and, in the case of the girls' schools, the Girls Public Day School Trust and other endowed day schools, they were therefore mostly single sex schools. A very important long term effect of these decisions was that although the new schools provided good secondary education for many of the boys and girls who formerly would not have experienced it, they did not remove the wasteful confusion referred to by Balfour. Because of the rejection of the idea of technical secondary institutions the great divide between academic and practical, general and vocational, pure and applied, was widened. The new secondary schools did not provide a second stage of education for all; they provided a route to higher education of the traditional kind for those who could pay the fees or who could win a free place. This meant there had to be selection examinations, often referred to as the 'scholarship,' which introduced another constraint, and relegated technical secondary education to second place.

The thirty years of educational history following the Act of 1870 were therefore formative, but the changes which took place were not the result of educational theory but of social and economic demand. The school buildings of the period also reflect these social attitudes and had little relation to educational theory. The four-decker elementary schools with high walls and high windows and inward-looking classrooms supervised from a central point on each floor are sometimes marginally reminiscent of prisons in which children could be instructed, watched or punished. After all, the children of the poor were often assumed to be actually or potentially like Fagin's pickpocket apprentices. As much was expected from the religious instruction given; ecclesiastical influence is also apparent in building styles. And of course ground space was expensive.

The new post-1902 secondary schools reflected a more liberal and gracious approach and many of the schools were planned on neo-Georgian lines; more outward-looking and with more space around them than the elementary schools. They were modelled on the public schools and therefore they had to have playing fields and gardens.

The thirty years which followed the 1902 Act saw steady growth in the numbers going to school and the length of the time they attended, whether in elementary or secondary schools; the 1918 (Fisher) Education Act confirmed this by making elementary education compulsory up to the age of 14 and laying the basis for day release after that age. The distance between the private (Public) schools and the state schools is clearly shown by the fact that even after almost half a century of public elementary education it was only in 1918 that

the legislators made the age at which their sons began study at public schools the leaving age for the majority of the nation's children.

In the 1920's and 30's more liberal concepts of education, as distinct from its practical uses, began to influence policy, and the Report of the first Hadow Committee on the Education of the Adolescent urged the establishment of a post-primary stage of education for all youngsters. Professor R H Tawney, who was a member of the committee, had actually written a book called 'Secondary education for all'. Of course, if the idea was to be realised the leaving age had to be raised from 14, as established in 1918, and Hadow (1926) recommended that it should be 15. In the event it was not raised until the 1944 Act and put into operation in 1947, but other results did follow the Report, and the Hadow reorganisation into primary and post-primary schools was widely adopted. If all were to have some secondary education and the majority still left school at 14, it was clear that secondary education could not begin before the age of about 11 in order that the secondary course could last for at least three years. The years before 11 were to be for primary education and the years after post-primary or secondary.

The Hadow committee reported again in 1931, this time on the primary schools and for the first time there was some recognition of children's needs, as distinct from the nation's needs. This report put its seal on those progressive ideas, still looked at askance today in some quarters, by the claim 'that the primary school is to be thought of in terms of activity and experience rather than of knowledge to be acquired and facts stored'. The philosophy of the post-primary stage had been outlined in the 1926 Report when the need was stated 'for well staffed, well equipped modern schools or senior departments with practical work and realistic studies' in 'the free and broad aim of a general and humane education which, if it remembers handwork does not forget music, and if it cherishes natural science, fosters linguistic and literary studies'. There are more fine words of this sort and it is sad to think that we are still struggling to find such a curriculum and philosophy for our secondary schools.

Hadow (1926), however, was concerned only with the post-primary years of those boys and girls, some 80% or so, who did not go to the secondary schools or the technical classes, and another commission was appointed under Sir William Spens to look at this area of secondary education. The Spens Report (1938) was severely critical of the conventionality and traditionalism of the grammar schools and the Board of Education for not fostering 'the development of secondary schools of quasi-vocational type designed to meet the needs of boys and girls who desired to enter industry and commerce at the age of 16'. Further, the report claimed

that 'the existing arrangements for the whole-time higher education of boys and girls above the age of 11 in England and Wales have ceased to correspond with the actual structure of modern society and with the economic facts of the situation'.

In the event the economic depression of the early '30s and the outbreak of war at the end of the decade inhibited any extensive action on the Hadow and Spens recommendations, but their thinking laid the foundations for the White Paper and the Act of 1944.

The war years 1939–45 demonstrated very practically the reality behind the aspirations of these education reformers who claimed that everybody could profit from and deserved a longer education, for young people who had left school at 14 responded quickly to the training and education required to become airmen, technicians, office workers and to reach high ranks in the services.

A committee of the Secondary Schools Examination Council, under the Chairmanship of Sir Cyril Norwood, Headmaster of Harrow, reported in 1943. He recommended that there should be three types of secondary school to meet the needs of the three types of children, which without research evidence and ignoring wartime experience of training they claimed to recognise. There were those 'who were interested in learning for its own sake' and who would enter the professions, those whose 'abilities lie in the field of applied science or art', and those 'who deal more easily with concrete things than ideas, who may have ability but in the realm of facts'. There was no analysis of the proportions of the children who might fall into each group, let alone whether the descriptions applied equally to girls as well as boys, or whether aptitudes might change as the child grew.

The Norwood Report was followed by the White Paper on Educational Reconstruction which laid the foundations for the Act of 1944. The Act did not follow the Norwood Report in recommending three types of school, but said that public education was to be organized in three stages, primary, secondary and further, and that efficient education throughout shall be available to meet the needs of the population of each area. The duty was placed on parents to cause every child to receive full time education suitable to *his* (sic) age, aptitude and ability. The abolition of the elementary code of expenditure and of all fees in secondary schools, and later a new basis for teachers salaries, cleared the way for the creation of a rational and just system of secondary education.

Indeed the Act of 1944 has been called revolutionary, but the revolution which should have followed has still not succeeded. There are several reasons for this. First, the imperative need to restore war damage, and to do it quickly, meant that there was no time to consider whether literal restoration of building and school style was the best course to take. Secondly, all authorities had to concentrate on providing additional primary school places for the 'bulge' in the school population, so that secondary school planning and building had to wait. Thirdly, the innate conservatism of the whole educational process inhibited far-reaching change. H C Dent, whose analysis of the Act at the time was vivid and penetrating, writes in his book 'A Century of English Education,' 'In England and Wales in 1945 few people wanted to be conservative; almost all were in favour of advance in every field of social welfare, in education, health, in housing, insurance ... the lot. What slowed things down was the almost universal fear, not overtly expressed but always there, of revolutionary change, of going too far, too fast, or both. This led inevitably to a tendency to hedge, to compromise, to doubt the wisdom of this, that or the other radical proposal, to delay, even to oppose'. This attitude led to another constraint on the new system in the retention of the Direct Grant list and the failure to abolish fees in the Direct Grant schools, as well as in the maintained secondary schools where, a fact often forgotten, fees had been paid for 50% of the pupils up to 1946.

However, the new Minister of Education, who had replaced the former President of the Board, proceeded to ask all authorities for development plans for providing secondary education for all. The responses to his request varied enormously and those of some like London or Sheffield really did start the wheels of change turning, because they decided that the best way to provide genuine equality of opportunity for all boys and girls of secondary school age was to establish large schools, with varied equipment and courses, to which all the children of the neighbourhood should go. The same pattern was developed in smaller and more homogeneous areas like Anglesey and the Isle of Man. Other local education authorities looked round at what they had got; such as an established secondary grammar school with, maybe, considerable prestige, junior classes in technical colleges, and several senior elementary schools or departments. They renamed and spent a bit more money on the ex-elementary schools and then tried to slot into the schools the Norwood Report's three types of child, regardless of the fact that the provision for each third was very uneven, with by far the greatest number of places for the type allegedly good with 'concrete things'.

This reluctance, or inability, to exploit the possibilities opened up by the 1944 Act and the improved economic condition of the majority of the public is also apparent in the post-war reports of the newly constituted Consultative Committees. Although far more analytic and realistic than the Norwood Report, neither the Crowther report on the education of the 15 to 18 year olds, most of whom did not attend school at the

time, nor the Newsom report which only dealt with half the pupils, broke really new ground or seemed to have the vision of their more far-seeing predecessors, Hadow and Spens.

None of the great reports, or Acts of Parliament, recommended the Comprehensive School as a means of establishing secondary education for all. Spens considered a multilateral organization to include technical schools but rejected it on the grounds of size. Crowther was only examining the education of the 15 to 18 year olds and Newsom, although he published at the time of Circular 10/65 (which required education authorities to prepare proposals for comprehensive education) and the peak of the comprehensive debate, made no recommendation on organization in order to avoid controversy and a split report. So it is not from central planning or national policy that the comprehensive school grew, but from the actions of certain forward-looking and powerful authorities. Of these the London County Council was a notable example.

The Comprehensive School was, and is, a splendid idea for secondary school provision for all the youngsters of the neighbourhood of the appropriate age; an idea which, if properly put into practice, could remove that 'wasteful confusion' referred to by Balfour in 1902 and wipe out the damaging three types of school concept. Furthermore, the Act of 1944 had prepared the way for it, though much needed to be done to make it a reality both in material and mental terms. First, existing schools needed to be reorganized, some closed, some expanded, some amalgamated, some adapted. Even more important than these physical changes, there had to be mental changes involving radical re-thinking about who and what the schools were for, about the curriculum and teaching methods, as well as the general style of school life and its relations with the community. Of course, the physical re-organization had to be embarked on first, and so powerful were the powers of resistance that the battle of reorganization is still not yet won today. The heads and staff of the established secondary schools dug in their heels and organized powerful emotional anti-comprehensive campaigns on the grounds that the move towards comprehensive secondary schools involved destroying good schools and generally 'levelling down'. Those very schools which had been criticised in the Spens report as being narrow, conventional and out of touch now claimed to be centres of excellence and adopted a 'noli me tangere' stance which had the effect of smearing the comprehenders with charges of educational vandalism. The unfortunate result of the concentration on the structural and organizational argument was that the basic educational issues were lost sight of, and it was left to the people actually in schools, which were at least nominally comprehensive, to work out in practice the theory of

going comprehensive.

So the spell of thirty years educational history following the 1944 Act is even more confusing than either the post-1870 or post-1902 periods, because of the nature of the challenge thrown down by the call for secondary education for all, and the enormous increase in scale in the whole educational process that this involved in sheer numbers of pupils and teachers, as well as in budgets and buildings. It was also complicated by the far greater sophistication required as the school population gets older and the standard of living of the population rises.

Immediately after the war the greatest need had been for roofs over heads, both in the Primary and Secondary sectors, so the first years were times of repair and restoration. However, it was clear that within five years there would need to be a vast increase in primary school building, followed by secondary schools five years later. The Hadow Report on the Primary Schools had both reflected and encouraged new thinking about young children's education and the post-war development of primary schools was relatively happy: planning, building and educational theory mingled.

The other great obstacle was that there were not enough teachers, and the emergency Teacher Training Colleges, often using army camps as buildings, were launched. The students were ex-service men and women, and others who because of the limited educational opportunity of the pre-war years had left elementary school at 14, or secondary school at 16, and gone into employment, and, of course, they were older. The Colleges were lively and forward looking and helped to inject new ideas about activity, discovery and child centredness into the primary schools.

It was in the secondary field, however, that the obstacles were most formidable because of the heritage of a divided system, for elementary and secondary education had not developed as two stages. For those over 11 it had remained as two types of education: secondary for a minority, open-ended and leading on to higher education, and elementary for the majority, short and dead-end, with a few trade and central schools in between the two. The Act of 1944 had cleared the ways for unifying the secondary stage of schooling by legislating for secondary schools for all and calling on local authorities to alter financial provisions so that all children over 11, whether in ex-elementary or ex-secondary schools, could have access to the same resources. Local education authorities, as we have seen, set about trying to transform their ex-elementary schools into secondary modern schools. When it is remembered that most elementary schools taught no foreign language, no science, arithmetic rather than mathematics, had asphalt yards rather than playing fields, and whose oldest pupils were 14, change was no mean task. And the immediate raising of the leaving age to 15 demanded enhanced resources and more teachers, some of whom came from the Emergency Training Colleges. The established secondary schools were changed in one major respect, the abolition of fees. Thus admission had to be by examination, the notorious 11 plus. They also suffered what many regarded as the indignity of being administered by the 'local' office which had formerly dealt only with elementary education. On the whole, though, they reinforced their former ways in curriculum and style and succeeded in keeping the two systems separate.

The role of the teachers was important in all this. The heritage of the divided system included the heritage of a divided teaching profession, for the elementary schools were staffed by teachers trained for two years in the Teacher Training Colleges, many of which had been founded by denominational bodies to train teachers for their voluntary schools. Secondary schools were staffed by university graduates who, if trained at all, and many were not, had spent one post-graduate year in a University Department of Education. The elementary 'teachers' belonged to the National Union of Teachers; the secondary school 'masters and mistresses' belonged to the Association of Head Masters, Association of Head Mistresses, and the Associations of Assistant Masters and Mistresses, known as the 'Joint Four,' and the two groups moved in different worlds. When The Burnham Committee met to re-examine teachers' salaries in the light of the Act they had taken the sensible step of recommending a basic scale for all teachers with additions for degrees and length of training. Formerly the elementary teacher, even if a graduate, as a very few were, was paid less than a similarly qualified colleague teaching children of the same age in a secondary school. The new Burnham recommendations, together with the Act itself, did help towards merging the two traditions of elementary and secondary education, but the conservatism and resistance to change of the teaching profession and many sections of the public was another great obstacle in the way of establishing secondary education for all.

In spite of these formidable obstacles progress was made and the 50's and 60's saw prodigious expansion and progress. Many authorities went ahead with reorganization plans, and comprehensive schools were established by a large number of local education authorities. Although the leaving age was not raised to 16 until 1973, the optimistic nature of the comprehensive school with its high expectations and wider opportunities meant that considerable numbers of youngsters stayed on voluntarily into the 5th and 6th forms and were entered for public examinations. This trend was encouraged by the rise in the general standard of living and full employment.

Teacher training was vastly expanded and the minimum course was extended from two to three years. Increasing numbers of pupils went on to higher

education; the splendid new comprehensive school architecture attracted attention not only in the United Kingdom but abroad. In fact, education became news and a whole new breed of educational reporters emerged who did an excellent job in keeping the public interested and informed.

Yet all was not well and progress was very uneven. A change of government in the '50's slowed up the rate of change and the new comprehensive schools found that they had not been joined by more similar schools each year. They were no longer on the crest of the wave but in the trough. The resistance of the grammar school lobby prevented many reorganisations of grammar—secondary modern groupings from taking place and the voluntary, usually denominational, schools particularly refused to co-operate. In new towns the problems were much less formidable, but in cities, where numbers of voluntary schools owned their buildings, even though these schools were maintained by the education authority, movement was minimal. Thus the organization argument went on and attempts were made to rationalize lack of progress by claiming that comprehensive schools could exist and grow alongside grammar schools; in practice this meant that comprehensives were large secondary modern schools, and residual to boot, as they were second choice to the grammar schools for the most of the 'abler' boys and girls. Co-existence with grammar schools is NOT practically possible for a 'Comprehensive' School.

In any case the continued existence of selective grammar schools perpetuated the 'historical bondage' of the two systems and kept comprehensive development in chains. Circular 10/65 did provide some release, but development following it was slower than the earlier expansion because there was no money, and possibly because the concept of comprehensiveness was blurred by the wide choice of schemes and the influence of opposition to change.

Meanwhile the heads and staff of comprehensive schools, as they struggled to release their schools, found that their claims to provide a better, broader and more relevant education for all young people fell on deaf ears. They were not praised for breaking new ground, but were condemned for not being as successful as the grammar schools in cultivating the old. So in self-defence they set out to show that they were as good as the grammar schools at the grammar schools' game; they too could achieve O and A level results. Thus energies were diverted from the second great need, that of renewal of curriculum content and teaching method and change of style, objectives and organization, and instead the comprehensives competed with the grammar schools rather than develop on their own lines. Educational conservatism and imitation, rather than change and innovation, were the order of the day and the old battle of reorganization

went on.

It was not only the success of those who resisted change which inhibited comprehensive development, for the slowing up of change outside the existing comprehensives made it more difficult for them to resolve their internal contradictions, and these were many. Never before had heads and teachers been faced with the problem of educating all teenagers up to the age of 16. The divided system meant that many had had no experience of teaching youngsters above the age of 15 and, until recently, 14. Other heads' and staffs' main experience had been teaching examination courses in grammar schools. The problems were legion and in the nature of things there could be no pause for thought about how to restyle technical education and give it equal status to traditional grammar education; about what was the place of modern language teachings; about how much science; 'maths for all;' 'to stream or not to stream;' to specialise or generalise? Indeed new thinking was essential if the two basic questions – what to teach and how to teach – were to be answered. And what about public examinations? If they are needed to round off secondary education, should all be submitted to them?

No survey of educational edvelopments over the century since 1870 can exclude critical comment on examinations for they are part of the 'historical bondage' already referred to which restricts freedom in so much of the system. Ironically enough when examinations were introduced in 19th century to select for the Civil Service, and later when elementary school schildren were examined for the 'scholarship,' the examinations were democratic instruments used to enable young prople to get on by their own merits and not because of their social and cultural background. But as secondary education expanded the competition for success at the age of 11 was yet another factor which inhibited growth of progressive education based on discovery and activity in the primary school.

In the secondary field, too, examinations have inhibited (stultified and prevented) curriculum development instead of fertilizing it, and teachers and parents have conspired to cling to the chains the examinations shackle them with rather than break free from them. The curriculum of the post-1902 secondary grammar schools was dominated by the School Certificate and Matriculation examinations. They were group exams and to gain a pass the candidate had to pass in all of five subjects, the five to include maths and french and for matriculation (admission to the university) latin. The introduction of the General Certificate of Education (GCE) in 1951 was meant to free the schools from these rigidities by introducing a subject-based exam at two levels, Ordinary at 16 and Advanced at 18. The examination was intended for qualifying purposes only and it was recommended that candidates need not be entered at Ordinary level for subjects which they were capable of taking at Advanced level. One of the more bizarre examples of educational conservatism has been the way that, instead of the examination being used as a door to freedom, it has been used in such a way as to make it as restrictive and dominating as the old system. Thus the scramble for 'O's and 'A's gathered pace as the cohorts passed through the secondary schools and, although originally the exam was not intended for pupils under 16, eager users got permission to enter 15 year olds and so the secondary modern schools joined in the sport as well.

Soon some in the grammar schools (in spite of having been selected at 11 for an academic course), as well as most of the modern schools, found the exam too difficult, and in every way inappropriate, geared as it was to university entrance. So began the demand, not for freedom from, but for yet another, lower level, examination at which more pupils might succeed. A committee was set up under the chairmanship of Robert Beloe, Education Officer for Surrey, to make proposals for a new examination, and the Certificate of Secondary Education (CSE) was the result. The new examination was to be recognised nationally, but administered by local boards whose committees and panels included a majority of teachers. The CSE has succeeded in introducing new techniques and concepts which allow course work to be assessed, and schools to make their own syllabuses and set and mark their own papers with appropriate safeguards. The new exam has possibly helped to heal the conflict between pupils' need and society's demands, but it has also served to widen the gap between the two traditions which have dogged secondary school development, since schools have found it necessary to separate the GCE 'sheep' from the CSE 'goats,' sometimes as early as the third year of secondary school. Plans for creating a single system of examining at 16 have been held up for uneducational reasons, such as the vested interests and autonomy of the examing boards, and a generalized fear among the traditionalists that such a change would inevitably mean a fall in standards. Questions as to whether a public examination at 16 is really necessary are not even listened to in spite of the saving of money and the education advantage the removal of this trauma would bring.

The most recent third of the century since 1870 has seen an unprecedented increase in the rate of change in the way people live and the range of opportunity open to them. Brighton, Blackpool and Bognor have given way to Spain, the West Indies and the Far East; 'steam radio' to multi-colour TV which brings the outside world into the living room; slow manual operations to micro-chip wizardry. All this, however, has not brushed off onto the schools which have,

on the whole, continued to look to the past for their models rather than to examine contemporary needs, let along future possibilities. This failure to change with the times must account for many of the strains from which the education system is currently suffering.

For example, an important result of the raised standard of living and other social changes has been the earlier maturity of young people both physically and, in many ways more importantly, socially. The fact that this should not prevent them from wanting to stay on at school longer would seem to show that they saw education as something they needed so that they could play their part to the best of their ability in the life of the country. Sadly, many of them from all levels of ability have not found what they were looking for and have become alienated from their schools and all that they stand for. Discipline problems and academic failure follow and the schools are blamed. Those who had always been against the changes in secondary schools seized on these signs of discontent, and one phenomenon of the sixties was the publication of a series of pamphlets under the heading Black Papers, by a group of minor academics and disgruntled teacher-politicians who asserted, without research or other evidence, that standards were falling, and that comprehensive secondary schools, together with primary schools which used activity and discovery methods, were the villains in the piece. Not surprisingly the arid controversies which followed further diverted resources and energies from educational development and were seized on by the media and certain politicians who made sure they subtly preyed on parents' fears that their children were losing out in the state system.

Thus in the seventies the brakes on educational progress were working harder than the accelerator and schools which had begun to flourish and blaze new trails in the expansionist sixties found themselves criticised for their educational stances and blamed for the ills of society. They were separated increasingly from the private sector, and more seriously, from those maintained schools which had resisted reorganization, retained a selective intake, and perpetuated the traditional pattern of the examination-dominated secondary school.

So the vast physical increase in scale in post-1944 education has not been accompanied by parallel great leaps in imaginative theory and practice. In spite of the greater social mobility of the population the maintained system has not achieved a complete or satisfactory synthesis of the two systems of elementary and secondary school it inherited, nor has there been any national policy or will to create a unified and truly comprehensive system such as exists in, for example, Sweden or even in France with her strong academic traditions. Furthermore, the habit of looking to the past has meant that instead of the

maintained and private (so-called independent) sector coming together they are drifting further apart, and Britain alone among the advanced industrial nations still recruits its top people from among the relatively small private sector. Importance is still attached to the school you went to rather than what you learnt there, so that curriculum reform and changed teaching methods struggle for recognition.

It is always difficult to compare recent history with that of the more distant past. Even so, it does appear that events and opinions seem to have moved on together towards inevitable and agreed change in a far more cohesive way in the first two thirds of the last century than in the most recent third. In this context it is perhaps significant to remember that the three great legislative steps forward, 1870, 1902, 1944 were not the monopoly of one political party. W E Forster was a Liberal, A J Balfour a Conservative, and though the reform of 1944 is often referred to as the 'Butler Act' the Conservative minister was not its 'onlie begetter,' as Chuter Ede, a Labour minister, shared in its preparation, for it was passed during the Churchill–Attlee coalition government.

There are various reasons for the fragmentation of the consensus, and indeed the polarization, of opinions which characterize recent educational history, and some stem from the widely different methods and time-scales employed by local authorities in interpreting the duties laid upon them by the 1944 Act. Then there is the unprecedentedly large scale of the whole operation and its greater complication in respect of pupil need, and the unfortunate party political disagreements about comprehensive schools. Another factor which can be seen, partly as cause and partly as effect, is the increase in the number and influence of the active participants or partners in the business of education. The Department of Education and Science (DES) is infinitely more powerful and involved than its predecessors. The Local Education Authorities (LEAs) have increased their financial commitment and their influence on educational developments as distinct from administration. Their local advisers, teachers' centres, in-service training courses, media resource centres all affect the life and work of the schools. But advice and suggestions also come from DES inspectors (HMIs) and, often on very different lines, from the researchers in Institutes and University Departments of Education. In 1960s an attempt was made to rationalize and concentrate work on the curriculum and examinations by the setting up of the Schools Council, and under its umbrella, teachers, inspectors, and administrators do work together to support the schools. But because of the English tradition of not telling the schools what to teach, in the name of so-called academic freedom, the Schools Council is not expected to actually produce an agreed curriculum, but only to give examples of good practice and make available to schools curriculum models and suggestions. It has in fact produced great numbers of valuable guides across a wide range of subjects which the schools are free to use, or not, as they wish.

Since the Newsom Report of 1965 there have been two nationally commissioned studies. The first on Primary Schools, chaired by Lady Plowden, and the later one on Special Education, that is education of the handicapped, chaired by Mrs Warnock. These were of course, widely publicised and discussed and have had some effect on educational policy, but the public and the educational world has also been bombarded by reports and surveys carried out by individuals or groups in universities and other research organizations which initially, at any rate, seem to be given the same status by the media as the major surveys. As they frequently offer contradictory views about what is happening the difficulty of getting an overview becomes greater than ever. The tendency of the press to seize on any section of such a report which will confirm any current prejudice is best illustrated with reference to what is known as the Bennett Report. This was the result of a fairly small scale study carried out by a lecturer in a department of education in Lancaster. In it there was some criticism of the activity methods used by some teachers. This was seized on as evidence of the failure of all progressive primary school teaching, the basis of whose philosophy is derived from Rousseau, Pestalozzi, Froebel, Hadow and, in our day, Plowden and others. Bennett's most interesting finding was that the best teaching he saw was by using formal methods: he has recently revised his views in the light of later statistical analysis by using the same basic figures to reach a quite different conclusion.

A later and much larger scale survey '50,000 Hours,' made a far less resounding splash in educational waters, but its findings were significant as it showed that it is not just buildings or environment or 'type' of school that determines its success in terms of good attendance, high morale and steady achievement, but some old-fashioned thing like ethos or spirit which characterises a particular institution.

In 1976 the Prime Minister, James Callaghan, called attention to some of the difficulties schools were experiencing in a speech at Ruskin College; he quoted some industrialists as saying that they were dissatisfied with the standard of the school leavers they employed; he also said that he had been impressed as he went round the country by the way school children spoke and by the nice letters they wrote to him. Of course, this last bit did not hit the headlines.

The Green Paper and the 'Great Debate' which followed the Prime Minister's speech, launched by Mrs Shirley Williams, the then Secretary of State, served rather to emphasize the number of parties in policy making and the difficulty of formulating a national view or policy, and thus it did not produce a generally acceptable chart for moving forward. It did however bring another group into focus: parents, who became partners in the education business as a result of the report by a committee on school governance chair by Tom Taylor.

In July 1980 Dr Harry Judge, of the Oxford Department of Education, warned the conference of chief education officers that the greatest threat to education in the '80s 'is an exaggerated and self-fulfilling pessimism'. It is a warning which must be heeded, particularly against the background of falling rolls, economic stringency and youth employment. There is nothing that so concentrates the mind as the approach of doom and already there are signs of rigorous and imaginative planning about how to cope with contraction, for example in realistic and exciting schemes for the 16–19 year olds, in cooperation with further education colleges; in the redeployment of teachers and the use of and search for resources; and in the design of flexible and adaptable buildings.

Furthermore, this new and, initially sad, heart searching does draw attention to what has been achieved. Full-time education for all up to the age of 16 is a far cry from Balfour's two fifths under the age of ten at school. There is, too, the much greater professionalism among teachers who now have a minimum of three years training; new degrees in education; no untrained graduates; and management courses for headteachers. And in the kaleidoscopic pattern of schools which has developed there are new and dynamic campuses like Stantonbury and Countesthorpe with strong links with adult education and the local community – heirs to Henry Morris and the village college of the thirties? Add to this exciting open plan school buildings, media resource centres and libraries, new concepts of school travel and international exchanges and a pattern of achievement emerges which is impressive.

What must not be forgotten in any short survey of educational history is that the whole operation is for people and the particular young people for whom the system is planned cannot wait in the wings while their elders argue about types of school and styles of teaching. They are *there* and they cannot have their precious five or seven years over again if the methods used during their time are deemed unsuccessful. Nor can they compare their experience with others either in the past, or currently in different schools, but their response to their experience is what matters. Those who do meet and deal with young people today are, far more often than not, vastly impressed with what they have made of their education. The immediate tragedy is that having educated them, contemporary society seems unable to employ them.

THE BOARD SCHOOLS

SCHOOLS

School Building 1870-1914

by Frank Kelsall

'We are so used to the sight of the handsome school buildings which are such prominent features in most parts of London that we are apt to think that the type has been long established. The fact is that, in 1870, a satisfactory plan for a school building was non-existent. The Board had to create it . . .'

So said Lord Reay, the Chairman of the School Board for London, in his valedictory address.[1] The Board had been brought into existence by the Education Act of 1870 and was abolished, with its powers going to the London County Council, by the Education (London) Act of 1903. Lord Reay's pride in the architectural achievements of the Board was well placed. Before 1870 the designing of schools has not been a matter of great concern; the main business of the architect was to dress up a simple plan in a currently fashionable style. But advances in educational ideas, especially those learned in Germany, and the pressing need to cater for the deprived children of the great cities, led to public intervention into the provision of schools which had long been necessary but constantly frustrated by the denominational squabbles which accompanied most educational advance in the nineteenth century. The school Board for London, the largest in the country and the recipient of great publicity, at once became a pace-setter in the design of schools. The Board's achievement was recognized by the *Builder* magazine when it reviewed the last London school designed by the Board's first architect, E R Robson. The elevation of the Latchmere School was a 'fair specimen' of Robson's School Board style, though not as picturesque as some of his efforts; 'it has, however, the merit, in regard to architectural expression, of looking like a school, and the nature and intention of the building could hardly be mistaken'.[2] This was a great compliment to Robson who had set out earlier his belief that 'a Board School should look like a Board School and like nothing else'.[3] The way in which these schools became not only notable landmarks but symbols of the late nineteenth century faith that education would provide the path to national progress was exemplified in a conversation between Holmes and Dr Watson:

'Look at those big isolated clumps of buildings rising up above the slates, like brick islands in a lead coloured sea. 'The Board schools.
'Lighthouses, my boy! Beacons of the future! Capsules, with hundreds of bright little seeds in each, out of which will spring the wiser, better England of the future.[4]'

The Education Act of 1870, which introduced education on the rates, was not the beginning of public involvement in the building of schools. From 1833

central government made grants, and from 1839 there was a specific committee of the Privy Council (which grew into the Education Department) which administered the money. But until 1870 public money was intended to augment that raised from other sources and it was spent almost entirely to aid the voluntary religious societies, especially the National Society and the British and Foreign School Society. These societies had largely supplanted the charity schools of the eighteenth century. They sponsored schools where the monitorial system permitted a large attendance to be controlled by one teacher in a large schoolroom; there were no problems in planning and it was suggested by the National Society that 'a barn furnishes no bad model and a good one may be easily converted into a school'.[5] The

style adopted by architects was related to the architectural prejudices of the day. In 1830 the St Martins National School was given a classical order by John Nash to conform with the West Strand Improvements of which it was part, though in a second application for a grant it was held necessary to advise the National Society that the elaboration of the ornament had been paid for out of subscriptions and not the first grant.[6] (Fig 1)

The Clerkenwell Parochial School of 1828 was built in a thin Tudor Gothic by William Chadwell Mylne, architect to the New River Company on whose land it stood; this was an early essay in a style which became increasingly favoured in mid-century. (Fig 2) Although religious (or perhaps denominational) enthusiasm and government assistance produced

1 *St Martin's in the Fields National School, 1830*
2 *Clerkenwell Parochial School, 1828*

many new schools in nineteenth century London, supply fell far short of demand and even further short of need. An attempt to supplement existing provision, and to cater for the least favoured children of London, was made by the Ragged Schools, but their educational and architectural contribution was marginal; an ambitious building, such as that at Lambeth (Fig 3), was exceptional for children often taught in cellars and railway arches. Of all the elementary schools provided in London prior to 1870 one stands out as a bold attempt to design a large school on a restricted site: E M Barry's St Giles's National School in Holborn was a precursor of the lofty Board Schools, raising infants, girls and boys schools in a multi-storey block (including a floor of residential accommodation a soup-kitchen in the basement) made necessary by the costs of an inner-city site and the attendance of some 1500 children of an overcrowded parish.[7] (Figs 4/5)

The St Giles' School was the result of an enterprise by the local rector, Rev A W Thorold, later Bishop of Rochester and Winchester. He was also one of the first members of the School Board for London. The Board was created by an amendment to Forster's Education Bill, which had first proposed smaller, local, education authorities for London. It was a directly elected authority, and the elections of November 1870 were a notable step in democratic advance, with women being allowed to stand for election and to vote, and the secret ballot being used. The result was a Board drawn from the area of inner London (more or less corresponding to the ILEA boundary established in 1965) of which the members were of the highest calibre. While some, especially the clergy, were there to protect their denominational interests many were elected because they had a specific interest in education. The ratepaying electorate knew what they could except, and T H Huxley's election address noted that

'it seems to be the fashion for candidates to assure you that they will do their best to spare the poverty of the ratepayers. It is proper, therefore, for me to add that I can give you no such assurance on my own behalf . . . my vote will be given for that expenditure which can be shown to be just and necessary, without reference to the question whether it may raise the rate a halfpenny.'[8]

Among other first members of the Board were William Torrens, the Member of Parliament whose amendment to the 1870 Bill had led to the creation of the Board and whose campaigns for Londoners included better housing as well as better education, and three other MPs—W H Smith, Lord Sandon and Samuel Morley. Emily Davies, founder of Girton College, and Elizabeth Garrett Anderson, Britain's first woman doctor, were the only two women on the Board. Benjamin Lucraft was pioneer trade union leader and, at

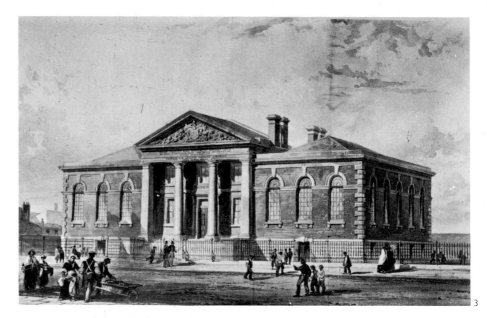

3

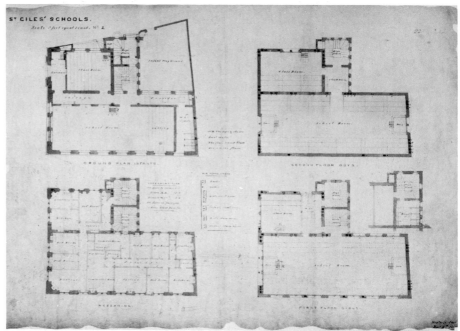

4

5

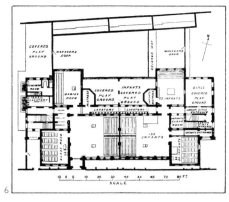

6

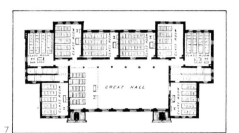

7

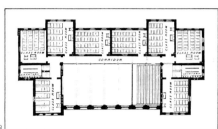

8

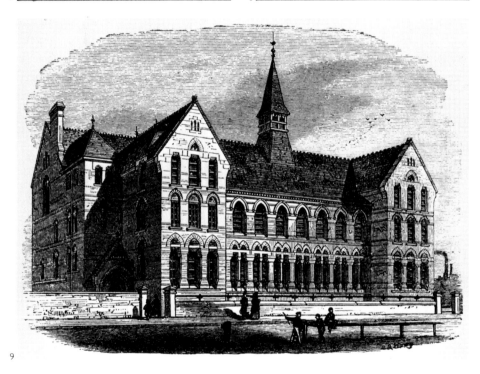

9

Surveyor to Liverpool Corporation. It was the opportunity offered by the 1870 Education Act which brought him back to London with the declared intention of becoming the country's expert on the design of schools. But his first tasks were to examine sites, survey existing school buildings offered to the Board as premises, and most importantly, to set out the terms of the competitions under which private architects were invited to submit designs for the new schools. It was not until July 1872 that Robson was given an increase in salary and the job of designing new schools. This was a recognition by the Board that school design had become more than an exercise in style; it was the expression of their own views on curriculum, on teaching method and on school management. Robson set out to acquire the necessary knowledge, visiting America and much of Europe. His observations overseas and his early work with the School Board for London led to his publication in 1874 of *School Architecture*, the first serious attempt in England to discuss the design of schools in terms of planning, use and fittings as well as style.

In his book Robson was able to review the early years of the School Board's work and the products of the limited competition system which had been first favoured. A number of architects had presented designs and two of their schools (both now demolished) were of special interest; one, Johnson Street, Stepney, for its planning and the other, Harwood House, Fulham, for its style.

The Board had decided in November 1871 to erect one school on the Prussian system, allocating one teacher to each class, rather than, as elsewhere, making do with a teacher with assistants and pupil-teachers for the whole school. This experimental school was designed by T Roger Smith and resulted in the Johnson Street School, opened in 1872 (Figs 6/9). The plan provided classrooms for girls and boys ranged round and entered from a jointly used central hall, the whole raised over the infants school; the novelty of the school's plan, if not its elevation, can be seen by comparing both with the design of Smith's other Board School, in Islington, which hardly differed from many of the voluntary schools of the period. (Figs 10/11) In 1874 Robson was not impressed with the Johnson Street plan; it was too big, it did not provide adequately for infants, and it was too expensive in its use of teachers and the building of wasted hall space when each teacher has a classroom: 'the Johnson Street School cannot, when critically considered, be regarded in the light of a success which invites general limitation.'[9] The problems which made Smith's plan ideal but impracticable in 1874 were overcome within the next fifteen years. Felix Clay's book *Modern School Buildings* of 1902 recognised it as 'practically the prototype of the modern Board School.'[10] By 1880 Robson could note that 'the proper planning of schools is better understood'[11] and in 1888, after

the other end of the social spectrum, the Board's first chairman was Lord Lawrence, former Governor General of India.

On 25 January 1871 the Board appointed a Works Committee for sites and buildings; this was chaired by Charles Reed (who succeeded Lord Lawrence as Chairman of the Board) and included in its membership Thomas Chatfield Clarke, the only architect elected to the Board. The Works Committee's task was to fulfil that part of the 1870 Act which required the Board 'to proceed at once to supply their district with sufficient public school accommodation.' After considerable fudging of the figures, to make them as manageable as possible, the Board decided that over 100,000 school places were to be provided; a more reliable figure in 1870 would have been

250,000, and that, of course, took no account of the capital's increasing population or of population movements within the Board's area. Whatever programme of building the Board decided upon there was no doubt that it would be extensive and prolonged, and that the sooner a start was made the sooner the shortfall would be made good. In fact the Board decided to build before they had precise figures of need. On 3rd May 1871 they resolved to erect twenty new schools in the most needy areas, and in July 1871 they appointed E R Robson as their architect.

Edward Robert Robson (1835–1917) had been articled to John Dobson of Newcastle; from 1857 to 1860 he worked in Gilbert Scott's office in London. He then set up on his own and secured appointments as Architect to Durham Cathedral and Architect and

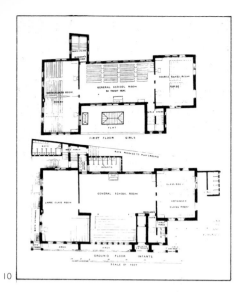

10 *Blundell Street School, 1873, plans from* The Builder.
11 *Blundell Street School, 1873, from* The Builder.

he had left the School Board for London, he acknowledged the merits of the hall and classrooms plan. The hall was 'the very pivot of the whole work;' it should be placed in the centre of the plan where 'its position there alone enables the school planner to get rid of cor-ridors.'[12] The large schoolroom developed into a school hall (which might or might not serve also as a classroom) from which other classrooms – for most of the Board School period intended to seat 60 pupils – were reached. This plan was ideal for a headteacher in schools where the abilities and self-sufficiency of assistants were in doubt; the glazed partitions between hall and classrooms facilitated supervision. In 1890 a headmaster noted that the central hall plan enabled him to 'see the state of discipline in each room without entering the room and disturb-ing the class at its work ... he may easily see what are classes where his assistance and presence is required by a weak disciplinarian or by some master newly appointed in need of help.'[13] Robson, unlike Clay, would not admit that the

central hall plan derived from German examples; it was an English plan, achieved through experience and observation of the benefits gained somewhat fortuitously at a school in Haverstock Hill; (Fig 12) here, in the only single storey school to have been built by 1874, the infants had a separate building and boys and girls schools were built on either side of what had been designed as a central playground for girls but which was floored and roofed and made to serve as a hall.[14] From 1881 the School Board insisted that a hall be provided in each school, and halls were often added to those schools of the 1870s originally built without them. Until 1891 the Education Department would not make a specific grant for a hall; this contributed to the erection of the large schools, for in them the cost of the hall could be spread among the greater number of pupils for whom a grant was payable. The hall became not just a central circulation space or means of supervision; it was a symbol of the school's unity expressed in morning assembly (which had no counterpart in

Germany), lectures or prizegivings, and examinations. (Figs 13/14)

As to the teaching methods, in the early years the supply of trained teachers who could be left in charge of a classroom without supervision was grossly inadequate and a problem which constantly exercised the minds of Board members.

It was left to T J Bailey, Robson's successor as Board Architect, to develop the school plan in the later 1880s and 1890s. Robson's early schools, frequently asymmetrical in plan and on a relatively small scale, were more informal in character than the schools usually regarded as typical products of the School Board for London. He usually designed for a school size of 700 to 800 pupils, only half the size which became usual in the 1890s. Many of the early schools were small and inadequate by the Board's later standards; by 1904 some 115 of the schools built up to 1884 had already been altered or enlarged, with the result that it is now difficult to find a Robson school where the original design remains clear. The Victoria Junior School, Hammersmith, relatively unaltered since its opening in 1876, survives as an example of the early Robson type, but even here a junior mixed school was added in 1894. (Fig 15) Bailey's schools are architecturally more coherent since he often designed for the maximum number of pupils (which he calculated at 1548) and then let the school be built in parts to meet demand. The planning requirements of the schools had become rather standardised, and Bailey set them out in a paper in 1899:

'The main line of classrooms should, if possible, face the playgrounds rather than a noisy road, and draw their light from the east, as that aspect suns up the rooms in the early morning and does not disturb them for the day. ... The hall, facing west, provides a good reservoir of sun-lighted air to help the classrooms, and, not being seated or reckoned in the accommodation, is a cheerful place into which to march the classes for recre-ation or collective purposes. Architecturally also this elevation, being the more broken up (comprising, as it does, the main lighting of the hall, the staircases, cloak and teachers' rooms and blocks, and gable end of wings) is more desirable for a street front than the long unbroken lines of classrooms, though the aspects of the site do not always allow for this.'[15]

Bailey's typical plan can be seen in a large number of schools; the Fulham Palace Road School, opened 1902, was selected by the Board to illustrate its final report; it provided on the first floor a girls school for 530 pupils in 10 classrooms. (Fig 16)

The difference in the composition of the elevations that the regular Bailey plan produced can be seen all over

12 *Haverstock Hill School, 1874, from* School Architecture.

London. The hall front of Kennington Road School opened in 1898, has its seven units clearly indicated and the separate bays emphasised by the fanciful turrets to the staircase towers and the shaped gables to the classroom wings. (Figs 17) The 'unbroken lines of classrooms' presented a greater problem if the range was not to become monotonous, and various methods were used to articulate this front; pilasters appear frequently, and at Thomas Jones School opened in 1880, alternate bays are treated as vestigial oriel windows and topped by plain gables enclosing flower plaques; (Fig 18) at Marion Richardson School, opened in 1907, two of the six classroom bays are emphasised by pediments. (Fig 19)

If Robson was not immediately enthusiastic for the central-hall planning of schools he very quickly adopted 'Queen Anne' as the style for their elevations. But he was not the pioneer. The first application of 'Queen Anne' to school design was the work of Basil Champneys at Harwood Road School, opened in October 1873; (Figs 20/21) in *School Architecture* Robson recognised it merits; its style

'is a quaint and able adaptation of old English brick architecture to modern school purposes ... this building must be regarded as possessing decided architectural character. The war between the rival styles has raged so long that we are in some danger of forgetting the existence of certain broad first principles common to the great architecture of all times and countries, and which are certainly never absent from the more conspicuous and representative examples. Among the first conditions of architecture must be ranked a regard for good form, good proportion, good grouping and, above all, good architectural character and good colour. ... The design in question must rank as thoughtful and artistic work, whatever may be our individual preference as to style.'[16]

Champneys' building was thoroughly old-fashioned in plan. It provided only a large schoolroom and one adjacent classroom; the infant school had a gallery of the type suited to regimental teaching of the very young and already being removed from the Board's schools before the end of the century. (Fig 22) An ambivalent attitude to style is apparent in Robson's *School Architecture* and was noted by another ciritic of 1874:

'Thus far the exteriors of the new

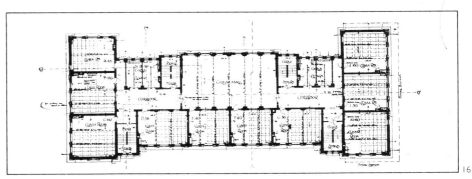

13 *Crawford Street School, 1884, interior of hall in 1906.*
14 *Crawford Street School, 1884, interior of hall in 1906.*
16 *Fulham Palace Road School, 1902, plan from the* Final Report of the School Board for London.
15 *Victoria Junior School, Becklow Road, Hammersmith, 1876.*
17 *Kennington Road School, Cormant Road, Lambeth, 1897.*

schools may be said to be Gothic in character, but very little has been expended upon ornament, everything being rigidly sacrificed to convenience and suitableness. We are not sure that some of them will not be found to be "when unadorned adorned the most." A chaste simplicity of style seems most conformable to a place for primary education.'[17]

In 1874 it can have been by no means clear that 'Queen Anne' would win the day. Winstanley Road School, opened in January 1874 (Fig 23) and described by Robson as having 'a more castellated character' is of a very different type to the Wornington Road School, opened March 1874 (Fig 24) and described by Robson as 'architectural design on the idea that, in London, good architecture of simple type may be produced on the model of the old brick architecture of London.'[18] It is reasonable to suppose that of these early schools Robson was responsible for the Gothic and J J Stevenson for the 'Queen Anne.' Robson's appointment as Board Architect did not preclude private practice and in 1871 he took Stevenson (whom he had met when both were in Scott's office) into a partnership that lasted four years. Stevenson had already built his own Red House in Bayswater Road, long recognised as influential in the change of taste in English architecture, and in 1880, in *House Architecture*, he made specific comment on the schools:

'Within the last year or two there has been a revival of the "Queen Anne" style for town houses and even for streets. The fashion seems to be spreading. It has received some accession of force from the schools of the London School Board, planted in every district of London, having been mostly built in that style. For the architecture of a few of the earliest of these I am responsible, having found by the practical experience of a house I built for myself in this manner that the style adapts itself to every modern necessity and convenience. In that case I made no attempt to follow any particular style, the style grew naturally from using ordinary materials and modes of work, and trying to give them character and interest.'[19]

Robson himself was less inclined to give Stevenson credit; in *School Architecture* he merely acknowledged 'valuable assistance' and Robson's son in 1917 noted that his father 'was occupied often in the afternoon rubbing out what John had done in the morning'.[20]

18 *Thomas Jones School, Latimer Road, Hammersmith, 1880.*
19 *Marion Richardson School, Senrab Street, Tower Hamlets, 1907.*
20 *Harwood Road School, 1873, from The Architect.*
21 *Harwood Road School, 1873, plan from School Architecture.*
22 *Oratory School infants gallery in 1905; this was not a Board School.*
23 *Winstanley Road School, 1874, from School Architecture.*
24 *Wornington Road School, 1874, from School Architecture.*

18

19

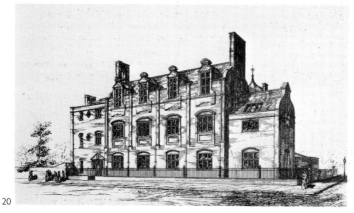

20

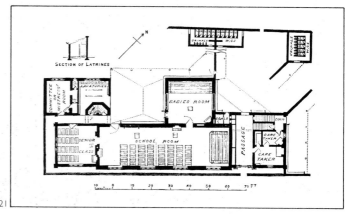

21

22

23

24

Nonetheless, Stevenson's 'Queen Anne', adapted to the needs of schools, dominated the 1870s. It was practical, it expressed 'civil rather than ecclesiastical character', and it no doubt satisfied those Board members who were drawn from the group of intellectuals to whom the new style represented progressive taste. In a paper read to an architectural conference in 1874 Stevenson justified the practical nature of 'Queen Anne':

'Take the ordinary conditions of London building – stock bricks and sliding sash windows. A flat arch of red cut bricks is the cheapest mode of forming a window-head: the red colour is naturally carried down the sides of the window, forming a frame; and is used also to emphasise the angles of the building. As the gables rise above the roofs it costs nothing, and gives interest and character ... to mould them into curves and sweeps. The appearance of wall-surface carried over the openings, which, in Gothic, the tracery and iron bars and reflecting surface of thick stained glass had taught us to appreciate, is obtained by massive wooden frames and sash bars set, where the silly interference of the Building Act does not prevent, almost flush with the walls, while to the rooms inside these thick sash bars give a feeling of enclosure and comfort. With these simple elements the style is complete, without any expenditure whatever on ornament. ... There is nothing but harmony and proportion to depend on for effect. We may, if we have money to spare, get horizontal division of the facade, in this style as in Gothic, by string courses and cornices, and we have the advantage over Gothic that we can obtain vertical division by pilasters. ... The style in all its forms has the merit of truthfulness; it is the outcome of our common modern wants picturesquely expressed. In its mode of working and details it is the common vernacular style in which the British workman has been apprenticed, with some new life from Gothic added. ...'[21]

The desire to combine this non-dogmatic, straightforward, style with the local vernacular led Robson to relate it to a specifically London context:

'Specimens of good and thoughtful brickwork in sufficient number still remain scattered among the old architecture of the city and its suburbs, to form the basis of a good style suited to modern requirements. Hackney and Putney, Chelsea and Deptford, all furnish old examples. In London, the plainer and less expensive buildings, forming by far the most numerous class, must always be constructed in brick.'

In terms of the period to be looked at Robson claimed that

'the only really simple brick style available as a foundation is that of the time of the Jameses, Queen Anne and the early Georges, whatever some enthusiasts may think of its value in point of art. The buildings then approach more nearly the spirit of our own time, and are invariably true in point of construction and workmanlike feeling.'[22]

This was an architecture which, by 1880, could be advocated by Robson with evangelical fervour:

'It must always be among the high purposes for which Art exists to make any home brighter and more interesting – nobler, if you will. We have seen how abject are the homes of countless thousands. If we can make the homes of these poor persons brighter, more interesting, nobler, by so treating the necessary Board Schools placed in their midst as to make each building undertake a sort of leavening influence, we have set on foot a permanent and ever active good. . . . The working man also appears quite to consider the schools in the light of a property peculiarly his own of which he may be proud, and not as an alien institution forced upon him by those of superior station. . . . They are simply common schools for the common people of the present time. We do not expect a costermonger to understand or appreciate the sonatas of Beethoven, the operas of Mozart, or the subtle perfections of Greek Art in the time of Pericles. We do expect him to comprehend a piece of practical advice about building, and to admire a lively tune, especially if well played on a good instrument for the benefit of his own children.'[23]

This enthusiasm for the Board Schools as 'leavening influences' in the squalor of the inner city or the uniform banality of more recent suburbia is clearly brought out in H W Brewer's drawings which accompanied Robson's paper. At Cranbrook Road (Fig 25) and Hanover Street (Fig 26) the schools rise dramatically above wharves and the canal; at the former playground space is found on the roof – made possible by the use of the best asphalts adds Robson in a practical note – and at the latter school the playground is under the whole building. At Caledonian Road School (Fig 27) the Board School style can be seen in transition from the informal schools illustrated in *School Architecture* to the large schools of the later years: the lofty symmetry and the vertical emphasis of the staircase towers with their cupolas are already present, but the school is without hall; circulation is provided by corridors, and the gables have the elaborate bricks details of the early schools.

It is unfortunate that of the schools erected by 1874 and illustrated in *School Architecture* the best surviving example, the Mansfield Place School in Kentish Town (now Camden Institute, Holmes Road) represents Robson's work before he had been convinced of the benefits of 'Queen Anne'. (Figs 28/29) The school was ingeniously planned to provide an infants school on the ground floor, with covered and open playgrounds for the infants, girls and boys; the junior schools, as was customary, were on the upper floors; each school has had its separate entrance, a standard requirement inherited from the voluntary schools. In 1874 Robson was proud of this school:

'Whether in completeness of plan or in character or architecture this schoolhouse must be ranked among the most conspicuous of those designed and contracted for during the first three years of the Board's existence. The fault lies in being somewhat beyond the mark of the elementary, and suggesting in appearance rather the uses of secondary or grammar school.'[24]

25

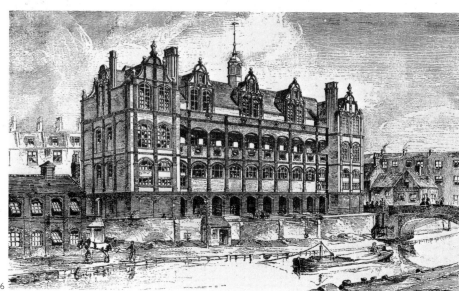

26

27

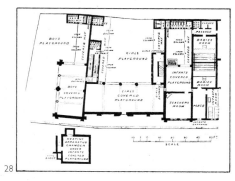

28

25 *Cranbrook Road School, 1881, from* Art Journal.
26 *Hanover Street School, 1877, from* Art Journal.
27 *Caledonian Road School, 1878, from* Art Journal.
28 *Mansfield Place School, 1874, plan from* School Architecture.
29 *Mansfield Place School, 1874, photograph taken in 1884.*

Robson left the School Board at the end of 1884 to become consultant architect to the Education Department in Whitehall; his letter of resignation noted that he had accepted the new post because 'the work is not usually carried on at high pressure, that the remuneration bears some relation to the work, and that I shall have more time for private practice'. But they were also suspicious over his management of the finances of some contracts. By the end of 1884 the Board had built 279 schools, and the 32 further schools that were opened in 1885 must also have been well advanced in design or construction; with over three hundred schools supervised, if not all designed, by him it is not surprising that Robson felt the 'high pressure'. His new appointment recognised this status as a specialist in school design, and his later private works included a stream of secondary schools, the People's Palace in the Mile End Road (later Queen Mary College) and the Royal Institute Galleries in Piccadilly. Robson died in 1917.[26] His successor as Board Architect was Thomas Jerram Bailey, who had been Robson's chief draughtsman since 1873. Bailey had served his apprenticeship with

R J Withers and had been as assistant to Ewan Christian before joining the School Board in 1872. Bailey was Board Architect from 1884 to the Board's abolition in 1904, and was then Architect to the LCC until 1910; he died a few months after retirement. His career is notable for the making of a reputation on the production of one type of building and entirely on work designed as a salaried employee of a public authority. Contemporaries were in doubt about Bailey's importance in his chosen field: he was

'a member [of the RIBA] whose influence on the evolution of school planning during the last 25 years can hardly be exaggerated. . . . There is probably no type of modern building which more nearly combines the merits of carefully thought out planning with an architectural treatment so thoroughly expressive of its purpose as a typical London Board School.'[27]

Bailey's standardising of the large school plan into two main ranges – a uniform classroom front and a more broken, usually seven part, hall front – has already been noted. The basis of the School Board style laid down by Robson

was developed by Bailey into a characteristic form that makes the schools, most especially the big three-deckers, so instantly recognisable. The elevations which the standard plan created were handled with a baroque symmetry in the mass and an immense fertility of invention in the detail. During the 1890s the Flemish influence of Robson's 'Queen Anne' gave way to more classical detailing. The cheerful gables on the wings of Primrose Hill School, opened 1885 and still with asymmetrical plan (Fig 30), were succeeded by weighty pediments, as at Montem School, opened 1897, or Rhyl School, opened 1898. (Figs 31/32). Other materials – such as Portland stone at Marion Richardson School (Fig 17) or terra cotta at Gordon School (Fig 33) – were introduced to maintain that variety in colour which from the beginning had been recognised as crucial to the Board School style and which had been first achieved in brick alone. The Gordon School, opened in 1904, is a classic three-decker although built to serve an area of new development where land cannot have been in short supply it is paradoxical that at Millbank (Fig 34), opened 1902, the school built to serve the lofty new

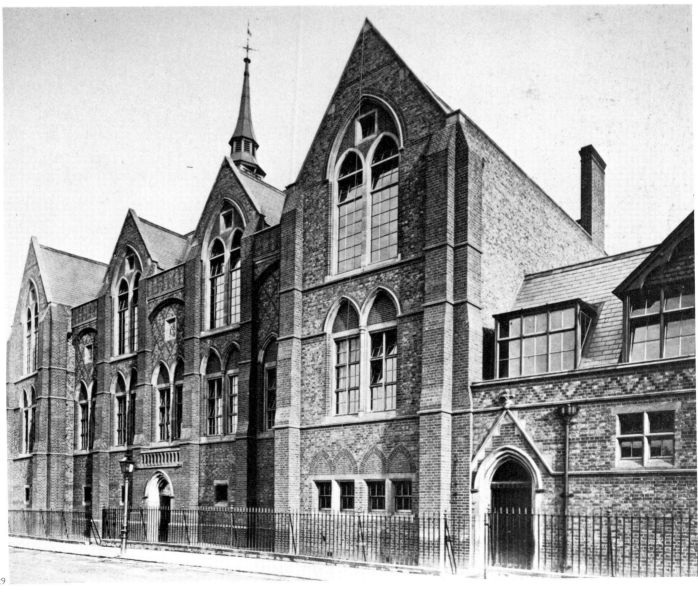

29

blocks of the LCC housing scheme in central London reverts in plan and character to the size and informality of the early schools, contrasting with the housing that it served in exactly the opposite way to the schools which Robson had used to illustrate 'Art as Applied to Town Schools' in 1880. Smaller buildings of this type had been a favourite device of Bailey's for the enlargement of earler schools; he found it easier in many cases to add a new (often mixed) school adjacent to but physically separate from the earlier building than simply to extend an older building, the integrity of which he respected.

The School Board's final report emphasised the concern for good architecture:

'The policy of the School Board has almost always been to give these buildings, as public buildings, some dignity of appearance, and make them ornaments rather than disfigurements to the neighbourhoods in which they are erected.... It was found that the difference of cost between bare utilitarianism and buildings designed in some sort of style and with regard for materials and colour was rather less than 5 per cent. At the same time this ornamental appearance may be secured either by richness of detail or by a dignified grouping of masses; it is the policy of the Board, while studying in the first instance suitable arrangements for teaching, not to set aside the dignity and attractiveness of buildings which the Board have always felt should be a contrast to their poor surroundings.'[28]

In fact decorative detail appears sparsely on the schools. A symbolic bas-relief of 'Knowledge strangling Ignorance' by Spencer Stanhope was occasionally employed, and there are a number of schools with flower plaques or other decoration. (Figs 35/36); the familiar date and name plaques were often the only ornamental details. In some of the very late schools an Edwardian richness creeps in, but in general the schools create their effect by the boldness of their massing and the interest of their skylines. It is a remarkable achievement to have created a succession of fine buildings, sustained over thirty years, with quality continued over very many of the nearly five hundred buildings for which the Board was responsible.

When the School Board's powers were taken over by the London County Council in 1904 the emphasis had changed from elementary to secondary education. In 1891 the School Board had begun to make provision for higher grade schools (those which taught children in standard 5 and above in the standards established by government codes of 1871 and 1882): The splendid Cassland Road School, in Hackney, opened 1902, with its terra-cotta decoration, is an example of this type (Fig 37). Instruction in specialist subjects was supported by the Science and Art

30

31

32

33

34

35

36

36

36

30 *Primrose Hill School, Camden, 1885.*
31 *Montem School, Islington, 1897.*
32 *Rhyl School, Camden, 1898.*
33 *Gordon School, Greenwich, 1904.*
34 *Millbank School, Westminster, 1902.*
35 *Decorative plaque at Victoria Junior School, Hammersmith, 1876.*
36 *Ornamental carved stone plaques at Park Walk School and Kingswood School.*

37

38

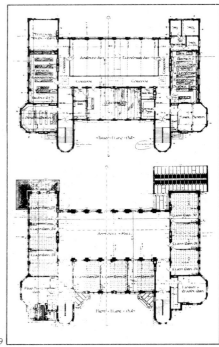

39

Department rather than the Education Department, but in 1900 the decision of Auditor Cockerton deemed the provision of such education under the 1870 Act an improper use of government funds. The confusion caused by this decision led first to the temporary reconstitution of some of the higher grade schools as higher elementary schools, second to a short Act regularising the situation created in good faith, and third to the total reorganisation of metropolitan education and the placing of all school provision from public funds under the control of the London County Council. The chief promoter of this new scheme was Sidney Webb who since 1893 had been chairman of the Council's Technical Education Board, with Dr William Garnett as the Board's secretary. Most of the architectural effects of the Education (London) Act of 1903 were not seen until after the Great War, and Bailey remained in charge of school building until 1910.

The building of primary schools continued without change, and the very early LCC secondary schools have a remarkable similarity in form to the Board Schools, the chief distinction being the smaller classrooms and the provision of more specialist subject accommodation. At Clapham Girls School (Figs 38/39), opened 1909, described as in a 'Free Renaissance' style though clearly a development of the School Board's version of 'Queen Anne', there is an extra floor on the standard three decker – though this was a single sex secondary school – which provided laboratories.

In the meantime, in the 1890s, the Council's Technical Education Board had been a promoter of further education rather than a direct supplier.[29] Its chief educational contribution was the creation of junior scholarships, enabling pupils from public elementary schools

40

to proceed to higher education. The Board's building activities were concentrated on Arts, Crafts and Technical subjects and much influenced by its Art Adviser, W R Lethaby. Lethaby became first principal of the Board's Central School of Arts and Crafts, founded in 1896 and eventually provided with a new building in Holborn. This building was associated with the London Day Training College, which was an endeavour by the Technical Education Board to aid the supply of teachers to the School Board: in 1902 the School Board took about 35% of the total national supply of trained teachers, and only a third of its requirement could be trained in London. The joint building (Fig 40) for School and College was attributed to the Council's architect, W E Riley, but four other architects on the Council's staff (P N Ginham, R M Taylor, A Halcrow

educational buildings was represented by its School Board inheritance, there were the beginnings of a more wider ranging service in design, both in the nature of the buildings to be provided and in the cross-fertilisation of ideas in the larger activities of the LCC Architect's Department.

37   Cassland Road School, Hackney, 1902, from The Builder.
38   Clapham Girls School, Lambeth, 1909, photograph taken in 1910.
39   Clapham Girls School, Lambeth, 1909, plans from The Builder.
40   Central School of Arts and Crafts and London Day Training College, Camden, 1907.
41   Hammersmith Trade School for Girls, Hammersmith, 1913, photograph taken in 1915.

41

Verstage and Matthew Dawson) were largely responsible.[30] The building was said to have been designed without adherence to any particular style[31] of the architects involved, R M Taylor at least had played a prominent role elsewhere in the Council's service – in the Housing Branch.

The Council's Education Department took over the Technical Education Board's policy of planting institutions in the less favoured parts of London. The Board's Camberwell School of Art (designed by Maurice B Adams as a commission and not by a staff architect) was followed by a similar school at Hammersmith; from this in 1913 grew the Hammersmith Trade School for Girls (Fig 41) which was designed by George Weald who had previously worked on the Council's cottage housing estate at Norbury.[32] The specialisms in school design, maintained until 1910 by Bailey's dominance in the Education Department, were breaking down. By 1914, although the bulk of the Council's

References

1 *Final Report of the School Board for London 1870–1904*, 2nd ed 1904, xxi

2 *Builder* 20 April 1889

3 E R Robson, 'Art as Applied to Town Schools', Art Journal 1881, 137

4 Quoted in Mark Girouard, *Sweetness and Light: the 'Queen Anne' Movement 1860–1900*, 1977, 64

5 Malcolm Seaborne, *The English School: its Architecture and Organisation 1370–1870*, 1971, 140

6 National Society file on St Martin's Schools.

7 *Builder* 22 December 1860

8 Cyril Bibby, *T H Huxley and Education*, 1971, 23

9 E R Robson, *School Architecture*, 1874 (reprinted 1972), 304

10 Felix Clay, *Modern School Buildings*, 1902, 309

11 *Art Journal* 1881, 137

12 *Builder* 11 February 1888

13 Quoted in Clay, *op cit*, 173 (in respect of secondary schools).

14 *Builder* 11 February 1888; *School Architecture*, 346–50

15 T J Bailey, 'On the Planning and Construction of Board Schools', *Journal of the Royal Institute of British Architects*, May 1899

16 *School Architecture*, 296–300

17 James Thorne, 'Architecture and Public Improvements', *British Almanac and Companion*, 1874, 193.

18 *School Architecture*, 310 and 324

19 J J Stevenson, *House Architecture*, 1880, Vol I, 348–9

20 P A Robson, 'Memoir of E R Robson', *Journal of the Royal Institute of British Architects*, February 1917

21 J J Stevenson, *On the Recent Reaction of Taste in English Architecture*, 187

22 *School Architecture*, 323

23 *Art Journal*, 1881, 140

24 *School Architecture*, 342–6

25 School Board for London Minutes, 20 November 1884.

26 *Journal of the Royal Institute of British Architects*, February 1917; *Builder*, 2 February 1917

27 *Journal of the Royal Institute of British Architects*, September 1910; *Builder*, 25 June 1910

28 *Final Report of the School Board for London*, 39

29 Annual Report of the Technical Education Board of the LCC, 1903–1904

30 *William Richard Lethaby*, ed A R N Roberts, 1957, 36

31 *Opening of the London Day Training College*, 1907 (An LCC ceremonial pamplet).

32 Susan Beattie, *A Revolution in London Housing*, 1980, 106

EDUCATION BUILDING IN INNER LONDON

1914 to the 1980's

by Ron Ringshall

Chapter 1
1914-1939

The outbreak of war in 1914 put an effective brake upon the growth of public authority housing developments and, with them, their associated educational buildings. Immediately after the armistice in 1918, however, the Lloyd George government tried to redeem their election promises with housing and town planning acts in an attempt to provide fitting homes for heroes. Inner city land values were high and the LCC was attracted by the cheaper suburban ring around London where a form of garden suburb could be provided influenced by Letchworth Garden City, founded in 1909. Housing estates such as Becontree, Bellingham, Downham and Roehampton were built and each required, as large developments, new shops, churches, playing fields and schools for their own needs.

At the same time that the Government was concerned with the future welfare of the fighting forces H A L Fisher, then President of the Board of Education (forerunner of the Ministry of Education), in 1917 stated his concern that the value of our educational system was being impaired by the low physical conditions of vast numbers of children, particularly the poor. His 1918 Education Act lead to social reform as it strengthened the education authorities, raising 50% of cost from central government thus reducing parental fees, abolished fees in elementary schools and reduced children's working hours and all exemptions from the leaving age of fourteen.

Sir Robert Blair, Chief Education Officer to the LCC, recognised in 1916 the healthy discontent with the educational system which the war had aroused and foresaw the call for 'the best possible education' with the need 'to place within the reach of every child a bright, attractive, well-planned and suitably equipped school building with a commodius playground'[1] as the first priority with the reduction of the size of classes as the second.

Educational philosophy was developing and the 1926 Hadow Report proposed expanded secondary education for all, with a break at eleven plus, and a leaving age of fifteen. The stimulus was to be practical work and realistic studies offering children 'the free and broad air of a general and humane education'.[2]

This would remember music along with handwork, cherish natural science whilst fostering linguistic and literary studies: training was 'to delight in pursuits and rejoice in accomplishments'[3] laying the foundations for recreation and leisure in maturer years. The long term aim was to awaken and guide the best and most highly trained skills of the country's citizens in order to fulfil the individual's requirements and attainments. But the national economy of the 1920's and 1930's was so bankrupt that these admirable objectives were not realised. Hadow recognised this by advocating 'simplifying School buildings and reducing their cost'.[4]

Another Hadow Report, 1931, upon primary education, shaped development in the late 1930's and early 1940's when the old elementary school was gradually transformed into the recognisable modern primary school. The educational aims were re-aligned 'in terms of activity and experience rather than of knowledge to be acquired and facts to be stored':[5] additionally, physical change was proposed with a demand for classes limited to 40 and school building standards were adumbrated. Special training courses were recommended for teachers of backward children, parental co-operation was to be welcomed in school affairs and competition between schools over 'free place' entrance examination successes was to be discouraged. Other reports urged courses for vocational interests, a proper tutorial system, employment of careers masters and a school leaving age of sixteen. The tripartite reorganisation of secondary education into secondary, central and senior elementary schools (in descending order of educational attainment) along the lines of Hadow, 1926, began in 1930 but was not formalised until the 1944 Education Act. Raising the school leaving age to fifteen, again a Hadow recommendation, to allow four years in secondary education was not ratified until 1947.

Hadow's recommendation reflected the general attitude of progressive teachers whose ideas were enlarged and encouraged. Heavy Victorian authority had been loosened by the common dangers shared between 1914 and 1918 and in the classroom this began to give way to a greater informality under Montessori's influence (see Chapter 8) but this was not reflected in school buildings which continued to provide rows of independent cellular classrooms. Although less formal than previously teachers taught a narrow curriculum from pedestals, or low platforms, at the front of the room using the blackboard constantly and perpetuating the division between themselves and the taught although it was alleged that 'changes in education have not changed the surroundings of education'.[6]

Further education outside the few universities and polytechnics adapted a wider demand for specialisation of courses to meet the expanding requirements of a modern industrial state. Nationally there was little pattern in the provision of technical education and institutions were set up in response to local demand for part time courses, their siting determined often by the location of a specific industry or the growing needs of a newly built and developing area: they developed mainly from trade schools eg Brixton School of Building, Westminster School of Catering or the Camberwell School of Arts and Crafts. In inner London a variety of institutions catered for a wide spectrum of studies with day continuation courses ranging from preliminary trade skills for fourteen year olds to degree level work. These represented the forerunners for

the great further education expansion of the 1950's and 1960's but in the intervening years they gradually grew and evolved to meet local needs usually demonstrating that their sites were finite and needing outposts and annexes to cope with their needs.

As the result of continual criticism the layout with a central hall based upon the 'Prussian system' used by Robson and Bailey for the London School Board and the LCC schools was no longer built although enthusiasts could not see 'how the plan can be much improved upon'.[7] But the practice of regular medical inspection, made law in 1907, had exposed the schools as being poorly ventilated and providing unhygienic environments for children. Concern over puny and feeble bodies had been noted[8] in relation to new schools and an open-air school movement had grown – most rapidly in Derbyshire and Staffordshire – as a consequence of international investigation into European school hygiene. Pavilion schools – classrooms single-banked along corridors allowing cross-ventilation and choice of orientation – were built in various parts of the country and by 1914 'English schools had obtained a distinctive character which was known the world over'.[9] Building regulations were changed in response to concerted pressure from doctors and architects and the central hall plan was replaced by 'single storeyed groups of rooms, arranged to let the sun and air into every corner'.[10] One of the pioneers of the open-air school movement in Northumberland, Topham Forrest, became architect to the LCC in 1914.

After 1918 the state of the national economy was so depressed that the pursuit of cheap construction for public buildings became a priority and short-life schools were advocated. A modern building economist would have pointed out that due to the rate of interest paid there is little saving in the costs of building construction if expected to last less than sixty years – 'shortening the lives of buildings reduces their value without reducing their costs'.[11] Lightweight, short-lived buildings were proposed as schools in order to save money with the Board of Education advocating asbestos roofs, plain brickwork and simple weatherboarding as cladding – 'the simplest form of construction'.[12] The Board later encouraged the building of single-storey schools of brick on flat sites with pitched roofs.[13] This stringency with its accent upon construction not being too strong or too permanent was noted by visitors.[14]

The suburban schools had larger sites than those in the central areas and generally they are one or two storeyed only: the buildings reflect the stultified educational approach being neat, hygienic and basic in their teaching arrangements. The use of neo-classicism for important public buildings produced a subtle infusion of classical ideas by architects who did not fully accept classical decorative form and this resulted in axial planning, symmetry and proportion but without a formal decorative vocabulary.[15] Construction is lighter than the earlier School Board buildings and the layouts concentrate upon providing as much teaching space with the benefit of south light as possible. There is space for trees, lawns, shrubberies and flower beds and play space is immediate and adequate. Although lighter, construction is still traditional,[16] but by the 1930's there began an intellectual demand among architects for change to mirror the spirit of the age with new technologies to be exploited and which adherence to traditional expression would preclude. There had been a continuous, if slow, development of the attitude stated in 1905 that architects should use 'the same fitness, the same science, the same unchallenged acceptance of modern material and modern conditions and the same sincerity'[17] as the designers of express locomotives. From the Continent came the belief that the modern architecture had a social role and that science should be dominant in determining its form: these beliefs found expression in white walls, flat roofs and

large windows and an exhibition at the RIBA in 1937 of schools designed by Leurçat, Dudok and Schumacher reinforced the beliefs.[18] The Modern Movement had arrived and had already demonstrated at Stuttgart in 1927 that it was an organised force intent upon re-establishing architecture from the first principles with the International Style.[19] The Movement was a necessary corrective to stylistic eclecticism coinciding with, and reflecting, a new supra-national cultural vision.

At the same time the training of architects had changed sharply from the system of pupillage, where the pupil absorbed the ethos of the master's office, to a wider attendance at schools of architecture where more radical views were pursued. Political change on the Continent brought to Britain an influx of talented adherents of the M.M. – Gropius, Mendelsohn, Breuer, Korn and Lubetkin – and they gave extra power to the development of MARS (Modern Architecture Research) the British offshot of CIAM (Congres Internationaux d'Architecture Moderne) with 'human need and new technology' as the watchword.

Functionalism was being pursued

among younger British architects in the late 1930's but this was expressed in a compromised less aggressive way than their European counterparts. Some writers are critical of the 'Continental fashion' pointing out that 'many of the architects involved were foreign'[20] whilst ignoring the fact that their preferred Renaissance style developed in fifteenth century Italy from antique Greek models and that the really acceptable English variant, Palladian, evolved in Vicenza: one might say that 'every genuine style has been international'[21] from classicism onwards allowing for local deviations. The need for a fresh, lighter approach to school design was recognised in the results of an open competition for new schools, urban and rural, with lighter construction, large glazed areas and simple lightweight classing.[22,23] Immediately there was a call 'for up-to-date industrial techniques'[24] to provide spaciously planned but cheap schools. Post-war architects owed a debt to these earlier colleagues whose dreams faded in 1939 but who had espoused 'a new attitude and a new method of work', (see Chapter 2(2)).

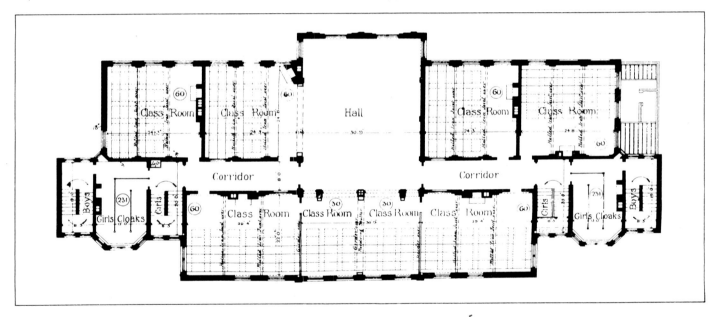

Athelney Elementary School

The schools for the LCC cottage estates were originally described as transitional whilst the local population moved in and grew and Athelney was built on what was road No 18 at Bellingham. It has an important site befitting an important local building being placed upon the main axis of the geometrically laid out estate closing the view down a long avenue of plane trees. It is a neat, modest design being light and open with the classrooms facing south off a single corridor: its modesty is reflected in the lack of an entrance hall as such – visitors

enter by a corridor. The estate symmetry is reflected in the axial plan with an assembly hall bisecting the equal halves of the classroom wings: senior classrooms were designed for forty pupils and the girls were kept separated from the boys by the assembly hall. Craft rooms were included at the extremes of the wings for woodwork and cookery.

The construction demonstrates a radical move away from previous heavy loadbearing modes through being largely single-storey: nominal brick walls, light steel frames and timber trussed roofs sufficed to give open, airy classrooms. Timber cladding indicates on elevation the lighter construction but red staffordshire bull-nosed sills anticipate

1 Latchmere School, First Floor Plan
The plan shows the central hall arrangement used by the School Board for London. Seating was stepped up towards the back of the classrooms, see Chapter 14, each of which contained up to sixty pupils. Supervision of each class by the head teacher was allowed by the use of glazed partitions to the corridors. Cross-ventilation was not possible, although vertical flues fed air vents in each room.

heavier use on the brick faced elevations to the playgrounds. Roofs are 45 degree pitch with red/orange clay tiles. The school is a marriage of economy and hygiene as cross-ventilation became the orthodoxy of the period. In comparison to the secondary schools it is 'cheap, functional and unpretentious':[25] it is the congenial, acceptable vernacular of its time.

Independent open air classrooms were built from timber in the playgrounds and were initially expected to cater for those delicate children from the inner city slums who required a more wholesome environment.

Bellingham estate was begun in 1921 and Athelney school in 1922. Both have matured and changed with some roads having avenues of fine mature trees. Athelney transitional school became an elementary school with a separate infant building but, after extensive rebuilding since bomb damage in 1940, is now a junior and infant mixed school with a nursery class added in 1975.

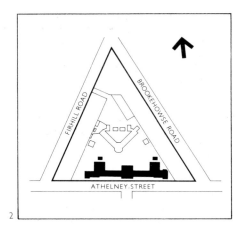

2   Site Plan
The development of the site is governed by the symmetrical placing of the school's assembly hall opposite an avenue of trees. A smaller building for infants and juniors pursues its own symmetry in a vee-shape upon a different centre line.
3   Ground Floor Plan
The central shared assembly hall (a second

one for girls only was never built) separates the symmetrical arms of the single storey classroom wings — eastern for girls and western for boys. Single banked classrooms facing South fulfilled the basic requirement of 'pavilion' schools as a reaction to the large, three storeyed, poorly ventilated Victorian and Edwardian schools. Each classroom was for forty pupils.
4   *The symmetrical plan is reflected in the massing of the building with the assembly hall and administration rooms over, providing a solid centre (1928). The door is not the main entrance to the school — entrances are at the extreme ends of the wings.*
5   *Main elevation facing south, 1928. Classrooms have large windows largely with timber cladding stained black under an orange clay tiled roof.*

The trees and grass in the foreground have matured successfully: the sturdy oak fence on the school boundary has lasted over fifty years but the school wing nearest the camera was demolished by a bomb in 1940.

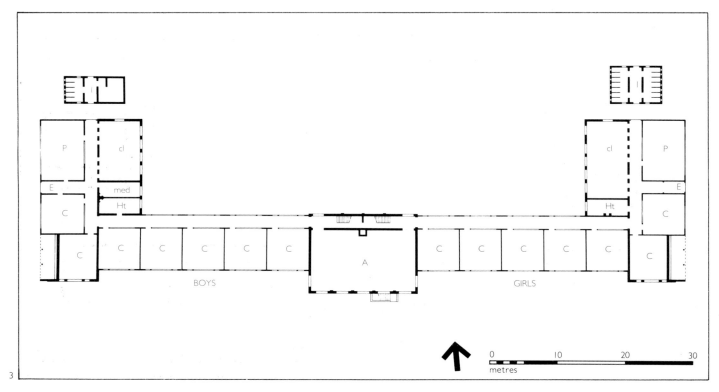

Red Lion Secondary School

Originally designed in 1925 as Red Lion Secondary School for boys the school later became Shooter's Hill Grammar School and, expanded, is now Eaglesfield Secondary, a comprehensive school – see Chapter 3. The secondary schools were conceived as being quite different from the elementary school such as Athelney, being much larger and having higher educational aspirations. These are reflected in the building's attempt at importance for there is an impressive entrance hall with a porter's room leading to a very large study for the headmaster. Again the plan is axial with a neo-Georgian approach to detail: the symmetry was deliberate as it was seen to demonstrate the acceptance of a given order of things.[26] Neo-Georgian represented an 'identifiable and clearly defined style of architecture', indeed, it has been said[27] that classicism is the architecture of the gentry – their own vernacular. The neo-Georgian was to assert prestige over the plainer elemen-tary schools[28] but a writer such as Pugin would have criticised the use of classical orders to mask and conceal under one monotonous front[29] instead of simply stating the building's 'convenience, construction and propriety'.[30]

It was not until 1945 when the Modern Movement became pre-eminent that the pretentious neo-classicism was broken. All types of schools thereafter reflected the same architectural tenets: the class had been taken out of classicism.[31]

In keeping with the educational objectives the architectural aim is gravitas having a heavy load-bearing brick structure with steel beams, filler joists and an in situ concrete first floor. Ceilings are high (11'0'': 3.35 m) for adequate ventilation and sensible hard wearing dados are universal in the wide corridors and classrooms. Lavatories are spacious, simple, well ventilated, durable and internal: elementary school lava-tories were external, detached and largely open to the sky.

The classrooms have a more intent air with thirty pupils each and the science/craft facilities are developed. A fully fitted gymnasium gives an early

6 Site Plan
The school was built upon a wide, flat area at the base of a steep slope falling from the South. The building parades its symmetry in front of the ample playing fields between it and the northern boundary.

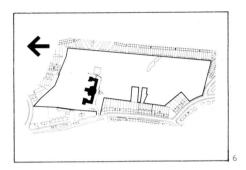

6

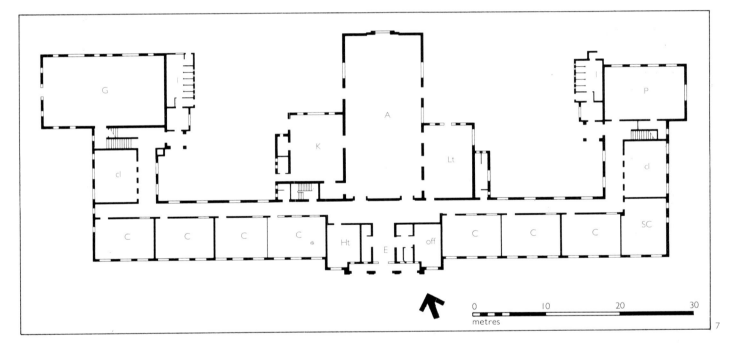

7

7 Ground Floor Plan
The layout shows the pavilion form for classrooms with larger elements placed to the North. The generous provisions of kitchens for school meals in secondary schools give an indication of their wide catchment areas.

8 *The main entrance, 1928, is given a heightened importance with the modelling of the building and the use of a stripped classical stone detailing.*

8

indication of the yearning towards the public school aim of healthy minds in healthy bodies and extensive adjacent playing fields complete the picture.[32] Lofty and dark with heavy timber king post roof trusses exposed and sombre panelling the assembly hall is intended as a shrine, a holy place, 'the atmosphere desirable ... touch of religious spirit'[33] where the school mystique can be communicated communally in a quasi religious atmosphere.

The secondary schools of the time are noteworthy for the provision of a full kitchen and dining service evidencing the fact that they were intended as centres of excellence drawing their 450 pupils from a wide catchment area. Large cloakrooms were necessary but all administration was carried out from a small office.

9

10

11

9   Although in a suburban setting, 1936, the school could be a rural boarding school due to the size of the site and the maturity of the trees.
10   A chemistry laboratory, 1936. Note the amount of natural ventilation possible using banks of hopper windows. The roof structure was apparently not considered in relationship to the room.
11   The gymnasium, 1936, was an advance upon the formal drill for boys which previously took place in school playgrounds.
12   The assembly hall, 1928, could seat the whole school with masters upon the platform.

12

Eltham Hill Secondary School

Designed in 1925 as a girls' secondary school Eltham Hill later became a grammar school and is now much enlarged as a girls' comprehensive school. Intended for the more able child the building attempts to convey a serious demeanour with a columned entrance hall controlled by a porter's room with ready access to a large study for the headmistress which contains one of the few open fireplaces in the school. Classrooms are generally single-banked off corridors and face south over an ancient park with the ground floor rooms each having direct access on to a terrace. Science and craft rooms indicate, for the time, the promise of better qualifications for the gifted. It was built for four hundred pupils with class sizes generally of thirty. The layout is asymmetrical largely due to a 5'0'' (1.50 m) fall across the site but an entrance court draws the visitor into the centre of the school which then presents a series of symmetrical neo-Georgian facades. This apparent regularity disguises the larger volume such as the assembly hall and gymnasium. The fall across the site does, however, allow a fine library to be included in the general massing with an oriel window overlooking the park: the placing and prominence of this room gives a hint of the pleasures and rewards of study and higher education yet to come.

The scale of the building is modest and construction is of load-bearing brickwork with steel and timber roof trusses supporting a 45 degree pitch clay tiled roof: the external walls are facing brick with powerful brick quoins to all external corners. Radiators are hospital pattern and are treated as specific features in rooms included as part of the general dado design. Windows vary from casement to sliding but it is noticeable that there are no fixed lights – all are intended to open for ventilation.

13 Site Plan
The secondary school site included sports facilities, in this case a hockey pitch and tennis courts, and was still large enough for formal gardens at the entrance.
14 Ground Floor Plan
Each elevation was seen as symmetrical in its own right, irrespective of function or volume contained behind it, and here the layout shows classrooms facing South as at Athelney but with larger elements included successfully.

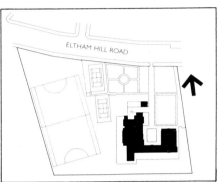

13

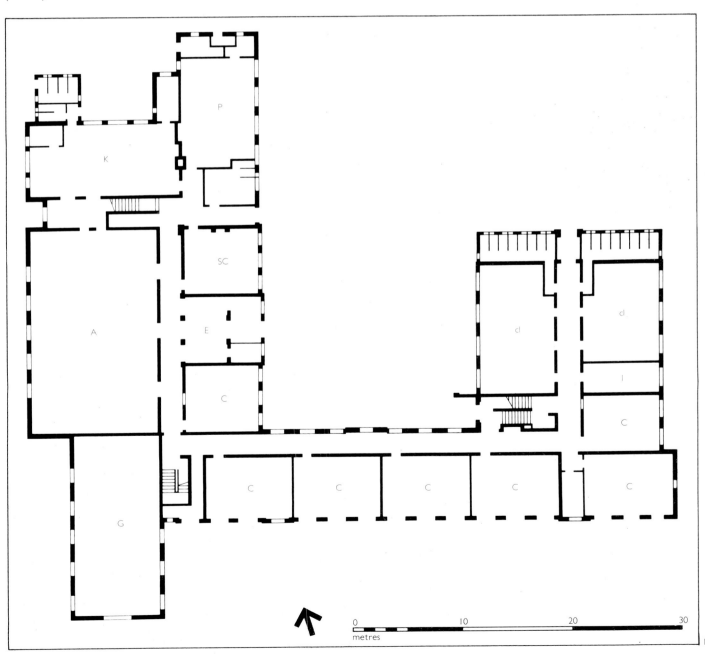

14

37

15 *Chemistry laboratory, 1936. This is evidently a place of work with painted brickwork walls and the most fundamental light fittings. Compare with figure 17, the library, as a place of study.*

16 *The entrance court, 1927, allowing a series of symmetrical elevations to an aseymmetrical plan. Smaller windows on the left are to light corridors only as classrooms face south.*

17 *The library, 1936, is shown to be a place of study with higher standards of finish: the walls are plastered, a more expensive light fitting is installed, full length curtains hang and a carpet provided.*

18 *The library, with its oriel window, sits above the gymnasium overlooking the park. Note that the library's side window is a repressed oriel barely breaking the line of brickwork but providing a centrepiece, nevertheless, for a minor elevation.*

15

16

17

18

Burlington Secondary School

Among the two hundred and twenty eight new schools built for the London County Council between 1914 and 1939 some showed the influence of imported styles of modern architecture. Burlington School for 500 girls (now known as Burlington Danes, a mixed comprehensive school) was designed by Sir John Burnet, Tait and Lorne in 1935 for a long, narrow site next to Wormwood Scrubs. An earlier proposed design (1931) for this school for a site at Streatham showed an axial, symmetrical plan similar in layout to the neo-Georgian secondary schools but also showing the growing 1930's concern with the fashionable international styles.

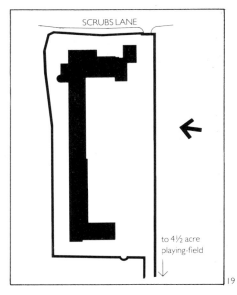

SCRUBS LANE

to 4½ acre playing-field

19

19 Site Plan
The site influenced the building development heavily with its extreme shallowness and southerly aspect.
20 Ground Floor Plan
Symmetry was difficult to pursue upon this site and the layout clearly shows each element expressed. Shallow classrooms are grouped together in four storeys whilst the deeper specialist rooms rise to three storeys with an open loggia over. New forms are introduced with projecting staircases, cantilevered porches and wide windows.
21 First Floor Plan
Essentially the accepted pavilion classroom layout is followed with the main entrance level reached by wide, handsome, external steps.

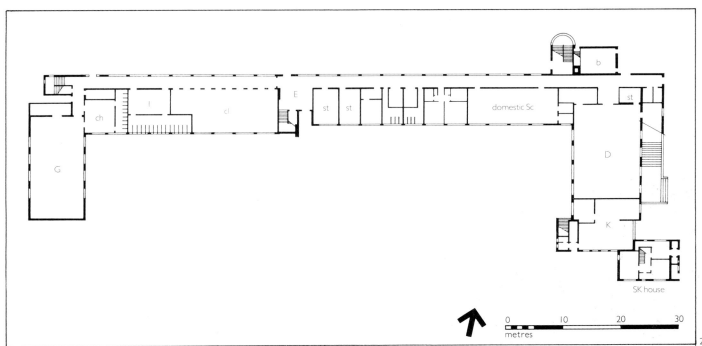

0 10 20 30
metres

20

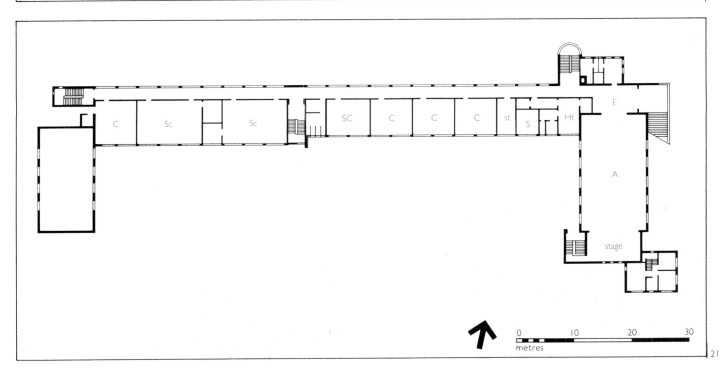

0 10 20 30
metres

21

Horizontal window bands and chic projecting corner windows betray the beginnings of an interest not yet given point in the planning.

The final narrow site, however, indicates how the architect was forced to plan asymmetrically and this loosening of the beaux arts corset produced a comprehensive 1930's international building heavily influenced by the Dutch architect Dudok.[34] The plan is long and narrow with a single corridor allowing all class-rooms to face south. Pupil's access is at ground floor level half way along the building and the entrance is made along a wide path flanked by flower beds: the plan forms widens at this point also as deeper specialist rooms and library are separated from the general classrooms. The school's main entrance and administration suite is at first floor level and is reached at the narrow east end of the site by handsome easy flights of steps.

Architectural expression comes from the articulation of the building form and it is here that those earlier interests come to maturity. Major runs of

windows in the 2″ light yellow facing brickwork are given great horizontal emphasis as the hitherto universal georgian square pane gives place to larger steel-framed fenestration and by the projection of concrete window heads and stone sills with the remaining solid piers between faced in glazed coloured tiles. Large circular windows are introduced, often arbitrarily, to give a contrasting vertical emphasis in company with projecting blocks containing the staircases but when large volumes, such as the assembly hall or gymnasium, are to be lighted then soaring vertical windows are let into plain brickwork. An interesting feature, and a reflection of a concern of the time, is the inclusion of a fully equipped film projection suite for the main assembly hall. The use of acoustic panels on the rear wall of the hall shows the growing concern with the technical performance of buildings. Furniture and fittings show that Modern Movement principles are carried right through the buildings.[35]

But the real interest is in the massing of forms, the piling up of the main

rounded staircase with the water tank rooms and the added articulation of the boiler room flue with 2″ dark brown bricks adding vertical emphasis: this major departure from earlier symmetries was followed through in the general detailing by the introduction of nautical handrails, flagstaffs, integral flower boxes by the main entrance stairs and a clock marking the main doors.

A major technical development assists the architecture as the horizontal expression of the four storey classroom wing and three storey specialist wing was only possible by the use of a reinforced concrete frame which allows the building's general flat roofed elegance. It was the development, use and expression of such structural properties which challenged the received ideas of proportion based upon ancient authority. They made previous visual assessment such as Alberti's 'compartition' meaningless whilst laying the foundation for structural expression after 1945.[36]

22

22 *The east elevation, 1936, demonstrates the powerful composition of the entrance, main staircase and assembly hall. Note the use of brick textures and coloration to add emphasis to the design.*

23 *The main entrance steps sharing the 2" brick and glazed coloured tiles articulating the horizontal window runs.*

24 *The library indicates a different style of design (see Fig 17, Eltham Hill School) being smoother with rounded and streamlined detailing reflecting the more powerful curves elsewhere in the planning.*

25 *A classroom shows a different range of finishes and furnishing from the ordinary LCC schools. The floor is a smooth sheet of linoleum and the reinforced concrete frame and roof slab obviate pattern staining (see Fig 14, Eltham Hill School). Flush doors, large fixed blackboard, integrated storage furniture, light fittings and steel framed furniture indicate the beginning of a new way of finishing classrooms.*

26 South Elevation
This indicates a new asymmetrical massing of forms made possible by the use of a reinforced concrete frame which allows wide, horizontal bands of windows and the building's general flat roofed elegance.

23

24

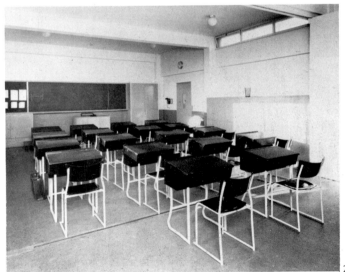

25

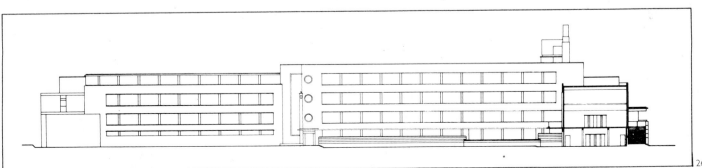

26

South East London Technical Institute

In 1929 a comprehensive technical college, the South East London Technical Institute, was designed and the courses catered for present a broad canvas of perceived need. Plumbing and gas fitting, woodworking, carpentry and pattern making and building science provided for basic trades and skills. There was a more advanced technical side also with an electrical laboratory, an electrical engineering power laboratory, a metal plate shop, a Post Office wiremen's training workshop, a strength of materials laboratory and a mechanical laboratory. Physics and chemistry as well as chemical and metallurgical laboratories were included and there was a range of drawing offices and general classrooms. Assuming that these subjects catered for men's further education, only women had trade and commerce options as well as needlework, cookery, laundering and a fully fitted domestic science flat.

The building form is bold and four-square being a heavy brick three-storeyed mass with a semi-basement lending dignity to the main entrance which is gained by easy going york stone steps. The structure is untoward being largely brick load-bearing with inter-mediate steel stanchions carrying steel filler joists and concrete floor slabs with a steel trussed roof. Rooms were designed to be hard wearing with deal floors, hard plaster to door height and fair faced brick over painted. Windows were steel, ungalvanised naturally, with georgian panes and wooden sills. There is an earnest, worthy air to the building with very little relief except at the entrance hall which has a terrazzo floor, artificial marble walls and half round arches leading off to corridors but the space is tight and workaday. Emphasising the non-academic needs of the occupants is a small central library. A gymnasium was included at basement level but only men's changing facilities were provided; however a great deal of detailed attention was paid to the high and handsome assembly hall which has a fully enclosed film projection booth among its columns, capitals and friezes. The subject rooms were laid out in such a way that the assumed men's and women's subjects were rigorously segregated in plan even to the extent of having two separate bicycle stores. The need for the kinds of education offered at this college is demonstrated by the leasing of a large building in 1948 to expand the building department, the incorporation of the newly built adjoining Wickham block (originally a college for further education) in 1974 and the addition of the Breakspears building completed in 1976 (see Chapter 15): the original college is now known as the Tressillian building.

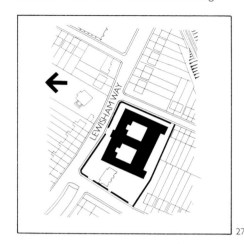

27 Site Plan
The site is not large and with existing buildings retained as part of the institute's accommodation the new building fits very tightly. Chapter 15 shows the enlargement into a college using adjacent sites.

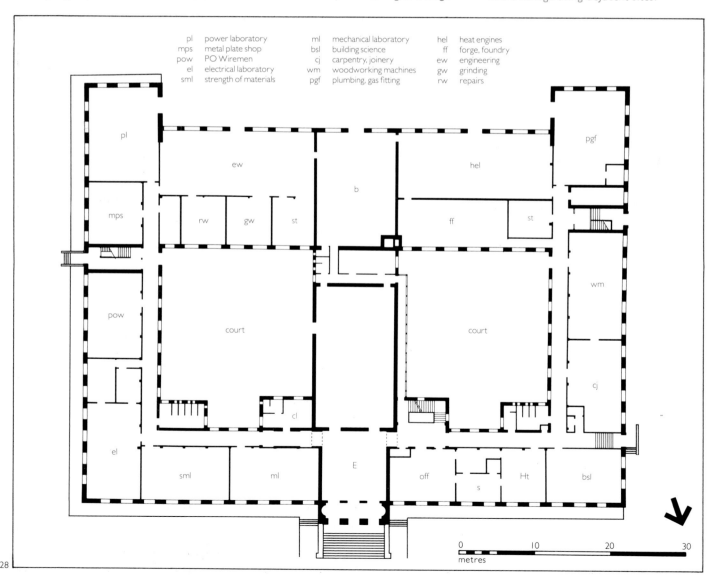

pl — power laboratory
mps — metal plate shop
pow — PO Wiremen
el — electrical laboratory
sml — strength of materials
ml — mechanical laboratory
bsl — building science
cj — carpentry, joinery
wm — woodworking machines
pgf — plumbing, gas fitting
hel — heat engines
ff — forge, foundry
ew — engineering
gw — grinding
rw — repairs

28 Grand Floor Plan
*Layout is formal, simple and symmetrical
with a large entrance hall giving on to
quite narrow everyday corridors. Cross-
ventilation to classrooms and laboratories
is possible through borrowed lights above
the corridor partitions following the single-
banked pavilion layout used in elementary
and secondary schools – see Athelney, Red
Lion and Eltham Hill in this chapter.*

29 First Floor Plan
*The general arrangement follows the
ground floor layout. A film projection room
and a library hint at the future expansion
of audio-visual aids in education even when
disguised with antique detailing.*

30 *The main entrance front, 1932,
showing the square, solid construction
enlivened by shield details on the gutters
and rainwater hoppers and large heraldic
panels between the first floor windows: see
Figs 34 and 35. The trees are now mature
and the spare nature of the building is
partially obscured.*

31 *Three heraldic panels being prepared.*

30

31

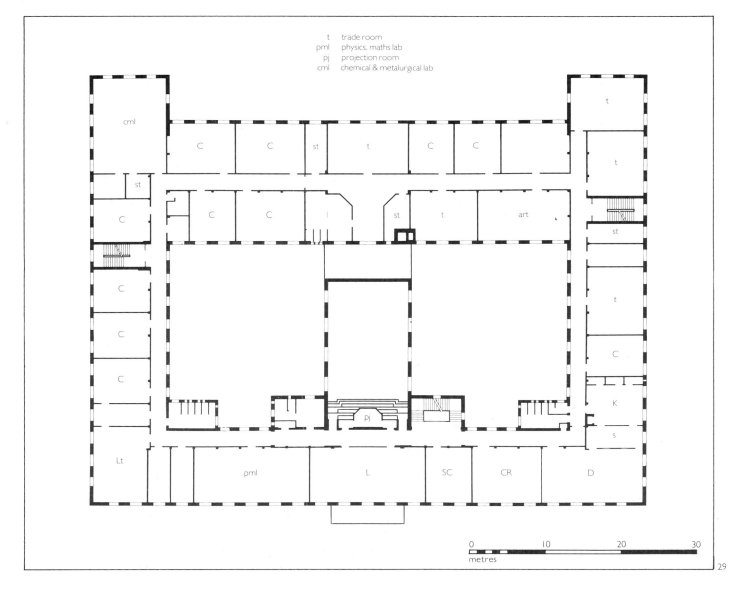

t   trade room
pml physics, maths lab
pj   projection room
cml chemical & metalurgical lab

0   10   20   30
metres

29

32

33

34

35

32 An heraldic panel by Nicholas Babb at the design stage as a clay model.
33 The main entrance hall, 1932, showing a range of good quality materials but without the volume to demonstrate them at their best.
34 The mechanical engineering workshop, 1939.
35 Cookery, 1939. The rooflight let into the main roof was repeated on the men's side of the building in the technical drawing offices.

Chapter 1: References

1 Maclure J S, One Hundred Years of London Education, 1870–1970 Allen Lane, 1970, pp 113–114.

2 Hadow Report, The Education of the Adolescent, 1926, Introduction to Report, p xx.

3 Hadow Report, The Education of the Adolescent, 1926, Introduction to Report, p xxi.

4 Architects Journal, 10 Februrary 1938, p 253

5 Hadow Report, The Primary School, 1931, p 93; the Report recommended that every school should have proper lavatory accommodation with hot water and drinking water, proper cloakrooms and drying facilities and school meals where necessary.

6 Architects Journal, 28 May 1936, p 797.

7 Clay F, Modern School Buildings, Batsford, 1902, pp 170–174

8 Rowntree B S, Poverty, A Study of Town Life, Macmillan, 1903, (3rd Edition), pp 209–216.

9 RIBA Journal, November 1921, p 34: G H Widdows, the Derbyshire County Architect, addressing the RIBA upon School Design dealing particularly with ventilation, daylighting and heating. The illustrations are particularly interesting with a section of a window showing how all elements open for ventilation whilst preventing draughts: this pattern was followed by the LCC until 1939.

10 Board of Education, Building Regulations for Public elementary Schools, HMSO, 1914.

11 Stone P A, Building Economy, Pergamon, 1976 (2nd Edition), p 27.

12 Board of Education, Circular 1175, September 1920.

13 Board of Education, Circular 1419, July 1932.

14 Architectural Record, 26 November 1926, pp 569–574: the economical designs for schools at Tooting and Downham are illustrated.

15 Macleod R, Style and Society, RIBA, 1971, p 122.

16 Watkin D, English Architecture, Thames and Hudson, 1979, p 130. 'traditionalism was the norm in architecture until the 1930's'

17 Architectural Review, July 1905, p 27: in 1931, Edmund Wilson also noted in 'Axel's Castle' p 39 that the 'ascendancy of scientific ideas' had already profoundly changed the basis of poetry.

18 Architects Journal, 28 May 1936: the whole issue is given over to school design and examples by Leurcat (at Villejuif) and Dudok (at Schullwersweg) are illustrated.

19 Frampton K, Modern Architecture, A Critical History, Thames & Hudson, 1980, p 163: The Werkbund Exhibition, Stuttgart, 1927, 'became the first international manifestation of that white, prismatic, flat-roofed mode of building which was to be identified in 1932 as the International Style'.

20 Watkin D, English Architecture, Thames and Hudson, 1979, p 192: Tom Wolfe in From Bauhaus To Our House, Farrar, Straus and Giroux, (New York) makes a similar point with reference to the influx of European architects fleeing political oppression and importing alien architecture into the USA.

21 Mumford L, The Human Prospect (Monumentalism, Symbolism and Style), Secker and Warburg, 1956.

22 Architects Journal, 25 March 1937, pp 511–544.

23 Architects and Building News, 26th March 1937, pp 387–396: both magazines published the results of the 'News Chronicle' schools competition which showed that the pavilion geometry (for an urban elementary school) was still the ideal plan whilst clothed in the new apparel of apparent function.

24 Architects Journal, 7 April 1938, pp 587–594: this was the summation of a series upon school design the remainder being – Nursery, 18 November 1937, pp 795–800. Infant and Junior, 23 December 1937, pp 1055–1060. Senior, 6 January 1938, pp 25–28 & 10 February 1938, pp 253–258.

25 Seaborne M, and Lowe R, The English School, its Architecture and Organization, Vol II 1870–1970, Routledge & Kegan Paul 1977, p 146.

26 Architectural Review, December 1933, p 222: paradoxically, in the same article, the headmaster of Marlborough – a public school – describes with pleasure his school's new science block as 'not so much an academic block, as generally understood, as an elegant factory'.

27 Allsopp B, A Modern Theory of Architecture, Routledge & Kegan Paul, 1977, p 13.

28 Seaborne M etc, as 21, p 142.

29 Pugin A W N, The True Principles of Pointed or Christian Architecture, 1841, p 60.

30 Ibid.

31 Architectural Design, May/June 1980, Post Modern Classicism, p 16.

32 Education, 19 March 1982, Digest 'Teaching Physical Education' p 208: this article sets out comparing the contrast between the children doing drill in maintained schools, p 1, who marched, wheeled and stamped to attention on concrete playgrounds before instructors (usually military) to instil discipline and obedience and those in public schools being taught games by Oxbridge blues in order to develop initiative and their 'natural' leadership.

33 Clay F, Modern School Buildings, Batsford, 1929 (3rd Edition) p 177.

34 Architects Journal, 21 January 1937, pp 137–141.

35 Architectural Review, January 1937, pp 8–9: p 6 states that 'it need hardly be said, with all the evidence there is around, how badly a revival of school building is needed.'

36 Allsopp B, A Modern Theory of Architecture, Routledge & Kegan Paul, 1977, p 22.

Key to drawings

A	assembly hall
AEI	adult education institute
AH	activities hall
C	classroom
CR	common room
D	dining
Dr	drama
DW	dining/work
E	entrance
G	gymnasium
H	houseroom
Hm	home bay
Ht	head or principal
I	infants
J	juniors
K	kitchen
L	library
Lt	lecture
M	music
Ns	nursery
P	practical area
PC	play centre
Q	quiet area
S	secretary
Sc	science
SC	staff common room
SH	sports hall
SK	schoolkeeper
Sw	swimming pool
W	waiting
YS	youth service
b	boiler
ca	covered area
ch	changing
cl	cloakroom
l	lavatories
s	servery
st	store

After the widespread tribulations brought about by the deep economic recession of the 1930's the shared dangers of the Second World War gave impetus to resolving new social systems. A humane society would be required with social security and a national health service and the Beveridge Report 1943, set these out as the foundations of the Welfare State. Wider opportunities would be made available to the general population through greater access to education.

In 1944 the Butler Education Act heralded an immense change in the objectives of education[1,2] and opened the way to a massive new school building programme. The Ministry of Education led the way in suggesting that the educational function should be paramount. New education methods – the user's needs – demanded new buildings and new functions coincided with new architectural forms.[3] Schools were one of the first building types in Britain to receive the analytical approach of the Modern Movement to user requirements: despite the Modern Movement's functional searchlight educational buildings did not conform to pattern as some may have assumed, and in 1959 it was said that 'the British school remains the most unpredictable in the world'.[4] This was evidence of vitality for each school design was subject to complete and systematic examination of human needs and change achieved through full use of modern technology whilst each architectural problem was reassessed constantly and thought out afresh.[5] The principles followed were to do with function and not with outward appearance:[6] the massing of the new buildings broke down the previous overemphasis upon formality, frontality, symmetry and monumentality. The new school buildings conveyed the message to the community that progressive, liberal education had arrived.[7]

Many elementary schools catering for the 5–14 year olds, with very little specialist accommodation apart from a woodwork shop and a teaching kitchen (see Athelney, Chapter 1), became primary schools with the intention that at eleven the pupils progressed to secondary education – 'a system of comprehensive high schools'[8] – having much fuller provision in the crafts and sciences. The post war increase in the school population and the need to replace obsolete buildings and rebuild war-damaged buildings necessitated over four hundred new schools in inner London by 1970.

The 1944 Act's triparite approach to secondary education (grammar, technical and secondary modern schools) consolidated proposals made by the Hadow Report, 1926, the Spens Report, 1938, and the Norwood Report, 1943, and resulted in the 1950's in pressure for change culminating in the call for common comprehensive education for all. The LCC in the 1950's adopted a long term strategy for comprehensive secondary schools basing size upon the number of first forms necessary to achieve a sixth form able to sustain economically the necessary numbers of specialist teachers. The strategy was founded upon a development plan for primary and secondary education[9] and a scheme for further education.[10] The belief grew that economies of scale provided a greater range of opportunities: large comprehensive schools were a culmination of this belief and initially ninety were proposed, each having 2,000 pupils.

Teaching attitudes had changed to the mutual benefit of those involved: the problems of socialising the young adult were recognised and it was seen as beneficial to pursue education in partnership. The size of the schools guaranteed educational benefits but also introduced arguments concerning the need to stream children of differing abilities.

All age or year based houses were introduced to cut across the segregation of ability and to provide full integration for all children. The introduction of the house system, based upon that used in existing schools, brought a fundamental change into secondary education for here the individual pupil, sometimes in quite large organisations, retained individual social significance and participation in and cooperation with the wider school community consequently evolved. This was the first attempt to match social accommodation with the maturing needs of adolescents.

Many architects working upon school design immediately post war were the first generation trained as non-traditional designers[11] for whom the whole world's contemporary style was an acceptable idiom.[12] They were fired with post war social idealism and the social need of school building provided fulfilment. Despite general austerity post-war construction was given impetus by pervasive optimism.

This brave optimism was demonstrated by the LCC Education Committee when patronage of the arts was seen to be a natural continuation of the exciting new architecture for the new educational expansion. Schools and colleges were given sculpture, fountains, mural panels and large scale textiles were designed especially for the large scale new volumes of assembly halls. It was a time of commitment and high purpose.

The Ministry of Education, acting as pace-maker and tutor, produced a succession of Building Bulletins which gave detailed information varying from the provision of school kitchens (school meals became a feature of school life after the 1944 Act) to the need for protecting the school and its occupants from fire. The beneficial use of colour in schools was set out and the dimensioning of school furniture and fittings was to become an art in itself. The Ministry pursued various development projects for primary and secondary schools and the findings were broadcast by the Bulletins. At the same time cost control was introduced in 1949 with the Ministry introducing limits of capital expenditure upon each individual project.[13] This operated in concert with the publication of statutory regulations for minimum sites, teaching areas, lavatory accommodation, etc.[14]

The immediate effect of cost limits was to force architects to seek the most economic building methods and to review, by functional analysis, the space available for each school pupil. Since 1945 circulation space had been lavishly provided but after 1949 primary schools tended to lose their corridors as classrooms were designed for forty pupils, being self-contained with their own sinks and lavatory blocks having direct access to the open air:[15] internal circulation space became largely unnecessary.[16] In order to maintain maximum teaching areas secondary schools had reduced circulation space and many ideas were pursued to maximise such circulation space that was retained: corridors were double banked with classrooms on either side limiting choice of orientation and preventing cross-ventilation (see Chapter 1 (10)). Sandwich corridors were introduced and dead end corridors were used in an attempt to reduce circulation areas to the absolute minimum: in conjunction with cost limits the minimum corridor with cheap finishes probably has created more problems in secondary schools (poor ventilation, casual damage leading to positive vandalism) and cost far more in terms of bad behaviour and repair bills than the margin initially assumed to be saved (see Chapter 11).

To reduce circulation to a minimum the exploded plan was evolved with short span and medium span spaces being separated into pavilions linked by covered ways. The workshop block was able to develop as an entity whilst the gymnasium and assembly hall with dining accommodation were different from the teaching block. Economic necessity gave impetus to the adoption of some basic tenets of the Modern Movement – separation and articulation.[17]

In the late 1940's and early 1950's building materials were in short supply with severe limitations upon imported timber and traditional steel work was not always available. One consequence was that new methods of exploiting available materials were progressed, but not all new technology was fully understood (see Chapter 10).

John Ball Primary School [18]

Immediately after the end of the War in 1945 stock was taken of the LCC education building needs and it was discovered that out of the 1,200 schools in use in 1939, 1,150 had been damaged or demolished. The rebuilding or replacement of primary schools was the most urgent priority and in the late 1940's and early 1950's the resources of the schools architects were concentrated upon these objectives. Acute shortages of traditional building materials and skilled building labour required a new approach to construction and the light steel construction system based upon development in the Hertfordshire

schools of the late 1940's, was developed to build a large number of primary schools upon an 8'3" (2.50 m) structural grid.

The site of 2.00 acres (0.80 hectares) overlooks a railway to the south and has a steep cross fall of 9–12 metres: large specimen trees on the periphery of the site were retained. The design was developed along the contours with the infant classrooms developed as single-storey pavilions opening on to a high terrace making a natural teaching extension. The administration block, with overtones of small scale Dudok influence, runs across the contours to link with the two storey junior class-room block located at the bottom of the site. Under the southern end of the administration block the natural fall of the site has provided a covered play

area. Circulation was reduced but a large separate dining room was provided. Lavatory accommodation is concentrated into internal blocks and quite separate from external play areas.

The whole design shows a confident articulation of shapes, levels and functions: one major new function is the provision of a kitchen and dining block and the flat roof signalled a break with the traditional, and what is now called vernacular, building. Wide, high windows demonstrate the influence of the requirement [19] for all teaching spaces to provide a 2% daylight factor. The new age of school building in inner London was launched when the design of this school, constructed in 1951–52, and its contemporaries were accepted by the members of the LCC Education Committee.

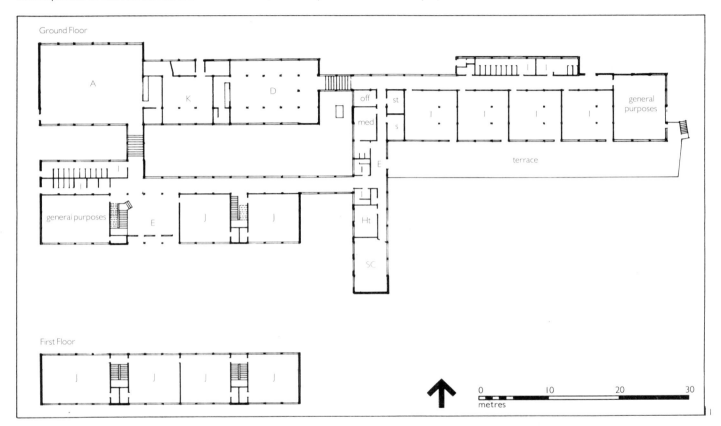

Ground Floor

First Floor

1 Ground Floor Plan
The site falls steeply from the North and the school is built across the contours. Planning shows the discipline necessary using a light steel constructional system originally developed by Hertfordshire County Council and later marketed by Hills Ltd: this was widely used to make good war damage in inner London.

Cellular classrooms, identical for juniors and infants, are served by long straight single-banked corridors and the plan form gives a very high and costly perimeter
2 *South elevation, 1956, showing the infants' wing on a brick faced terrace with the administration block providing a covered space at playground level.*

3 *Infant classrooms developed as separate pavilions built from a light steel constructional system and opening out directly on to a terrace.*
4 *Infants' wing with terrace immediately available as an extra external work space.*
5 *The infant classroom shows the utilitarian nature of the steel constructional system. Despite the large windows rooflights have been found necessary to meet daylighting requirements.*

It is noticeable that by 1956 the formal teaching approach was beginning to dissolve in favour of the group method even if the furniture available had to be used in a radically different way from its design.

3

4

5

Brooklands Primary School

With the development of Blackheath as a new private housing area, mainly Span with Eric Lyons as the architect, came the need for new schools for as many as forty new houses replaced one large private house. The school site itself, 1.84 acres (0.73 hectares), replaced a large house and had a fine array of specimen trees around which the design was progressed. It was completed in 1957 and provided eight classrooms for 320 children.

Apart from the steel framed assembly hall a standard form of construction had developed using brick cross walls with prestressed concrete beams carrying concrete floors and wood wool roofs.

The steel cladding system was developed as a window wall based on a 3'4" (one metre) grid giving a light and elegant appearance.

Classrooms were large (71 m²) from the specified class size and were built in pairs, each with its own lavatories, to reduce circulation space;[20] there was no direct connection with external play areas. The cellular design being based upon load-bearing walls limits future flexibility and does not convey the ease of adaptation thought normal ten years later. The assembly hall was placed to act as a link with other elements of the school again to reduce circulation. Articulation of the plan and separation of the elements makes an attractive design but paradoxically is profligate, due to the high cost of cladding, in view of earnestly sought economies.

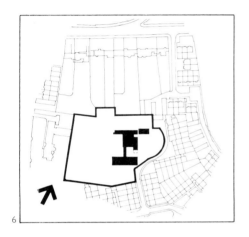

6 Site Plan
It was possible to assemble generous sites in some parts of London – in this case Blackheath – due to the size of the original housing plots from which they were formed. The large sites to the North were giving way to the new private housing (SPAN) from the South.

7 Ground Floor and First Floor Plans
The plans illuminate the simplicity of approach with separation of function for the teaching block from the hall and administration. The site is large enough for the layout to make obeisance to a large cedar of lebanon. Classrooms follow the earlier precept of the pavilion plans and face due South.

Already the circulation space has been drastically reduced and it is necessary to go through some classrooms to reach others whilst lavatory and cloakroom accommodation is contained within the classroom volume: this arrangement later led to the development of practical areas. Infant and junior classrooms are identical and interchangeable. Simple cross wall construction is used except for the assembly hall which has a steel frame.

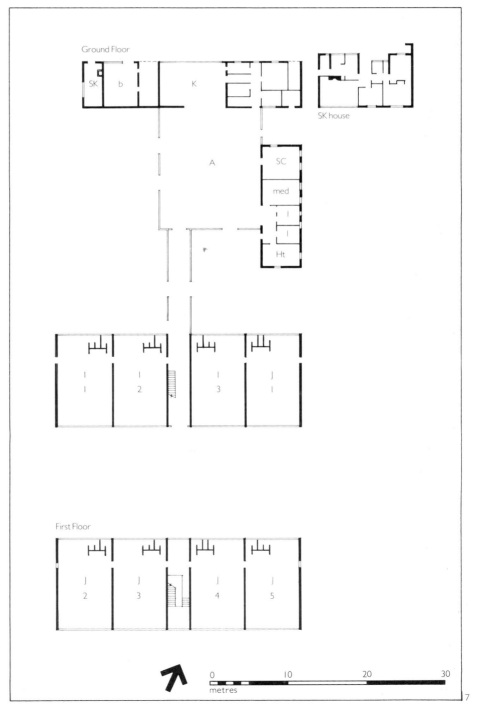

51

8

9

8 West Elevation
The low, elegant simplicity is established here as a foil to the large cedar tree.
9 *The assembly hall from the west shows an early form of glass box with minimal glazing bars to mark its periphery. The junior classroom block is linked directly to the hall which acts as circulation space.*
10 *Crosswall construction is clearly shown in the junior classroom block although it is expressed only at the flanks with the window wall cladding mastering the intermediate party walls. The panels below the windows were usually finished in bright primary colours.*

10

Garratt Green School

In 1955 Garratt Green School for secondary girls was designed upon the basis of what later would have probably been described as a campus plan: the blocks are separated into types with upper and lower teaching blocks, upper and lower house blocks, an assembly hall block, a staff block and an administration block with a system of wide covered ways connecting all. The monolith is avoided by fragmentation and, despite its size, it has an informal humanity.[21]

The social intent is clear with a fully equipped dental surgery and recovery room incorporated into the administration suite whilst the assembly hall also contains specially designed music practice rooms.

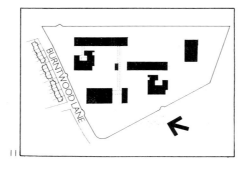

11 Site Plan
The plan demonstrates separation and identification by function with the long teaching blocks connected by covered ways to the house blocks: a further link continues to the administration and assembly hall blocks. The swimming pool/gymnasia alone stand remote.

12 Ground Floor Plan
Pursuing the spirit of the age the new secondary school includes specialist accommodation for science and music whilst the assembly hall is akin to a fully equipped theatre.

The house blocks each provide four age related rooms served by a kitchen: the four-storey teaching blocks are also age related serving the lower or the upper school.

13 First Floor Plan
The upper floors of the teaching blocks demonstrate attempts to reduce circulation by shortened corridors although the full range of support areas (cloakrooms, rest rooms, medical rooms) were left intact. A planning grid of 3'4'' (one metre) was used throughout being reflected both in the structural expression and the fenestration of the buildings.

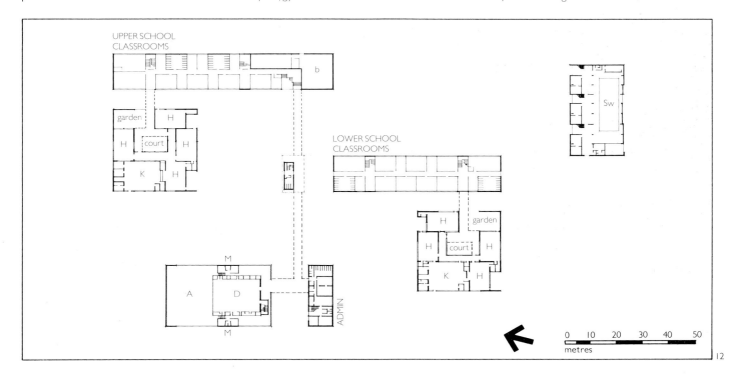

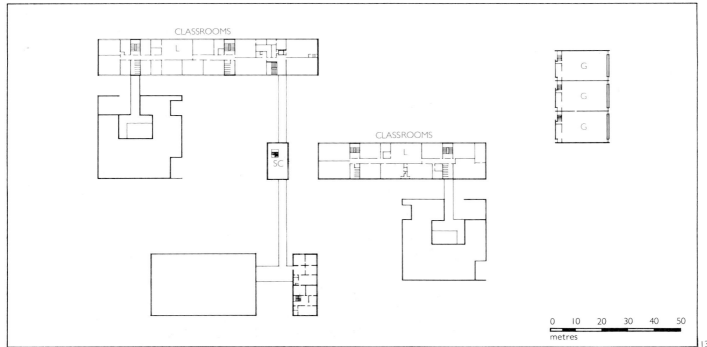

To reduce the impact of size upon the individual in a school designed for 2,200 pupils the house blocks are related by age and are single storey, each containing four houserooms with one self-contained kitchen each: each has a tuck shop also to extend the measure of individual independence and a very wide corridor for intentional occasional contact ensures careful integration into the school society. A cloistered garden provides a calm contemplative centre to the block.[22]

Each teaching block is completely equipped for the new intention of full secondary education for all: a full range of science laboratories and art and craft rooms complement the general teaching rooms which are grouped throughout the two buildings. The gymnasium block begins to reveal the real scale of provision with three fully equipped gymnasia at first floor level above changing rooms an indoor swimming pool: the changing rooms are banked in

such a way with associated staircases that movement of large numbers of girls within the block can be directed without confusion. All blocks have wide corridors, generous open staircases and full cloakroom and rest room provision indicating that at this stage cost limits were still a desirable objective and not a reductive and inhibiting mechanism.

The various blocks are treated as individual buildings but finished with similar cladding to give an overall, if somewhat diffuse, unity: they are clear, light, simple forms constructed around the now ubiquitous in-situ reinforced concrete frame, having wide spans of steel framed windows with face brickwork and precast concrete cladding with marble aggregate. Attempts at expressing rationally the function of various rooms and suites had begun to be exploited and, in consequence, the elevations convey a balanced abstraction closely related to the 3' 4'' (one metre) dimensional grid underlying both the

rooms and their enclosure. Roofs are generally flat except for wider spans where structural necessity shaped the resulting curve. Due to the intricacies of servicing required for this group of buildings electrical and mechanical consultants played a larger role in the development of the project and to make a rational provision, whilst easing future maintenance, a complete network of accessible ducts, including some crawl ducts for the major routes, was included under the ground floor slab with large rising ducts associated with the staircases.

One of the most noticeable developments of this site is the success of the landscaping. There is sufficient space among the network of buildings for a wide range of planting (some of the original trees are now handsome mature specimens) of different natures and the hard finishes for paths and playspaces demonstrate imagination.

14

14   *Three gymnasia are placed over an internal swimming pool. Construction is straightforward being based upon an in-situ reinforced concrete frame which is allowed expression by omitting precast cladding panels.*
15   *Interior of swimming pool indicates the scale of provision thought appropriate for the new generation of secondary schools.*

15

16 The reinforced concrete frame is not expressed upon this teaching block as it is obscured by window wall panel junctions. Different room functions demand different window expression and the mass of the building is reduced.

17 The 3'4" dimensional grid was used throughout the design and is demonstrated upon elevations of quite different types of building in different ways. View from the west showing the main entrance with the assembly hall to the left and the upper teaching block in the background.

18 The assembly hall interior demonstrates a new approach to structure with mild steel, tubular section trusses supporting softwood rafters.

William Penn School

The construction of this large comprehensive school in 1955 for boys only demonstrates the concern still felt for the separate education of boys and girls. Like Garratt Green this school is developed using the exploded plan form but it shows a totally different approach in producing a parallel establishment.

In their distribution the blocks follow a far more formal layout with the imposing main entrance effected under a bridge with the assembly hall immediately and axially available as in the earlier neo-Georgian plans: this is the public face of the school and it offers order and a secure environment. The separate buildings have no simple connection except for the workshop and house blocks which frame the entrance by having a suspended corridor at first floor level, otherwise circulation between them is in the open air. Science, art and the humanities are taught in the large four storey block where corridors are truncated for economy but staircases are treated as sculptural forms, freestanding cantilevered exercises in structural engineering expertise with tiled panel murals to enhance them.

The scale of provision can be gauged by the assembly hall and the games block where three gymnasia can be expanded into a vast sports hall. The numbers of pupils to be moved and accommodated is shown by the scale of the lobbies of the assembly hall where multiple use for drama and music is conjectured by the raked gallery over the entrance and the music suite beneath the hall itself. The fully glazed side walls with few opening lights require the battery of extract fans on the roof to make the hall habitable on warm days.

A 3' 4'' (one metre) grid is used throughout the school and this is reflected in the layout and general planning of the individual blocks. It finds expression externally in the elevations where again the phrase 'window wall' expresses the simple infilling between internal partitions and demonstrates the freedom conferred by the reinforced concrete frame. Paradoxically, the frame is expressed at ground floor only where it shows the lightness of construction and a pursuit of the earlier ideal of buildings raised off the ground by piloti; notionally, the unencumbered volume resulting would allow the free flow of space defined by the building but in the 1950's the lowest concrete frame was used to permit articulation of a multi-storeyed building down to ground level with a ground beam expressed above gound level.

The tank room, mounted on the highest block, is of a large enough volume to require apparent reduction in size by the use of balconies. The power demonstrated by the close confines of the courtyard is diluted by the use of different cladding materials: in addition to brick and precast concrete panels, presenting an apparently solid facade, the inclusion of vertical boarding and vitrolite panels serves to undermine the unity of the design.

The use of other materials provides information about the building industry at the time: floor finishes are largely solid oak block or terrazzo but the suspended floors are of precast, prestressed concrete beams illustrating a shortage of basic material being met with intelligent structural economy.

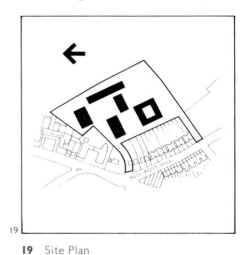

19

19 Site Plan
Although the site is quite large by urban standards the exploded plan form — separated by function as is Garratt Green School, see Fig 11 — uses the space available in providing smaller scale areas between the buildings. As the site falls from South to North these areas form playgrounds with different levels.

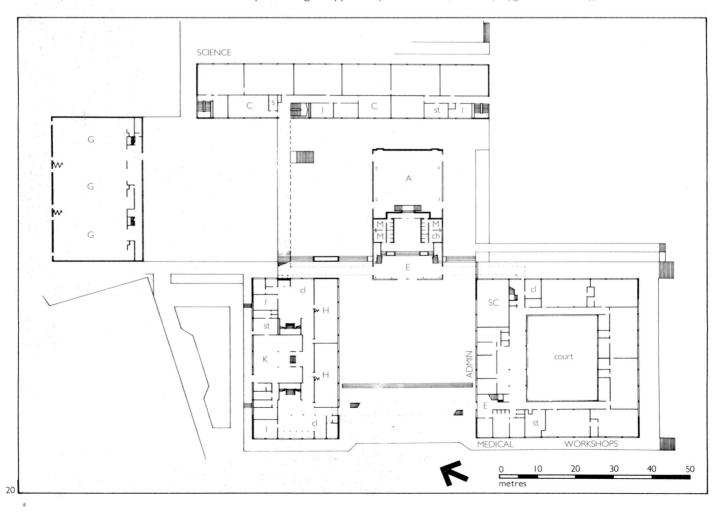

20

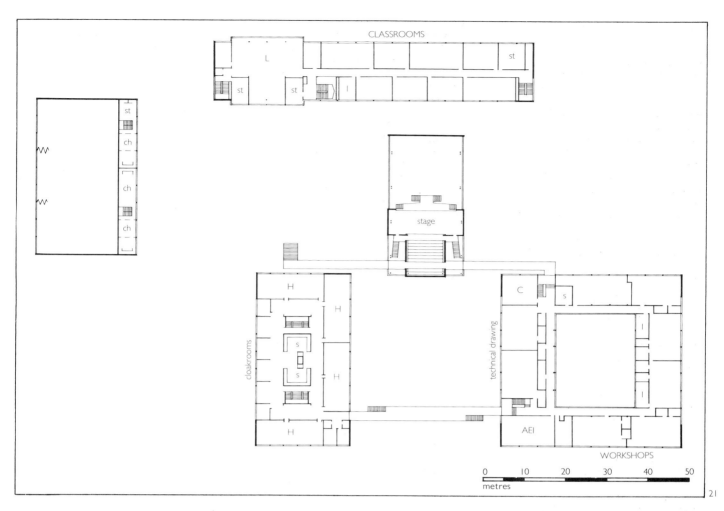

CLASSROOMS

stage

cloakrooms

technical drawing

WORKSHOPS

0 10 20 30 40 50
metres

21

20 Ground Floor Plan
The differing volumes of the house block and the workshop block are carefully placed to provide a sunken, symmetrical, main entrance court closed by the main public building, the assembly hall. Three gymnasia are planned to form a games hall together and a four storey slab block contains all teaching, general and specialist. The playground to the gymnasia is a storey lower than that around the assembly hall.
21 First Floor Plan
This layout reinforces the specialist nature of the separate blocks demonstrating the use of bridges to ease communication. Stores for the Evening Institute are included in the workshop block.
22 *Art was taught to a larger number of pupils than previously in well-equipped spaces such as this pottery room.*
23, 24 *In the large new secondary schools all pupils were expected to study science (Fig 23) and the size of the school enabled special provision to be made for the sixth form (Fig 24).*

22

23

24

25

27

26

28

29

30

25 The school size made it possible to have large, fully-equipped libraries available to all pupils.

26 Staircases were in-situ reinforced concrete structures and were seen as potentially sculptural: thus the flights were cantilevered and these hard wearing areas were given tiled walls to protect and enhance them.

27 A school catering for so many pupils required three gymnasia which could be transformed into one large games hall as shown here: the dividing partitions can be seen folded back against the side walls.

28 The main teaching block window wall allows the reinforced concrete frame to be seen, unlike that at Garratt Green (see Fig 16); the main entrance to the block is signalled by a panel of bright tiling. Service and tank rooms proved problematical and many were disguised with pergolas and balconies in an attempt to reduce their bulk.

29 The workshop block provides an oasis of calm with its enclosed courtyard. The window wall has developed its own elegance and white framed opening lights are used to articulate the neat geometry of enclosure.

30 View from the west over the entrance bridge indicates the impact of the axial assembly hall block in this close confined area.

Franklin Delano Roosevelt and John Keats Schools[23]

In addition to remoulding the aims of general education the Butler Act also extended the duties of education authorities in the provision of special education. On one site two schools were constructed catering for children with differing diabilities. Roosevelt was provided for 160 physically handicapped and Keats for 180 delicate children. The site is flat and has many mature, handsome trees which further planting enhanced. The schools were designed 'simply and boldly'[24] in 1955 and are similar in many respects both having an 'elegant courtyard plan, condensed but of great charm and practicality':[25] The construction is load-bearing brickwork except for the steel framed assembly halls but whilst Roosevelt has a pre-stressed concrete roof slab Keats has a hollow pot in-situ concrete roof. Windows are softwood with steel opening lights with under-sill panels in cedar boarding.[26] In essence these two schools are very similar to contemporary primary schools with minor special differences: Roosevelt has a medical suite with a remedial exercise room whilst Keats has the maximum number of opening windows and a heated floor. In 1978 this enclave for special education was completed with the addition of the Frank Barnes School (see Chapter 13) which is radically different in function and appearance from the two earlier schools.

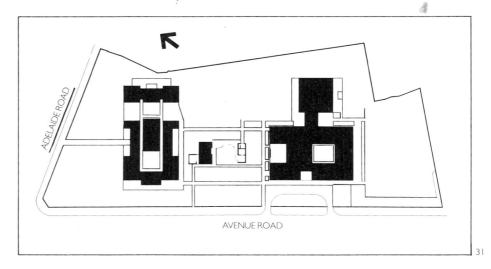

31 Site Plan
The site is shared by the two schools and together they maximise the wide sweep of grass and mature trees in an exclusive neighbourhood.
32 *The school sits comfortably in a handsome, mature, park-like garden which its simple elegance enhances.*
33 *Large trees frame the main entrance and this view shows the simple load-bearing construction with cedar fascias.*
34 *Like the neighbouring Roosevelt school this building is contained in a garden site.*
35 *An enclosed courtyard flanked by the assembly hall and classrooms.*

Chapter 2: References

1 Education, 10 July 1981, p 27: *illustrates the radical nature of the Act as 'it envisaged an extension of compulsory schooling from 14 to 15 and eventually to 16. It aimed at a sufficient supply of nursery schools. All school leavers up to the age of 18 were to benefit from technical education or part-time study in county colleges. The Act also laid firm ground rules for transport of pupils, school meals, medical services, maintenance grants for students and special education.'*

2 The Times Educational Supplement, 12 March 1982, p 3: *in an obituary notice Lord Butler's Act is described as revolutionising British education 'by sweeping away the concept of elementary education as an inferior system for the poor and replacing it with primary and secondary education as a continuous process, free and available to all.'*

3 Architects Journal, 27 January 1982, p 32: *speaks of the public and political 'will' for change paralleled by new building methods and images.*

4 Architects Review, May 1959, p 306.

5 RIBA Journal, May 1967: *Leslie Martin's 'An Architect's Approach to Architecture' speaking of the scientific approach of the 1930's and on p 191 speaks of a 'new attitude and a new method of work'. Dr Martin is here referring to an article in the Journal of the Society of Historians, March 1965, by Catherine Bauer-Wurster 'The Social Front of Modern Architecture in the 1930's'.*

6 Cantacuzino S, Howell, Killick, Partridge and Annis: Architecture; Lund Humphries, 1981, p 10.

7 Architectural Review, November 1956, pp 302–324: LCC, New Standards in Official Architecture by Furneaux Jordan.

8 White Paper, Education Reconstruction, 1943, was the basis of the new LCC Secondary School Principles.

9 The London School Plan – a development plan for primary and secondary: LCC Annual Report 1947. See Appendix A for provision.

10 The London Scheme for Further Education: *LCC Annual Report, 1944, p 14 describes the scheme as 'one of evolution not revolution'. See Appendix B for expenditure.*

11 Watkin D, English Architecture, Thames and Hudson, 1979, *'traditionalism was the norm until the 1940's' p 190.*

12 Esher L, The Broken Wave, Allen Lane, 1981: the first part 'Consensus' illustrates the influences which changed architectural and social attitudes.

13 Ministry of Education, Circular 209, 1949.

14 Standards for School Premises Regulations, No 345, 1945.

15 Seaborne M & Lowe, The English School, Its Architecture and Organisation, Vol II, 1870–1970: *see p 161 for comparative reductions (eg primary 1949 total area per child 69 square feet including 27 for teaching: by 1957 these figures had changed to 43 and 29 square feet. In secondary schools 44 square feet per pupil in 1949 required 102 gross but by 1957 the secondary pupil had 45 square feet of teaching space out of gross total of 70 square feet.*

16 Official Architecture, September 1966, Trends in School Design, p 1279, *reported that cost limits in 1966 were still the same as in 1949 although building costs had risen 45%. Generally, the ratio of teaching to general areas had changed from 40:60 to 60:40.*

17 Cantacuzino S, Howell, Killick, Partridge and Annis: architecture; Lund Humphries, 1981, p 11.

18 Architectural Design, June 1959, p 225.

19 Standards for School Premises Regulations, No 345, 1945.

20 Architectural Design, June 1959, p 226

21 Architectural Review, Two Comprehensive Schools, May 1959, pp 306–313.

22 Architectural Design, June 1959, pp 229–231.

23 Architectural Design, June 1959, p 228.

24 Architects Journal, 12 March 1959, pp 411–424.

25 Architectural Review, November 1956, p 323.

26 The Builder, 26 September 1958, pp 524–525.

Key to drawings

A	assembly hall
AEI	adult education institute
AH	activities hall
C	classroom
CR	common room
D	dining
Dr	drama
DW	dining/work
E	entrance
G	gymnasium
H	houseroom
Hm	home bay
Ht	head or principal
I	infants
J	juniors
K	kitchen
L	library
Lt	lecture
M	music
Ns	nursery
P	practical area
PC	play centre
Q	quiet area
S	secretary
Sc	science
SC	staff common room
SH	sports hall
SK	schoolkeeper
Sw	swimming pool
W	waiting
YS	youth service
b	boiler
ca	covered area
ch	changing
cl	cloakroom
l	lavatories
s	servery
st	store

In the optimistic years following 1945 there was a continual, rolling and developing wave in educational building. Initially the primary schools were the most urgent priority in inner London due to war damage and the requirements of the 1944 Education Act. Resources concentrated upon these were then used to design and build secondary schools as the initial pressure eased. By the late 1950's the pattern was beginning to change once more as the emphasis was now placed upon providing buildings for further education.[1] Education provision for those over compulsory school age was sporadic throughout the United Kingdom and there never had been any uniform pattern of further education. Outside of the universities and polytechnics technical colleges had grown up in response to local demand and their siting had been largely dictated by the location of industry. In 1956 the White Paper on Technical Education set out a five year plan proposing the establishment of colleges of further education, area technical colleges, regional technical colleges and colleges of advanced technology. Systematisation by levels of work was gradually established and these ranged from supplying education to students under eighteen, to providing more advanced courses and regional centres offering advanced courses on a full time basis up to colleges of advanced technology (CATs) until these last were transferred from local authority funding to direct state grants in 1962. Optimism was widespread and the nation was told that 'you've never had it so good'[2] by Harold Macmillan, the Prime Minister, before the 1959 election campaign.

Whilst the post war boom in education building had met inner London's most urgent needs, a second wave of primary and secondary schools was designed and built in the late 1960's and these show initially an independence of architectural spirit, for, although they met the needs of the same brief, attitudes were changing in educational philosophy.[3] A series of significant reports – Crowther, 1959, 15 to 18: Newsom, 1963, Half Our Future; Plowden, 1967, Primary Children and their Schools – reflected changing ideas and teaching methods each having a large influence in the development of school buildings: the last named setting the seal upon the movement towards open plan primary schools which had been evolving in this country since the beginning of the century and reflected in the Hadow Reports of 1931 and 1933.

Political change altered the inner city with the 1963 London Government Act which terminated the London County Council and created the Greater London Council (GLC) with a vastly enlarged area. Whilst each outer London borough was responsible for its education welfare services the old London boroughs, now inner London, controlled welfare services but a special committee of the GLC was set up under the Act to provide educational services in inner

London – the Inner London Education Authority (ILEA). This arrangement provided for a continued and unified education service covering the same area as the School Board for London, 1873, and confirmed by the Balfour Act, 1902; this Act restructured local government and thereafter the London County Council continued to provide the educational service for inner London. The Authority consists of the 35 GLC members for inner London constituencies together with 13 other members, one from each of the inner London Borough and City of London Councils. The full Education Committee consists of a further 17 members described as 'persons of experience in education and persons acquainted with educational conditions prevailing in the area for which the Committee acts': 5 of these are teachers employed by the Authority. The ILEA came into being in 1965 and, although architectural services remained unaltered from those of the LCC, an Education Architect was appointed specifically for the Authority's work. Each borough became the planning authority for its area and consequently might not necessarily view educational requirements in the borough with the same eyes as the ILEA. As London had largely repaired or replaced its bomb damage and as interests vied with each other to obtain options on land for development, serious problems arose in providing new or enlarged sites for schools. In 1965 the Ministry of Education changed its name to the Department of Education and Science (DES) in response to the call for a coming 'white hot technological age'.

Cost limits upon new school building were tightly administered by the DES and school plans became deeper to reduce the ratio of external enclosure to enclosed area as the former was demonstrated to be a highly expensive element with the advent of better cost information. Some education authorities with particular problems met these by rationalising their construction into system building: some architects were already demanding windows as efficient as those in motor cars – the gasket was added to mastic and factory production was proposed. The DES encouraged the use of system building upon the grounds of initial value for money (that is, a greater area of building provided for the same cost that traditional could provide), speed of construction and adherence to education building programme timetables – a dream arrangement for a centralised bureaucracy. By 1970 the consortia[4] were constructing 41%[5] of school building but by 1973 it was 35% and declining rapidly.[6] The best known is the Consortium, for Local Authority Special Programme (CLASP) and the acronyms grew – SCOLA, SEAC, METHOD, CLAW, ONWARD – but none suited construction in inner London as, at the time, the London Building Acts contained more rigorous requirements than other building regulations. In 1966, however, a rational-

ised building system (RBS) was developed by ILEA architects for single storey schools and twenty eight were constructed as there was a continuing and urgent need for primary schools in certain areas, notably Hackney, due to population movement: some special schools were built in this manner also. The continuation in system building was desired and fostered by the DES and the Metropolitan Architectural Consortium for Education (MACE) was set up in 1967 with the ILEA, Surrey County Council and many smaller education authorities as members. Twelve primary schools, one special school and a large secondary school were built for the ILEA in MACE and generally the architects designing the schools were critical of the system. Like other systems MACE reflected the well-intentioned utopian enthusiasm for good quality and high technical performance which can be obtained through high spending. The schools could be designed and placed in contract very quickly and they were built rapidly but they demonstrated the technical consequences of mass provision when no prototype had been allowed upon cost grounds. Apart from their initial inferior technical performance they provided an unacceptable architectural image – a uniform, box-like standard which suspended individual taste, wit and humanity – ubiquitous but nowhere in particular. Although the MACE schools were built for the ILEA between 1971 and 1974 they are part of the thinking of the 1960's and represent part of that busy decade.

Whilst architects had from 1870 provided hundreds of educational buildings they had not influenced the development of the educational brief and this is witnessed by the almost unvarying Victorian plan, however, the detailed appearance varied, and the repetitious, cellular layouts up to 1940. After 1945 designers were preoccupied in making – and being invited to make – bold architectural statements which met the brief. From the mid 1960's, however, the rapid rate of educational change required a far greater contribution from the architect in progressing with the client the development needs of a particular school or college. Thirty years after the statement 'Ideally, every school building should be a skin, or shell, that will change and grow as the living organism within changes and grows' was made there was a renewed demand for flexibility of use – initially in the primary schools but later in the secondary schools also.[7] This decade was the busiest for education building this century.

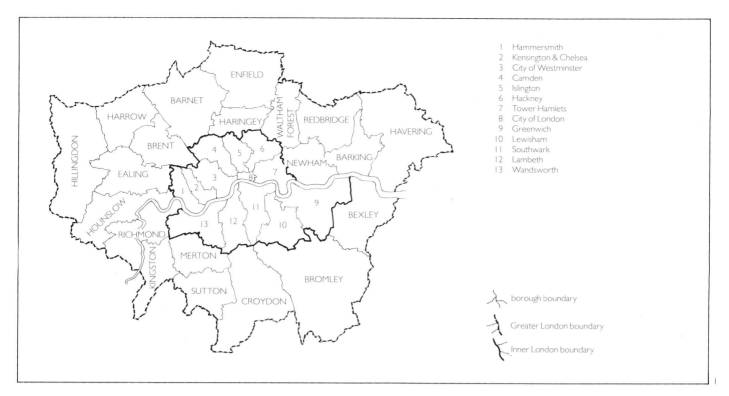

1   Map of the ILEA area
With the formation of the Inner London Education Authority under the London Government Act, 1963, a continuing link *with the original School Board for London, 1873, was preserved as the inner London Boroughs and the City of London share the ILEA's unified service.* *The same Act expanded Greater London with the formation of twenty outer London Boroughs.*

The map legend reads:

1 Hammersmith
2 Kensington & Chelsea
3 City of Westminster
4 Camden
5 Islington
6 Hackney
7 Tower Hamlets
8 City of London
9 Greenwich
10 Lewisham
11 Southwark
12 Lambeth
13 Wandsworth

borough boundary

Greater London boundary

Inner London boundary

Brixton College

Originally Brixton Day College this was intended to become one of the LCC's first county colleges but this policy was not pursued. The level site is 2.50 acres (1.00 hectare) with some good trees on the Brixton Hill boundary.

A primary concern was to create the impression in the minds of the day release students that they were not returning to school and a recognisable collegiate layout resulted, the plan attempting to create the atmosphere of a secluded and calm traditional quadrangle in a modern building.[8] The inner quadrangle is surrounded by a two storey building with the kitchen and dining accommodation under the assembly hall: the remainder of this block contains administration, general teaching, library and schoolkeeper's flat. A link at first floor level contains changing accommodation and connects with the double gymnasium which is built above the workshop block.

Construction is generally in-situ reinforced concrete with steel framework for the gymnasium block.[9] An existing gymnasium in the north east corner of the site was retained. The College was completed in 1960 and in 1980 a further small teaching block was built next to the old gymnasium.

2   Site Plan
The site is level in a residential area only a short distance from the centre of Brixton. It already contained a hutted gymnasium and some mature trees.

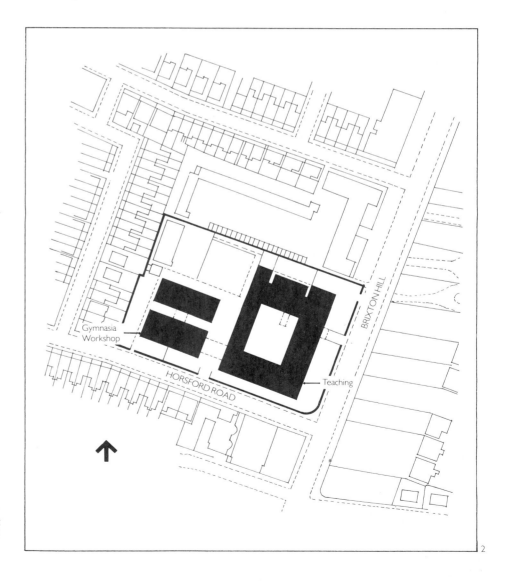

Gymnasia
Workshop

HORSFORD ROAD

BRIXTON HILL

Teaching

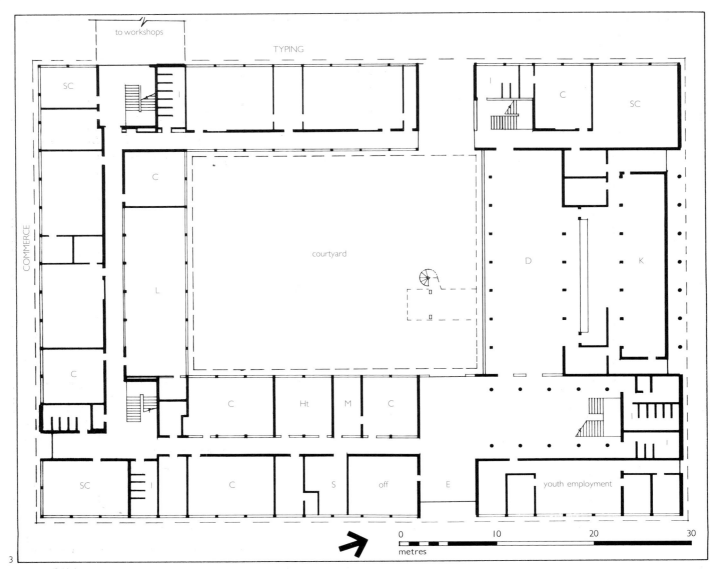

TYPING

to workshops

SC

COMMERCE

C

L

C

SC

C Ht M C

C S off E

courtyard

C

SC

D K

youth employment

0　　　　10　　　　20　　　　30
metres

3

3, 4 Ground and First Floor Plans
The accommodation is set out in a relaxed manner with a generous entrance hall, staircases and foyers. A full range of technical and commercial subjects is set out around a placid courtyard with a youth employment bureau located by the entrance.

To the West at ground floor level are the workshops and above these with a connection at first floor level are two gymnasia with changing rooms.

5 *The elevation to Brixton Hill describes the College as neat, modest and considerate. Articulation is made by a mosaic clad spandrel and steel windows to the ground floor and a slightly projected first floor with a timber framed window wall with steel opening lights.*

5

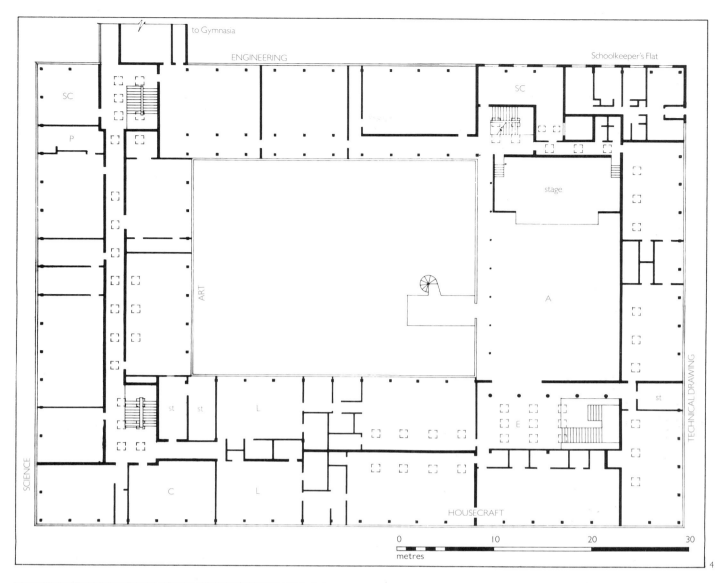

to Gymnasia

ENGINEERING

Schoolkeeper's Flat

SC

P

SC

stage

ART

A

SCIENCE

st st L

L

C L

E

st

TECHNICAL DRAWING

HOUSECRAFT

0   10   20   30

metres

4

6

7

6 *The quadrangle offers repose with the three teaching wings completing the enclosure with the assembly hall/dining area to the left. The circular staircase gives direct access to the hall.*

7 *Main staircases provided the focus for much design activity being regarded as major communication links: the main strings are in steel with precast terrazzo treads and the tiled background celebrates the space afforded.*

London College of Printing

Built on a 2.50 acre (1.00 hectare) site at the Elephant and Castle it was a major element in the comprehensive re-development of this heavily bombed area.[10] The College had previously occupied leased accommodation and annexes near Fleet Street and the rebuilding was to draw all of the departments together.

The College consisted initially of three buildings. Instruction in the printing trades and processes is carried out in the four storey workshop block. The assembly hall, lecture theatre, library, kitchens and other service areas are in the two storey communal block. Above this block is a thirteen storey teaching tower which contains classrooms, laboratories, design and photographic studios.

The workshop block expresses the heavy nature of its work and structure with an in-situ reinforced concrete frame and slabs with glazed panels infilling between beams and columns. The communal block demonstrates its enclosed nature with the in-situ concrete construction having an exposed aggregate facing. In-situ reinforced concrete provides the lift and staircase core of the teaching block whilst floors, perimeter columns and beams are precast: aluminium framed curtain walling glazes most of the block. The contract was completed in 1964.

A further five storey teaching block[11] was built over the car park in 1973.[12]

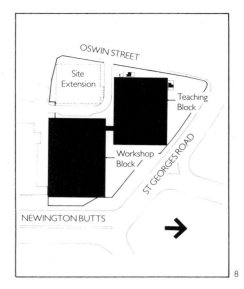

8

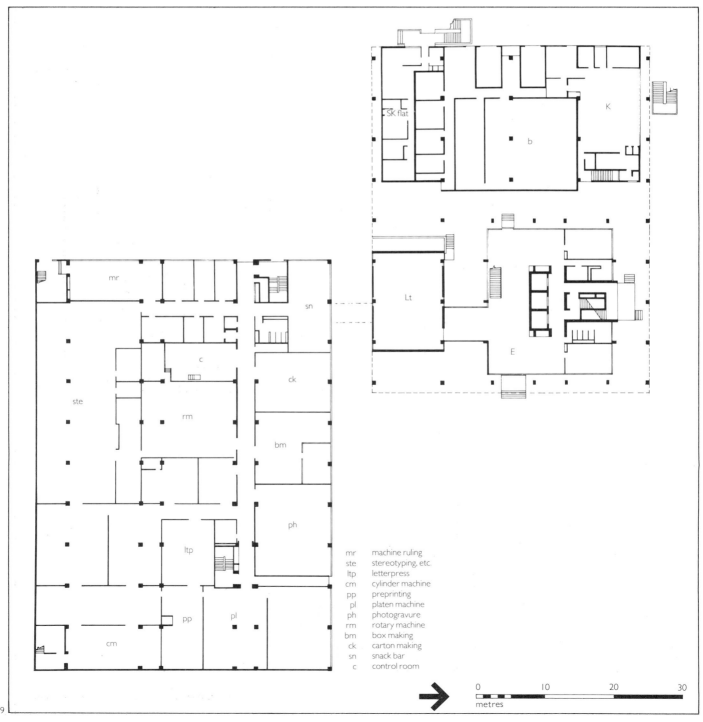

mr	machine ruling
ste	stereotyping, etc.
ltp	letterpress
cm	cylinder machine
pp	preprinting
pl	platen machine
ph	photogravure
rm	rotary machine
bm	box making
ck	carton making
sn	snack bar
c	control room

9

0   10   20   30
metres

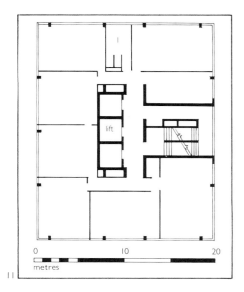

8 Site Plan
The college occupies an important position in the comprehensive redevelopment of the war-battered Elephant and Castle. It adjoins a well-known surviving building, the Metropolitan Tabernacle, and neighbouring sites have large scale housing and shopping developments. There is no boundary fence around the site as the original design envisaged public piazzas around the buildings.

9 Ground Floor Plan
With the heavy workshop to the South and service areas to the North, the main entrance demonstrates the separation by function.

10 First Floor Plan
Circulation space is generous where the workshop block abuts the communal block. The communal block plans show the use of interpenetration of structures, solids, and voids to provide ideas of the spaces contained.

11 Second Floor Plan
The tower block contains thirteen storeys of general teaching with specialist science and administration subjects.

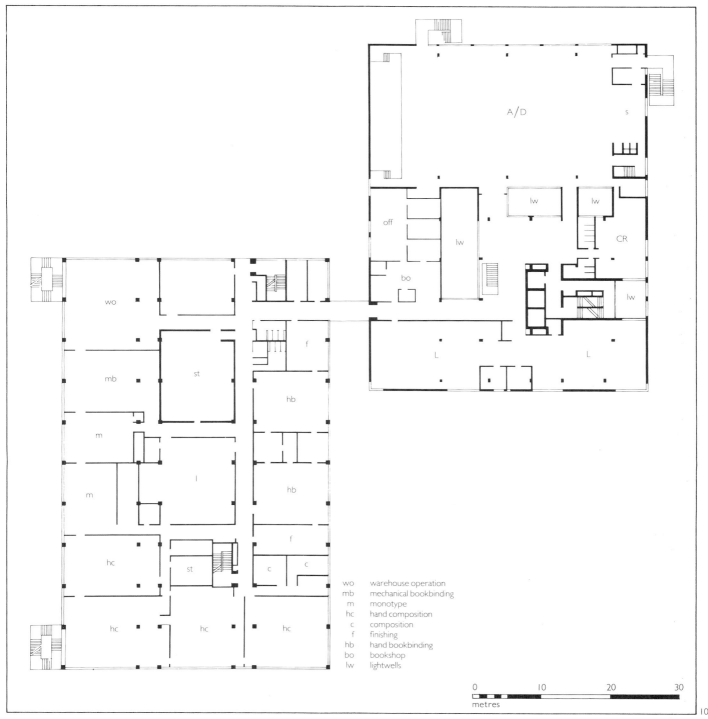

wo	warehouse operation
mb	mechanical bookbinding
m	monotype
hc	hand composition
c	composition
f	finishing
hb	hand bookbinding
bo	bookshop
lw	lightwells

12

12 Seen from the south the teaching tower balances lightly over the more solid communal block. The railings to the pavement indicate the sort of road system that the Elephant and Castle has become and with which the College must cope.

13 The workshop block expresses its heavy engineering content in its structure. Here the junction of the open, modelled, escape staircase with the adjoining Spurgeon's Tabernacle is illustrated – a good comparison of style and scale.

14 The main entrance to the College is through the communal block: this block balances in function and appearance between the lightly clad teaching tower and the solidly engineered workshop building. Mosaic cladding gives way to carefully cut fenestration demonstrating the function of the lighted spaces.

13

LONDON COLLEGE OF PRINTING

14

68

Garnett College

In 1960 the opportunity arose to rebuild this College on a beautiful falling site between Roehampton Lane and Richmond Park. It is unusual for a teachers' training college as it takes mature students from industry who wish to diverge into education: there are only three such establishments in the country.

The site is semi-public and unenclosed and is effectively two separate areas linked by a broad swathe of open grassland cutting through the Roehampton housing. The upper area contains Downshire House, a listed historic building of 1770, and the new teaching block which is two storey, becoming three with the slope, built around two small courtyards. Downshire House was rehabilitated to contain administration and common rooms associated with the teaching block. The teaching block is constructed of an in-situ concrete frame with aluminium sliding windows and light-weight undersill panels.

Mount Clare, 1772, by Robert Taylor with portico, 1780, by Columbani, dominates the lower area astride a knoll 400 metres away from Downshire House and is the College's communal and residential centre. Whilst Downshire is immaculate red brickwork, Mount Clare is pristine white stucco and its adjoining blocks make obeisance both in scale and colour. The large dining block with a street of staff flats over has a concrete frame to first floor and then the load-bearing upper structure is white painted brickwork interspersed with storey-height glazing which serves to break up the apparent size of the building. Residential accommodation is contained in two storey blocks with a brick load-bearing structure painted white. There are fifteen blocks of twelve study-bedrooms grouped in five clusters of three linked blocks. A single storey residence for the principal completes the layout, linking visually with the staggered, terraced local housing, having an eighteenth century temple at the end of the garden.

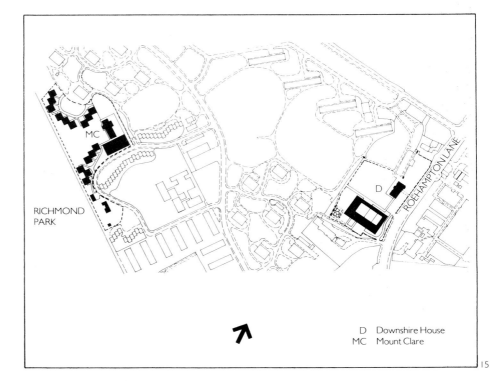

15 General Site Plan
The site is most unusual for being in two separate parts, approximately 400 metres apart, across the rolling parkland of the Roehampton housing development. Teaching is centred at Downshire House and the residential/communal centre is at Mount Clare adjacent to Richmond Park. Boundaries are generally left open in this area.

RICHMOND PARK

MC

D

ROEHAMPTON LANE

D   Downshire House
MC   Mount Clare

15

16 Downshire House Site Plan
Downshire House, 1770, serves as the administrative centre for the new teaching block. The ground falls away to the West and the two storey teaching block gains a storey from the House terrace.

Downshire House

New Teaching Block

16

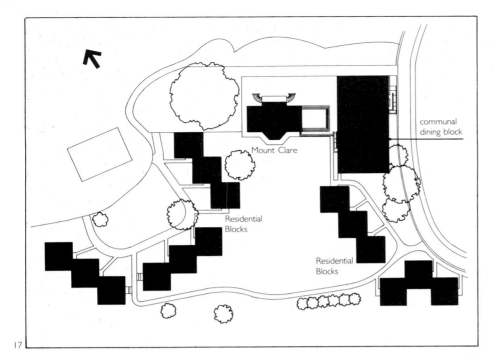

17 Mount Clare Site Plan

17 Mount Clare Site Plan
Residential and communal accommodation is centred upon Mount Clare, 1772, with the simple two storey brick residential blocks in echelon. The dining block is also treated very simply to avoid competing with the older building.
18 *The red brick of Downshire House is linked by covered way to the teaching block on the right. The sculpture is The Watchers by Lynn Chadwick and stares across to Mount Clare.*
19 *The falling site is obvious as the teaching block in the background gains a storey from the terrace of Downshire House.*
20 *Mount Clare, the nucleus of the residential part of the College.*
21 *Newer blocks are set out in sympathy with Mount Clare. In the foreground is an echelon of old people's houses with the communal block rising over them.*
22 *Mount Clare in closer juxtaposition to the dining block, centre, and one of the residential blocks to the right. The upper part of the dining block has been designed in small elements so as not to compete with the older building. White painted brickwork is used sympathetically with the aged, but restored, stucco.*

21

22

Hungerford Primary School

When it was decided to redevelop the existing handsome three storey primary school with the addition of a 240 place infant school plus 80 nursery places it was intended as the first stage of a 600 place primary school.

The site is large (2.08 acres, 0.83 hectares) and a single storey building sits easily in its space contrasting its horizontality against the bulk of the existing school. Three main teaching areas are trapezoidal in plan and provide for each infant year radiating from the administrative centre of offices, dining and main entrance: each area is self-contained with practical, resource and quiet spaces further emphasised by extending the radiating walls out into the playspace providing small, inter-linked playcourts instead of one large playground. Covered external work spaces are shared. The hall is radial also and isolated to provide insulation for noisy and quiet activities.

The walls are load-bearing masonry blockwork,[13] which is exposed internally and externally,[14] with timber framing to window walls and monopitch timber trusses for the roofs. The roof sheeting is dark blue and some of the lightweight cladding to window walls is vermillion coloured sheet. The contract started in 1968 and completed in 1970.

25

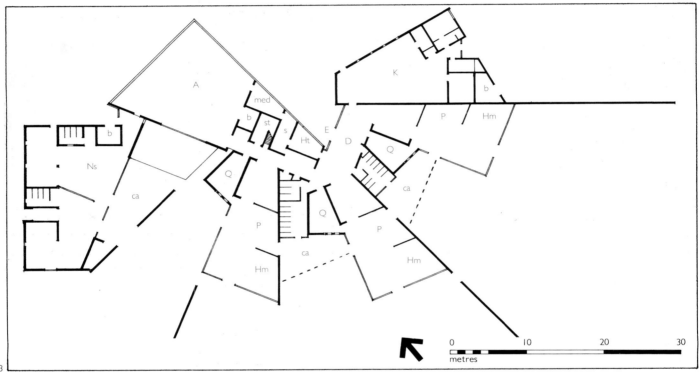

23

24

26

23 Layout Plan
Upon a larger, flat site the school plan spreads and here displays three similar teaching bays for a total of 240 infants. Each bay is for one infant year and provides a large practical area linking a home/quiet area with a home/resource area. Two covered work areas are shared.

The radiating walls running beyond the building perimeter identify enclosed playcourts closely associated with particular teaching bays. The assembly hall is isolated allowing noisy and quiet activities.

Load bearing walls and framed timber window walls carry monopitch timber roof trusses allowing the deeper sides of the plan to have continuous clerestory lighting.
24 *View from the south with the original school building in the background. Load-bearing walls, of concrete block, are extended externally to form playspace divisions. Window walls are made from structural timber with bright coloured lightweight sheet to unglazed areas.*
25 *Interiors are warm and domestic even though the scale of materials used is unusual. The use of plain blockwork throughout gives a unity and the timber structures provide a glow of natural elements.*
26 *The interior of the assembly hall shows the scale of the timber trusses and the straightforward use of materials.*

John Evelyn Primary School

With the growth in the numbers of young children in Deptford it was planned in 1967 to expand the existing three storey school to provide 560 places. The existing site was small but with Lewisham Borough Council's intention to redevelop the area comprehensively roads could be closed and a site extension assembled. The junior school would remain in the existing block and the new building would provide for the infants initially: the

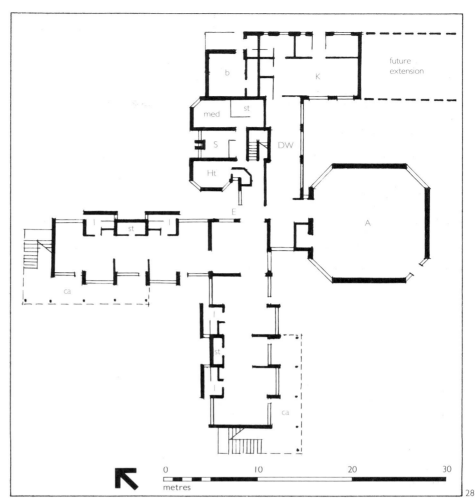

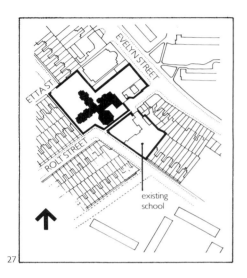

27 Site Plan
The site demonstrates the general problem of extending existing schools on small sites. The existing School Board building takes up half of its site and the new building must be designed to be extended into the existing site when the old building is demolished. Evelyn Street is a main feeder road for the A2 and is very noisy and with the necessity to maintain pedestrian links between Rolt Street and Evelyn Street and Rolt Street and Etta Street the new site use is heavily circumscribed.

28 Ground Floor Plan
Designed early in 1968 the plan shows a further move away from the cellular classroom without providing a totally open plan. At this stage the brief called for a range of different types of space which could be defined on a day-to-day basis by the school: the provision of small, domestic scaled spaces was emphasised and from this the 12'0'' (3.66 m) load-bearing bay developed with the articulated plan expressing and fulfilling the brief.

This building was designed for juniors but is used by infants in the absence of the second stage development of the site. The kitchen/service area acts as a barrier against traffic noise and the work/dining area was developed as a pullman arrangement.

29 First Floor Plan
The teaching space is identical in intent and layout with the ground floor with direct access to the covered work areas by enclosed staircases.

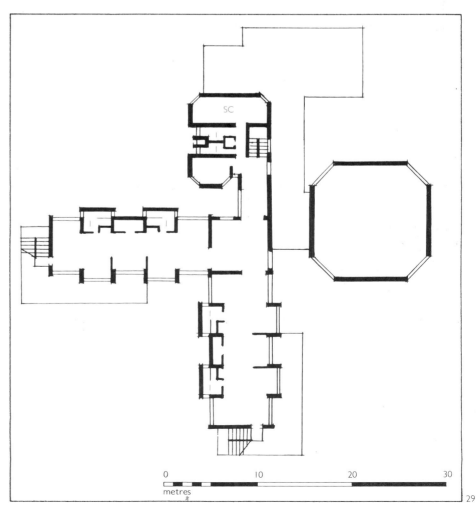

shape and size of the site extension precluded a new single storey school but this was seen as the first stage of complete rebuilding upon the demolition of the old school.

The flat treeless site of 1.50 acres (0.60 hectares) is separated from the original building by a public pedestrian way and has a high traffic noise level from the north. The assembly hall is isolated from the main two storey teaching areas to provide for quiet or noisy activities: teaching areas are long, articulated spaces with stores, lavatories and main construction providing a series of domestic scale bays for flexible use with minimal enclosure. The dining area is designed as a main work space and both levels of the buildings have a central undesignated space for development by the school.

Construction is load-bearing brickwork with in-situ reinforced concrete beams crossing the building and supporting concrete floor slabs or flat timber roofs.

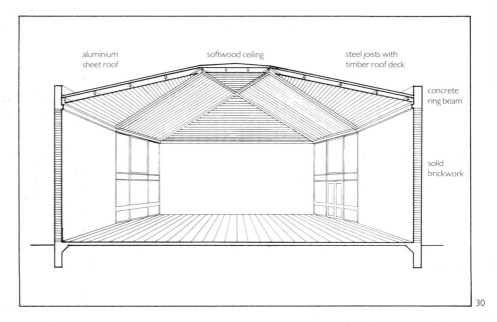

30

30   Assembly Hall
The assembly hall demonstrates the constructional principles of separation of material and their articulation. Solid 13½" (363 mm) brickwork is raised in freestanding panels on mass footings with an expressed in-situ reinforced concrete ring beam providing restraint at the wall top. The main roof construction is in standard rolled steel joists carrying a timber deck with an aluminium sheet finish. Internally, the brickwork is painted and a softwood ceiling echoes the general structural planes whilst revealing the steelwork.

31   *The long teaching spaces are articulated by structure and partitions and the school uses them as a series of linked bays: curtains which were originally required to close the openings in the brick partitions have been removed providing the option of more open continuous space instead of smaller enclosures.*

32   *This view from the north-west shows how tightly the form of the school fits the available site. On the left is the adjoining church and in the background is the original school building now used for juniors only. Mature trees were retained and incorporated into the layout.*

The simplicity of construction is demonstrated with in-situ concrete beams spanning on to load-bearing brickwork: the articulation of the plan is evident in the modelling of the elevations.

31

32

Rationalised Building System (RBS)

This system was developed in the middle 1960's to meet a large programme of primary schools – it is suitable for single storey construction only – in a relatively short space of time. Eventually twenty eight were built but whilst rationalised they are by no means standardised.

The original intention was to provide a light, cheap, swift method of construction and the consequence was a simple structural solution. Essentially the ground slab was designed like a road – ballast rejects consolidated in a scraped depression with a concrete raft, reinforced with steel fabric, poured directly over a bed of sand containing a polythene damp proof membrane. A 100 mm × 100 mm square section mild steel frame on a module of 12'0" (3.60 m) was bolted into plates set in the slab. The roof was constructed of stressed skin plywood box girders made into insulated punts spanning between the steel frames. Internal walls were not load-bearing being of lightweight building blocks surfaced with pin-up boards: careful siting of electrical service points gave opportunity for almost universal future flexibility. Heating was usually by means of small, local gas-fired heaters circulating warm air in ducts at high level over suspended ceilings with outlets typically above windows.[15] Since completion it has been found possible to swiftly install or remove partitions, add or delete areas, to the everyday advantage of the school in question.

33 Rationalised Building System (RBS)
The typical section of the original system shows its clarity with a concrete slab, reinforced with steel fabric, poured on to a bed of sand containing a polythene damp proof membrane, the whole set on consolidated ballast rejects.

Square section mild steel columns, usually at 12'0" (3.60 m) centres were bolted to plates in pockets left in the slab with rolled steel beams carrying plywood 'punts' as the structural roof deck. The fascias at low level and roof level were factory-produced plywood boxes with the actual external finish varying with the tightness of the cost limits. Originally a plastic faced, profiled aluminium sheet was intended for cladding but cost eroded this and it was succeeded by horizontal ship-lap boarding or painted plywood.

Ceilings were usually proprietary suspended brands and windows normally were vertical or horizontal sliders. The system responded swiftly to cost requirements as not only was it possible to economise as necessary upon external cladding, windows and ceilings but the basic 12'0" grid could be reduced marginally to effect area reduction.
34 Rationalised Building System (RBS)
This isometric shows the complete system including the construction of clerestorey windows to the assembly hall.

The system was neat, simple, rapidly constructed but bloodless.

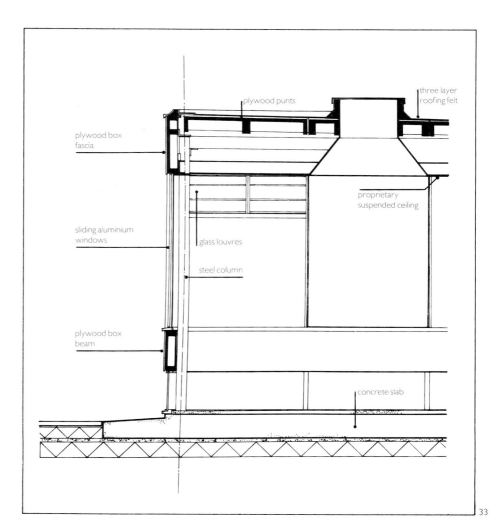

plywood punts

three layer roofing felt

plywood box fascia

proprietary suspended ceiling

sliding aluminium windows

glass louvres

steel column

plywood box beam

concrete slab

33

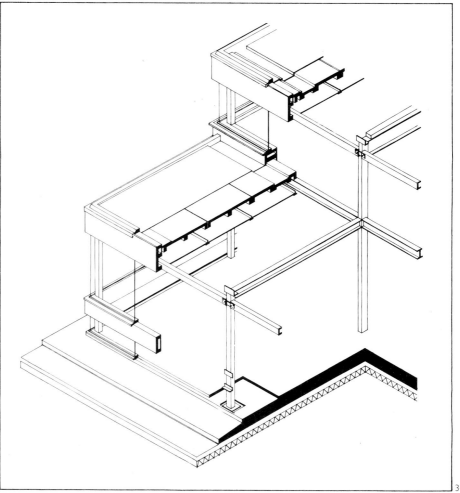

34

External walls varied considerably. Originally a timber framed system similar to the roof construction was used with the intention of using a plastic faced, profiled aluminium sheet for cladding but this was gradually eroded by cost limitation and several claddings resulted. Horizontal timber shiplap painted was succeeded by external quality plywood painted and various other readily available materials all sufficiently light for their loading to require nothing more than the original concrete raft but the time came in 1970 when brickwork proved cheaper than any of these finishes. Brickwork required a footing but even with a reinforced concrete downstand to provide this, destroying both the simplicity of the concrete raft and the original conception, it was more economical using a cheap facing brick than softwood, or its derivatives, the price of which had soared on the world market. Windows were generally aluminium vertical or horizontal sliding sashes with horizontal centre-pivotted lights at high level for assembly hall clerestoreys. Rooflights were used to provide natural lighting to the backs of teaching areas as, to save costs, the ceilings were reduced to 8'0" (2.40 m) and the ordinary window could not produce sufficient daylight to meet the 2% factor required by the DES.

No more RBS schools were designed after 1970 with the advent of MACE.

Grazebrook Primary School

35 The simplicity of the Rationalised Building System (RBS) is apparent here. The edge of the concrete raft provides a margin around the building and almost any lightweight cladding was acceptable from plastics, aluminium, plywood or shiplap timber as used on this school. The fascia used is also shiplap.
36 The early RBS schools showed a cool elegance evidenced here in the assembly hall. Compare with Fig 42 to see the erosion by cost limitations.

35

36

Prior Weston Primary School

When Prior Weston[16] was built upon a 1.17 acre (0.47 hectares) site in the Barbican, City of London, in 1968 it provided almost 45 square feet (4.16 m²) gross per child: subsequent primary schools over the following years progressively provided less under economic constraint until in 1973 they had reached 32 square feet (3.00 m²) per place. Size, however, is not the important element in this school. It was also the prototype for the ILEA's rationalised building system (RBS) but more than this it demonstrates how flexible in use a school can be.[17]

The Plowden Report, 1967, had urged the need for flexibility in use, domesticity in scale and changes in teaching attitudes: the basic tenets were that 'children learned by activity starting from their own surroundings and being taught to conduct their own investigations'.[18] ILEA primary school planning was already producing looser, open layouts for teaching areas and this important document gave absolution to the theory. A flexible shell was provided as an educational backcloth and the school staff have breathed life into it sowing the seeds for wider-ranging developments in succeeding primary schools in the 1970's. The plan shows two groups of large square classrooms clustered around communal areas with wide access openings but it also shows the beginnings of the open plan: use has demonstrated the problems encountered by the inability to shut off areas acoustically and the limits to flexibility that this imposes. Later plans are more specific in open areas and fully enclosed spaces but the wider environment fosters educational exploration and discovery by the individual child, having a domestic scale with soft furnishings, carpets, curtains and cushions. The layout permits team teaching, with the teacher as the hub around which education revolves, giving three teachers for 120 children rather than one to 40.

39 This view into the head teacher's room indicates the domestic environment sought in primary schools. It also demonstrates that, in the provision of pictures, cushions, etc, user interest must be engaged.

37 Large square classrooms for both infants and juniors were required in the 1965 brief for this school but large shared spaces providing resources for practical work, wet and dry, were included to meet an expanding teaching requirement. A distinct library is included in the junior area. A further class space was added at a later date between the infant and junior wings.

38 This was the first of the twenty eight schools built in RBS and the photograph shows the library, in the background, viewed from the junior resource area. It demonstrates how open the planning of primary schools was in 1968 and how the depth of plan required rooflights to provide the necessary daylight factor.

The use of curtains, carpet and wallpaper (put on to pin up areas by the teaching staff) shows the concern for a domestic-type environment. Compare with John Ball (Chapter 3, Fig 5) photographed in 1956.

Holmleigh Primary School

This building was designed in 1967, in RBS, as the first stage of a 520 place school with seven distinct classrooms – three for infants and four for juniors – with the infants sharing a constricted space labelled 'utility' for practical work whilst the junior rooms had large folding/sliding partitions connecting them directly to their resource/circulation areas which served for practical work. The plan has developed since Prior Weston was designed but both show the assembly hall beginning to be incorporated into the main block – unlike Hungerford and John Evelyn – in an attempt to reduce the perimeter of the school and thus reduce cost.

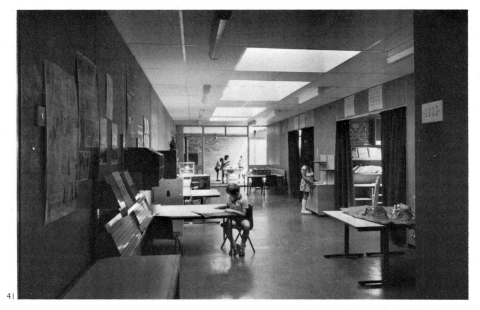

41

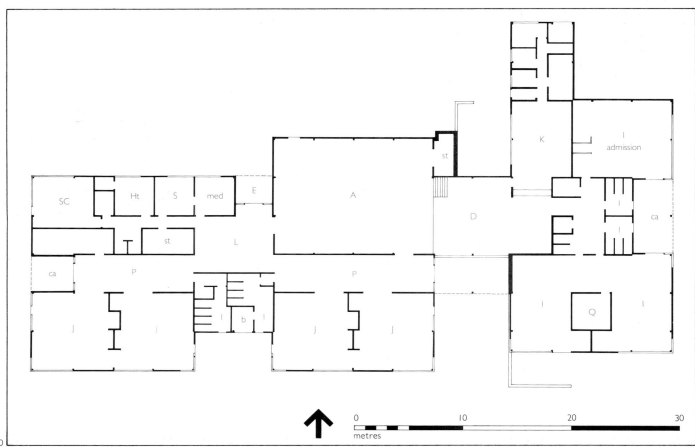

40

40   Layout Plan
When this was designed in RBS in 1967 the infants' admission group still required an enclosed classroom with limited access to a utility area but the other infant areas had already acquired a shared, top lit, quiet area. Juniors still had classrooms for all ages, with tentative links between them, and shared dry resource areas for practical work. Circulation space is tightly constrained with the main entrance doubling up as an attractive library.

42

41   *This is the junior resource area demonstrating that it offers a base for various activities including those undertaken in the external covered work area in the background. To the right are the junior classrooms with wide, ready access to the resource area.*
42   *The exterior was finished in external quality plywood painted: the fascia is the same material.*

Torriano Primary School

Originally required to extend the existing school this RBS school demonstrates several things very clearly. By 1969 the teaching arrangement had developed into distinct paired home bays (practice) having direct access to quiet areas and shared practical space: there are no doors within the three teaching areas, curtains only are used to close off spaces. The quiet rooms are disposed to take advantage of a secluded central courtyard which became normal upon many projects to light otherwise deep plans. As ever, in inner London, the site played a crucial role in determining the building layout: the site is generally two metres lower than the road, which implies setting back from the pavement, and a block of flats strikes across the site making the natural service connection to the future second stage very tenuous. By 1969 cost limits necessitated lowering the hall ceiling height by 2'0'' (600 mm) and the omission of all external covered work areas: by this time brick cladding proved to be the cheapest.

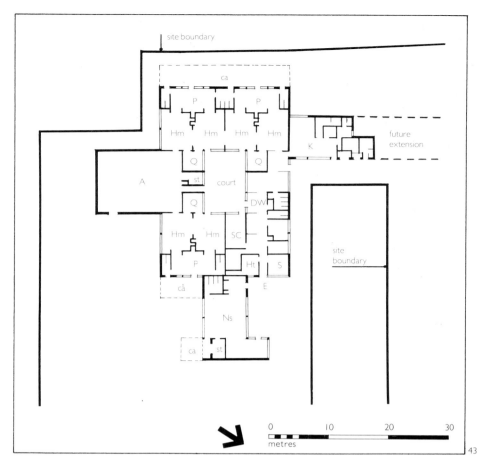

43   Layout Plan
By 1969 infant teaching arrangements had developed into distinct paired home bays (noted as practice) with direct access to a shared quiet room and a practical space leading to the outside: the outside work areas should have been covered but savings to meet tight cost limits almost invariably led to the omission of the covers and they have not yet been provided.

The urban site's effect upon the layout is evident again with a very awkward shaped site falling from East to West and the need to provide for kitchen/service connection to a second stage for juniors which has not been realised as the original School Board building still stands some distance away.

Wilberforce Primary School

44, 45   *Built at the same time as Torriano (see Fig 43) it was finished in 1972 and shows the final phase of RBS construction.*

The assembly hall has a lower ceiling to save costs and cheaper louvre windows have been introduced. Heating is by warm air from the horizontal duct below the windows: compare with Grazebrook, Fig 36.

External cladding was brickwork as this became cheaper than any of the lightweight claddings.

Metropolitan Architectural Consortium for Education (MACE)

The system developed by MACE for school building was based upon a one metre grid and provided a complete method of construction and finishes.[19]

Foundations were short, in-situ concrete piers with precast edge beams acting as permanent shuttering to the power floated concrete slab: this had the polythene damp proof membrane below and required no screeding to take finishes. The perimeter enclosure could be precast concrete, exposed aggregate, load-bearing walls or light steel frames with lightweight plastic-faced plywood cladding: there was an interesting vertical jointing detail which became the MACE symbol. Internal load-bearing walls were smooth-faced precast concrete slabs placed where necessary to support the roof. The roof was a steel space-frame type of construction which provided a deep ceiling void for the circulation of services and which did not require regular supports. Prescreeded woodwool roofing slabs were laid quite flat and a single layer synthetic rubber membrane provided the waterproofing: fascias were precast concrete or plastic-faced plywood. Windows were aluminium sliding sashes but clerestorey windows were horizontally centre-pivotted or louvres. Partitions were 50 mm solid chipboard. Lavatory units were pre-plumbed and standardised upon the one metre grid.

Electrical services were all run down walls, from the ceiling void, in broad flat plastic conduits which had socket outlets, light switches, radio and television connections, etc., already available upon them. Heating was by warm air which was introduced into the rooms through the ceiling: the ceiling panels had thousands of small holes punctured through them at selected places over windows and when the ceiling void was pressurised by fan units the warm air was intended to be forced out downwards. No water tanks were required as water storage tubes were laid in the roof structure holding the necessary litreage.

The system demonstrated that a one metre grid is too coarse a tool for designing relatively small buildings: 300 mm was seen to provide greater flexibility for the architect. When the grid is used rigorously for all building elements inequities abound: a ceiling tile one metre square and 2.40 m above floor level assumes a crushing potential and lavatory planning is severely circumscribed. The grid had an electrifying effect upon primary school plans and the typical meandering ILEA layout was quite suddenly forced into rectangular discipline and rectitude – a premonition of the coming espousal of classicism by writers.[20]

Other aspects of the system required early correction. The single layer roof membrane had to be replaced with traditional three layer roofing felt and the flat roofs did not drain as the rainwater outlets, due to minor building settlement, tended to be higher than the membrane: attempts at introducing falls failed as standard upstands to clerestoreys and rooflights were not high enough. Due to the difficulty in sealing the periphery of the roof void fascias, insufficient pressurised warm air was forced into teaching areas and positive ducting was introduced into the roof void with outlet grills placed as required. Town planners would not always accept the offered external appearance and brick and horizontal timber cladding were introduced as options.

Twelve primary schools, one special school and a large four storey secondary school (Lewisham, see Chapter 9) were constructed in the system. Systematic consortium building requires a firm continuing programme and as the national economy faltered in 1973, with rising oil prices, the previous certainty of school provision faltered under a DES moratorium and in 1974 the ILEA left MACE.

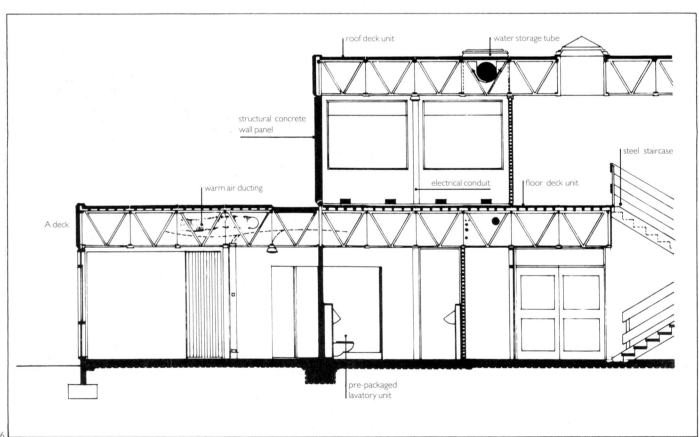

46 MACE. The System
The essence was to reduce to an absolute minimum the amount of site work required and consequently once the in-situ ground beams (if any) and power floated slab were in position (edge beams were precast, sitting on concrete piers) the remainder of the building could be delivered with various factories supplying structure, cladding, steel A frame roof, partitions, door sets, lavatory units, staircases, ceilings, etc, ready for site fixing. Apart from groundworks, drainage and external works most elements were able to be pre-packaged for installation.

Ashmead Primary School

Whilst primary schools built in traditional or RBS construction showed an articulation of plan the introduction of MACE produced rectangular layouts and this school for 240 pupils has a perfect square plan. In 1970 the quiet room became fully enclosed and the practical areas are more generalised. The formal plan required a central courtyard to provide the necessary daylight levels to teaching areas but it is noticeable that the assembly hall is now fully integrated within the building giving rise to problems of noise. Built upon a steeply falling site the school occupies the only flat plateau available as previous houses left uneven basements. High traffic noise from the adjoining main road has been minimised by the detailed planning and the building of a sound baffle wall.

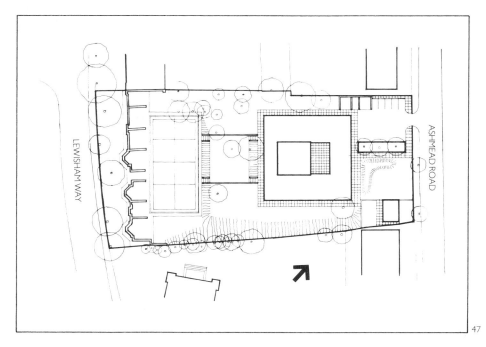

47

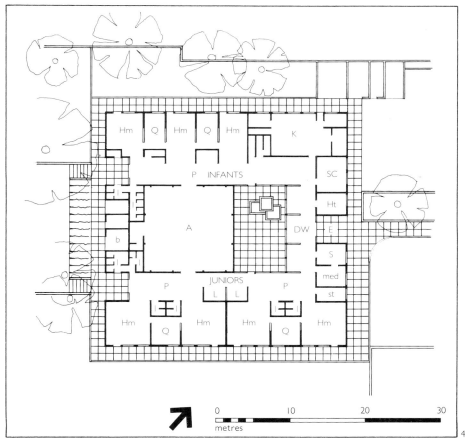

48

47 Site Plan, 1970
The site falls steeply from the South and high levels of traffic noise emanate from Lewisham Way. The school is sited upon the only flat ground available – the MACE system did not cope well with changes of level.

As the drawing shows, the main front walls of existing houses were intended to be used as a sound baffle, but they proved to be structurally unsound and were demolished. Lewisham Borough Council required a link wall in the same position to repair the visual damage to a terrace of Victorian houses and this can be seen in Chapter 12, figs 8 and 9.

48 General Layout, 1970
The introduction of the MACE system is reflected here (see also Paxton, figs 52 and 53) with powerful rectangular geometry: seeking to reduce the external perimeter. Quiet rooms become fully enclosed with glazed panels for visual continuity but the home bays open directly on to the wide, corridor-like practical areas. The combination of site and MACE limitations produced a square building with a square assembly hall almost totally enclosed by teaching space.

49 The Metropolitan Architectural Consortium for Education (MACE) produced all of the elements necessary for school building with the exception of the ground floor slab. This view from the south-west shows the precast textured concrete cladding panels and door assembly on a two metre grid with plastic cover plates to the vertical joints and lead dressing from the plastic faced plywood fascias over the cladding elements.

50 View of the courtyard. Steel construction was available in MACE as well as load-bearing panels and this was often used for the assembly hall, on the left, in conjunction with plastic faced plywood cladding: the small slots at low level are pressure relief flaps which were to work in conjunction with the warm air system operating from the roof void.

51 An infant home bay. The deep plan and the one metre square ceiling panels give a feeling of heaviness. On the window wall are two flat vertical electric conduits which carry switches, socket outlets, radio and television aerial sockets, etc. This school was used temporarily for secondary girls and this explains the formality of the furniture.

49

50

51

Paxton Primary School

The site played a major part in the placing and development of the plan on this project to replace an existing Victorian school. A steeply falling site provided the minimum flat area for building. In 1971 teaching terms the layout for 240 pupils is similar to Ashmead but the play centre and central assembly hall prevent direct communication between junior and infant areas. Two courtyards are required consequently to light teaching areas and the vital floor area to wall area ratio rises eroding the money available for building. When the new school was completed the original building was demolished to low level providing an adventure playground.

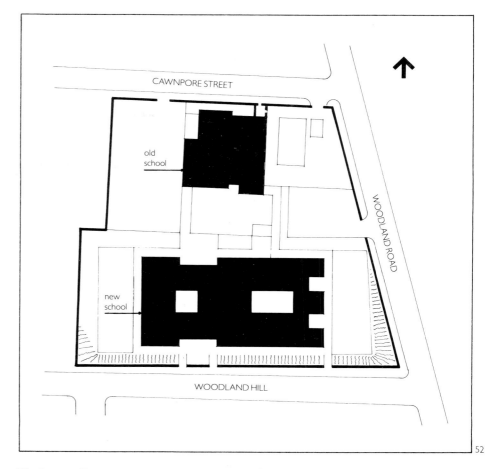

52

52 Site Plan
The site falls steeply from South to North towards the original School Board building leaving a narrow plateau for the replacement building. The original building was levelled to provide an adventure playground.

53 Layout Plan
Built in the MACE system in 1972 the layout shows close affinities to Ashmead Primary School (see Fig 48) with the teaching arrangement but demonstrates also the effect of extra accommodation – a play centre, requiring direct access from the outside and to the assembly hall – upon a narrow site.

In order to provide the prescribed daylight level two courtyards were included to light the centre of the building.

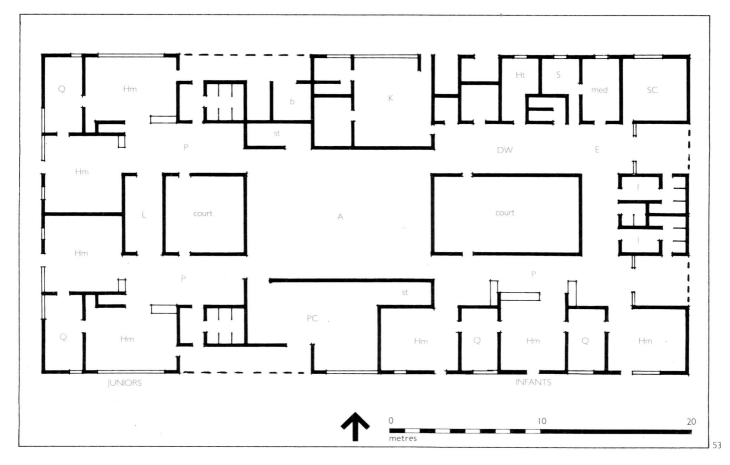

53

Scott Lidgett School

The 5.10 acre (2.00 hectares) site for this 1400 place secondary boys' school is flat and, being formed by closing off existing roads, has retained existing avenues to provide a tree-lined walk. Designed in 1965 with the Newsom Report very much in evidence the buildings have been arranged in groups to provide the required, low key environment.[21] Specialist accommodation is arranged in separate buildings with links at ground and first floor levels connecting the art, communal, general classroom, science, library, sixth form and games blocks together. The effect of this is to reduce the apparent size of the school thus providing a more individual sense of place for the pupil. A comparison with Pimlico (see Chapter 5) shows a different sort of site and interpretation of the brief.

The design is generally two or three storeys high and keeps in character and scale with its surroundings.[22] The separation of buildings has created interesting glimpses and views within and without the site and the roofs have been designed to give a varied but cohesive roofscape either in silhouette or when seen from surrounding high buildings.

The structure is an in-situ reinforced concrete frame with columns on a 10'0'' (3.00 m) grid. Finishes are simple and few. Windows are rationalised to two standard types only, fitted between columns. Concrete edge beams are expressed with warm brown brick cladding below window sills. Bright colour has been used on the structural steel work to some roofs and covered ways to give emphasis at certain points.[23]

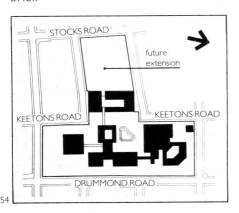

54

54 Site Plan
Typically of inner London, the site was formed by closing roads. Some sports facilities were included in addition to the games block and a future site extension promised further resources.

An existing avenue of plane trees along Keetons Road was incorporated into the main layout of the school.

55, 56 Ground and First Floor Plans
In 1965 the various educational functions were still developed separately (classroom, science, crafts, VI form, games, youth service, communal, music and drama and art) but no longer in the isolation of the

mid-1950's – see Chapter 2.

Generous covered connections ensure the full interdependence of the departments and at first floor level classrooms, science laboratories and VI form accommodation are linked by the library with the main communal/arts block in close proximity.

57 *View from the south with the sixth form and administration block to the right and the communal block in the centre with the open air theatre stepping down between them. The retention of the avenue of plane trees from the original Keetons Road adds a mature quality to the development.*

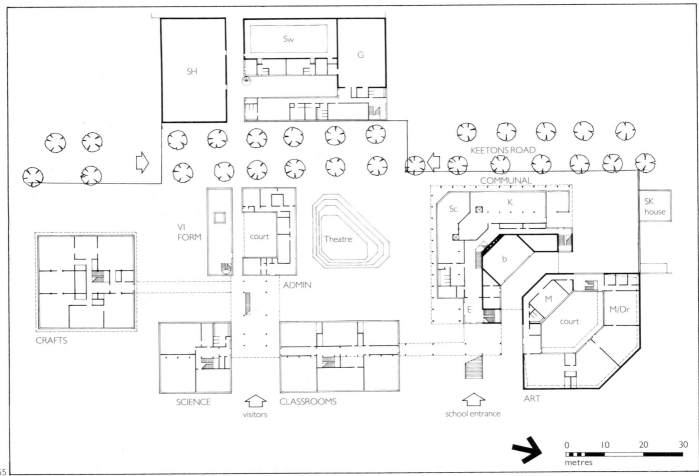

55

57

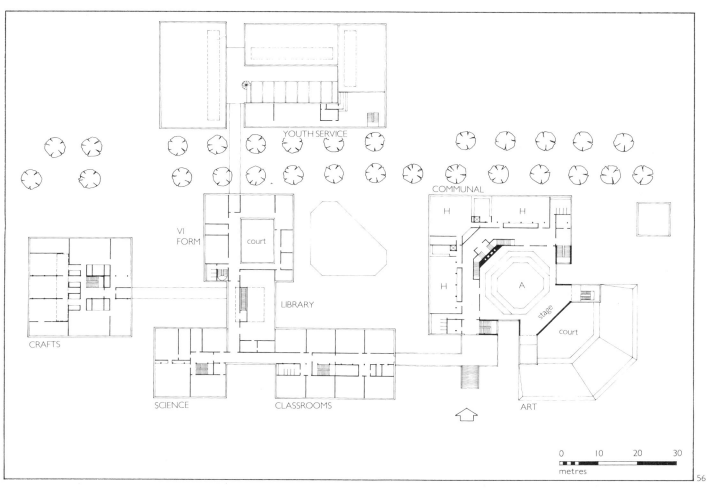

YOUTH SERVICE

COMMUNAL

VI
FORM

court

LIBRARY

H   H

H   A   stage

court

CRAFTS

SCIENCE   CLASSROOMS   ART

0   10   20   30
metres

56

58 View from the east – the main entrance with the art rooms to the right and the houserooms and assembly hall at the top of the steps. The enclosed corridor leads left to the classroom block.

59 View from the south of the sixth form block showing the rationalised window system – two standard types only fitted between columns – with precast facings to concrete edge beams and warm brown brick cladding. The ground is paved with in-situ concrete and triple rows of paviors, a pattern which unifies the centre of the site.

60 Covered ways between blocks are painted scarlet and serve to mark the entrances to the buildings: this is the link between the sixth form block, on the right, and the games block.

61 The assembly hall which doubles as a drama workshop justifying the theatre lighting hung from the exposed steel roof trusses.

59

60

61

Eaglesfield School

In 1968 the ILEA decided that the existing Shooters Hill School (formerly Red Lion School, see Chapter 1) should be expanded from 550 secondary boys to ten form entry plus a sixth form of 255 – a total of 1755 places. The site is 17.00 acres (6.80 hectares) and in 1962 a new science block had been added: although the site is large it is attractively wooded and a steep slope posed considerable problems. To retain the existing playing fields the new buildings were developed rising up the hillside. The contract was completed in 1975.

The original building was adapted for fifth and sixth form use and contains accommodation for art, drama, music and commerce. An adult education institute is housed at the west end of this block.

New accommodation was grouped into three blocks. The main teaching block is four storeys high, stepping down the hill, and contains the main classroom accommodation and dining areas (in house rooms) with the main library centred at the core of the

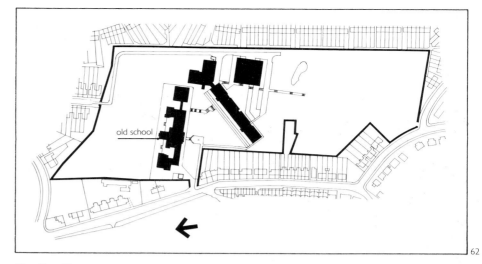

62 Site Plan
The site is large but slopes steeply from the South where the land is heavily wooded.

The existing building (see Red Lion School, Chapter 1) occupies the only flat area and the adjacent games pitches were to remain uncontaminated by more buildings. Closely attached to the East of the original building is a new science wing completed in 1964.

In order to maximise the potential of the existing, the new buildings had to be built down the slope.

63 Ground Floor Plans
Due to the falling site the ground floors are at differing levels but all are shown here to indicate their basic juxtaposition.

The original building was remodelled in order to meet the School's new overall requirements.

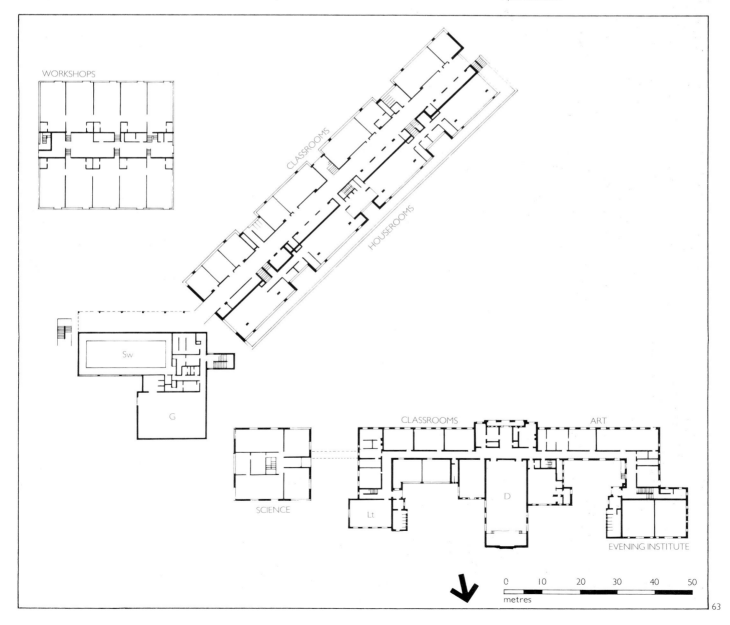

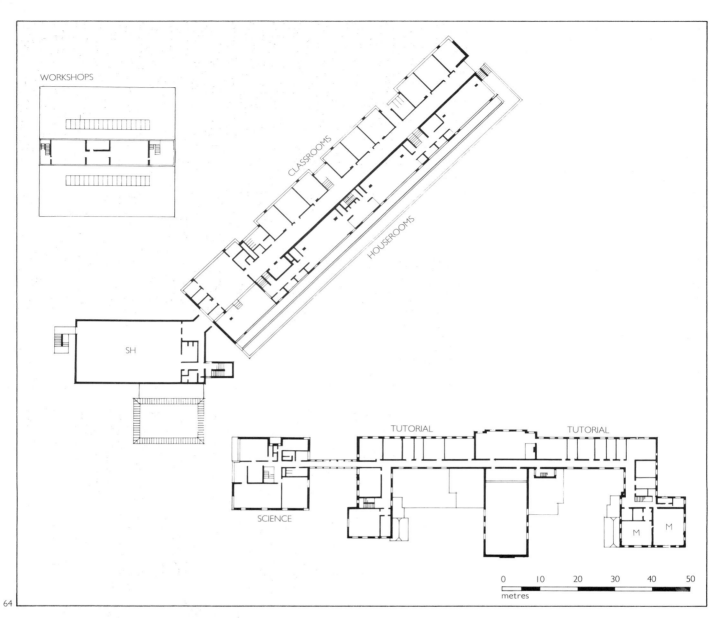

WORKSHOPS

CLASSROOMS

HOUSEROOMS

SH

TUTORIAL   TUTORIAL

SCIENCE   M   M

0   10   20   30   40   50
metres

64

development. At the focus of the school is the games hall (which can provide for school assembly), gymnasium, swimming pool and youth service areas.
Workshops are contained in a single storey building which steps up the hillside in three levels. The imploded layout of the four blocks has provided a new centre to the enlarged school with circulation links kept as short as possible within the limits of the terrain.

Foundations had to be piled to support in-situ reinforced concrete frames to the teaching and games hall blocks and steel frames to the workshop block. Whilst the two smaller blocks have facing brick cladding the teaching block is of bush-hammered concrete. All blocks have steel windows with top-hung opening lights.

65

64 Upper Floor Plans
*The new teaching block shows the
progressive stepping-back upon the North
side as it eases down the slope whilst the
physical education suite has a games hall
which can provide for school assembly.*
65 *The contours under the teaching block
drop progressively away and ground had to
be excavated to provide a playspace. The
bridge link connects the second floor of the
block with a higher level leading to the
workshop block. In the distance the roof of
the games hall/swimming pool, lying
further down the slope, can be seen.*
66 *View of the teaching block from the
south. Generally the block is three storeys
high but beyond the distant railing a
further floor steps down to house the boilers
and the kitchen. Walls are of bush-
hammered concrete with top-hung opening
steel window frames. For further
information concerning the solar shading
louvres see Chapter II.*
67 *The teaching block section steps
sideways down the hill and changes in level
laterally are made by half flights of stairs
opening off this central concourse. At the
upper level is the enclosed corridor serving
the second floor.*

66

67

Chapter 3: References

1 Description of the LCC scheme for College for Further Education Official Architecture September 1967 p 443–445. See Appendix B for growth in expenditure.

2 The Times 22 July 1957; Macmillan was addressing a Conservative Party rally in Bedford.

3 Official Architecture September 1966: Trends in School Design p 1279–1363.

4 M Seaborne and R Lowe: The English School – Its Architecture and Organisation Volume II 1870–1970, Routledge and Kegan Paul 1977 (see p 165 for graph).

5 Machiavelli N, wrote: 'There is nothing more difficult to plan, more doubtful of success, nor more dangerous to manage than the creation of a new system. For the initiator has the enmity of all who would profit from the preservation of the old institution and merely lukewarm defenders in those who gain by the new one.' This is particularly apt for architecture for there are untold numbers of architects who have in their portfolios a fully-evolved system of design and construction just awaiting recognition and application whilst knowing that they would never deign to use a system designed by another architect.

6 Education 7 June 1974 p 687.

7 Architects Journal 28 May 1936 p 810–812

8 Architectural Design June 1959 p 224

9 The Builder 2 August 1957: Four Education Buildings for the LCC p 196–198

10 Architectural Design June 1959 p 227

11 Building 13 December 1974 p 65–72.

12 GLC Architects Review: Academy 1974 p 40–42.

13 Concrete Quarterly July 1972 p 31–34.

14 Building Specification July 1972 p 31–34.

15 Frampton K: Modern Architecture – A Critical History: Thames and Hudson 1980 p 248: describes an objective very similar to the aims and intentions of RBS with the 'International Style's stripped planar form ... implied technique, synthetic modern materials and standardisation ... using modular parts so as to facilitate fabrication and erection. It tended as a general rule towards the hypothetical flexibility of the free plan, and to this end it preferred skeleton frame construction to masonry.'

16 Deutsche Bauzeitung April 1973 p 369.

17 Architects Journal, 4 April 1973, p 778–781.

18 Times Educational Supplement, 4 September 1981, p 2 argues that 'after fourteen years the discussion of "Plowden practice" is still open.'

19 Architecture Design, May/June 1980, Post-Modern Classicism p 12.

20 Russell B: Building Systems Industrialisation and Architecture, Wiley 1981, p 561–583, gives a very full description of aims and effects of MACE.

21 Design, August 1972: A Challenge to Bermondsey p 25–29.

22 Deutsche Bauzeitung, April 1973, p 370–371.

23 Architecture and Urbanism, February 1974, p 127–130.

Key to drawings

A	assembly hall
AEI	adult education institute
AH	activities hall
C	classroom
CR	common room
D	dining
Dr	drama
DW	dining/work
E	entrance
G	gymnasium
H	houseroom
Hm	home bay
Ht	head or principal
I	infants
J	juniors
K	kitchen
L	library
Lt	lecture
M	music
Ns	nursery
P	practical area
PC	play centre
Q	quiet area
S	secretary
Sc	science
SC	staff common room
SH	sports hall
SK	schoolkeeper
Sw	swimming pool
W	waiting
YS	youth service
b	boiler
ca	covered area
ch	changing
cl	cloakroom
l	lavatories
s	servery
st	store

Chapter 4
An Introduction to Changing Attitudes

There was a time when it was believed that humankind had access to 'almost unlimited supplies of energy'.[1] When the 'Oil War' of October 1973 erupted it signalled several different things: the major and universally recognised one was the future emphasis upon energy conservation, as the world's fossil fuel reserve was recognised to be finite[2] but ecological and economic crises were in close attendance. Local authorities[3] were told that 'the party's over' meaning that the optimism and expansion of the 1960's would not continue. In the new era of scarce energy, architectural concepts would need to be transformed returning to basic principles: to the use of more cheaply produced materials[4,5] and the further development of the deep plan (see Chapter 3, p 3). The one consequence immediately recorded in inner London was the freezing of the current school building programme due to the resultant economic stringency: new procedures emanating from the DES presaged a downturn in ILEA building programmes and the subsequently cancelled building programme was the last one which included normal, steady replacement of obsolete schools with new.[6] In addition to economic and energy considerations, by the late 1960's young architects were beginning to question seriously the need to demolish the old School Board buildings when their replacements were often inferior in many respects. Since 1973 the ILEA has been replacing primary schools at a rate of two each year instead of twelve, and complete new comprehensive schools are unlikely to be seen again. In 1973 the projected population of England and Wales for the year 2000 was reduced from 64 million to 52 million.

Apart from national economic crises inner London has been suffering a particular decline shared with other established cities – that of population.[7] The ILEA serves the twelve inner London boroughs and it is precisely these where the population is falling: an education service, such as the ILEA, must be able to adapt its structure and policies to meet the changing social, economic and demographic conditions and; since 1965, inner London has seen radical change in these areas. In 1965 inner London's population was 3,160,000 but by 1980 this had fallen to 2,600,000: in the same period required school places fell from 393,000 to 331,000.[8] One immediate advantage was the reduction in the size of classes giving the ILEA very favourable teacher:pupil ratios. Of necessity, existing school buildings came under scrutiny also in the search for balanced provision.

As education authorities' major building programmes are now based upon demonstrating the need for new provision, ie for developing and expanding areas of the country, and inner London has one such area only, Thamesmead, the provision of new schools is limited except to replace old buildings which cannot be adapted, rehabilitated or extended economically and the clear fact is that the ILEA has nearly two thousand existing buildings containing over 48 million square feet (4,363,000 m²) of floor space. Matched with falling school numbers the need for new buildings has declined. At the same time that the number of schoolchildren has dwindled there came an increase in the requirements and expectations of a whole range of groups both directly and indirectly associated with educational buildings. Amenity and conservation societies began to press for the improvement of the environment requiring better quality building materials, external works, planting and boundary fences. Strong action was called for from building users for internal improvements and better servicing. Laws were enacted and the Fire Precautions Act, 1971, requiring, in due course, that all buildings should achieve higher standards was followed by the Health and Safety at Work Act. 1974, which again focused upon the use of buildings and their potential danger.

One of the particular problems in inner London is that one third of its schools are pre-1914 construction on very small sites: additionally, the old School Board for London buildings have a massive, brooding image which is part of the neighbourhood and not readily substituted by a newer, more accessible, better serviced but smaller school These old buildings' range of shortcomings[9] include being on at least three high storeys with inadequate staircases, inflexible layouts with wasted circulation space and an unsuitable scale for young children. Unimaginatively treated external areas[10] are unsuitable for teaching some play activities and almost all have external lavatory blocks without proper washing facilities. But they are often handsome, always solid and, with an enormous amount of accommodation, represent a tremendous potential for a new existence as the ILEA, by remodelling them, makes the best of what it has.[11] Economy must be considered between replacement or remodelling: where there are additional benefits to be gained these 'should exceed the amount by which the annual equivalent of the installation costs and the running costs of the renewal exceed the running costs of the existing component".[12]

The educational wheel has completely turned and Victorian architecture is being translated, with imagination, into a modern resource for current educational needs. What could be described in 1936 as 'disastrously permanent'[13] is now considered to be a valuable resource.

In 1967 the Plowden Report, 'Children and Their Primary Schools', recommended that positive discrimination should favour education provision in areas where children are most handicapped by their home conditions. The Report suggested that modest sums of money could be spent advantageously in these educational priority areas by transforming old schools which had adequate space of the wrong description into buildings suitable for current teaching practice and, by making these community schools providing day, and evening use for children and parents. The ILEA's serious intent is demonstrated by its careful garnering of monies from maintenance, inner city and energy conservation funds in order properly to preserve and remodel many of its old schools. Whilst the three primary schools illustrated here were the pioneers of this intent, more have now been remodelled and a full review of all sites and building accommodation has given a rational base for decision making.

By October 1973 the great wave of new further and higher education colleges and polytechnic buildings had begun to recede (see Chapter 15) but the need for more accommodation had not lessened. The majority of older inner London colleges for further education are to be found confined upon small sites and the consequence is usually that expansion, due to local demand, is made possible only by leasing buildings in the vicinity or by using other ILEA buildings as annexes to cater for new courses of study. This naturally has led to fragmentation and duplication of administrative effort and the two further education projects described here have not only reduced this but have made positive physical impacts upon their neighbourhoods by recycling interesting older buildings into the wider urban fabric.

Secondary reorganisation has also proved to be a catalyst in the remodelling and rehabilitation of old school buildings restoring them to new life whilst providing better sites, new expanded facilities and making a positive focus for local community education and recreation. One is described in Chapter 6 (Clapton) and another is in Chapter 7 (Langdon Park).

Another major influence already in secondary education – only 24 ILEA schools out of 170 do not have on-line micro-computer facilities – is the wider availability of high speed logical capacity. Exploitation of this provides modelling and simulation, data base enquiry, dynamic problem solving and automatic process control which will lead to corresponding social, economic and, finally, cultural transformations. Buildings will again need to be reassessed in the light of needs and uses of this powerful addition to basic educational provision, for primary and special schools are to have microcomputers too, bringing further changed attitudes and enhanced expectations.

1970–80 proved to be a decade of change[14] producing many pressures to drive architecture forward: energy, preservation, revitalisation, conservation, consumerism, public participation and media interest all served to create a new populism exposing architecture to wider debate than ever before.

Compton Primary School

As a direct result of the Plowden Report the ILEA, in conjunction with the Goldsmiths Company, held an open competition[15] in 1968 for improving and upgrading this typical three decker primary school built in 1881 for 928 pupils. The competition was a great success attracting 120 entries demonstrating a general release of ideas with the winners' alterations revitalising the whole building. The winning architects were Farrington, Dennys and Fisher and they carried out the remodelling.

Facilities were poor with a very limited unextendable site, almost all lavatories being external and away from the building. The alterations are designed to provide for a nursery group and seven other groups of forty children and allow for a gradual reduction of numbers in groups as teacher: pupil ratios improve. The competition was intended to encourage the opening up and linking of interior spaces in old school buildings, to avoid perpetuating the classroom cell of forty children with one teacher whilst providing for greater variety in group sizes and activities available and the Compton remodelling demonstrated all of these principles.

From an economical viewpoint Compton provides 2145 m² enclosed floor space against a maximum of 1394 m² in a new building for a comparable number of pupils. The major element in relaxing the tightness of the old school plan is the new central staircase which rises right from the new entrance, with parents' waiting area and bookstall, up through all three levels: this also allowed the removal of an ugly external fire escape. Breaking through non-structural partitions it is possible to use most of the existing corridors and achieve transverse as well as linear groupings. The introduction of mezzanines enables the reduction of scale in large areas and provides additional work space. The alteration of overwhelming scale is most important in the remodelling of the old Board Schools but the sheer volume of existing buildings and classrooms allows enjoyable change, and enclosure, and elevation for small children using raised bays and platforms: this is particularly noticeable in the delightful shared story telling area in the centre of the ground floor which is snug, low ceilinged and dark. When the large enclosed central volumes are opened up to the side windows there is a great release of clear light into the heart of the school giving long vistas and lofty views.

Traffic noise nuisance from Compton Street to the north has been reduced by a barrier of service rooms on each floor whilst all lavatories have been brought indoors and closely associated with teaching areas. The central staircase breaks down the apparent size of the

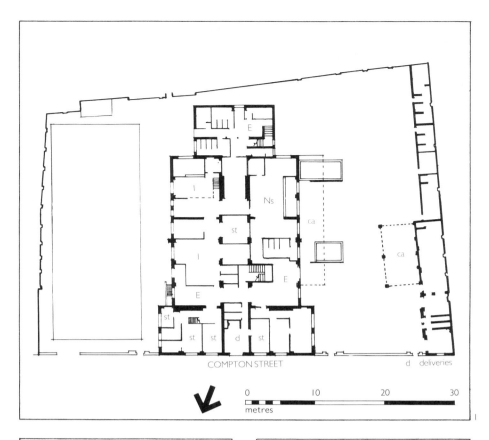

COMPTON STREET

d   deliveries

0   10   20   30
metres

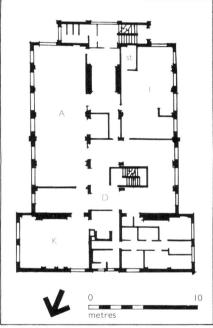

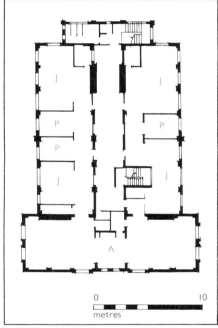

0   10
metres

0   10
metres

1 Site and Ground Floor Plan
The tightness of the original accommodation can be judged from the site area which has not altered with remodelling.

The main construction was retained but most partitions were removed to provide more accessible spaces for the infant groups which were moved to the ground from the first floor. A mezzanine floor has been included along the length of the central corridor linking with the new work balcony over the infants' area: the mezzanine contains a library. Replanning service areas along the northern side has provided a noise barrier to Compton Street.

All external lavatories were replanned inside the building and their clearance has

provided a good sized games area in the eastern playground. Old outbuildings along the western boundary were retained for new uses.

2 First Floor Plan
The relocation of the kitchen on this floor allows the nursery class and infant groups the use of the ground floor although one of the latter is still at this level providing a natural link to the junior groups on the second floor.

3 Second Floor Plan
Junior groups have more formal layouts than the infants although groupings of 40 or 80 are possible: rooflights over the central area enables it to be used for general work and study.

dining area allowing smaller scale eating areas around it.[16] Rooms are generally paired and are so arranged as to be flexible within pairs: this allows nursery children careful access to infant areas. The mezzanine library is placed to allow easy flexibility and is intended for teaching large remedial classes or for children working independently.

Compton School alterations were completed in 1971, and several years later it became St Peter's and St Paul's Primary School.

4 *A timber framed mezzanine was introduced into the high Victorian classrooms providing extra space, changing the scale and, here, allowing a library area.*
5 *Cellular classrooms can be opened up to provide a freer plan form.*
6 *Large volumes are reduced by mezzanines or false ceilings and with softer, more domestic, finishes provide an acceptable background for current primary education.*
7 *The shared story telling area is a snug, attractive space.*
8 *A new scaled primary school has replaced the old with a new teaching format.*

Montem Primary School

Montem's history is typical of one of the original Board Schools: built in 1895 for 1,179 pupils and managing upon its very small site hardly to keep pace with educational developments until, in the mid 1960's, HM Inspectors could describe it only in terms of inadequacy and unattractiveness whilst the efforts of the staff were highly praised under trying and unsuitable conditions. With the basis of a sound building and an enthusiastic staff a brief was developed[17] for extensive remodelling in 1968 to provide a flexible environment[18] at the same time as the Compton competition was being held.

The project was progressed with the express aim of providing a flexible environment which could serve the entire community. Accommodation was required for a nursery class of forty, an infants school for three hundred and sixty and a junior school of four hundred and eighty. Parents were to be encouraged to participate in all school activities and the local adult evening institute (Holloway AEI) proposed courses for two thousand evening students. New gardens would be made in the extended site (enlarged by the demolition of an adjacent obsolete police station) being available to all including old age pensioners.

The building was depressing being short of wash basins, indoor lavatories, hot water. Windows were mostly too high with bleak corridors and crowded cloakrooms. Montem was not equipped to meet normal educational demands made upon it and the school could hardly compensate physically for the surrounding impoverished quality of decayed urban life and social deprivation.

In 1971 the remodelling contract was completed[19] and Montem has a new lease of usefulness for at least thirty years. To utilise all available areas corridor partitions and doors are removed increasing available teaching space and allowing a greater commonalty between previously rigidly enclosed classrooms.

Due to the great storey heights it is possible to use the existing mezzanine levels of the staircases to insert resource balconies and group rooms whilst altering the scale of the volumes: the balconies were seen as libraries and reading areas, the school has found extra uses for them. All the existing cloak-rooms are converted into internal lavatories, stores or helpers' rooms: trolleys within each class base carry coats.

Carpet is widely used and complementary colour is used to decorate the varied arrangement of multiple use areas. The care is extended outwards with bold, colourful patterns on play grounds and play walls designed by an artist, David Cashman, and carried out with the children's help. Covered play areas abut the ground floor nursery and infant areas and a garden has been provided between play pitches.

The social intent of the school is obvious as facing the main gate is a new entrance which opens into a parents/school meeting point.[20] Apart from offering parents seeking advice a welcome, the area serves as an exhibition space for children's work, a stall for children's books and an extra teaching space. An acute case of Victorian affliction has been cured, becoming a neighbourhood centre.[21]

9 Ground Floor Plan
The ground floor is largely given over to infant classes which are linked together by new openings and corridors are incorporated into the accommodation. The inclusion of a distinct parents/school meeting point at the entrance portrays the social attitude of the school.

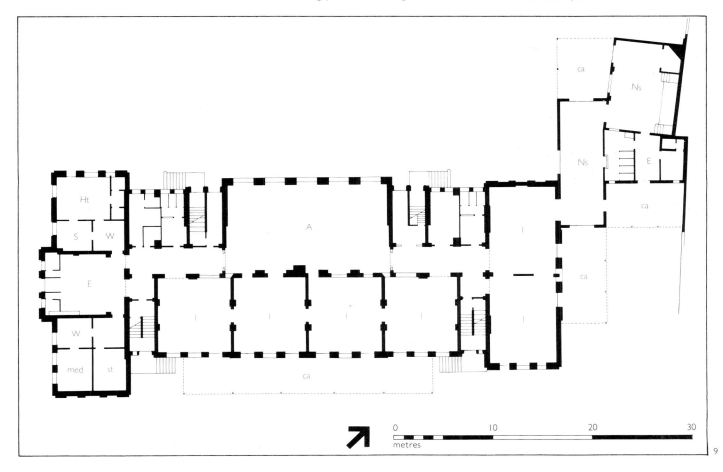

9

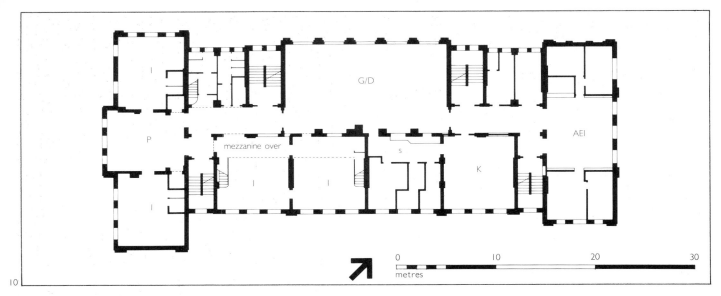

10

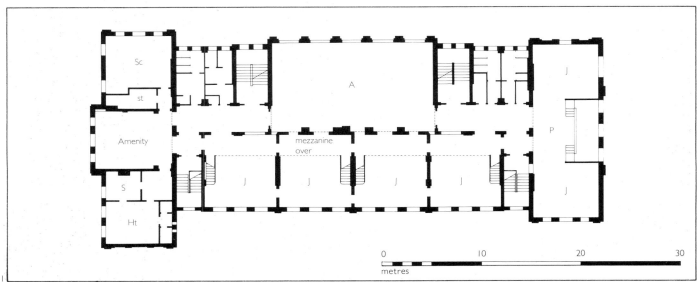

11

12

10 First Floor Plan
Infant class bases, each of which has a practical area, share a large resource space. The kitchen was already on this floor and is adjacent to the Adult Education Institute for future servicing.

11 Second Floor Plan
The junior floor is more formal than the infant layouts with class bases which can be enclosed with sliding screens and the provision of fixed chalkboards.

The two upper floors have had mezzanine balconies included in the remodelling taking advantage of the very high ceilings of the original building.

12 *Cleaned, painted and restored the school presents a refreshed image to its neighbourhood.*

13 *The overbearing proportions of Victorian classrooms have been altered by the insertion of mezzanine balconies providing spatial variety and giving access to the original mezzanines which were previously accessible only by the main staircases.*

14 *Mezzanines become libraries and reading areas.*

15, 16 *The removal of partitions on the top floor has provided a great burst of light into the interior of the building. Juniors are provided with resource platforms for group work.*

13

14

15

16

Sebright Primary School

In 1973, Farrington, Dennys and Fisher were briefed to remodel Sebright, a three decker school built in 1892. The school site was incredibly small with four streets closely hemming in the buildings but the closure of the two to the east and the west in the general redevelopment of the neighbourhood provided approximately three times the site area.

Even with the availability of more building land the architects persevered with the principles behind remodelling and planned as much as possible within the existing building. This put a premium upon ground floor accommodation

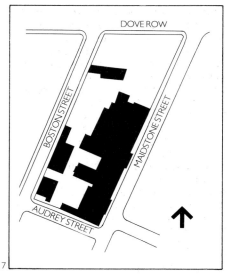

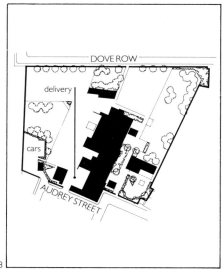

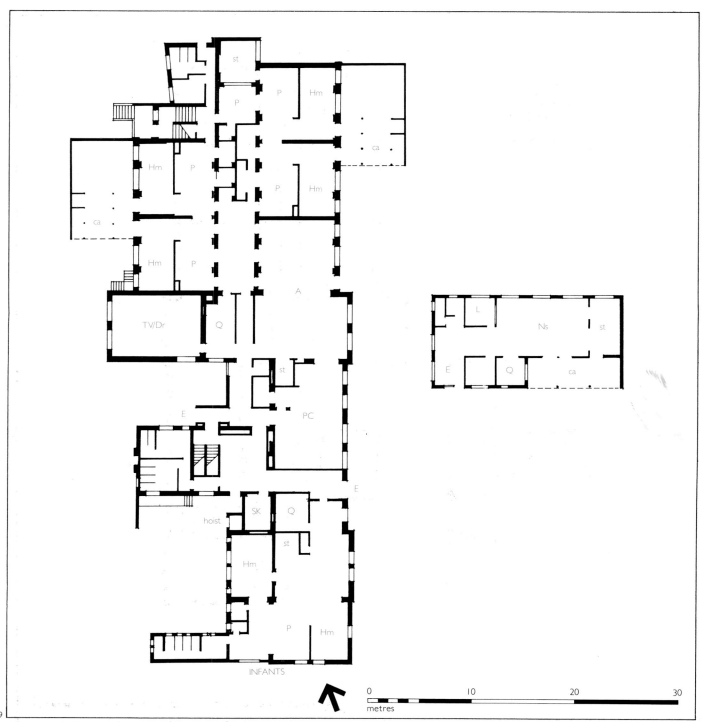

which was required for the three infant years: the existing nursery class was rehoused in a new self-contained building with close proximity to the infants. This was seem to be important as the whole school is treated as a progression from the informal nursery through the relatively informal ground floor infants up to the more formal layout of the junior school.[22]

As at Compton School the architects have provided new kitchen and dining arrangements on the first floor which is effectively a sandwich of shared resources for infants and juniors. Sufficient internal lavatory accommodation already existed and this was completely re-furbished giving access from associated teaching areas. The adaptation of the existing block has provided areas in excess of the current minimum and has

given the schools separate halls, dining rooms, a TV/drama room and a hand-some library for the juniors.

The existing plan was cellular with square, high-ceilinged classrooms opening off a central corridor. Structural alterations were minimal with a link constructed at first floor level between the south stair and the north cross corridor. New teaching areas are formed from two or three old classrooms linked by new openings in cross walls and the removal of partitions. Although the teaching areas are open, each year group has an enclosed quiet area. The replan-ning has taken the most useful, attrac-tive and character-filled spaces for special purposes such as the library, drama room and halls. Floors are made cohesive by broad bands of colour at door height joining different areas and

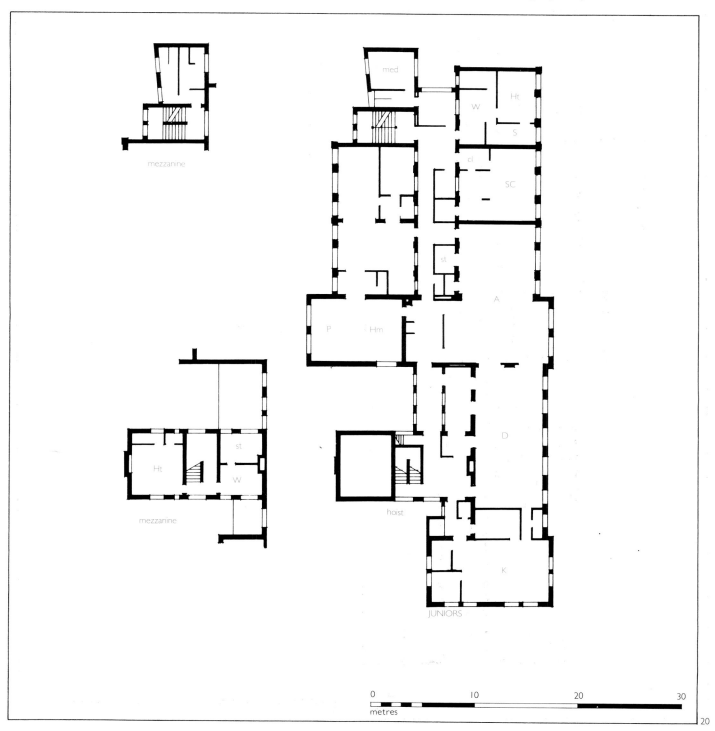

21   Second Floor Plan
*The original cellular classroom
arrangement has been broken down and the
juniors are centred around a library. By
making full use of the existing mezzanine
levels all lavatory accommpdation is closely
associated with teaching spaces.*
22   *Building a new detached nursery class
immediately adjacent to the old school
building released the whole of the ground
floor for the three infant years.*

22

Hm

Q

P

Hm

display

P   Hm

TV/Dr

st

L

Hm

Q   P

P

Hm

21

0   10   20   30

metres

linking with new lower level partitions and screens. With fully utilised pin-up the areas below these bands focus attention upon the lower areas of the high rooms and provide a more appropriate scale. The contract was in two stages to allow the schools to function continuously and finished in 1977.

Both infants and juniors have ample hard play space adjacent to the school buildings and the enlarged site has allowed ample parking and service space whilst contributing, with broad bands of peripheral planting, to the generally improved environment.

23 *The glazed roof of the original top corridor provides daylighting for the juniors' display area: it demonstrates how necessary it is to get daylight into the centre of the large, old school buildings – see Figs 15 and 16.*
24 *New, open teaching areas are formed by linking the original cellular classrooms with new openings in their cross walls. Here, the juniors have two home bays linked with a central shared project area. The scale of the high Victorian classrooms has been altered by the broad, horizontal bands of colour at door height.*

23

24

101

Westminster Technical College

One of Baroness Burdett-Coutts social initiatives was the founding of Battersea Polytechnic which was designed by E W Mountford and completed in 1894. A memorial library was added in 1910 and other extensions of varying architectural merit were added in the next forty years. As a result of the Robbins Report. 'A Committee of Enquiry on Higher Education', 1963, Battersea became the University of Surrey and in 1969 moved to new purpose built accommodation at Guildford, Surrey. The ILEA made the site in Battersea Park Road available for Westminster Technical College and a stringent economic analysis was undertaken to determine whether to proceed with the comprehensive adaptation of the existing building or whether to demolish the old building and rebuild behind the 1894 frontage, listed as being of historical interest. It was decided to keep and adapt the entire complex and reconstruction started in 1973.

Work was completed in 1977 and the revived building permitted the College work to be better concentrated, provided for the urgent expansion of the catering courses, stabilised the hotel school courses at its original building in Vincent Square, Westminster, and enabled leased accommodation to be given up. At Battersea the departments of civil engineering, mechanical engineering and home economics and

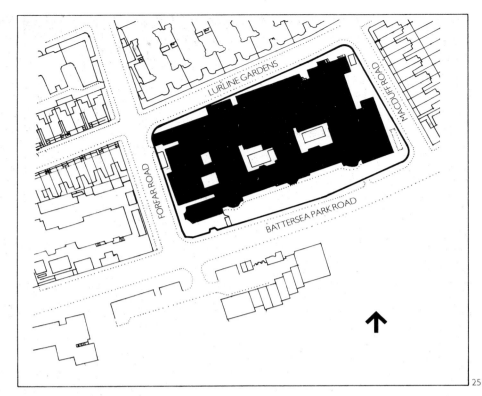

25 Site Plan
By the time that the site became available in 1973 it had been almost totally developed by the original Battersea Polytechnic building (E. W. Mountford, 1894) and other additions and extensions since.
26, 27 Ground and First Floor Plans
There was no space for further development upon the site and the College is an exercise

in adaptation for changed use with two new lifts and a link bridge included to achieve better circulation and improved means of escape.
28 *Some areas, such as the dining room shown here, had to be completely refurbished in this case with a cedar ceiling containing a new mechanical ventilation system. New flooring and servery provide a resource comparable with a new building.*

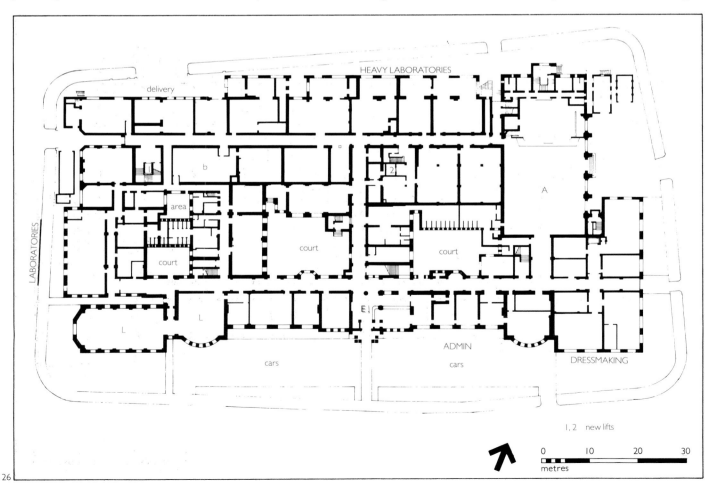

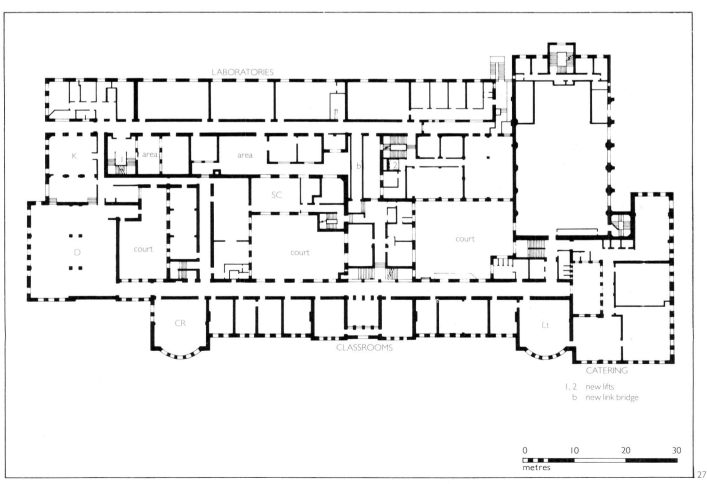

LABORATORIES

K

area

area

SC

b

1 2

court

D

court

court

court

CR

Lt

CLASSROOMS

CATERING

1, 2   new lifts
b   new link bridge

0   10   20   30
metres

28

27

catering are located but there are strong community links with young school leavers taking further O-level examinations, vocational links with local schools, home management tuition and training courses for social workers from neighbouring boroughs.

Over half of the cost of rehabilitation was spent upon maintenance of the fabric and whilst this reflected the complexity of the structure to be repaired it demonstrated the rapid ageing and deterioration which follow from underuse of old structures. Without the existence of a single, unified user prepared to occupy the whole building the premises would probably have remained empty and

deteriorated rapidly. The existing layout was deficient in circulation and means of escape and two lifts and a link bridge were necessary to achieve a functional solution. Internally, the appearance was transformed by modern materials and the bold use of colour. Externally, changes were kept to a minimum but brick and stone were cleaned and fittings painted. A total of 15,349 square metres of handsome space was provided for half the cost of building new.

Originally must doubt existed as to whether a structure of this age and variety of elements could be successfully adapted but it is seen as a successful building project which is a restoration of quality in Battersea.

29, 30 *Staircases and halls have had their robust Victorian detailing highlighted by the use of equally bold colour.*
31 *Cleaning brickwork and stone dressings followed by routine maintenance painting have reasserted the former grandeur of this large building in its neighbourhood providing a punctuation of quality in an otherwise unrelieved road.*

29

30

31

St Martin's School of Art, Long Acre

As the original Covent Garden Market moved to Nine Elms there was a danger that the vacuum left by old empty warehouse buildings might encourage comprehensive redevelopment and scatter the local community.[23] When T Walton and Sons, fruiterers, moved also, a feasibility study was made into adapting their warehouse, running between Long Acre and Floral Street, for elements of the St Martin's School of Art. Typical of many London colleges the School of Art had expanded with new departments to meet an increased demand and these were accommodated in expensive leased premises in Soho near the parent building in Charing Cross Road. The original warehouse was erected in 1922 and extended in 1934.

The feasibility study had to balance the continuation of these leases against a different type of agreement: the warehouse owners offered a full repairing lease incorporating a system of rent free and reduced rent periods to partly compensate for the costs of conversion. The owners provided all finance for the works of adaptation and improvement and were to be re-imbursed by the Greater London Council. The ILEA decided to proceed with conversion and rehabilitation of the warehouses and construction started in 1978 finishing in 1980 and the project of 2,300 square metres has provided 1,100 square metres net increase of accommodation at a low total rental balancing the surrender of the Soho leases.

Three departments are accommodated in the building which is quite near the main School: graphic design, painting (part) and the film/video unit. The plans show the full complexity of studios, workshops, processing rooms and support facilities. Original panelled offices have been retained and re-furbished and the main staircase extended whilst a large goods lift had to be included to serve all five floors. Artificial ventilation was necessary and the basement needed air-conditioning. The use of the flat roof was extended by adding railings and making it a fully paved terrace with a greenhouse and a flammable materials store.

A large proportion of the cost was spent in repairing and maintaining the fabric: the asphalt roof was renewed, steel windows replaced, electrical and heating installations renewed and special plastic flooring used. Internally, a cheerful atmosphere has been achieved by modern materials, services and colour. Externally, the redecorations are in keeping with the original building largely by restoring the original materials and appearance.[24] The school name is incorporated in the main elevation using letters matching the original warehouse lettering. At an early stage the local residents and planners expressed the wish that some of the

School's work should be visible to passers-by at street level and this has been achieved by glazing the ground floor photographic studio facing Long Acre and providing facilities for display-ing sculpture, paintings and graphic work.

Conversion of these warehouse premises not only gave a new lease of life to a building which might have fallen into disrepair, but has also introduced a new element, art students, into the varied and colourful community of Covent Garden.

32 Site Plan
Typical of the warehousing in Covent Garden the site was totally developed with access from two sides – Long Acre and Flora Street.

33, 34, 35, 36, 37, 38 Basement, Ground Floor, First Floor, Second Floor, Third Floor and Fourth Floor Plans
The original structure remains with exposed steel columns now protected against fire and all services have been renewed. A new goods lift with direct access off Floral Street serves all floors and pedestrian access is off Long Acre. Windows have been replaced to match the original pattern and stonework has been cleaned. Whilst the original panelled offices have been retained and refurbished the new partitions are universally demountable.

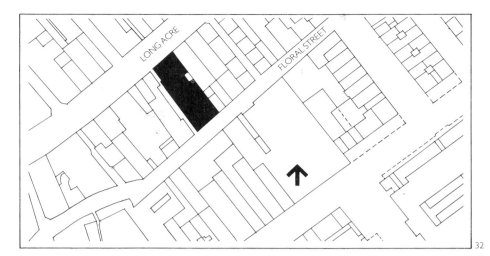

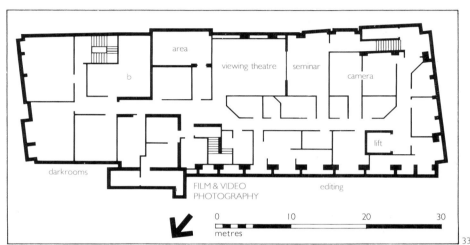

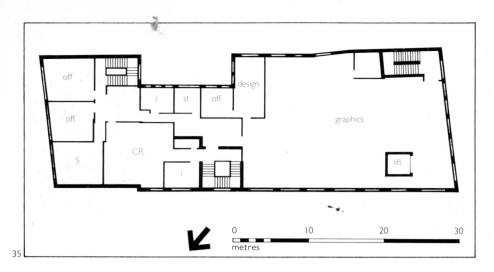

S
l st off
CR
l
design
graphics
lift

0   10   20   30
metres

35

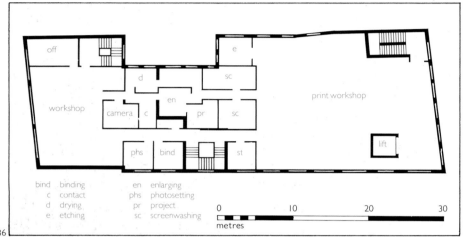

off
d
workshop
camera c
en
pr
sc
e
sc
phs bind
st
print workshop
lift

bind   binding   en   enlarging
c   contact   phs photosetting
d   drying   pr   project
e   etching   sc   screenwashing

0   10   20   30
metres

36

off
graphics
graphics
lift

0   10   20   30
metres

37

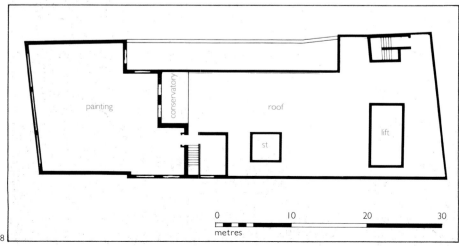

painting
conservatory
roof
st
lift

0   10   20   30
metres

38

39   *The original Long Acre elevation.*
40   *The basement contains the film/video unit and air-conditioning was necessary in areas such as the viewing theatre, shown here. New construction is quite straightforward with painted brick walls, a plastic floor finish and simple suspended ceilings but the unit's technology is very advanced.*
41   *The roof offers a further resource with railings added to the periphery and paving to the asphalt surface: the two additional blocks represent newer technology than the original building with steel framed enclosures for flammable substances storage (foreground) and lift motor room.*
42, 43   *The original staircase rising to the fruit company's directors' offices and boardroom has had its panelling restored, Fig. 42, and has been extended to the upper floors with new construction, Fig. 43.*

39

41

42

40

43

44

44 A secondary staircase has needed a higher handrail to meet current regulations and the steelwork is painted chrome yellow. All windows have been replaced in galvanised steel matching the originals. The grid patterns on the wall come from the original entrance doors to Long Acre (see Fig 39): many items from the original building (e.g. external lettering now redundant with the new name) have been transformed into decorative artifacts by Brian Yale, a GLC artist working with the architects.

45 The Long Acre elevation restored (see Fig 39). Portland stone has been cleaned, windows replaced and the new entrance has been opened up to the street providing an exhibition space visible by pedestrians. With other buildings being imaginatively restored also – note the neighbouring antique booksellers shop – Long Acre is becoming an interesting street again.

46 A side door gives access to Banbury Court – one of Covent Garden's warren of alleys – and is marked by an original gas lamp and a new entrance porch.

45

46

Chapter 4: References

1 Banham R, Theory and Design in the First Machine Age, Architectural Press, 1977, p 9: *this phrase would have been generally acceptable when the book was originally published in 1960. The RIBA Journal, January 1973, p 23 had reported the debate for buildings having 'Long Life, low energy, loose fit', started by Alex Gordon, President of the RIBA.*

2 Management Today, Feburary 1981, What Energy Crisis? pp 5–11; *for an alternative view of energy supply and energy costs.*

3 The Times, 10 May 1975, Anthony Crosland speaking on the Social Contract at Manchester Town Hall.

4 Stone P A, Building Economy, p 259, Pergamon (2nd edition), 1976: *for a comparison of the energy required to produce different building materials. The development of the deep plan was necessitated partly in order to reduce to a minimum the heat-conducting periphery of many types of buildings: as Building, 3 April 1981, p 5 points out 'more than 50% of the nation's total energy usage is expended in its buildings'. The other major reason was to reduce the costly external cladding of buildings.*

5 Building, 12 Febuary 1982, p 29: *states an uncertainty about an energy shortage but continues that 'cheap steel, cheap cement and cheap bricks are the products of cheap coal and oil'. There will be a shift in the relative costs, however, as different sources of energy are depleted.*

6 This is illustrated by the ILEA total new building programmes sanctioned by the DES (at November 1969 prices):

1970–71	£4,323,000
1971–72	4,574,000
1972–73	3,520,000
1973–74	2,302,000
1974–75	1,325,000
1975–76	596,000
1976–77	536,000
1977–78	284,000
1978–79	644,000
1979–80	862,000
1980–81	759,000

This graph indicates the dramatic decline of new building but this is increasingly complemented by a matching increase in rehabilitation and remodelling work.

See also appendix A for provision in new schools 1947–74. Appendix B for pattern of expenditure 1947–74. Appendix C cost per place (primary) and resultant areas.

7 Census Returns, 1981, HMSO indicates that the total population of Inner London declined by 18% since 1971 to 2,425,630.

8 Education, 16 October 1981, deals with falling school rolls and building costs and states that the school population in England and Wales is likely to fall from a peak of a little under nine million in 1979 to eight million by 1983; with a further decline to below seven and a half million by 1990.

9 RIBA Journal, December 1968: John Kay (DES) upon the success of the Compton competition.

10 A Study of School Building, DES, 1977, 5:64, states that 'few pre-war primary schools . . . have welcoming sites; in urban areas few have anything but hard asphalt surfaces surrounding them'.

11 GLC Architects Review 2, Academy 1976, pp 34–38.

12 Stone P A, Building Economy, Pergamon (2nd edition), 1976, p 250.

13 Architects Journal, 28 May 1936, p 797.

14 Architectural Record, January 1981, p 52.

15 Architects Journal, 9 June 1968, pp 1359–1361.

16 Architects Journal, 31 March 1971, pp 702–703.

17 Bauwelt, 26 April 1971, pp 702–703.

18 . Architectural Design, July 1973, p 466.

19 Building, 11 May 1973, p 67: Remodelling of an 1895 Board School.

20 Architects Journal, 21st November 1973, p 1236.

21 Design, June 1973, pp 74–77, Cure for Victorian Afflictions.

22 Surveyor, 31 January 1975, p 12–16, Second Chance Schools.

23 Building Refurbishment and Maintenance, April 1980, p 46, Modern Art: Fruit Warehouse Is Now Art School.

24 Building, 7 November 1980, p 34, There's Still Life.

Key to drawings

A	assembly hall
AEI	adult education institute
AH	activities hall
C	classroom
CR	common room
D	dining
Dr	drama
DW	dining/work
E	entrance
G	gymnasium
H	houseroom
Hm	home bay
Ht	head or principal
I	infants
J	juniors
K	kitchen
L	library
Lt	lecture
M	music
Ns	nursery
P	practical area
PC	play centre
Q	quiet area
S	secretary
Sc	science
SC	staff common room
SH	sports hall
SK	schoolkeeper
Sw	swimming pool
W	waiting
YS	youth service
b	boiler
ca	covered area
ch	changing
cl	cloakroom
l	lavatories
s	servery
st	store

Chapter 5
Experimental & Innovatory Schools

It is an often repeated truism that schools are not ultimately dependent upon their physical containment and this can be reinforced by identifying highly successful and popular schools inhabiting the most awkwardly arranged, ancient, badly serviced and recalcitrant buildings. There is little correlation between a school as an amalgamation of teachers and taught and the building which houses it. There is a far wider debate as to whether the reality of a building is in its finite, identifiable elements such as . walls and roof or whether it is in its enclosure, the space enveloped by such elements. Since 1945 there has been a continuous, sometimes acrimonious dialogue, between architects and educationalists to establish a common ground for their differing objectives from which to advance triumphantly together in the provision of school buildings: sometimes when mutuality has been established the resultant building has within a short time proved obsolete because of a change of educational emphasis or a national development in curricula. And so the dialogue continues with schools resulting in bold architectural statements or fully flexible, fully serviced, indeterminate envelopes.

From 1920 to 1944 the teaching space was universally recognised as the cellular classroom designed to contain thirty or forty pupils. It was designed to face south and opened off a single-banked corridor which allowed cross-ventilation through a series of opening lights. Even buildings such as Burlington School[1,2] (See Chapter 1) which is viewed as a very advanced architectural work for Britain in 1929 or Impington Village College, 1936,[3] bearing the fame of adventurous educational aims and Walter Gropius as its architect did not attempt to depart from the accepted geometrical enclosure in an attenuated plan form.[4] The vast majority of secondary schools in inner London reflect this unchanging requirement and right up to 1969 new schools were assumed to contain arrangements of simple classrooms sometimes heavily serviced and specialised for science, but mostly of a general description their own speciality – art, language, geography or history – being defined by furniture and fittings. Workshops were treated as independent units. Whilst the two schools described in this chapter exemplify how buildings are made to meet their briefs by architectural resourcefulness and by the integration of specialist consultants' skills, they also indicate that the rapid movement and development in school needs overtake the reality of the provision. It is unlikely that either sort of school will ever be built again in inner London for even as the fundamental need for large new secondary schools no longer exists no educational brief is likely to require either the enclosures of Pimlico or the wide, open spaces of Waterfield. Both schools, and the thinking which developed them, have been influential in subsequent designs, however, and this is illustrated in chapters 7 and 8.

Pimlico School

When Pimlico was designed in 1964[5] the brief was based upon the finite class and class size which was not necessarily relevant in 1970 when the building was completed. 1725 secondary pupils, boys and girls, were to be contained upon a site of 4.50 acres (1.82 hectares) only which is 10'0" (3.00 m) below the surrounding roads on all four sides of the rectangular site. The consequence is a large but very compact building of three and four storeys with its very size (200 separate rooms) apparently reduced internally by the simple accessibility stemming from a single first floor major circulation route, the concourse, from which frequent stairs give direct access to teaching, administration, social and sports facilities. Having solved the problem of internal movement[6] it was necessary for the architect to determine the nature of the accommodation in the light of the density of site use. The solution lay in providing a deep plan and to meet the premise that all teaching accommodation must be naturally lighted the narrow ended classrooms have a most complicated cross section in order to permit daylighting by deep rooflights.[7,8] Very wide cantilevers were required to support the projecting floor slabs and these in turn needed monolithic concrete cross walls to sustain them: flat slab construction in lightweight insulating concrete was used without downstand beams. A direct consequence of the compact plan giving good accessibility is the total inflexibility inherent in the cross structure and briefing assumptions were said to have been overtaken by events.[9]

The concourse is the social core of the building which, in a school of this magnitude, enables immediate identification for routes and gives the individual a chance to relate to the whole organisation with the library the core of an excellent circulation conception. There is, however, complete separation of academic from specialist and practical accommodation: this has led to the isolation of art from craft and engineering from science ultimately prohibiting the easy development of linked projects. Due to its inflexibility and the problems of glare and solar radiation inherent in the narrow end lit classrooms the building has been criticised for, as the brief became obsolete, so did the building. Schools change with their administration and the house system has not been used as designed.[10] Despite the criticism the school is internationally famous upon architectural grounds because of its boldness in the use of materials – these are limited externally to well-detailed concrete and patent glazing[11] – and its sheer ingenuity. It is a building of presence and humanity and its architectural success is based upon its social organisation, circulation and departmental structure which make the school 'an important architectural landmark'[12] with its 'glinting facetted form'.[13]

1 Site Plan
The plan shows the compact development of a four storey building upon a sunken island site.

To the East is St George's Square giving the relief of an open treed space whilst to the South is Dolphin Square which is arguably the most dense residential development in central London. The remaining buildings around the site are mostly stucco early nineteenth century six storey terraces.

2 Ground Floor Plan
Sunk below the surrounding roads the plan shows how fully the site has been developed with a self-contained workshop wing.

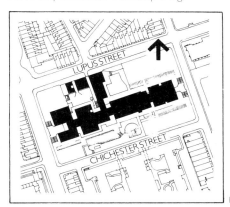

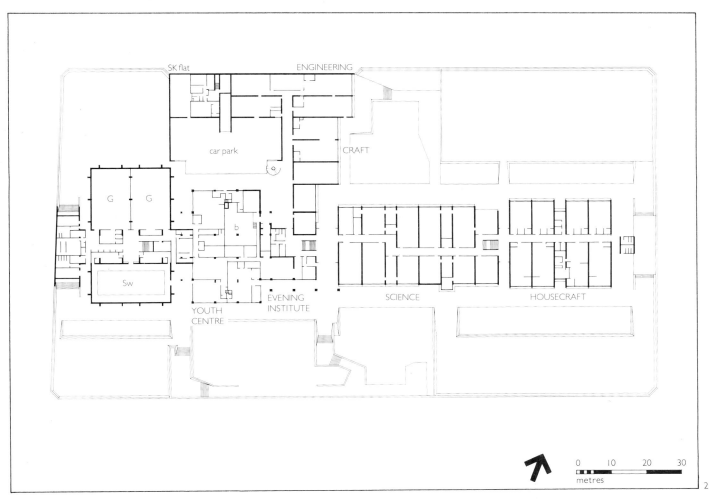

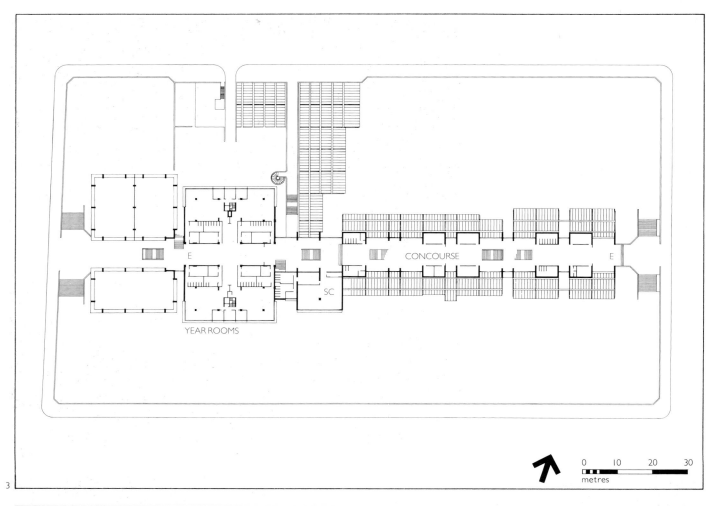

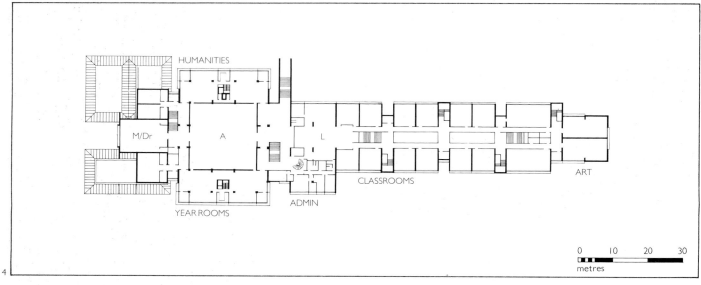

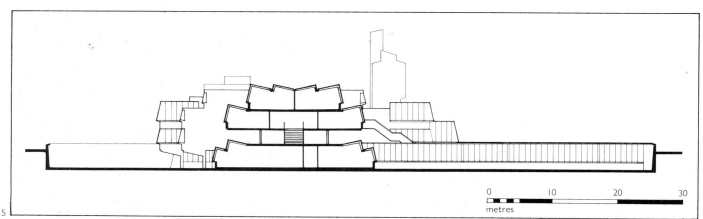

3 First Floor Plan
The importance of the concourse is demonstrated showing it not only as the main access artery but the main street also.

4 Second Floor Plan
Typical classroom layout with the houserooms grouped around the assembly space. The constructional cross walls demonstrate the fixity of the plan.

5 Section
The section demonstrates the importance of the concourse in providing a spacious and successful means of circulation.

6 *The size of this large school upon a very small site is concealed as the ground level is three metres below surrounding roads.*

7 *The form of the building is necessitated by the daylight factor required in teaching spaces in a deep plan.*

8 *The main entrances at pavement level lead directly to the central concourse at the school's ground floor level.*

9 *The limited use of materials — well-detailed in-situ concrete with patent glazing — provides a bold integrity.*

6

7

8

9

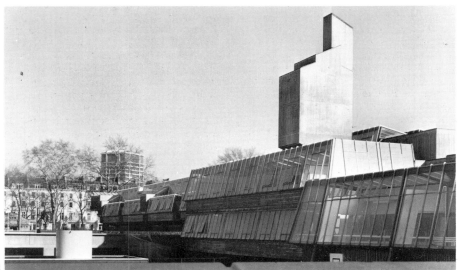

10　The library.
11　The assembly hall is a multi-purpose space including possibilities of theatre in the round: unity is provided internally by simplicity of a limited range of materials.
12, 13　In context the building fits well with its diverse neighbours. Its scale is a triumph.

Waterfield School

A school such as Pimlico could have been placed upon its difficult site by developing the design as a two or three storeyed building of exceptional depth with a highly sophisticated comprehensive servicing system permitting plug-in servicing enabling science and workshop provision to be made virtually anywhere within the building envelope. The Pimlico brief assumed that the traditional class of 30 pupils would remain the basic grouping for teaching purposes: even as it was being constructed greater emphasis was being placed upon individual and independent group work as well as upon larger groups of 120 for team teaching following the successful development of this method in primary schools.

Studies for a new and innovative secondary school were begun in 1969 by a joint group of architects and educationists which was set up to identify requirements for future trends in secondary education and to translate these into a brief for architects. The brief was originally to be for the rebuilding of Thomas Calton School and when this did not proceed it was developed for Waterfield School at Thamesmead. The school, being at the proposed business/communal central area of Thamesmead, was to be integrated into the main community facilities. When the design had been completed the ILEA decided, in the light of projected growth of population at Thamesmead, to build in two phases with the first accommodating 750 children. The upper school portion was completed in 1976 as the first phase.

The studies were for a mixed secondary school of 1450 pupils on a site of 10.40 acres (4.21 hectares) and the brief was designed to encourage new teaching approaches.[14] The identification of a distinct lower school allowing group and individual learning in an informal atmosphere, similar to the modern primary school practice, for children in their first three years in secondary education was one. The raising of the school leaving age to sixteen, envisaged in the 1944 Act and made concrete in 1973, enabled greater emphasis upon more adult organisation for the older pupils with an expanded curriculum giving greater individual choice: new subjects, developed as a result of the Newsom Report, 1963, Half Our Future, which proposed a broader approach for the less able pupil in technology, the humanities and social science and new teaching techniques were becoming more widely accepted.[15] The social system was to be organised by year or interest groupings and its more tightly arranged dining requirements would be replaced by an informal cafeteria having six sittings. Topics would be studied which crossed traditional subject boundaries and so there is a drama studio instead of an assembly hall, arts and crafts rooms are integrated to form

design/technology areas and the library becomes a resource and study centre. In addition to a greater emphasis upon guidance and counselling there was to be an increased use of educational technology.

Against this background of fundamental investigation the architects contributed a great deal because of their ability to analyse problems and to illustrate proposed solutions in such a way that the briefing group could arrive at well-informed decisions about the general organisation of the school as well as the physical relationship of its parts. One of the main characteristics of secondary education in Britain has been a high level of subject specialisation which was reflected in large areas of the school building being of limited, but highly specialised, use. By defining spaces in terms of activities rather than in terms of subject the group found that it was possible to provide a high proportion of general teaching areas, both enclosed and open-planned, allowing greater flexibility in use:[16] this presupposed that some specialised teaching would be carried out in non-specialised areas. The ability to re-organise the layout as teaching methods evolve was seen as essential. The need for close relationships between all parts

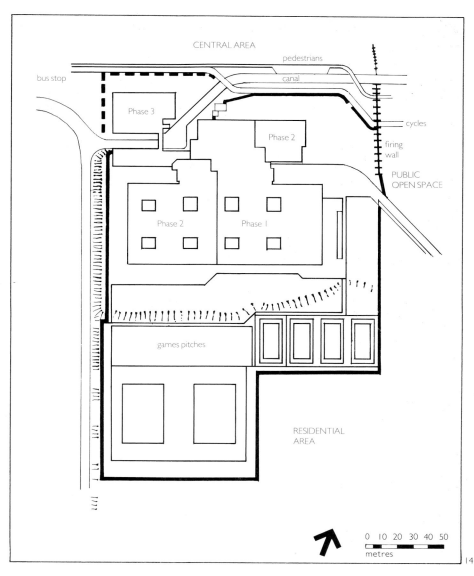

14 Site Plan

The site is large enough for the development of a single-storey, deep plan teaching block which is designed to be built upon an existing plateau (3 m) higher than the adjacent canal side to the North.

A canal initially was to have separated the proposed phase 3 development (swimming pool, community centre, etc) from the main school buildings as shown here but later it was proposed that the canal ran on the North side of this too. The plan shows how the school links into the pedestrian and cycle ways which are fundamental to the Thamesmead movement system.

The firing wall is 'large, brick, monumental structure 10 metres high built for the Royal Arsenal which originally owned most of the Thamesmead area. Canals are a necessary part of the total development to ascertain that the water level, in a swampy environment, remains constant.

of the school and the emphasis upon the use of mobile equipment developed a single-storey, deep plan which gives a long life with a loose fit.

Originally the brief was developed for an eight form entry secondary school providing accommodation for 240 pupils per year and it was decided, for the lower school, to organise these into half year groups of 120. Each group would be organised as a social/academic unit with its own home base consisting of a large multi-purpose area, a group room, a tutorial area and a social area. A specialist area will provide for art, craft and science facilities for the first two years and equipment will be trolleyed from there into the multi-purpose area which will be equipped for light practical work. In the centre of the lower school will be its library/resource area sharing facilities, such as the recording studio and teachers' preparation room, with the upper school.

A more complicated arrangement exists for the upper school. General teaching areas, grouped around the library/resource area, will consist of two multipurpose spaces which will be used for team teaching in the humanities, English, language and mathematics with groups of up to 60 pupils: as in the lower school these areas will be carpeted and have light, movable furniture for simple rearrangement. Tutorial, seminar and group rooms as well as social areas for 30 are provided adjacent to the multi-purpose spaces. An enclosed room for student activities is available for use by the sixth form or as a base for clubs. To encourage the development of team teaching, staff work rooms provide places for team meetings as well as individual work spaces. The specialist facilities include a suite of linked spaces for housecraft, art, crafts and science each with bays for specialist equipment or activities: this arrangement offers integration between subjects and links between activities.

Teaching areas are single storeyed with a steel framed structural grid at 9.00 m centres giving wide flexibility in use. Specialist areas, which are grouped together, with fixed layouts have been reduced to a minimum with social areas

15 Layout Plan
The plan form demonstrates the simplicity of the teaching block as a deep, single storey volume enclosing a variety of spaces – social, multi-purpose, group, tutorial, seminar and staff rooms. The first phase, shown here in detail, demonstrates the integration of housecraft, arts and craft, science and general teaching with the library resource placed in what will be the centre of the completed school.

Peripheral rooms have natural ventilation but the main volume is air-conditioned. Courtyards provide visual variety with paving and landscape.

The teaching volume is placed upon a low plateau with the shared/community accommodation on two levels to the north: the latter contains the noise generating parts of the building – music, activities hall, gymnasium, changing, kitchen/dining and common rooms.

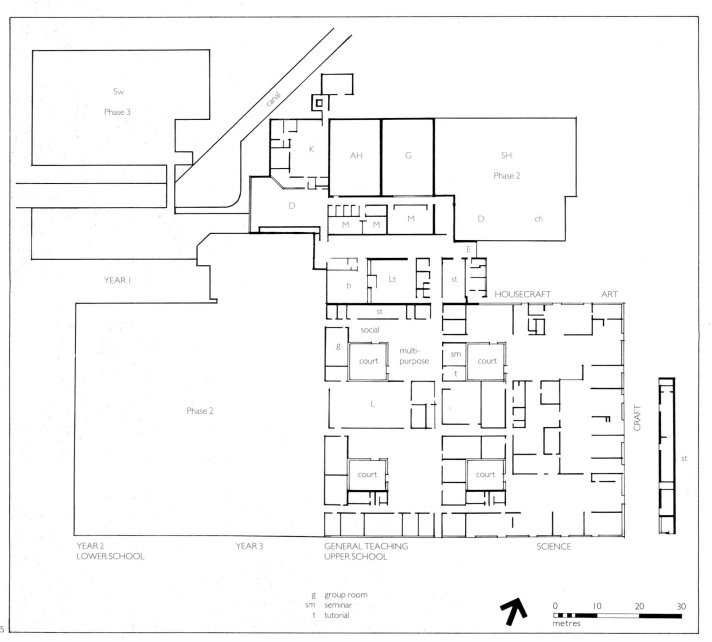

g   group room
sm seminar
t   tutorial

providing informal extensions to teaching areas. The building has been designed for the long term need for flexibility and adaptability and this is reflected in the use of steel faced demountable partitions and mobile equipment: even fixed partitions are easily altered being stack bonded blockwork only. Servicing arrangements are eminently variable with electricity, water and gases widely available from the ceiling void feeding, via service booms, areas having a grid of potential drainage points in the floor. Immediate variation is provided by the articulation of locker or storage units which can convert areas upon a day to day basis. The need for adaptability dominates the design solution.

Along with the wide, deep teaching space the need for limited, specialised volumes remains for reasons of servicing or acoustics: these volumes are for music, drama, dining, the kitchen and physical education. This differentiation is marked by the placing of these elements together in a two storeyed block running parallel to the teaching area: this enables easy access and sharing by the lower and upper school as well as the community. A change in site level allows this element to be half a storey lower than the teaching block with a wide ramped mall making a common entrance focus. The enclosures of the specialised volume are marked externally by the use of stack bonded blockwork.

A concept of deep plan, largely open single storey spaces raised a new range of technical issues unusual in normal school building with special emphasis upon lighting, heating and acoustics. However deep the plan it is considered desirable for all teaching spaces to have a view to the outside of the building or into a courtyard and to reduce glare to these areas the glazing is mostly translucent ply glass with a continuous horizontal viewing strip. The deep plan could not provide sufficient daylighting to all teaching areas and a permanent supplementary artificial lighting installation (PSALI) was required to achieve an illumination level of 450 lux. This level of artificial lighting would produce glare from the fittings and to reduce this a proprietary suspended ceiling system is used consisting of a series of deep troughs which conceal the light source when viewed from a distance providing a diffused illumination.[17]

The perimeter rooms have natural ventilation but the majority of the volume is air-conditioned. Heating and ventilation is provided by a combined system with hot water convectors

16

17

18

16 *Informal cafeteria displaces usual school meals provision.*
17 *Specialist areas, such as workshops are grouped together: the structure is clearly expressed.*
18 *Waterfield was the first school to make full use of the ILEA's specially designed storage range: see Chapter 14 for details.*

installed at external walls and package air-handling units on the roof provide heated or cooled air as required.

Deep, open planning raised problems of noise and a workable acoustic environment is achieved in the large areas by carpeting the floor and providing a suspended sound absorbent ceiling. To prevent sound transference from noisy to quiet areas the acoustic properties of the demountable partitions were checked and adjusted. The air-handling equipment upon the roof is isolated from the main steel structure to reduce sound transference whilst at the same time it is tuned to provide an adequate background noise level in the open planned areas.

The form of the school reflects the prime concerns and the teaching areas are bounded by a tight glass skin drawn around the perimeter with a neat gridded fenestration of clear glass and white insulated panels framed in black standard steel sections – 'an immaculate example of the exposed steel frame and blockwork idiom'.[18] The steel structure is expressed in red and the effect is cool and classical. The depth of plan that was required to fulfil the brief could have resulted in an unrelieved, windowless interior but all spaces have views through with internal courtyards providing points of vivid landscape. Great care was taken with the interior design with a dynamic colour scheme in primary reds, blues and yellows to add point to the general functionalism and environmental comfort of the block: the building reflects the bold, optimistic brief.

19 *Flexibility and future adaptability are demonstrated in the physics laboratory which has easily movable furniture, fittings and partitions whilst overhead services and flexible drainage enables easy variation to a different mode or even subject.*
20 *A ramped mall at the entrance connects the main teaching spaces to the right with the two storey block on the left which contains enclosed spaces for music, administration, gymnasium, etc.*
21 *Packaged air-handling units on the roof express the designs reliance upon immediately available technology.*
22 *Cladding is a tight, white, insulated glass skin drawn around the perimeter in black standard steel window sections with the main steel frame, trim and doors painted scarlet.*
23 *South terrace.*
24 *South elevation.*

19

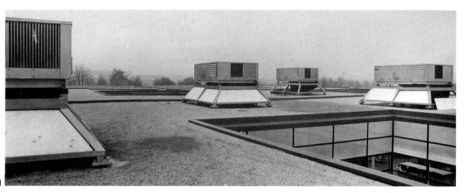

21

20

22

23

24

Chapter 5: References

1 Architects Journal, 21 January 1937, pp 137–141.

2 Architectural Review, January 1937.

3 Architectural Review, December 1939, p 225.

4 Architects Journal, 10 February 1938, pp 253–258: *illustrated many varieties of school layout but always based upon the square classroom as an isolated cell.*

5 Architectural Design, April 1966, pp 176–177.

6 L'Achitecture d'Aujourd'hui, February–March, 1971, pp 48–49.

7 Architectural Review, July 1971, pp 9–22.

8 Architect, December 1974, p 50.

9 Architects Journal, 14 April 1971, pp 9–22.

10 Architectural Design, November 1970, pp 556–557.

11 Architect, May 1975, pp 50–51, Claddings.

12 Architects Journal, 31 March 1976, pp 627–638, Building Revisited.

13 Architectural Design, April 1966, p 177.

14 Architects Journal, 9 March, 1977, pp 443–454.

15 Industria della Construzioni, December 1978, pp 66–71.

16 Airoldi R, Innovazione Didattica e Spazi, ISEDI, 1977, pp 92–101.

17 Casabella, September 1976, pp 54–59.

18 Design, August, 1977, p 40.

Key to drawings

A	assembly hall
AEI	adult education institute
AH	activities hall
C	classroom
CR	common room
D	dining
Dr	drama
DW	dining/work
E	entrance
G	gymnasium
H	houseroom
Hm	home bay
Ht	head or principal
I	infants
J	juniors
K	kitchen
L	library
Lt	lecture
M	music
Ns	nursery
P	practical area
PC	play centre
Q	quiet area
S	secretary
Sc	science
SC	staff common room
SH	sports hall
SK	schoolkeeper
Sw	swimming pool
W	waiting
YS	youth service
b	boiler
ca	covered area
ch	changing
cl	cloakroom
l	lavatories
s	servery
st	store

Chapter 6
The New Balance

Simultaneously with the development of the secondary school as an infinitely flexible volume with full potential for servicing variations to cater for future requirements, as heralded by Waterfield School (see Chapter 5), there was a slower, steadier strand to be discerned in educational policy. The idea of l'uomo universale had faded over the last hundred years with the rapidly increasing rate of information and although the schools of the 1950's (Garratt Green and William Penn see Chapter 2) recognised this and presented an heroic front with large scale workshops, separate science wings and art facilities they are to be seen as pioneering attempts to provide wider educational options for the average pupil as envisaged in the 1944 Education Act. The significant point about these schools was that their large departments were insulated from each other, each subject being taught in isolation and usually in separate buildings. During the 1960's it became plain that the boundaries of specialities had blurred as the flood of information required a wider and looser physical framework with greater opportunities for cross-fertilisation between different disciplines. It is worth noting that in 1888 it was proposed 'that the methods of Kindergarten teaching in Infants' schools be developed for senior scholars throughout the Standards in schools, so as to supply a graduated course of Manual Training in connection with Science teaching and Object lessons'.

By the late 1960's it was clear that recent primary schools (see Chapter 3) could offer successful working examples of flexibility in use without the expensive, sophisticated technology[2] at that time being pursued in the United States of America.[3] The use of the home bay/informal teaching area proved attractive, particularly with the lower years where a home base was more appropriate in a large school than the more traditional vertical house groupings which separated a child from many of its contemporaries. A new balance between specialist and non-specialist accommodation was proposed and, as a consequence, the architect became a member of the briefing group with the education inspectors, the school's head and staff and the administrators seeking to set the enlarged provision into its local context. Accommodation was required to allow the development of a range of curricula as new teaching patterns emerge during the lifetime of the school building: initially this was seen as closer integration of subjects, team teaching (ie more than one teacher being directly involved with a group of pupils engaged in specific work; eg the chemical consequences in studying food and nutrition, or the physical properties apparent in metal working) and block timetabling but it also encompassed the change in emphasis from direct instruction by a teacher to learning by the pupils and the resulting modes of imparting information.

By this time it was clear that inner London would no longer require complete new secondary schools, except at Thamesmead, and from 1970 onwards expansion by new buildings, rather than new schools, would be the pattern. The architect was presented thereafter with the need to extend an existing school upon an urban site to provide for a new educational flexibility with architectural virtuosity. The three secondary schools illustrated here demonstrate totally different but equally successful approaches to extension: Hydeburn the separated new provision of a radically different layout and appearance and Clapton the firmly integrated and extended school sharing the apparently informal and formal concepts respectively, whilst Blackheath Bluecoat, upon a smaller scale, comes halfway between the two offering neat enclosure in a radical fashion.

1 Site Plan
The site is banded on the South by a main line railway embankment with a primary school immediately to the West.
The existing buildings form the lower school as they had little specialist accommodation.

2 Ground Floor Plan
The taller, less sensitive volumes provide a noise shield against the railway: one split level corridor serves a classroom arrangement where workshops merge with art and craft continuing to suites of seminar and tutorial rooms grouped around large home bays as general teaching centres. The library resource area is located centrally and the music suite is isolated from other teaching areas.

Hydeburn School

At Balham there existed a four form entry secondary boys' school in a series of old buildings and in 1969 it became possible to extend the site with a further 5.50 acres (2.20 hectares) to the south against a main line railway embankment. The old buildings were to remain as the lower school for the traditional cellular classrooms would provide ample general teaching space, whilst a new block for the upper school would provide specialist areas and enlarge the school to a six form entry mixed school.

An intensive survey of current educational trends by the architect, inspectors and school staff demonstrated a need for closer inter-relationship of subjects in the new building. The plan instantly reflects this with a series of large home bays,[4] acting as year centres and general teaching space, closely associated with the central library

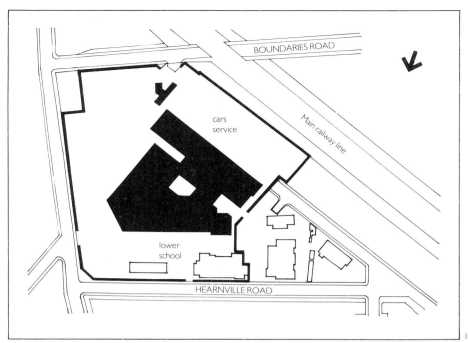

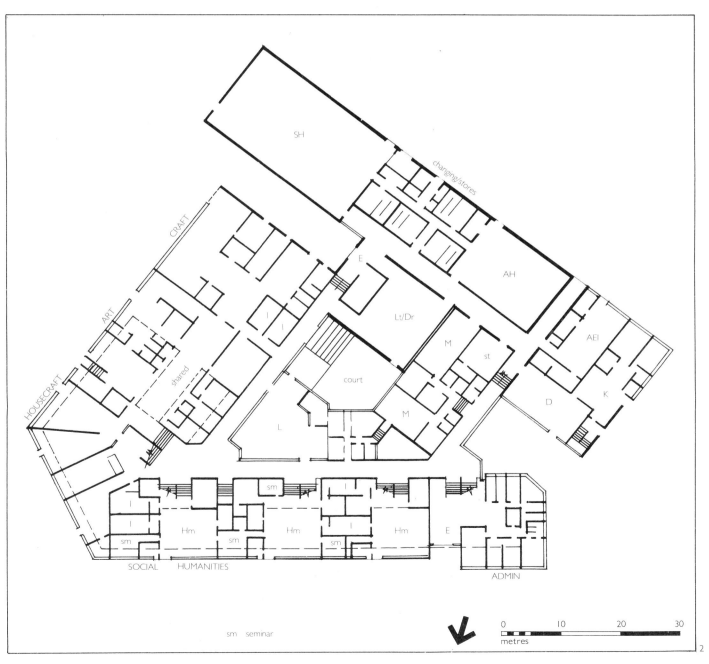

sm seminar

resource: a variety of room sizes with seminar and tutorial rooms provide immediate in-use flexibility. On the ground floor are the workshops, art and craft suite and housecraft rooms closely related together with a centrally planned shared activities area. Immediately above this is the science department. Separation of the two floors is minimised by the use of a single split level corridor set midway between the floors allowing short flights of stairs to link upwards and downwards and providing an apparent immediacy.

In broad terms the accommodation follows the boundaries of the wedge-shaped site with the taller noisier volumes of games hall, activities hall, youth service facilities and main kitchen presenting a solid face to the railway and providing a noise shield to the re-mainder of the building. The main teaching areas, already described, are ranged along the quieter perimeters of the block whilst the protected centre contains, in addition to the library

resource, a lecture/drama theatre, music suite and a recording suite. The latter areas are air-conditioned. A small central courtyard can be used for open air drama.

The superstructure is an envelope of white acrylic aluminium panels and brown tinted patent glazing in bronze coloured bars, carried by steel portal frames clear of internal partitions to allow for the partitions easy future removal, if required. The first floor is carried on an in-situ concrete coffered slab with walls, inside and out, generally fairfaced, stack-bonded masonry blocks. Where suspended ceilings are used they are acoustic and floors are carpeted including all circulation.

When completed in 1976 extensive areas of planting had been established to relieve the monotonous faces of the neighbouring streets and the sleek new buildings provide a 'quietly distinctive addition to the surrounding environment'.[5]

3 First Floor Plan
The built-in flexibility layout continues with the general teaching areas' multi-purpose rooms whilst the science specialist rooms have a direct link with their associated subjects on the ground floor.

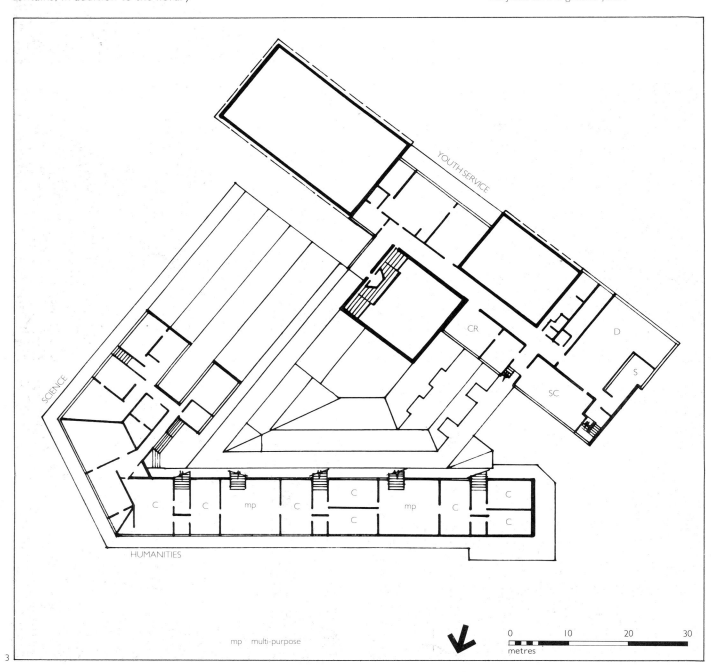

mp   multi-purpose

0   10   20   30
metres

4 A home bay on the ground floor demonstrating the more informal layout possible with a square shaped room. In-situ concrete coffers are used for the first floor slab.

5 The library resource area is in the centre of the plan readily available to all subject areas: with largely glazed partitions it can be seen as accessible from adjacent circulation areas. Suspended ceilings are metal faced acoustic panels.

6 The shared activities space which lies between and connects housecraft and the craft areas although it forms a major element of the art department with immediate access to painting, drawing, sculpture and ceramic areas. There are two large rooflights lighting the ends of the space.

7 The biology laboratory sharing the interior of the roof peak utilising all of the available volume to provide adjustable overhead service booms permitting future change and flexibility.

8 The main circulation is the split level corridor which serves ground and first floors with short flights of wide stairs: the stairs lead up to multi-purpose areas and down to large home bays. Floors are carpeted and the ceiling is a rooflight of bronze tinted glass with the main steel structure exposed.

4

5

6

7

8

127

9 The main entrance area viewed from the entrance desk shows the split level circulation arrangement and the simple consistency of the building materials: stack bonded concrete block walls, exposed steel structure, coffered concrete slabs and rooflighting patterned by patent glazing.

10 Looking south towards the sports and dining accommodation which acts as a screen for the teaching areas to noise from the adjacent railway lines. The stack-bonded blockwork used as a boundary wall (on the right) is the standard partition detail throughout the school.

11 From the south looking towards the original building, now the lower school.

Clapton School

The original building dates from 1912 but in 1960 a two storey classroom block was added and later a three storey extension was completed in order to provide accommodation for raising the school leaving age. In order to allow enlargement to its current size for a six form entry secondary girls' school the adjoining area to the south east was purchased which included the Salvation Army's Congress Hall, the facade of which was listed and had to be retained in the new design.

The brief was developed again with the architect, inspectorate and the existing school and one of its bases was the recognition of three broad categories of accommodation necessary. The least flexible type of specialised space was designed for teaching one subject only. Activity specialised areas providing

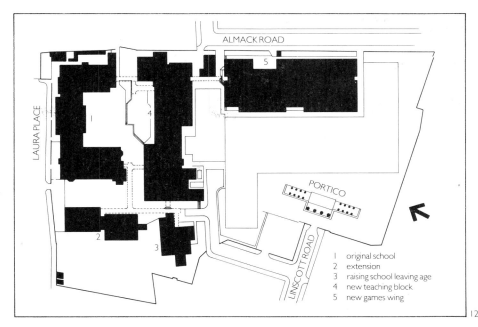

ALMACK ROAD

PORTICO

LAURA PLACE

LINSCOTT ROAD

1 original school
2 extension
3 raising school leaving age
4 new teaching block
5 new games wing

12

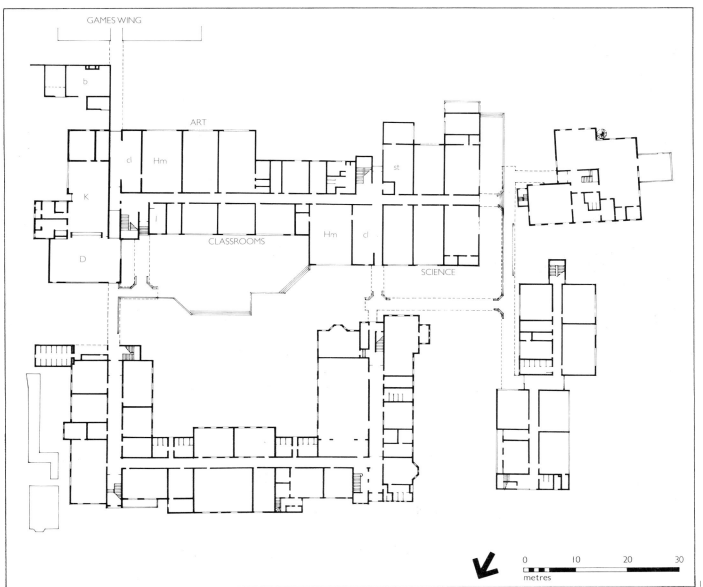

GAMES WING

ART

CLASSROOMS

SCIENCE

0   10   20   30
metres

13

12 Site Plan
The original school building is complemented by the new teaching wing providing a large central courtyard. A new games wing protects the games pitches from the North and the listed Congress

Hall portico remains to close a vista on an adjoining road.
13 Ground Floor Plan, Teaching Block
Science and arts and crafts are closely associated but in large enclosed areas rather than the more open approach used

at Hydeburn or George Green's (see Chapter 9). Large home bays adjacent to suites of classrooms provide a range of room sizes for future flexibility. The first floor layout is similar but the floor area is smaller.

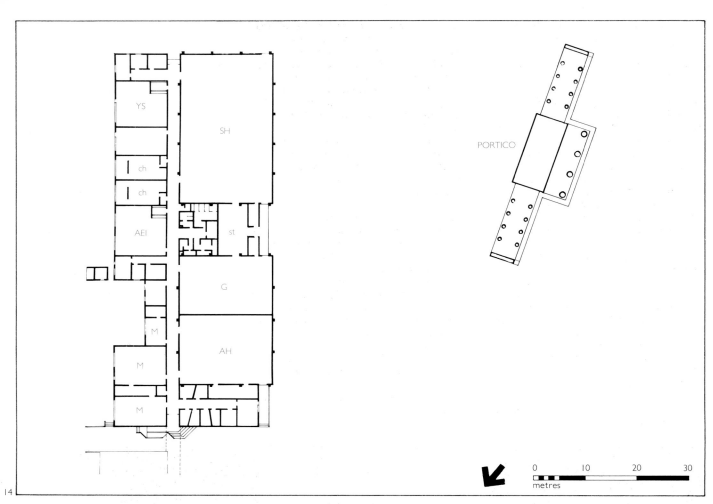

YS

SH

ch

ch

AEI

st

G

M

AH

M

M

PORTICO

0   10   20   30
metres

14

15

for a special activity applicable to more than one subject, such as the library resource centre, would increase the overall flexibility of the school with general teaching space providing the most flexible accommodation.[6] The outline design was agreed in 1974.

Unlike Hydeburn School the form of the original building has, in effect, been completed by the new teaching wing providing the enclosure to a large central courtyard and this has made the whole concept much more formal. A new games wing protects the enlarged sports area from the north. All existing and new blocks are separate but are linked by a comprehensive system of covered ways.

Science areas are placed centrally to the enlarged school on two floors and the art and craft suite is a series of large enclosed areas. New classrooms and large home bays (each being the social base for 180 pupils and the tutorial base for two groups of 30) complete the suiteing and mixture of accommodation with pastoral tutors' rooms and other staff rooms giving a range of room size for future flexibility. A lecture/drama theatre is isolated to prevent noise disruption to teaching areas but in close conjunction with them. The main library

resource centre is located in the original block and is a handsome two storeyed space with mezzanines associated as working areas: it has a sound recording studio and dark room en suite. The new music department is part of the games wing as the massive load bearing structure for the activities hall and gymnasium provides isolation and quietude. An adult education institute and youth service accommodation adjacent to the sports hall complete this wing allowing for totally separate use as necessary.

The architectural intention was to merge as far as possible the new accommodation with the old, requiring a phased construction programme of four stages completing in 1979, and matching the original building in general terms. Two storeyed blocks resulted with matching brickwork and pitched roofs to the new teaching wing with the large scale games wing massing describing its structure. A simple corridor system mirrors the existing and provides a continuity for the movement of large numbers. The newer existing blocks were of such diverse styles and massing that they were excluded from aesthetic consideration.

14   Ground Floor Plan, Games Wing
A fully fitted music suite sits naturally in this block due to its isolation and massive load-bearing structure. This wing can be totally separated allowing for full use by the adult education institute and the youth service both of which are centred here.
15   *The old and new buildings form a large courtyard and looking south one sees the merging of the new teaching block on the left and the original building to the right joined by a covered way built like a pergola. The taller distant block was erected in the early 1970's to provide extra accommodation for raising the school leaving age.*
16   *A new library was formed from the assembly hall of the original building with mezzanines associated as working areas.*
17   *Part of the doric portico remaining from the Congress Hall frames another massive structure – the sports wing with the games hall on the right and the gymnasium and activities hall to the left.*
18   *The new teaching block seen here from the east has a quality sympathetic to the old building in the background. This end of the new block contains the science department.*

16

18

17

19

20

19 The architectural detail of the new blocks is shown in this view over the covered way linking the sports wing with the teaching block in the background. The boiler house is on the right.

20 The load-bearing structure of the sports wing is massively explicit in this view showing the external brick piers. Floodlighting is for the games pitch to the right.

21 The general development of the new buildings shows a low key architecture with significant forms expressed at particular points. Here, the boiler house marks the transition from the mass and scale of the sports wing on the right to the more domestic scale of the teaching block to the left (see Fig 20) connected by a covered way.

21

Blackheath Bluecoat CE School

The existing school, built in 1911 and extended in 1934, had an ample 5.00 acre (2.00 hectares) site for its size although land-locked by small suburban houses and a large sports ground. There were good mature trees and the school was sited on the western boundary leaving most of the remaining site clear.

It is a voluntary maintained school and the governors selected Stillman and Eastwick-Field as architects in 1970 to provide expansion on the site from a two form entry to a six form entry secondary school. At an early stage the architects offered two options: a conventional school with cellular classrooms off corridors or a radically different approach to teaching arrangement which, by juxtaposing related subjects, and by locating spaces of varying sizes in adjacent areas, would allow for groups of two or three classes to be brought together on occasions, leaving other spaces free for smaller

22 Site Plan
The site had the original building only upon it and the position of this left the maximum space available for further development as indicated here with the addition of five new teaching blocks and a games block. The disposition of these blocks and the surface treatment of the resulting courts give variety of finish and enclosure.

23, 24 Ground Floor Plan, First Floor Plan
The dispersal of house rooms to the pavilions makes them available as teaching/social centres and, with the association of a mix of different sized rooms, offers the opportunity of wide flexibility allowing expansion and extension as desired. The original building is treated in the same way.

Although the structure is load-bearing few internal partitions are structural and heating/electrical servicing has been rationalised so as not to inhibit future radical adaptation.

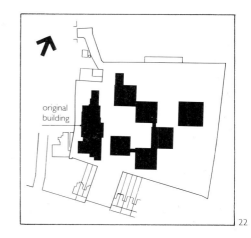

original building

22

CRAFT

b

SK house

cl

cl

VI FORM

ART

cl

SH

G

GAMES

Dr

NEEDLEWORK

ACTIVITIES

GEOGRAPHY

ADMIN

0   10   20   30
metres

23

groups. Organisation of this sort assumed team teaching as the teachers and pupils would straddle normal subject boundaries and a flexibility responsive building was required to accommodate the varying sized groups.

By selecting the second option the school and governors made it necessary for the architects to vary many other items in the standard ILEA brief which was otherwise to be followed. These proved significant in the development of the design and affected the architectural response profoundly.[7] Whereas the normal brief required an assembly hall of 839 m², which could not accommodate the whole school, a lateral approach was concluded by assuming the use of Greenwich Town Hall for these formal occasions when the whole needed to be gathered simultaneously. An immediate benefit of this was the provision of a classical block box for drama fully equipped with multiple lighting and control systems, high level catwalks and all supporting storage and preparation areas. By combining this black box with the varied music areas much greater potential has been lent to the original idea.

In the standard brief four house rooms were included in which dining would take place in two sittings: the house rooms were also required for teaching and social purposes. The school preferred separate dining/teaching areas having cafeteria service with the possibility of service from heated trolleys to adjoining rooms if necessary. This allowed the dispersal of the house rooms, freed from dining constraints and available as teaching/social activity areas, around the school and not grouped around the main kitchen. It was also decided to provide five house rooms, four in the new building and one in the old, each accommodating 180 children with the sixth form common rooms providing a base for a further 150. Initially it was required that the house rooms should provide for vertical organisation but the provision of five makes it possible to switch to year based groupings if later this is seen to be desirable.

Each house room is closely associated with a group of subjects such as science, geography/history, mathematics/commerce, religious education/languages, and art/craft/technical subjects. The house rooms provide a large central social area each served by its own lavatories and cloakrooms and, in conjunction with the associated subject rooms, provide a distribution of large spaces throughout the school with adjoining rooms available for immediate expansion and extension.[8] Careful planning, the balance of saving on having a drama space rather than an assembly hall and reducing circulation to a minimum has provided a larger total

SCIENCE

MATHS
COMMERCE

GAMES

ACTIVITIES

social
teaching

HISTORY

LANGUAGE

sb subject
t tutor

0   10   20   30
metres

teaching area than the statutory requirement.

Future flexibility has been assumed and very few partitions are load-bearing with first floor slabs designed to allow re-positioning of partitions. Roof construction has connections built in for future fittings and the location of partitions. Services match this approach with radiators on outside walls only and electrical trunking is fully accessible adjacent to main structural beams whilst switching is limited to the permanent walls.

Assuming that use would be made of a public pool for swimming the school decided that instead of having the standard requirement of two gymnasia, the provision of one sports hall and a smaller gymnasium would meet the school needs more closely.

Architecturally, the result of all of these interlocking decisions is a low key, brick clad, two storeyed series of five interlinked teaching pavilions which, in conjunction with the original building, enclose two interconnected paved courts of quite different character with the detached sports building dividing the two outdoor play areas. This relaxed arrangement and consequent enclosures spring directly from the option originally taken to pursue a more flexible educational approach and the architects have reinforced this with their small scale, individual, non-hierarchial detailing of the buildings.

25 *The activities hall is an enclosed black box fully equipped with multiple lighting, control systems and high level catwalks. Here it is being used as a further teaching space.*

26 *A corner room in the language department. Glazed screens allow views into the central shared social/teaching area which has further teaching bays off it: the central area also acts as a house room. Precast roof beams have connections built in to allow re-positioning of partitions: all services are placed upon permanent walls.*

27 *The sports hall is fully enclosed with a space frame roof deck supported upon load-bearing brickwork walls. An adjoining gymnasium completes the physical activities suite.*

28 *Looking north towards block A with the sixth form room on the ground floor opening directly on to the paved courtyard. The original building, on the far left, was converted to provide an arts and crafts block with workshops which connect directly by bridge to the furthest new block containing the science laboratories.*

29 *Looking south to the main administration block which has the language department on the first floor. On the left is the sixth form common room with the bay window, having mathematics and commerce above. To the right is the activities block for music and drama: it is connected at first floor level to the language department by a tutorial area.*

The spare, square aesthetic of the plan form is carried through into the low key detailing of sills and parapets.

Chapter 6: References

1 Maclure J S, One Hundred Years of London Education, 1870–1970, Allen Lane, 1970, p 46: *new curriculum proposals adopted by the London School Board in 1888.*

2 Architectural Design, July 1965, pp 324–339.

3 Architectural Design, November 1967, pp 495–506.

4 Architects Journal, 4 May 1977, pp 810–812, Top Glass.

5 Architects Journal, 4 May 1977, p 810.

6 Building Design, 5 January 1979, p 14, Makeshift & Merge.

7 Building Design, 5 March 1976, p 17, Comprehensive Transformation.

8 Interior Design, April 1976, pp 156–157.

Key to drawings

A	assembly hall
AEI	adult education institute
AH	activities hall
C	classroom
CR	common room
D	dining
Dr	drama
DW	dining/work
E	entrance
G	gymnasium
H	houseroom
Hm	home bay
Ht	head or principal
I	infants
J	juniors
K	kitchen
L	library
Lt	lecture
M	music
Ns	nursery
P	practical area
PC	play centre
Q	quiet area
S	secretary
Sc	science
SC	staff common room
SH	sports hall
SK	schoolkeeper
Sw	swimming pool
W	waiting
YS	youth service
b	boiler
ca	covered area
ch	changing
cl	cloakroom
l	lavatories
s	servery
st	store

Chapter 7
The Secondary Reorganisation Programme

As a result of the DES circular of 1965, requiring an end to selection in secondary education, the ILEA progressed plans to reorganise all of inner London's secondary schools upon a comprehensive basis but these did not come to fruition until 1975 in order 'to resolve the contraditions of a mixed economy of selective and allegedly comprehensive schools existing side by side'.[1] At the same time the opportunity was taken to reorganise many existing secondary schools upon a more rational basis. The Department of Education and Science sponsored a Special Programme to Assist Reorganisation (SPAR) which was intended to meet both of these object-, ives and which operated over several years.

In the previous twenty years many inner London secondary schools had additional accommodation built either as a first phase of a long awaited replacement scheme, or the inclusion of previously non-existent science resources. After the Newsom Report, 1963, (Half Our Future), the emphasis was upon raising the school leaving age to sixteen and providing a wider range of subjects for the ordinary pupil and the direct consequence of this was that the majority of schools required more or varied accommodation which was generally completed by 1973. The typical small inner London school site is thus not sufficiently large to enable extra buildings to be added easily and for the amalgamation of further extensions larger sites had to be secured or radical adaptations effected. The nature of the available site extensions has played a large part in the architectural consequences of reorganisation: in this programme the arbitary financial timing of the work has sometimes had a significant effect upon the construction of the buildings but the most abiding element is that here the architect had to be involved at a very early stage, often before the formulation of a brief, in designing for the new educational process.

Langdon Park School

It could be said that this represents the archetypal inner London secondary school. The original three decker teaching block was built in 1907 upon a small site within a very tight pattern of narrow east London streets in an area appearing yearly to be ever more deprived: the schoolkeeper's house was the adjoining terrace house to the west. During the 1960's an expansion was required to cater adequately for school dinners and a single storey prefabricated timber framed block was provided. Replacement plans, phase 1, provided a new detached concrete frame science and crafts block across the road from the school site in 1957 and in 1963 the projected raising of the school leaving age required another, two storey block to be designed in the already small playground adjoining the original block. Further classrooms were contained in an annexe some distance away. There was no space for formal games on the site and pupils had to travel by coach for shortened games sessions.

In 1977 two projects were raised, with a third to follow, with the intention of focusing the main secondary school for boys for the area upon Langdon Park. Many houses in adjoining streets to the south were acquired in order to provide a sufficiently large self-contained site of 8.00 acres (3.20 hectares) and the Borough of Tower Hamlets obtained the site adjoining the school's north east boundary: this left only the public house of St Leonard's Road in recognisable continuity for the new square site. The Inner Cities Programme contained the first project which was the provision of a sports hall and SPAR would provide a new block for the sixth form and for remedial teaching. These projects required to be run as one contract and needed to be started by April 1978 and completed by April 1979 due to quite arbitrary government spending requirements. When announced in 1977 the architects were very short of time and information and they worked very closely with the school in developing the foreseeable school needs upon those sites which were becoming immediately available: limited construction time dictated the type of structure that would be used.

The major work is now completed. Both the sixth form block and the sports halls have standard steel portal frame structures with heavily insulated plastic-coated rolled steel sheet cladding running completely over roofs and walls down to a sloped plinth of precast concrete slabs around their bases. The building form is smooth and unbroken, except for windows in the classrooms and this is given further emphasis by the transition from roof to wall plane by means of curved sheets flowing across the junction: rainwater is allowed to run down the face of the buildings to be collected in continuous channels at the foot of the plinths. The games hall is a

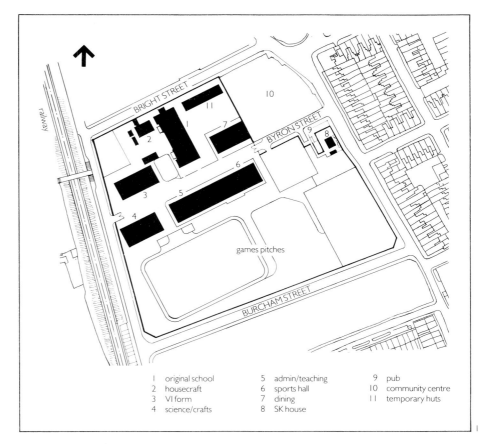

1	original school	5	admin/teaching	9	pub
2	housecraft	6	sports hall	10	community centre
3	VI form	7	dining	11	temporary huts
4	science/crafts	8	SK house		

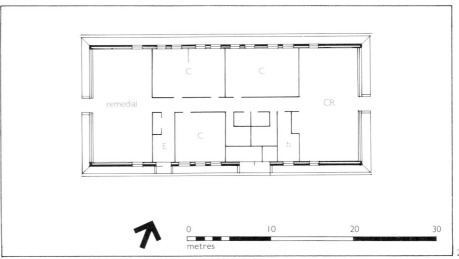

1 Site Plan
This site almost represents the history of London school provision in its own right. The main teaching block (originally upon a very small site) dates from 1907 with a concrete framed science and crafts block built across the road from it in 1957. During the 1960's the expansion of school meals required a prefabricated timber framed building whilst the projected raising of the school leaving age in 1963 required a further two storey block in the already small playground.

The 1977 decision to focus the secondary education for boys upon the site led to the closure of the tight network of surrounding streets providing an 8.00 acre site. New teaching blocks for sixth form and arts are complemented by a games hall, the extension of dining accommodation and a new house for the schoolkeeper. Huts are required as a temporary expedient to

provide accommodation over the secondary age 'bulge'. With the development of large hard play areas to the South only the public house survives from the original street layout.

The London Borough of Tower Hamlets has now built a new community centre upon the adjoining site to maximise the school's expanded resources.

2, 3 New Teaching Blocks
The form and construction was very much dictated by space available for construction during the long process of closing roads and the need to meet very tight spending programmes.

As a consequence standard steel portal frames were used with plastic coated rolled steel sheet cladding. Only windows and doors interrupt the smooth covering and the games hall is a windowless volume. Many items, e.g. staircases, are standard, off the shelf, material.

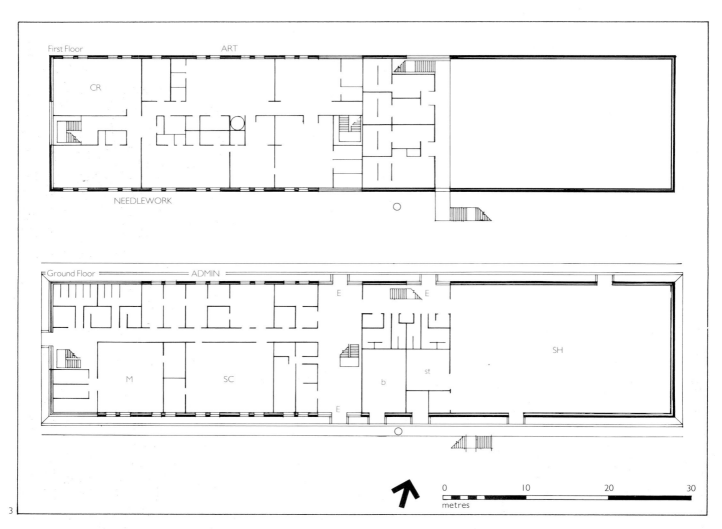

First Floor   ART

CR

NEEDLEWORK

Ground Floor ══════ ADMIN ══════

E   E

M   SC

b   st

SH

E

0   10   20   30
metres

3

windowless volume with two storeys of changing rooms at the west end. The structure is celebrated internally with bold colours and all services are allowed to demonstrate their presence: staircases are treated as an extension of the 'off the shelf'' but refined industrial mode whilst partitions are solid blockwork.

Whilst the first phase was under construction the second phase was being prepared: the dining block was extended in the same timber system as the original, the schoolkeeper's house was replaced with a new building, the original three decker school had extensive modifications carried out, adaptations were made to the science/crafts block and a large two storey teaching block has been added to the new sports hall following the same construction and classing. The enlarged site is now being laid out with all-weather pitches and landscaping: existing plane trees preserved along the former Byron Street will be added to and the new campus will represent the concentration of educational and architectural effort. Above all else it will be the local community school as the Borough completes its town community centre on the adjoining site.

4

5

4 The new sixth form block with the original School Board building in the background. With a structure of standard steel portal frames the new block has plastic-coated rolled steel sheet flowing over the building form to a plinth of precast concrete slabs. A continuous grating covers the drain taking away rainwater both from the building and the path.

5 The high technology construction mode is carried through to the interior of the sixth form block with all structure and services clearly displayed and picked out in bright primary colours. Teaching rooms have smooth plaster ceilings following the general curve of the steel cladding.

6 The interior of the games hall with a solid block internal lining up to 2.7 metres to provide rebound for ball games. The gallery in the background gives access to the changing rooms.

7 Entrance detail to the sixth form block.

Access is indicated by the runway lights set into the paving with vivid green guard rails over them: the doors and lights are scarlet.

8 The use of standard industrial elements is exemplified by the boiler flue and the escape staircase from the changing rooms. The windowless volume of the games hall is relieved externally only by doors, extract fans mounted on the ridge of the roof and air inlets to the heating convectors as shown here above the first handrail standard.

9 With the closure of the former Byron Street the school now has a campus for intercommunication between buildings. A new arts block completes the new sports hall wing.

10 A range of school building types is shown here with the original building to the right, a concrete framed structure in the centre background built to allow the raising of the school leaving age and to the left the new sixth form block.

7

6

8

9

10

141

Geoffrey Chaucer School

One of the more celebrated architectural projects of 1958 was the construction of this complete new secondary school (originally called Two Saints later known as Trinity House) for girls in Southwark by Chamberlin, Powell and Bon. The site was sufficiently large, access was good and the architects celebrated the implications of liberal education with a renowned design employing powerful architectural forms. It reflected the educational spirit of the time by having the academic block distantly separated from the practical block by administration and kitchen blocks flanking a central library overlooking a placid courtyard and a range of three gymnasia. It enjoyed new structural freedoms with hyperbolic paraboloid concrete shell roofs[2] over the raised pentagonal assembly hall and the steel braced catenary roofs over the gymnasia.

When, in 1976, it was decided that, due to falling school numbers locally,

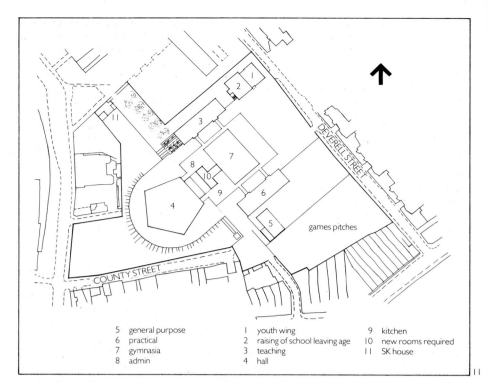

5	general purpose	1	youth wing	9	kitchen
6	practical	2	raising of school leaving age	10	new rooms required
7	gymnasia	3	teaching	11	SK house
8	admin	4	hall		

11

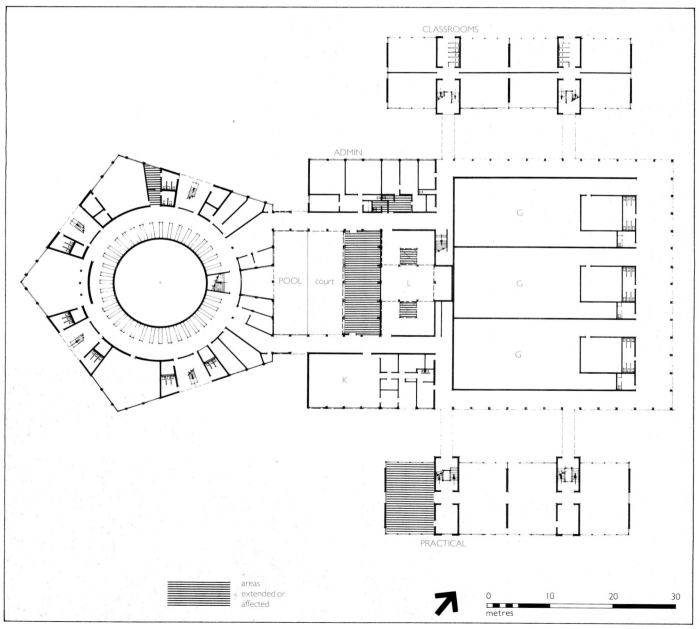

CLASSROOMS

ADMIN

POOL court

L

G

G

G

K

PRACTICAL

areas
extended or
affected

0   10   20   30
metres

12

amalgamation with Paragon School for boys was necessary a fundamental problem became apparent. In the years since 1958 a youth wing and extra teaching accommodation to raise the school leaving age had been built on the site but as a separate entity, not in conjunction with the original design. More accommodation however, meant that the existing building would be directly affected. In addition to the need to convert lavatory accommodation to cater for girls and boys a new block was required next to the practical block to provide for teaching technology and science metalwork and a covered external area for larger project work. More areas for teaching, and media

resource were necessary and these were located above extra staff rooms placed in the courtyard. Due to the existing structure, including steel tie rods from the gymnasia roof, the architect had to pursue a predetermined discipline: due to the strong architectural expression of the existing building many decisions were already made – the structural bay was copied, the window pattern extended and the new brickwork and fascias match the original. In this way, and by careful modelling of the extension and connection between old and new, the school is now transformed with little apparent alteration but by great effort and very careful stitching.

11 Site Plan
The site plan shows the typical 1950's approach to secondary schools with the functional separation of academic and practical areas by the administration and kitchen blocks. The latter also separated the three gymnasia from the pentagonal block which contained specialist rooms and a large radial cloakroom under the assembly hall which has a hyperbolic paraboloid roof. The hall block was separated from the administration centre by a fountain court.

12 Ground Floor Plan
Buildings added since the original – a youth wing, accommodation for raising the school leaving age (ROSLA) and a general purpose block – limited the remaining choices for siting the new accommodation in 1978. Its functions required a central location and so it was built into the fountain court with a new staff room at ground floor level: at first floor level are new teaching rooms, a media resources room and music practice rooms, all connected by existing galleries in the gymnasia block to the academic and practical blocks.

13 *The original pentagonal hall with its dramatic hyperbolic paraboloid roof set a tremendous architectural problem when further accommodation was required upon an already crowded site in 1976.*

14 *The new block set into the original fountain court complements, without matching precisely, the existing building elevations.*

15 *The new T-shaped block sits above the original roof level between (left) the hyperbolic paraboloid roof of the pentagon block and (right) the roof of the gymnasia. At this level the new block had to incorporate the steel bracing rods of the gymnasia roof.*

16 *View from the North sharing the curved gymnasia roof with the new block in front at lower roof level.*

17 *Another view of the fountain court at ground floor level.*

13

14

15

16

17

John Roan School

Upon reorganisation of a secondary school it is usually necessary to increase its size on a single site to vouchsafe specialist staff levels and resources. When an existing selective school, such as Roan Grammar School for Boys (there was a distant sister school for girls), is reorganised it may be found that the original building for three form entry will adequately fit the needs for an upper school – the fourth, fifth and sixth forms – with specialist accommodation well established and could be left virtually undisturbed.

Therefore for the Roan reorganisation a complete new lower school for a six form entry mixed school was required on a nearby site: the local Charlton School completes the amalgamation of the two Roans. Before the brief was finalised many comparisons were made with existing ILEA schools and those as far away as Berkshire and Leicestershire and by this means the education inspectorate and the architect were able to perceive a required balance of flexibility and enclosure. The standard, stereotyped schedule of accommodation was scrapped and in 1976 the brief began to develop. Upon the assumption that the building would be used well into the twenty-first century the intention was not to predetermine teaching methods but to pursue forward looking rather than restrictively conservative attitudes in the design.[3] Flexibility in design to assist flexibility of curriculum approach was essential to avoid imposing a straitjacket upon the freedom of the headteacher and staff: this implied the possibility of varied approaches, both inter-disciplinary and single subject, at all levels with or without co-operative teaching. Activities such as art, pottery, woodwork, metalwork, home economics and needlecraft were seen in juxtaposition to allow integrated work without imposing it. Social areas – soft carpeted spaces – were to provide for relaxation between work periods whilst being integrated into the teaching area. Although the lower school is self-contained it still contains 540 pupils who require a smaller social organisation and so year grouping was requested, each year having its own centre being complete with year tutor's room, cloakroom and lavatory facilities. The centres were to be grouped around a central library/resource area. It was specifically requested that dining accommodation should be used for that purpose only and not a joint dining/teaching area: as a consequence a relatively small area was designated and up to six sittings organised by means of cafeteria service.

The completed school is radically different from any other ILEA secondary school and the briefing was only one factor in producing this. Local conservation pressures were intense. The site contains many fine trees and is on the periphery of natural heathland. Before

any design work was started the GLC Parks Department made a careful survey of tree condition and before the contract started dead trees were removed and surgery undertaken where necessary. All retained trees were carefully protected. Because the whole of the site was not immediately available the location and development of the building was to some extent determined. Whilst the brief called for a single storey building two storeys became necessary in one limited area and this relates well to handsome adjoining properties. Large Victorian villas, due for demolition to provide the education site, were retained in residential use.

Siting and educational requirements influenced the form of the school and finally the scale integrates well with its surroundings whilst not compromising its present and long term functions.[4] The deep plan provides flexibility in use

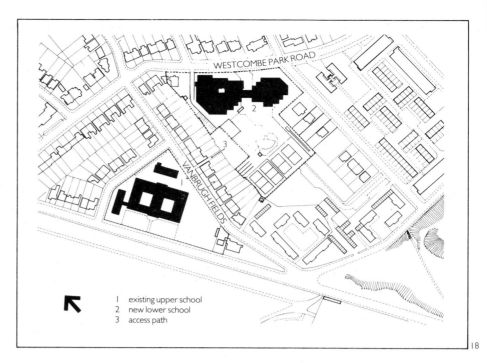

1	existing upper school
2	new lower school
3	access path

18

19

18 Location Plan, 1977
The proximity of the new site for the lower school allowed the existing upper school to remain virtually undisturbed whilst allowing ready access and interchange.
19 Site Plan, 1977
The site contains many fine mature trees and the large adjoining Victorian villas provided scale and materials of quality which required to be matched.
20 Ground Floor Plan, 1977
The deep plan allows the proximity of related subjects – art to crafts, crafts to science, etc – rather than the separated departmental approach.
The adult education institute is fully integrated into the building with outpost accommodation in most subject areas.
21 First Floor Plan, 1977
A second storey became necessary in one limited area but this assists the local scale of the school building compared with neighbouring villas.

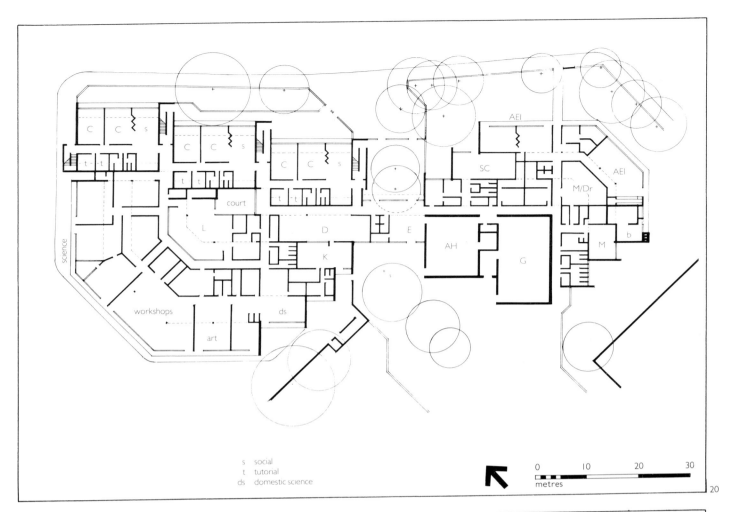

science

C C s
C C s
t t
court
L
D E
K AH
workshops
ds
art

C C s
t t
t t

AEI
SC
M/Dr
AEI
M
G
b

s   social
t   tutorial
ds domestic science

0   10   20   30
metres

20

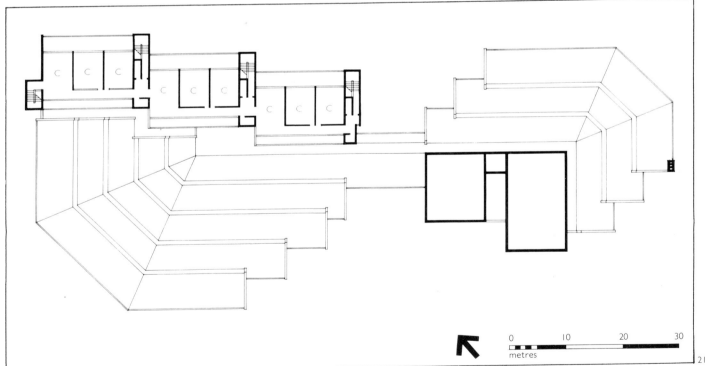

C C C
C C C
C C C

0   10   20   30
metres

21

22 Section 1977
Laminated timber beams carry the wooden monopitch trusses over the deep plan areas: the beams span on to steel columns and allow continuous clerestorey lighting throughout the ground floor.

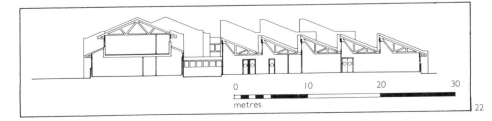

0   10   20   30
metres

22

with science and art and craft adjoining each other with the promise of blurred boundaries if required. Previous open plan arrangements being found wanting in some respects the year centres provide enclosed classrooms for language, mathematics and the humanities.[5] Dining accommodation links with the main entrance foyer to serve adult education activities in the smaller block allowing the activities hall (multipurpose and equipped for dramatic productions with a projection room) to have refreshments adjacent for public performances. Music rooms are isolated from teaching areas to prevent disturbance and the adult education institute is self-contained whilst having the school's resources available.

Deep plan areas are roofed by wooden monopitch trusses spanning on to laminated timber beams supported by square steel columns. Clerestorey windows, most of which face north east, are incorporated between the beams to provide natural lighting and permitting cross ventilation. The two storey classroom area has an in situ coffered concrete slab supported by concrete columns whilst the gymnasium and hall are in load bearing brickwork. Brickwork is medium red to reflect the weathered reds of adjoining properties and whole design is unified by blue grey pantiles which sweep down over windows with wide overhangs providing solar shading.

The brief called for a building of human scale: reorganisation of the Roan and Charlton Schools has provided a building handsome in its completeness whilst developing a lovely site to the full in meeting this fundamental requirement. It is a civilised success socially, educationally and architecturally.[6]

23

24

23 The roof form demonstrates the sectional development with a deep plan relying mainly upon clerestorey windows for good natural lighting: see Fig 27. In a residential area of some architectural quality the scale is significant and successful.

24 This block containing the Adult Education Institute turns a broad, sweeping corner matching the road's easy bend.

25 Interlocking paving blocks and elegant steel fencing provide an inviting main entrance of some quality.

26 The sectional detail demonstrates the solar shading effect of the powerfully expressed overhanging eaves.

27 The dining area is situated in the centre of the plan with no ordinary windows but the clerestorey provides successful day lighting.

146

25

26

27

Chapter 7: References

1 Maclure J S, One Hundred Years of London Education, 1870–1970, Allen Lane, 1970, p 180.

2 Architecture and Building, April 1958, pp 146–148, Progress with Hyperbolic Paraboloid Roof.

3 Architectural Review, January 1978, p 56, Preview 1978.

4 Building, 30 November 1979, pp 39–42, Extra Curricula: Open Plan Design for Roan Charlton Comprehensive School.

5 Architects Journal, 27 January 1982, pp 31–48 recognises many of the advances made by the John Roan School but does not always understand some specific, basic requirements of the client's brief.

6 Building, 27 November 1981, p 30–31, Forms to Fit.

Key to drawings

A	assembly hall
AEI	adult education institute
AH	activities hall
C	classroom
CR	common room
D	dining
Dr	drama
DW	dining/work
E	entrance
G	gymnasium
H	houseroom
Hm	home bay
Ht	head or principal
I	infants
J	juniors
K	kitchen
L	library
Lt	lecture
M	music
Ns	nursery
P	practical area
PC	play centre
Q	quiet area
S	secretary
Sc	science
SC	staff common room
SH	sports hall
SK	schoolkeeper
Sw	swimming pool
W	waiting
YS	youth service
b	boiler
ca	covered area
ch	changing
cl	cloakroom
l	lavatories
s	servery
st	store

Chapter 8
The Nursery Class & Primary School Programme

The nursery class is an essential bridge between the shelter of the family within the home and the outside world with its growing opportunities for independence. Nursery education provides an environment which facilitates learning, promotes physical and mental health through sensory experiences, the fostering of curiosity and imagination, and opportunities for social interaction in aesthetically pleasing surroundings: 'an appreciation of beauty and an understanding of the group relationship'.[1]

Before 1944 education authorities had the power but not the duty to provide for nursery education and schools were provided in areas of social priority. The Hadow Report, Infant and Nursery Schools, 1933, stressed the value of making special provisions for the under fives, especially in overcrowded areas: between 1939 and 1945 there was a considerable expansion in this provision enabling the mothers of young children to work. Under the 1944 Education Act it became the duty of education authorities to provide nursery education but shortages of resources prevented implementation and the post war increased birth rate led to such pressure upon accommodation in existing primary schools that nursery classes virtually disappeared.

It was not until the Plowden Report, Children and Their Primary Schools, 1967, that the matter received strong recommendation and consequently, for the first time, a number of proposals for nursery places, specifically for educational priority areas, were approved in that year's building programme. Urban Aid programmes were introduced in 1968 designed to assist areas of social stress in inner city areas. Since 1968 the ILEA has consciously included either a nursery class or space for a future nursery class on every new primary school site: for the nursery class is part of the main school system and close proximity eases the transition for children at the age of five. See Appendix A for EPA provision and B for spending consequences of the Plowden Report.

National policy changed radically in 1972 with the publication of the White Paper 'Education: a Framework for Expansion' which envisaged the expansion of nursery education up to 1982 by which time the Plowden Report recommendations would be met: 90% of four year olds and 50% of three year olds would be catered for. The economic climate of the late 1970's has prevented this fulfilment and the nursery programme has been severely curtailed.

To meet the aims of nursery education the architect must meet a simple brief with an apparently simple building: it must be domestic and carpeted whilst allowing the exploration by small children of paint, water, sand and other potentially destructive materials. Mess must be accommodated but there must be the opportunity to become clean. Parents are to be welcomed to the premises with a sheltered external area

to encourage contact which must lead to an involvement or commitment within the building: this veranda leads from the playroom out to a hard paved area where large toys can be used and enjoyed the whole year round. Lavatories must provide personal modesty whilst permitting ready assistance. Playrooms have to allow for a multiplicity of activities, some quiet, some noisy, with odd corners affording bases for privacy: a small, enclosed, carpeted area is required to act as a snug or den for story telling.

Before the ILEA nursery construction programme really got under way architects and researchers had evolved a type of provision with scale models and the close interest of the nursery inspectorate so that when it first came into operation the job architects had a ready brief immediately available. Initially an almost standard form of class was able to be constructed upon available primary school sites using a steel framed building system: some traditionally constructed nurseries were completed too but as the available sites dwindled and the school population declined internal adaptation of a whole range of school buildings dating from 1870 to 1970 followed. And when it was impossible to find space in an existing school building adjoining buildings such as disused laundries or workshops were readily converted to a new life. The nursery class building programme in inner London has shown that identical briefs developed on dissimilar sites within the same time span have produced a wide range of provision evolved to suit differing conditions by maximising opportunity.

Until 1973 the inner London area had a steady programme for constructing new primary schools: they were required either to replace a thoroughly obsolete building or to make new provision in areas where, often due to wholesale housing redevelopment, insufficient places existed. This programme consisted of ten or twelve new schools each year and in 1967 the Plowden Report gave fresh impetus with its recommendations concerning special treatment of educational priority areas: this gave greater need to develop new types of primary schools able to support the changing needs of educators. Whilst Thring, the Victorian headmaster of Uppingham School, could say that the almighty wall 'was the supreme and final arbiter of schools' a contemporary teacher might say that 'the building made the teaching method'.[2] Of course, some say that the school layout – cellular or open plan – has a direct correlation with the measurable results of children at the school and the attitudes developed by the teachers[3,4,5] What is generally agreed, however, is that the examination of human needs and constant reassessment of requirements inherent in the brief 'inspired the main success of post war British architecture, the new primary schools, whose design assisted the free development of

the child'.[6] See Appendix C for decline in area per place as building costs rose in the early 1970's.

The brief for primary schools was developed upon the knowledge of child growth and learning processes. From the early development of muscular activity and control come the growth of finer, manipulative skills and, parallel to these, intellectual skills grow and mature. Confidence is established and experience is broadened and enriched: the growth of the imagination is widened and the world of feeling is explored. The variety of children's needs and the resultant range of activities require a similar variety in the size of groupings in which children and teachers work.

Initially the change from the domestic scale has to be allowed for and many children play alone at first but with maturity they begin to explore social relationships and group play increases. The range of groupings is from one, the individual reading, to a construction group of four, through ten working together upon a project, a whole class listening to a story, finishing with the whole school at morning assembly.

Many teachers hold differing views as to the value of different age ranges working together and their mutual benefits. The flexibility of allowing team teaching to be exercised has been extended by different opinions concerning the transfer age from infant to junior. There are more adults available in primary schools now for, in addition to the teaching staff, parents may be assisting and there may be more ancillary staff if the school so chooses.

To meet this complex of needs, skills, grouping and availabilities and to provide, above all, flexibility, primary schools must be educationally useful immediately and throughout their economic life (which might be considered as sixty years – but could be one hundred) acceptable to a wide range of attitudes and experiences: whilst Thring commented upon the determinism of buildings, another Victorian, Pugin, took quite another view.[7] The development of the primary school plan derives directly from new teaching approaches which have evolved over a considerable time from 'activity' and 'interest based methods' through project and discovery methods and the open availability of libraries all leading to the integrated day with 'less talking by the teacher and more participation by the child'.[8] The Montessori teaching method was published in 1912 and was responsible for the gradual erosion of the idea of the discrete class as a teaching unit. By 1920 comparisons were being made between the bondage of the old methods and the calm, happy, absorbed atmosphere of a Montessori class which enabled children to work independently in the same room at the same time. American experience in the later 1920's imported 'child centred' learning and demonstrated the integration of old and new teaching methods and the progressive educationalists began to view the teacher as a guide, a director, with children learning through experience rather than the false incentives of rewards and punishments. By 1939 the progressives were in the majority – certainly the staff in the training colleges – and classroom teaching was heavily criticised: teaching methods developed further and classroom activities were extended. Before 1940 the primary school plan was similar to that used for elementary schools (see Athelney, Chapter 1) and after 1945 there was over-provision of space in school plans. Rationalisation of building design after the introduction of cost limits in 1949 resulted in the reduction of overall area whilst maintaining the actual teaching space (see Chapter 2 (7)). The over-articulated plan of the late 1940's became economically unacceptable with tight compactness finally resulting from the use of system building – the apotheosis of rationalisation (see Chapter 3, Ashmead). When the new educational ideas and new architectural trends came together the open plan primary school began to develop.

It was assumed that as teaching practice would continue to exhibit considerable variation and as educational ideas would continuously develop the building must offer future adaptability without sacrificing spatial and environmental standards. New teaching techniques required greater flexibility and, initially, this could be provided ideally in the primary school as a natural response to teaching organisation for it provided maximum opportunity. Building use and need will change again with the current installation of computers into the ILEA's primary schools.

Since 1967 it has been accepted that each class group (not exceeding thirty five) will have an exclusive home base

with its own identity. A general work space will be shared with the rest of the cooperative teaching group. There must be for this larger group a fully enclosed, acoustically separated space for quiet work. Each teaching centre will offer access to wet-work areas to all of its users. This total arrangement is called the teaching centre and is considered suitable for seventy children under eight years old but eleven year old pupils may be found in groups of 105. Juniors have their own library/resource centre and the assembly hall is shared with the infants. Some primary school layouts – Hungerford, John Evelyn, Prior Weston, Holmleigh, Torriano, Ashmead and Paxton – are shown and discussed in Chapter 3 with John Ball and Brooklands in Chapter 2: these schools demonstrate a development of the plan which is further progressed by those shown in this Chapter. The possible provision of the open plan in Victorian school buildings is illustrated in Chapter 4 with Compton, Montem and Sebright. In 1973 the generic brief encapsulating this information about the functions of primary schools was developed and circulated with the specific brief for each primary school – new or remodelled – and has formed the development basis for an evolutionary layout.

Inner London developed the use of home bays – firm in the 'belief that young children not only needed a physical "base" in the school but also "their own" teacher to give them a greater sense of security'[9] – along with quiet areas and shared, robust practical areas. The educationally acceptable minimum limits of teaching area had been reached by 1970 and the economic limits of cost control by 1973 whilst the concept of open-planning had probably reached its maximum acceptable level at

the same time. 'Flexibility is now seen as the facility founded on an initial variety of usable spaces rather than the monotony of prairie areas'[10] describes perfectly the ILEA approach of 'initial variety'.

Apart from its fundamental function the primary school may include a nursery class, a play centre, a youth centre or an adult educational institute. Circulation space is minimal but this presupposes the use of teaching space for movement. Sites, and their shapes, often are the final arbiters in the building layout but even with the use of a fairly standard specific brief the primary schools demonstrate ingenuity and resource in providing a fitting environment for the education of the young: Pestalozzi's idea that 'the classroom should resemble a living room' has been fulfilled by the creation of teaching areas of warmth, comfort and the right scale, promoting well-being. Pin-up areas promote display and this is 'a continuous celebration – of facts acquired and skills applied'.[11] The primary schools shown here indicate that the statement, made in 1959, that 'British schools are the most un-predictable in the world'[12] is still valid and demonstrates that ingenuity and vitality necessary in building evolution to match educational expectation.

1 Basic Nursery Provision
A scale model evolved from discussions with teachers and education inspectors which categorised the various areas and uses of a nursery class. This general arrangement was followed in using a standard steel construction system to provide the first classes upon suitable, flat sites. A pitched or a flat roof was available in the system.

2 Hillmead Nursery Class
This hexagonal plan was used successfully and the photograph illustrates the variety of spaces and materials used in meeting a rapid building programme. The space under the carpeted platform is for storing folding beds.

3 Haselrigge Nursery Class
The original building was a cookery classroom, 1891, and provided the right balance for nursery use with the addition of some new windows and a covered play area.

4 Haselrigge Nursery Class
Detail of the new bow window: it was designed with a deep internal sill low enough to allow children to use it as a window seat.

5 Woodhill Nursery Class, Layout Plan
Although initial investigation into nursery class needs evolved a standard of provision (Fig 1) this was not suitable for all available sites and the Woodhill plan shows variations from the norm to meet local conditions.

Designed in 1978 upon an existing concrete slab at ground level the site is closely circumscribed by an adjacent high brick wall on the North side and falls steeply from the South. The playroom has interesting nooks and crannies for young children and the carpeted quiet area can be shut off very simply for story telling. Food trolleys are brought in to the wash up/servery from the adjacent primary school.

Built from load-bearing brickwork the nursery has a generous covered area serving as sheltered entrance and play space. The entrance is defined and changing levels are retained by brick walled planting areas.

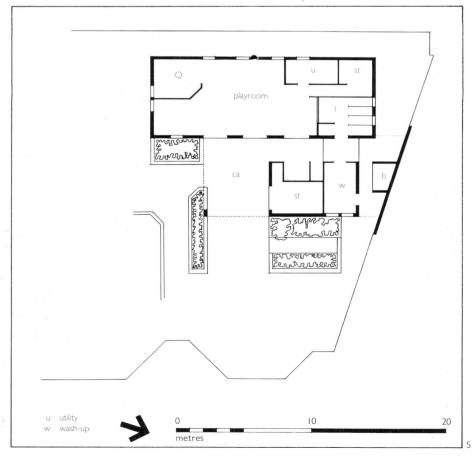

Q
u
st
playroom
l
ca
b
st
w

u utility
w wash-up

0   10   20
metres

Maxilla Nursery Centre

When the elevated section of Westway Motorway was constructed large areas of ground beneath it became unusable and the immediate neighbourhood was physically divided. At one point there is an area of social deprivation which had a great need for nursery care: this was made available under the auspices of the Westway Nursery Association when the ILEA provided a nursery school for sixty children and the Royal Borough of Kensington and Chelsea (with the Home Office through Urban Aid) a day care toddlers' room with thirty places and a baby room for eight. Additionally a parents' centre was provided by charitable trusts, largely the Vanessa Lowndes Trust, giving facilities for a clinic, adult education and advisory services. A recently erected public laundry was already on the site and the centre serves a defined catchment area from 8.00 am to 6.00 pm practically every day of the year. A specially built community hall attached to a new office block completes the development and the intention of the centre, opened in 1978, is to establish a strong link with the community and to serve its needs fulfilling 'an important social function in the area'.[13]

For administrative reasons the two nurseries have to be separate but the parents' facilities provide a central focus: these facilities are suitable for a multiplicity of uses and, designed as main circulation also, it is functionally and visually the core of the building. The nurseries share a large hard paved play area and a large garden and together 'clearly provide a happy and secure environment for children'.[14]

The plan shape was evolved by the requirements of parties other than the client bodies: road engineers required that the structure should not touch the underside of the motorway and that maintenance access be afforded to the columns whilst stringent fire precaution was called for to protect the motorway above. The nurseries are timber framed with some load bearing blockwork whilst the two storey parents' centre is steel framed. No special noise insulation was found necessary and so finishes are simple with the external lightweight cladding with masonry paint. When the design started in 1974 it was clear that any design could not compete with the dominant form of the motorway and the intention was to present a building with its own individuality and integrity scaled for its main users and welcoming to all.

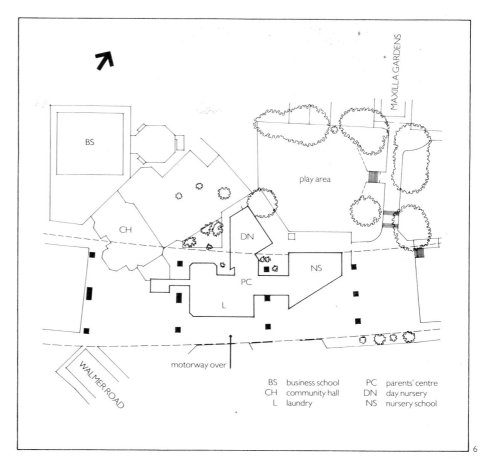

6 Site Plan
Being built under the Westway Motorway the Centre had to avoid contact with any part of the structure for engineering, maintenance and fire precaution reasons. Its juxtaposition to the community hall – a planning gain from the erection of the business school – and existing laundry makes it a community focus and this is strengthened by the inclusion of a parents' centre donated by charitable trusts.

The day nursery is provided by the Royal Borough of Kensington and Chelsea and the nursery school by the ILEA but with the parents' centre and kitchen wing serving the community centre all were included in one design and one building contract of some complexity.

BS	business school	PC	parents' centre
CH	community hall	DN	day nursery
L	laundry	NS	nursery school

7 *A site was available under the motorway – as long as the road structure was still accessible for maintenance and no fire hazard was introduced.*

8

9

10

8 View of the Day Nursery, 1978
9 *The parents' centre is open all day and provides many resources otherwise unavailable in the vicinity: being directly under Westway there is little natural light.*
10 *Construction is very simple being mainly timber framed with lightweight cladding. In the foreground is the nursery school (ILEA) linked by the glazed two storey parents' centre to the day nursery (Royal Borough of Kensington and Chelsea).*

Michael Faraday Primary School

In 1974 when this school was designed to replace an old obsolete building the earlier, tentative explorations into relationships between home bays, practical areas and quiet rooms had begun to crystallise.

This is a large school with two hundred and ten infants and two hundred and eighty juniors plus a playcentre. Despite its size the planning is compact with the infant and junior elements expressed as distinct wings: the infant grouping is based upon pairs of enclosed home bays flanking a quiet room with access to a large practical area sub-divided by low partitions. The junior layout is similar with enclosed areas clustered round a shared, divided practical space with fewer quiet bays and a full library. The central practical areas are lighted and ventilated by continuous high level clerestorey windows as are the dining/work spaces. Home bays and quiet rooms have small windows on the periphery with clerestorey lighting at high level on the opposite side to provide cross ventilation. Due to its size the school has two halls which have been treated as having different functions, one for dancing, music and drama and the other for physical education.

Construction is of load bearing brickwork with light steel trusses supporting monopitch roofs over main areas allowing the clerestorey windows long uninterrupted runs. There is no formal entrance but visitors' access is assumed to be made to the administrative area via the parents' room or the dining/work areas. Normally one would expect to find lavatories dispersed around the building but for economic reasons it was necessary to provide almost all such accommodation in large centralised blocks which are directly accessible to teaching and play areas.

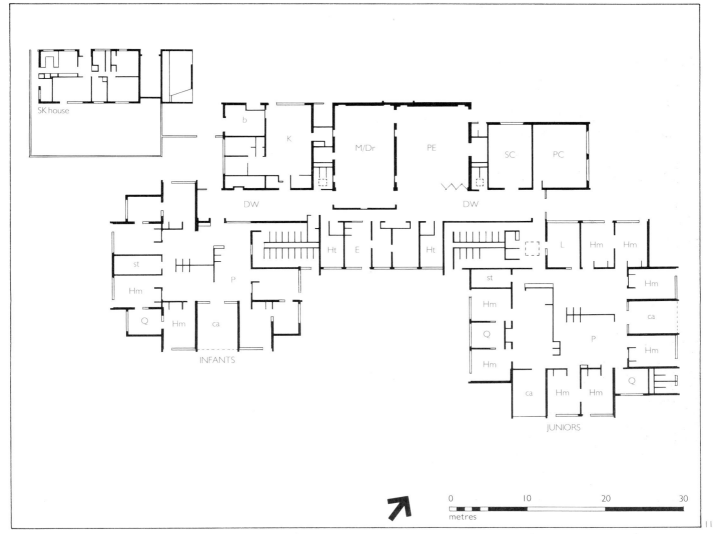

11 Layout
This large school was designed in 1974 for 210 infants and 280 juniors plus a playcentre. Compact planning defines the infant area with home bays and shared quiet areas grouped around a large shared practical area with low central partitions to break up the space into usable areas providing services. Junior areas are similar with fewer quiet spaces but with a library. All dining spaces are assumed to be used for work also. The practical areas have large roof monitors for daylighting.
12 *Two interconnecting junior home bays which give, with the other home bays and quiet areas, a variety of enclosable spaces.*

13

14

13 The large, central practical activities area in the junior wing is divided by low partitions into three spaces, each relating to a junior year with its quiet and home bays.

14 The top junior year's quiet bay is equipped more like a working library space.

15 The junior practical activities area has a high level of daylighting, even though placed centrally, due to the continuous clerestorey on all sides. The infant practical area is similar but smaller. Along the far wall is the main convector unit with the curtained entrance to a home bay adjacent: the double doors lead out to a covered area.

15

Elm Lane Primary School

Designed in 1976 upon a flat 1.40 acre site (0.42 hectares) adjoining a playing field 245 infant and junior places were required with a 30 place nursery class. Due to the proximity of the playing field and the lack of other local youth organisations it was decided to include a play centre and a youth centre in the project with an enlarged, floodlit playpitch.

The consequent proposal shows two infant teaching centres (140 children) and a self-contained junior centre (105)

both representing deep plans independently. The nursery is separate also. A separate dining hall serves as the main entrance to the school as well as the games area for the playcentre in close conjunction with the main hall. Due to site constraints the youth centre is at first floor level but the very density gives the design its formal architecture for the plan form is a split square with a wide covered area separating the teaching centres from the remainder of the school. The glazed top would provide year-round amenity for teaching and other activities: the area virtually eliminates circulation space for it was conceived as part of the hard paving requirement for the school. More

interest has developed recently in the use of glass roofs to enclose the school environment as Elm Lane heralded.[15]

Construction was to be in load-bearing red brick with domestic wooden trusses supporting black roof slates: elevational details show small windows with some rooflighting and sheer gables and eaves. The central hall has circular windows at high level and with its dense formalism the design appears to be an early runner in the new eclecticism.[16] Unfortunately, revised demographic projections could not support the need for a further primary school in this area and the contract was not proceeded with.

16 Site Plan
The site is not large but it is adjacent to an ILEA playing field to the South.
17 Ground Floor Plan
The infant and junior teaching centres are very similar in arrangement with a growing degree of enclosure to quiet and home bays: dry and wet practical areas are also firmly identified with the latter giving direct access to a common, glass roofed, internal work space. This isolated the teaching centres from other school activities giving the opportunity for noisy and quiet lessons to proceed simultaneously. With the inclusion of a play centre and a youth centre the hall would be used regularly in the evenings and week-ends requiring more separation for the teaching areas.

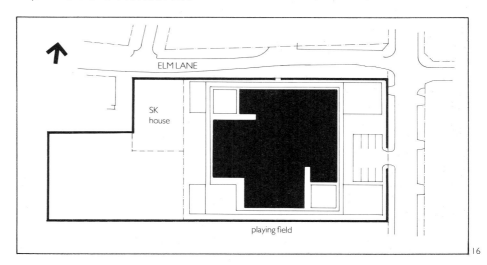

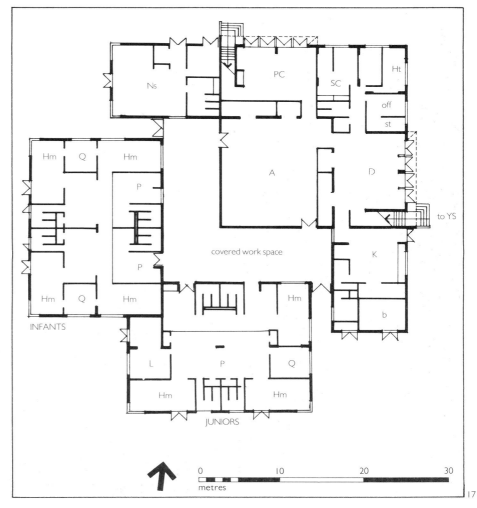

157

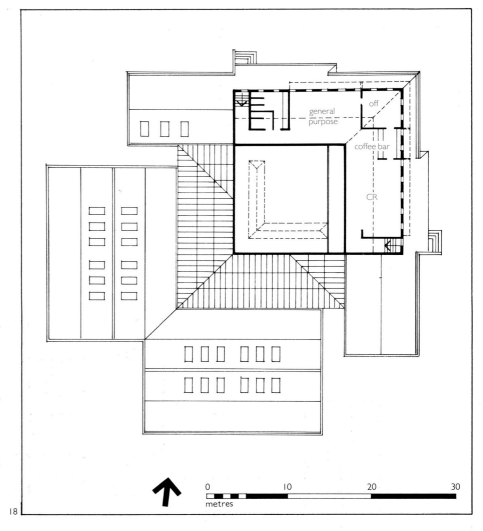

18 First Floor Plan
The main accommodation for the youth centre was on this floor with the shared use of areas on the Ground Floor.
19 East Elevation
The small site and large amount of accommodation produced a dense, formalist design which is expressed as early eclecticism in the elevational treatment.

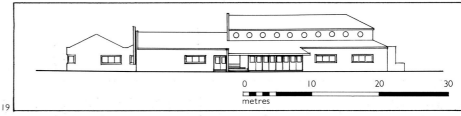

Linton Mead Primary School

The first element, the infant school and double nursery class, was completed in 1978 and is part of a school for four hundred and ninety children with a youth centre: the junior school and youth centre will follow as population growth in Thamesmead demands.

There are four teaching centres each for seventy infants each centre having a clearly defined area with two largely enclosed home bases giving access to a fully enclosed quiet room. The practical area is of a good proportion with the wet work area opening out on to a covered external space. What is significant is that the arrangement of the four centres allows a recognisable corridor separating them to reduce distraction to their occupants by people

circulating in the school. A similar layout is proposed for the junior school but with the quiet areas raised above other work areas.

Dark load bearing walls and a handsome exposed structural timber roof deck make this a building of some quality with good lighting levels maintained in the deep plan by north facing roof monitors supplementing the minimal windows.

20 Layout Plan
Four identical infant centres have given rise to a formal, symmetrical plan: the centres each have large practical areas which, however, are not contiguous as at Michael Faraday (see Fig 11) but are significantly separated by a recognisable corridor arrangement. The deep plan has small peripheral windows but is well lit by north-facing rooflights.
21 *A practical area with curtained access to home bays on the left and, on the right,*

the deep wings forming an opening to the central access spine. Unlike Michael Faraday Primary School (see Figs 13 and 15) the clerestorey faces North only. The roof deck is structural timber spanning three metres between standard timber trusses.
22 *Described on the overall plan as 'dining project' this space serves a variety of functions in the completed first stage including assembly hall and gymnasium.*
23 *Construction is straightforward with dark load-bearing brickwork externally and standard timber trusses supporting a slate-like roof. View is from the South West.*
24 *View from the South East with the kitchen and service area to the left and the dining-project area rising over it. In the middle a typical teaching centre indicates the central quiet bay with long windows flanked by two home bays: the covered work area links across to another teaching centre.*

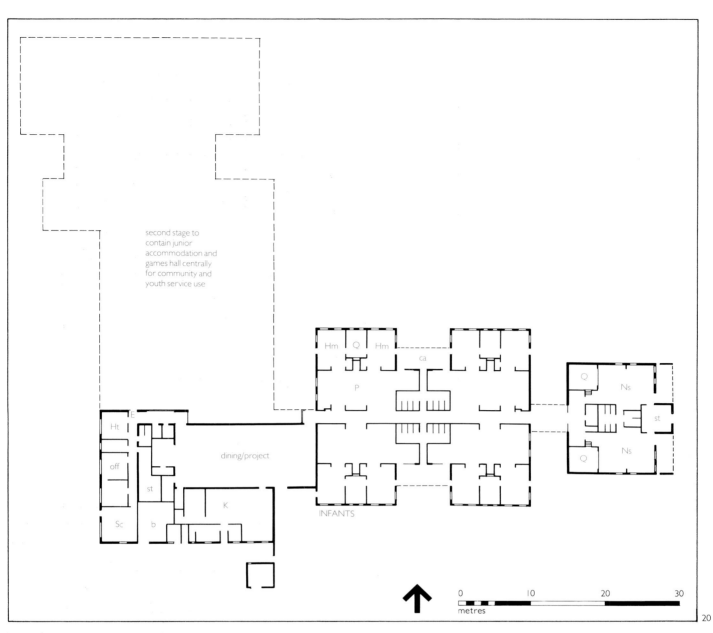

second stage to contain junior accommodation and games hall centrally for community and youth service use

E

Ht

off

st

Sc

b

K

dining/project

Hm Q Hm

P

ca

INFANTS

Q Ns

st

Q Ns

0 10 20 30
metres

20

21

23

22

24

Nightingale Primary School

Site opportunities and limitations have been exploited in the construction of this building completed in 1978. A northward fall across the site effectively has meant teaching centres at the higher level with service, administration and a nursery class at the lower level.

Two infant centres, each for seventy pupils, are elevated above the entrance and provide fully closed quiet rooms and largely enclosed home bays opening into well-proportioned practical areas which provide immediate access to small enclosed external courts. The three junior home bases are well enclosed and their practical area is split naturally into wet and dry activities by the contour line. Linking the two schools are the library and assembly hall which provide some lateral circulation space but a beneficial feature is the welcoming entrance area which is also used for dining.

As the school is within a General Improvement Area materials and scales were adopted in keeping with the local fabric.

A domestic scale has been provided by a load bearing structure with exposed standard timber trusses giving north light into the deep practical areas. The roofs are generally tiled and the site is walled to maintain the existing road perspective whilst reducing traffic noise. Siting the building close to the southern boundary has formed small and large external spaces which relate directly to the ages of the children using them.

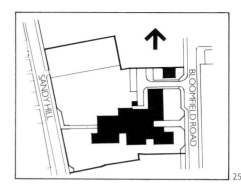

25

26

25 Site Plan
The site slopes from South to North and the school progressively steps down the contours. As the adjoining roads are narrow but busy, entrances have been set well back into the site giving generous sight lines. The boundary walls are in brick complementing the existing domestic fabric whilst maintaining the existing road perspective.

26 Layout Plan
By 1975 the open plan was exhibiting a higher proportion of enclosed areas within it. Here the infants have fully enclosed quiet rooms and the home bays are almost enclosed opening on to generous shared practical space.

Junior home bases are practically enclosed with a fully enclosed quiet room but, as with the infants, the practical space is open and the site contour line makes a natural break between wet and dry areas. Directly associated with the teaching areas are a variety of small and large external spaces on the southern side of the building.

The library and assembly hall are shared by infants and juniors and provide through circulation at different levels.

27 One of the teaching centres showing the single construction and the high quality of natural lighting through north-facing clerestorey windows. In the centre the brick flanks and handrails to the stairs leading down to the practical area can be seen.

28 As the school is built on a steeply falling site the section of the building steps down the contours. From the higher level of the teaching centres stairs lead down to the practical areas where there are workbenches and sink units.

27

28

Olga Primary School

Designed in 1979 to replace an 1874 building whose fabric was rapidly deteriorating the layout indicates the effect that site shape can have upon a standard primary school brief: a long narrow configuration was essential to provide sufficient immediate playspace to the teaching areas and the outline is broken down to create a domestic scale in keeping with the neighbourhood.

There is a single junior teaching centre for one hundred and five pupils and two infants centres for seventy each with an almost detached nursery class. In addition to a playcentre there is an adult education institute accommodation integral with the school: this means that the hall, which terminates a circulation spine, will be used by the school during the day, the playcentre in the late afternoon and the institute in the evening. With this wider use, access and lavatories for the disabled have been included in both school and institute. The financial arrangements reflect the school's varied population with money

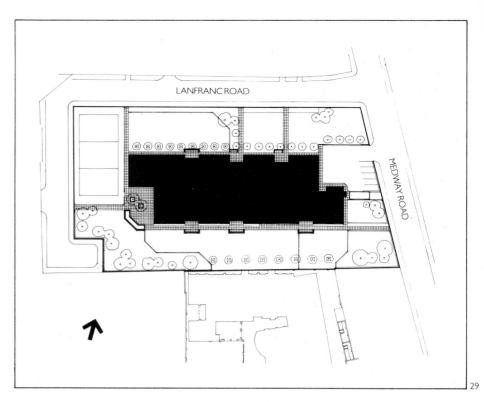

29

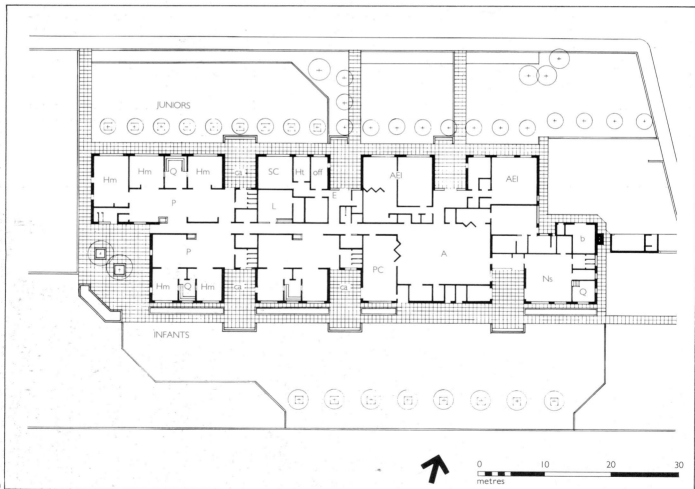

30

29 Site Plan, 1979
The tight urban site has conditioned the building form with the need for teaching areas giving direct access to playspaces. Nursery, infants, juniors and adult education institute each have separate entrances in addition to the main school entrance.

30 Layout, 1979
The open plan is shown here to be returning to enclosure, not the earlier cellular arrangement but a variety of spaces: the large general work area in the infants' areas gives access to curtained home bays and totally enclosed quiet rooms whilst the juniors have a large enclosed home bay —

similar to a classroom — and a pair of curtained home bays.

The hall is contained totally within the building but separated from teaching areas and available to all organisations using the building.

coming from at least four different building programmes.

The teaching centres are very similar in concept to Linton Mead being dispersed along a spine to reduce the totally open nature that full open planning produces and provides some general enclosure for the groups: each centre has an external covered work space immediately accessible from the practical area.

Construction is from load bearing brickwork with monopitch, tiled roofs on timber trusses ensuring, with clerestorey windows, daylight and ventilation into the deep plan: the roof perimeters are extended to provide shading. The building was completed in early 1982.

31 Perspective, 1979.
This illustrates the essentially domestic scale of a large building with standard timber trusses on load-bearing walls and clerestorey lighting to a deep plan.
32 *The roof perimeter is extended to provide a measure of solar shading to all teaching spaces. Larger covered spaces, accessible from teaching centres, give protected external work areas: this allows a wide range of outside activities to continue despite weather conditions.*

Bellenden Primary School

Although the basic brief has hardly varied over the last six years the primary school layouts have progressed and evolved so that no two plans are quite similar. In many cases the site shape has much to do with this, sometimes offering a falling site, occasionally a very narrow site which serves to channel the plan along determined lines (see Olga). Sometimes additional accommodation for a nursery, a play-centre or an adult education institute determines the disposition of teaching spaces.

The site for Bellenden School had roads on three sides with almost a quarter of the remaining area already occupied by a small block of flats: the resulting shape is a square with just sufficient additional space to make a junior playpitch. One consequence of this is a primary school 37.80 m square. Another is that this school, designed early in 1980, had much fuller proportions for the teaching areas giving almost square shapes for the school's activities.

Apart from siting consequences the plan indicates a further development in

arrangements for teaching. These are divided into four separate blocks and what can be quickly discerned is the smaller size home bays which are still relatively open to the practical areas: the quiet rooms for infants and juniors are, however, larger than previously and much more like a small classroom to meet the request for more enclosed spaces. Another significant point is that the infant reception class is separated from the main infant centre to enable a closer relationship with the nursery class – this allows the bolder nursery child to experience infant life and the new infant entrant can occasionally savour the nursery environment.

The intention is to allow a natural and gradual transition through the school. To augment this, the central courtyard acts as the core of the building with the library and library resource unit easily accessible and simply supervised from the staff room.

Construction is from a series of standard steel industrial portal frames with a pitched roof of heavily insulated steel decking which oversails the walls to give protection from sun and rain and provides covered work areas for all teaching centres leading out to enclosed play spaces. External walls are insulating blockwork rendered. The use of such a

structure, along with the well-known St. Paul's Primary School at Bow Common,[17] fulfills an earlier opinion that 'a barn furnishes no bad model and a good one may easily be converted into a school'.[18] The school was completed in early 1982.

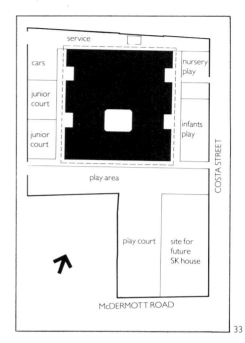

33

33   Site plan
The usable site is essentially square in plan with one arm containing a playpitch which is available out of school hours.
34   Layout Plan
The square site has had a formative effect upon the building development as each of the four teaching areas is square, reflecting the general shape of the main spaces. By 1980 when this school was designed there was a requirement for greater enclosure of quiet rooms and, at the same time, these grew larger resembling small classrooms.

The plan demonstrates the progression of children from nursery through infant stages to the junior levels of the school without a solid physical barrier separating different age groups which, however, still maintain the advantages of privacy.
35   *The roof structure stands free of the main building providing an extended perimeter to shade the teaching spaces and allowing external covered work areas: exposed steelwork is coloured chrome yellow throughout.*
36   *The standard steel portal frames are expressed internally: apart from the roof and clerestorey lighting the main windows are to the left of the photograph.*

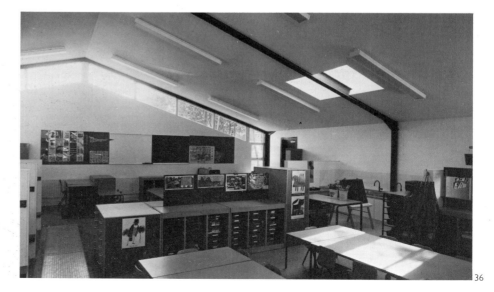

35

36

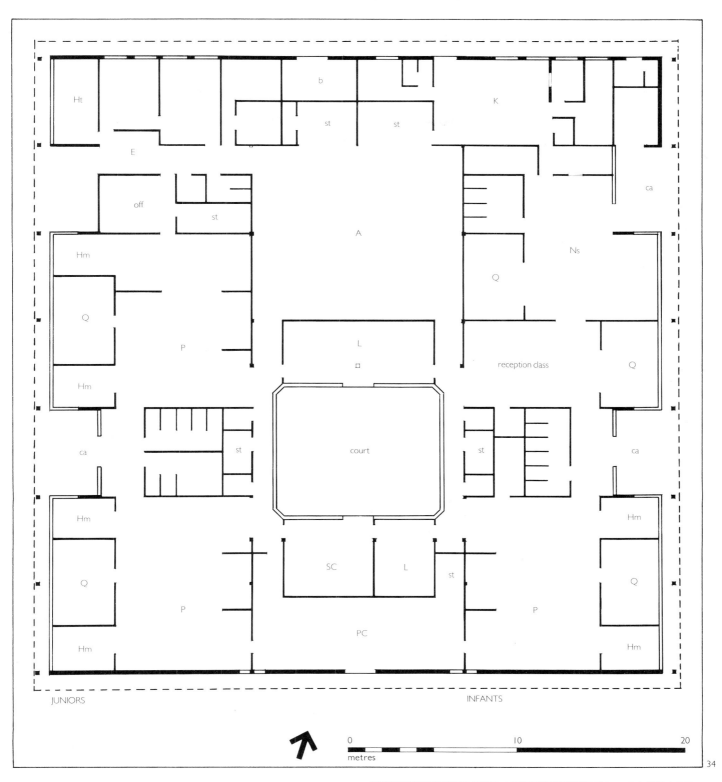

Ht

E

b

K

st   st

ca

off

st

A

Ns

Hm

Q

Q

P

L

reception class

Q

ca

st

court

st

ca

Hm

Hm

Q

Q

SC   L

st

P

P

Hm

PC

Hm

JUNIORS

INFANTS

0   10   20

metres

34

37 *A view of an internal courtyard: walls up to sill height are rendered insulation block with standard steel cladding to the gables. Steel cladding is silver grey, doors are painted red.*

37

Chapter 8: References

1 GLC Architects Review 2, 1976, Academy, p 39.

2. Seaborne M, Primary School Design, Routledge & Kegan Paul, 1971, p 1.

3 Open Plan Schools: Teaching, Curriculum, Design. Bennett N, Andreae J, Hegarty P, and Wade B NFER, 1980, p 84: *Chapter 1 of this book contains an excellent resume of the philosophical and historical background of open plan primary schools but secondary school experience is not included despite the book's title.*

4 Education, 25 September 1981, p 252, *East Morton Revisited, refers to limitations in teaching practice imposed by the building layout: for instance the open plan 'limits the teacher to group teaching which may not always be right'.*

5 Educational Research, NFER, vol 24, no 2: *This pre-school study carried out by the University of Strathclyde (S Neill and E Denham) concludes that 'The effect of building type seems to be to inhibit or facilitate the expression of existing child behaviour or staff policy – room openness and noise levels being the most potent factors'. In no case did the staff say that building design determined behaviour.*

6 MacEwan M, Crisis in Architecture, RIBA, 1974, p 16.

7 Ecclesiologist, vol vii, p 3, concerning school design: *Augustus Pugin inveighed against classical form for not reflecting 'Reality' where internal arrangements contradict external appearance. For him, each element was explicit and should be expressed. Prairie-like 'flexibility' would be inimical to his required expression of function.*

8 Inspectors' Report upon Senior Schools, April 1939.

9 Seaborne M, and Lowe R, The English School, Its Architecture and Organisation, vol II, 1870–1970, Routledge & Kegan Paul, 1977, p 177.

10 Architects Journal, 7 January 1981, p 22.

11 TES, 18 December 1981, p 13.

12 Architectural Review, May 1959, p 306.

13 Education, 28 November 1980.

14 The Observer, 16 April 1978, Under the Motorway Arches.

15 RIBAJ, February 1981, pp 46–47.

16 Jencks C, The Language of Post Modern Architecture, Academy Editions, 1977, p 87.

17 Architects Journal, 9 August 1972, pp 309–324.

18 Seaborne M & Lowe R, The English School, Its Architecture and Organisation, vol I, 1370–1870, Routledge & Kegan Paul, 1971, p 140.

Key to drawings

A	assembly hall
AEI	adult education institute
AH	activities hall
C	classroom
CR	common room
D	dining
Dr	drama
DW	dining/work
E	entrance
G	gymnasium
H	houseroom
Hm	home bay
Ht	head or principal
I	infants
J	juniors
K	kitchen
L	library
Lt	lecture
M	music
Ns	nursery
P	practical area
PC	play centre
Q	quiet area
S	secretary
Sc	science
SC	staff common room
SH	sports hall
SK	schoolkeeper
Sw	swimming pool
W	waiting
YS	youth service
b	boiler
ca	covered area
ch	changing
cl	cloakroom
l	lavatories
s	servery
st	store

Chapter 9
Community Education

By the 1970's schools were beginning to be recognised not as finite arrangements of buildings but as local resources potentially available for all. Had not Cambridgeshire provided village colleges available to all in the 1930's?[1] The original community school was seen as 'a village with a school as its heart'.[2] The question was posed whether schools should be open for a small part of the population for seven hours a day and for two hundred days a year only or should they be accessible for the total community, in many different groupings, with differing purposes for, perhaps, 24 hours a day:[3] 'schools should not be remote educational ghettoes in which neither education contributes to the community nor the community to education'.[4] In inner London there is a long history of schools with thriving evening institutes and these had had their own requirements included in schools during the 1960's making the adult education institutes available during the school day also.[5] The social content of a secondary school embraces many smaller groupings (house system, year bases, lower school, upper school, sixth form) but these all depend upon the shared use of the whole accommodation, teaching, administrative, formal and informal, for their activities. Shared resources, it was argued, could be extended to benefit the surrounding communities: the most immediately available facilities are sports centres and playing fields, kitchens and cafeterias, libraries and audio-visual aids centres, music and drama centres, and arts and crafts provision and these are the areas initially seen as most desirable by the community at large. The advantages are encompassed in three concepts: a closer bond is created between school and home, parent and teacher, teacher and taught, school and community: the school is provided with a wider range of human and physical resources by siting schools with ready access to community resources: and the overwhelming economic need to make the maximum use of scarce resources. Sporting facilities jointly provided for school and community use are generally more economical than those provided separately.[6] What has been observed in the fully integrated community school is that the school element begins to lose its identity and evolves into a centre for the community, a resource in a more general sense, requiring a full, overriding management structure of both school and community elements.[7,8] School management cannot always meet the need for this with equanimity.[9] Architects can make a positive contribution to community education in a way that few external factors can, but ultimately the community itself must evolve into an 'education society'.[10]

Beyond these widely accepted principles, however, stands one fundamental factor. Whereas the outer London boroughs are fully responsible for education within their boundaries and have the duty to provide welfare services also, the ILEA covers inner London for education only: the inner London boroughs are responsible as welfare agencies for provision in their areas. Therefore, when, for example, the outer London borough of Hounslow decides to make a joint provision of education and welfare upon the same site or in the same building this can be determined relatively simply within Hounslow's committee structure. When the ILEA in conjunction with, for example, the inner London borough of Lewisham decides to include recreation and education upon one site there may well be intractable problems between the different authorities over timing, balance of capital provision to erect the building and balance of revenue necessary to share the resources available in an equitable manner. Central government programming, ostensibly to make funds available, has not always managed to provide a sufficiently firm bridge to produce a mutually agreed community school in inner London in joint programmes. The three following schools are examples of agreement but it should be noted that in the Borough of Tower Hamlets, a site adjoining the newly enlarged Langdon Park School (see Chapter 7) is being developed by the Borough for its own community centre, which demonstrates the possibilities of maximising joint opportunity where full integration is not possible due to financial and programming difficulties. The White Paper, Policy for the Inner Cities, 1977, set up local partnerships arrangements for reducing serious urban stress. Under the partnership agreements with specific London boroughs (eg Lambeth, Hackney or Islington) the ILEA now formulates specific policies for the extra provision of nursery classes, sports accommodation, playspace extensions, youth centres and adult education institutes with the express intention of making education premises more widely available for the community.

1   Location Map
The school is sited on the edge of Ladywell Park where two railways diverge near Catford Stadium. Already located in the Park are a well-known athletics track, bowls rinks, tennis courts, cricket grounds and football pitches. The Crafton Leisure Centre,, built in conjunction with Lewisham Borough Council, complements these with further internal games and training areas.
2   Ground Floor Plan
The plan indicates the disparity in volume of the two elements and the need to treat them as separate elements.

The main entrance/ticket office to the Leisure Centre is at the focal point of the two buildings. Pedestrians crossing the Park enter from the South up a wide staircase. A large car park to the North gives entrance by a ramp, thus allowing disabled persons access to all facilities, and the school has a direct link from the West across its open, central atrium.

Lewisham School

This school is unique in several different ways. Firstly, because the site is on the periphery of the beautiful natural Ladywell Park which runs for a mile almost from the centre of Catford towards the centre of Lewisham. It is a linear park along a rolling hill flanking two railway lines and it already contained a well-known athletics track whilst fronting a famous dog racing stadium: there are good facilities for tennis and bowls. Secondly, the school building is the only example of a four-storeyed construction using the MACE system (see Chapter 3). Thirdly, but most importantly, the London Borough of Lewisham decided at an early design stage to ask ILEA to include, upon a joint basis, a sports complex to be shared by the school, the adult education institute, the youth service and the Borough: this complex would crown the other facilities immediately in view and plans, were laid for its further extension.

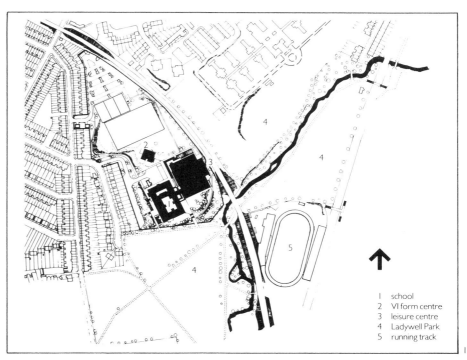

1 school
2 VI form centre
3 leisure centre
4 Ladywell Park
5 running track

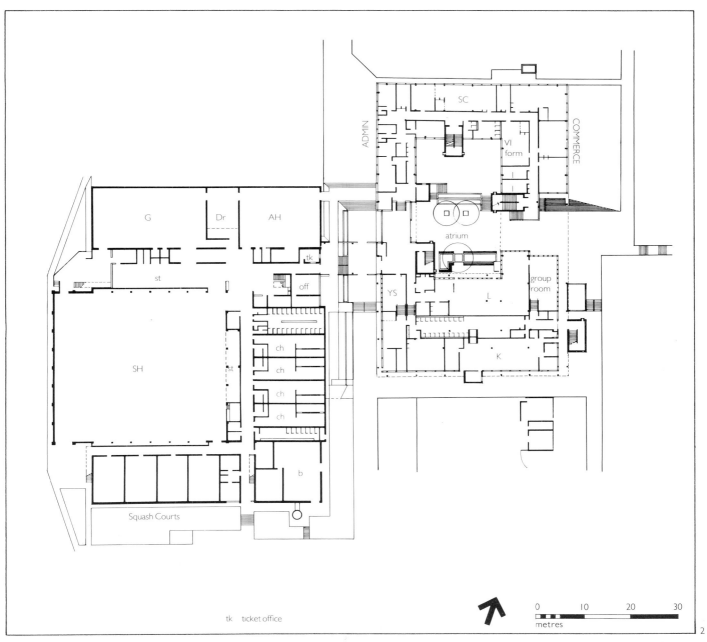

tk   ticket office

0   10   20   30
metres

169

Thus it can be seen that there already existed a long-standing and well-recognised recreational area and the Borough Council consolidated that reputation with a more formal provision whilst providing for a totally different range of activities. The park setting is allowed to flow into the school site and the heavily treed, sloping area sets off the school to advantage: this is rectangular in plan and presents a very clear simple architectural statement relying upon the in-situ white concrete staircase and service pylons to provide punctuation to an otherwise classical composition.[11] But it was not possible to incorporate the volume necessary for a modern sports complex into the school itself. The sports hall itself is 36.00 m × 24.00 m and 9.00 m high and the proportions of a school cannot hope to contain such spaces: although it does contain purpose designed youth service facilities and an adult education institute. In addition, it was accepted that the sports centre should be capable of operating separately from the school thus avoiding the problems of general access into teaching areas. Normally a school of this size would have two gymnasia but these are absorbed into the complex where there is a drama workshop, activities hall, training hall and four squash courts. Six large changing rooms give the option over the balance of men and women attending for particular activities and a creche, clubroom and bar with servery transform the building into a family attraction. Access to the two main floor levels is simplified by the natural slope of the ground and ramps down to the main hall level and up to the supporting activities are easy going for the fit and the handicapped.

The great contrast is in the appearance of the buildings themselves.[12] Whereas the school is white and cool and floats among the tall trees, the sports complex sits in a hollow and is built from load-bearing red brick in an attempt to totally differentiate their structures and uses for, in 1970, MACE had not developed sufficiently to cope with large cellular buildings, and the sports brief had not been finally determined at tender stage: it was felt that late changes in requirements, due largely to government programming, would be more easily dealt with in traditional construction rather than with an inflexible system. The separation is completed by naming the sports complex the Crofton Leisure Centre but the joint community aspect is reinforced by the entrance, for the school is constructed around a hollow rectangle which acts as a grand atrium and most sports centre users traverse this on their way to physical endeavour.

3 First Floor Plan
At this level there is no connection between the separate parts, the school providing a courtyard entirely enclosed by classrooms whilst the upper voids of the Leisure Centre have galleries, a bar, cafeteria, clubrooms and a creche.

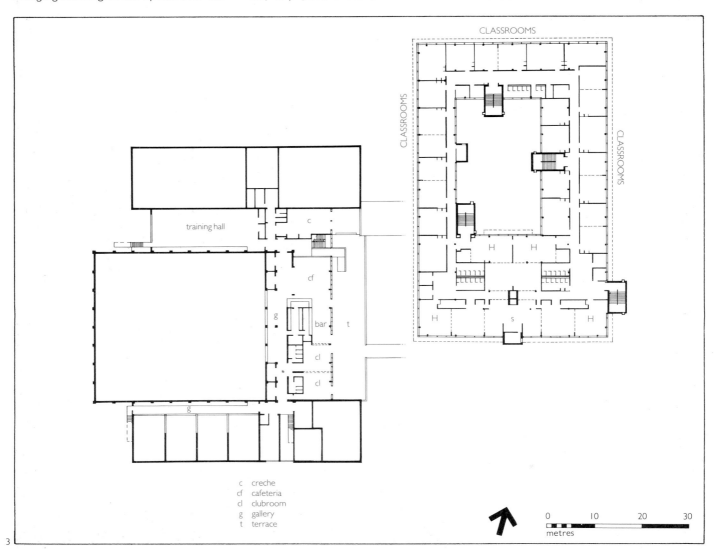

c creche
cf cafeteria
cl clubroom
g gallery
t terrace

0   10   20   30
metres

4 A photograph of the model shows the scope of the school and leisure centre: the site falls steeply from the houses at the top to the railway on the right. The four storey school is built in the MACE system with the leisure centre closely clad in red brickwork.
5 View from the West. The park has many superb mature trees which knit together the various leisure elements contained in it.
6, 7 The main games hall showing facilities for different sporting activities with bleacher foldaway seating available on two sides.

8 The school's drama workshop contained in the Leisure Centre: this is a two storey high space fully equipped for stage sound and lighting.

9 In addition to a creche and clubrooms, a bar en suite helps the transformation from a school sports complex to a leisure centre for the family.

10 View from the South showing the four storey school constructed in the MACE system. To the right, beyond the school, can be seen the roof of the sports centre. For a description of MACE see Chapter 3.

11 *From the North the school is seen in relationship to the sports centre. There is a pedestrian link between the two buildings at car park level.*

12 *The elevation of the sports complex (Crofton Leisure Centre) facing the school and the main car park. Construction is from dark red load-bearing brick with steel space frame roof structures to the larger volumes.*

13 *Whilst many Leisure Centre users arrive by car and enter the centre through the school, an alternative for pedestrians is across Ladywell Park and up these broad steps from the South.*

Waterfield School

Waterfield School (see Chapter 5) stands just beyond the present furthest point of the Thamesmead development and house construction is approaching from the east and south-east. Eventually the adjoining site will form the Thamesmead central area. When the Waterfield brief was being developed for quite a different site (Thomas Calton School at Southwark) community use of the school was part of the educational ideal. The school's first phase has been constructed and the second is in preparation and each contains elements of communal use but phase three will include full sports and social areas which will be run as communal facilities.[13]

The school is separated from the central area to the north by one of Thamesmead's necessary canals and it is against this barrier that the most easily shared facilities are placed. Originally, when it was proposed to build the school in one contract, there were to

have been, in addition to the gymnasia and sports hall, squash courts, a sauna bath and, serving as a direct link to the central area, a swimming pool across the canal.[14] Many of the shared facilities were to have been provided by the London Borough of Greenwich but this proved impossible in the general economic climate of the early 1970's and they did not proceed. The emphasis upon the northern approach was reinforced by the placing of the main public access from the north where there would have been large car parks and public transport terminals serving the central area shops, businesses, offices and welfare agencies.[15]

In entering from the north, at first floor level as a continuation of the central area's shopping centre, there would be immediate access to a mall which links the school's enclosed specialist areas for music, drama, dining and physical education with the open plan of the main teaching space.

The mall, which is the focal point of shared activities, is a double height

volume and it contains easy going ramps which give access for the physically handicapped to all school and communal facilities.[16] In the original plans the adult education institute and youth centre were given immediate access from the north: further emphasis was given to this area by placing the dining area immediately over them with a view westward along the canal. The whole of the shared specialist facilities are contained in a two storey block which can operate independently during evenings, weekends or holidays.

14 *The school is being built in phases as indicated with the completed first phase shown in detail. Main public access will be from the North where the Thamesmead central area is planned to have large car parks and a bus terminus. Originally a high level walkway was designed to link the central area's shopping centre with the school at first floor level. The most used shared facilities lie to the North of the mall with the Youth Service and Adult Education Institute at a lower ground floor level.*

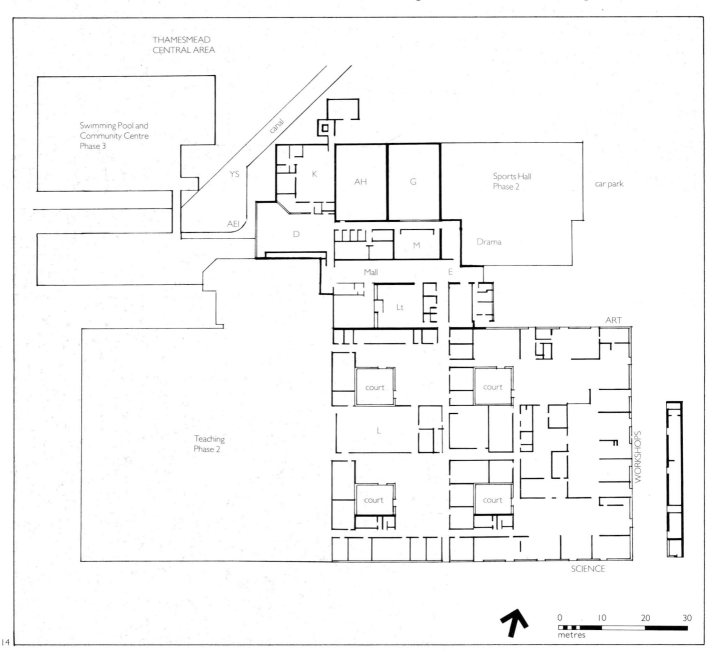

15

15   In community schools one of the areas most popular with the public is the workshop as it contains equipment far beyond domestic application. The benches shown are specifically designed for the ILEA by industrial designers working in the GLC Architect's Department.

16   The library represents another fruitful resource for the local community with a wide range of studies available: easy chairs are standard and the floor is carpeted.

16

George Green's Centre

The Isle of Dogs occupies a unique site in central London. It lies on the north bank of the Thames and is close held in a great, slow, southerly loop of the river facing Greenwich with its accumulation of handsome classical buildings: across the northern ends of the loop large docks were constructed in the nine-teenth century, and road access to the Isle itself is by a series of lifting bridges across these docks. This has produced over many decades the feeling of independence and community among the islanders as they are aware of the slender nature of physical communi-cation to the mainland and their voluntary isolation should they so desire.

There was one secondary school serving the Isle, George Green's School adjacent on the mainland, and it was a two form entry voluntary controlled mixed school which was not sufficiently large to accommodate all of the local secondary pupils. To remedy the problem of island children travelling some way to other schools, in 1972 the ILEA approved the design for a new George Green's School, relocated upon the Isle, for nine hundred with a large enough site for extension to eight form entry as new housing on the Isle developed. The new school would be wholly maintained by the Authority.

Apart from the need to provide more secondary school places on the Isle, the local borough, Tower Hamlets, recognis-ing the relative isolation and apparent independence of the islanders agreed to enlarge the purely educational require-ment on the site by increasing the school

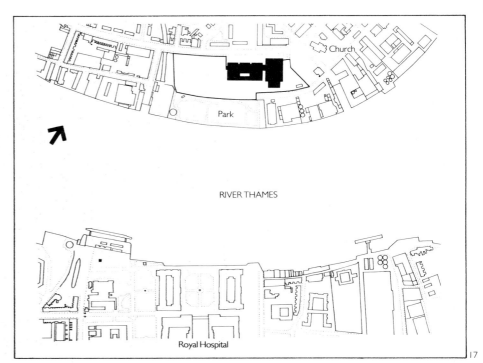

Church

Park

RIVER THAMES

Royal Hospital

17

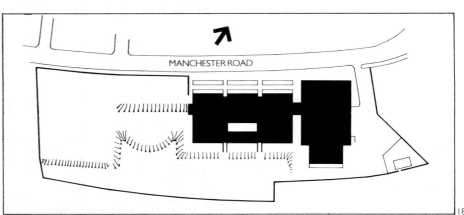

MANCHESTER ROAD

18

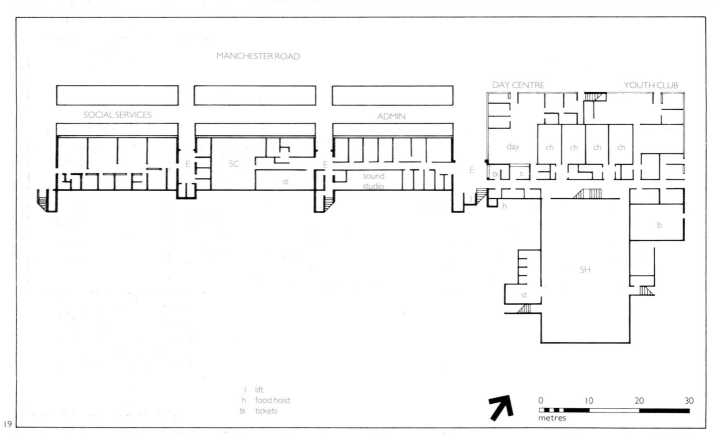

MANCHESTER ROAD

DAY CENTRE　　　　YOUTH CLUB

SOCIAL SERVICES

ADMIN

day　ch　ch　ch　ch

SC

st　　sound studio

tk　s

h

b

SH

st

l　lift
h　food hoist
tk　tickets

0　　10　　20　　30
metres

17 Map
18 Site Plan
The site lies directly across the Thames from Wren's Royal Hospital. The land is mounded and sits behind a small park with handsome, mature trees.
19 Floor Plan, Level One
The building sits back into a low natural plateau as it develops southward from Manchester Road. At this level the local social services, old people's day centre, youth club, school administration and the main entrance serving the shared sports accommodation are clearly defined and readily accessible from the street.
20 Floor Plan, Levels Two and Three
Due to the natural site contours the main building is developed as split level plan with half flights of stairs joining differing levels. Thus the single-storey science, housecraft and art and craft departments are closely associated and one flight of stairs up from the main road: the classrooms are one storey above the road. The more usual shared facilities are grouped around the sports hall and on the floor above are the theatre's green room, music suite and dining room with a bar.
21 *The school presents a calm face to Manchester Road with the four main staircases articulating the building mass and indicating direct access at street level to the Borough services. The projecting wing contains the day centre and the youth centre at ground floor level and gymnasium, theatre and activities hall above in the enclosed portion.*
22, 23 *The main entrance hall serves both the school and the leisure activities. The art department has provided the trompe l'oeil paintings to balcony front and walls depicting the historic activity of the area — shipping — with elements of the old and the new schools.*

21

22

23

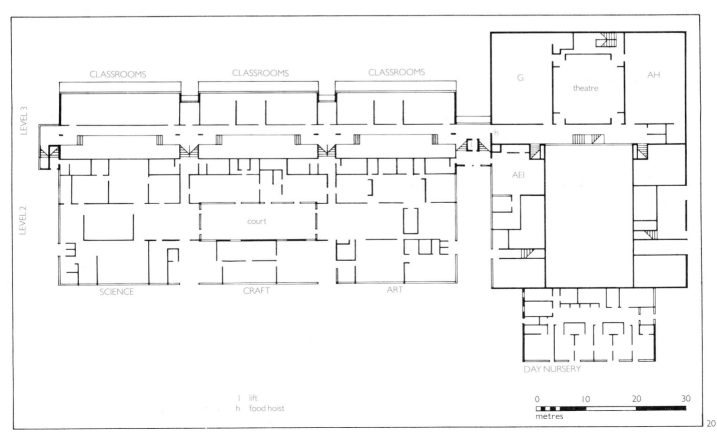

CLASSROOMS   CLASSROOMS   CLASSROOMS   G   theatre   AH

LEVEL 3

h

AEI

LEVEL 2

court

SCIENCE   CRAFT   ART

DAY NURSERY

l lift
h food hoist

0   10   20   30
metres

20

provision with social services and recreational resources.[17] The consequence is that the school has become a focal point for the Isle for it contains many borough services beyond those normally included by the ILEA.[18] To further demonstrate their integration the building was not developed as a series of separate blocks, each one identifiable as the province of a particular provider, but as a single extensive block overlooking the heavily treed Island Gardens, to the south, fronting the Thames. Additionally, the design did not attempt to isolate the school in the centre of its site, as is often the case with large secondary schools, but presents itself boldly on the main building line of Manchester Road a ready and resourceful servant of the community. The main entrance hall doubles as the access for the majority of recreational activities with a ticket office controlling the entrance to the wing which has a sports hall which includes spectator provision. In addition to the hall the wing also has a gymnasium and an activities hall which are served by a large range of changing rooms allowing for the variety of timing and use necessary for school and community sharing. The inclusion of a fully equipped theatre in the round is supplemented by a green room and the school servery/dining area has extended use with the inclusion of a bar set in the middle of the community provision. To facilitate the serving of food throughout this complex the kitchen is placed at roof level with lifts serving isolated serveries.

Facilities which are in more immediate use by the public are ranged along the pavement with individual entrances marked obviously by the building's articulation and placement of the staircases. There is a self-contained youth centre with an access to the sports facilities, and an old people's day centre which has its own servery provisioned from the main kitchen. A social services suite with individual interviewing facilities is, again, self-contained but not isolated.

School administration is immediately accessible off Manchester Road but the day nursery for fifty toddlers is located independently on the southern side with the park instantly available. The ILEA has included an adult education institute which not only provides courses during the day but makes the full facilities of a modern secondary school accessible in the evenings and during school holidays. The centre 'invites the local people to use it as casually and informally as they would the row of shops opposite'.[19]

One of the most important facets of this building is its apparent simplicity and, despite its size, its human scale which enables its location on an ordinary street without making its mass overwhelming: it welcomes and serves efficiently.

24

25

24 A full size sports hall would not normally be included in a school of this size but was part of the recreational facilities provided by the Borough of Tower Hamlets. The hall is windowless but has North lighting through monitors in the roof construction. The balcony on the left leads directly off the snacks and bar area.

25 The school drama provision is increased by the Borough's input and becomes a fully-enclosed 'black box' with a wide range of lighting effects available from a main control console and foldaway bleacher seating gives another dimension of flexibility. Unusually for a school a green room is adjacent.

26 Normal school meals provision was increased to include snacks and a bar in order that the leisure centre could provide full facilities for adult use: it was also placed in close proximity to the theatre and games provision. The furniture chosen for the dining room is not that normally associated with school dinners. Tables on the right overlook the sports hall.

27 The southern side of the school shows a very informal face with only the staircases, which indicate entrance from the main road, illustrating any hierarchical organisation. The main school areas are on the left arranged as terraces falling to the south: they are linked to the shared recreational facilities on the extreme right by a common entrance hall and access stairhall containing a lift.

26

27

Chapter 9: References

1 Architectural Review, December 1939, p 225. Comp.

2 Architects Journal, 19 March 1980, p 572: *the article with concurs a later view (Leon Krier's) of the school with a village at its heart.*

3 The Teacher, 8 April 1972.

4 Education, 26 July 1969, p 137.

5 The Times Educational Supplement, 5 March 1982, p 23: *Harry Rée says that school has regained its original Greek meaning: a place for worthwhile leisure.*

6 TES 18 December 1981, p 5, Sharing does work: *The economic and social costs and benefits of joint and direct sports provision, sports council survey.*

7 Nisbet J, Hendry L, Steward C and Watt J, Towards Community Education; An Evaluation of Community Schools, Aberdeen UP, 1979.

8 Municipal Journal, 14 August 1981, p 653, *notes that in the Crewe Community School, Cheshire, a 'space manager' was included in the original concept being responsible for management and maintenance of facilities including the sharing out of time and space between school community and adult education.*

9 Architects Journal, 11 November 1981, p 33 states *'the attachment of the word "community" would mean that people living in the neighbourhood actually contribute to their own education by organising a multitude of activities for themselves'.*

10 Architects Journal, 4th November 1981, p 893, Harry Rée quoting Henry Morris the founder of the Cambridge village colleges.

11 Surveyor, 1 August 1975, p 19–20, Learning for All.

12 Building Design, 4 July 1975, p 3.

13 Architects Journal, 9 March 1977, p 443–454.

14 Casabella, September 1976, p 54–59.

15 GLC Architects Review 2, 1976, Academy, p 66–67.

16 Industrial delle Construzione, December 1978, p 66–71.

17 GLC Architects Review, 1974, Academy, p 39–40.

18 Casabella, September 1976, p 52–53.

19 Architect, January 1978, p 27–30, Down in the Docks.

Key to drawings

A	assembly hall
AEI	adult education institute
AH	activities hall
C	classroom
CR	common room
D	dining
Dr	drama
DW	dining/work
E	entrance
G	gymnasium
H	houseroom
Hm	home bay
Ht	head or principal
I	infants
J	juniors
K	kitchen
L	library
Lt	lecture
M	music
Ns	nursery
P	practical area
PC	play centre
Q	quiet area
S	secretary
Sc	science
SC	staff common room
SH	sports hall
SK	schoolkeeper
Sw	swimming pool
W	waiting
YS	youth service
b	boiler
ca	covered area
ch	changing
cl	cloakroom
l	lavatories
s	servery
st	store

Chapter 10
Technical Problems & Solutions

When we consider the apparent ease with which the original London Board schools were erected we sometimes wonder how and why differences exist between their bold and confident designers and architects today. We are aware that working drawings were minimal, giving general profiles and dimensions only, and recognise that due to technical developments over the last sixty years the architect now needs to describe the minutest detail with the utmost care to avoid contractual delays and disruptions and to make the buildings perform as desired. Clients' ultimate requirements do not change, however, and it is possible to obtain much relief from reading the annals of the construction of Blenheim Palace, now universally recognised as a national monument, and the everyday correspondence between the architect, John Vanbrugh, and his client, Sarah Churchill, Duchess of Marlborough. It is as well to be aware also that not all Victorian architecture and engineering survived its construction long despite John Ruskin's injunction that 'when we build, let us think that we build for ever' – MacGonagall's 'Tay Bridge Disaster' still rings in our ears and the original foundations are visible today – whilst new laws and procedures were developed to meet new needs. New technology opens new vistas of opportunity in design but not all disadvantages are equally apparent as more recent bridge technology has amply shown.

From 1870 until 1940 the school building technique employed in inner London developed slowly and with no great new principles of design required to meet the provision of simple educational needs. The grand, solid, load-bearing walls of the Board's gave way to the lighter, suburban constructions all based upon well-recognised patterns and details and, although the roof structure changed from solid wooden king post trusses to lighter mild steel trusses the roof pitch was covered in similar clay tiles. Brickwork varied from solid 18″ (450 mm) walls to 11″ (275 mm) cavity construction but both were within the techniques known and practised by the building industry. In the 1920's, however, a new breeze began to blow from the continent of Europe and it carried the exciting message that the expression of function would create great, new architecture with bold new forms and that science should be pre-eminent in

its technical solutions: the primary recognition of this new approach involved the use of flat roofs, horizontal bands of windows and white walls. Very few London school buildings – see, however, Burlington School, Chapter 1 – pursued these principles and modest, traditional architecture continued generally to be designed and built until 1940.

The end of World War II signalled several things in educational building, the major one being the introduction of a new attitude to education emanating from the 1944 Education Act. This expression of liberal ideas into the slowly developing world of education was paralleled by the new breed of architects – most of whom were not trained in traditional construction methods – who were inspired by the new national zeal for social provision: this zeal was matched on their part by their pursuit of the international ideals of the science-based Modern Movement in architecture. Despite their inclination towards rational design decisions and detailing many decisions were made upon incomplete information and sometimes upon the lack of application of chemical and physical knowledge. After some years of shortage of building elements many new materials became available, often with unknown properties, and new building techniques were developed to stretch the minimal resources available.[1] Continuity of traditional knowledge was severed and normal development discontinued leading to a lack of that 'homely knowledge'[2] upon which building had been founded for hundreds of years: in the same vein another commentator finds that 'knowledge seems to be mislaid from time to time'.[3] It has been said ironically that 'building construction was based on practice, building technology is based on science'.[4] It might be added that technology is a servant, not a master.[5]

In architectural terms the flat roof can contain any shape or volume, however awkward the plan form: the pitched roof is a much more formal response to a usually more formal layout for it must be supported at its periphery and thus describes and contains the discrete form beneath. The new school plans were not formal and in London grew into meandering layouts, often to suit restricted or awkwardly shaped sites, and the flat roof was a simple response to enclosure:

much of the liberation of the primary school plan and latterly, the secondary school also, was possible through being able to discount the problem of roofing geometry. The pitched roof came to be associated with old-fashioned thinking as it inhibited freedom of planning: the flat roof was easily applied and after 1945 became universal except for some exotic assembly halls and gymnasia where a truly scientific structure of arcing steelwork or hyperboloid concrete would demonstrate the finite volume below. The major technical problem[6] with flat roofs in London's climate is that they do not shed rainwater quickly enough, exposing any weaknesses in jointing to the constant presence of moisture – see Chapter 12 – combined with this fundamental problem is the steady diminution of quality too as the specification was steadily reduced to meet ever more stringent cost limits. The solid three coat asphalt finish on a solid screed laid to falls above a concrete roof slab[7] gave way to lighter roof decks of strawboard – which sometimes sprouted into life when damp – and woodwool slabs which had three layer roofing felt as a finish. As the new, cheaper materials replaced the older flat roof coverings – lead, copper and zinc installed by experienced craftsmen – the heating and ventilation habits of building users changed, producing a new range of performance requirements which were not fully appreciated. Traditional methods of detailing had also been forgotten, giving problems at upstands and junctions. There was a dramatic moment in 1958 when the 20 year guarantee for three layer roofing felt was reduced overnight by its manufacturers to twelve months but this was exceeded by the 1971 MACE specification for a single layer plastic sheet which did not survive the investigative pecks of seagulls. Flat roofs began to lose favour both with architects and building users. The major solution to the roofing problem has been to revert to pitched roofs and this has been matched by the motives of many

1 Burlington Secondary School, South Elevation
This was the first school in inner London to use a reinforced concrete frame for its main structure and it enabled a new architectural vision to be expressed: the flat roof and horizontal bands of windows were an expression of functionalism.

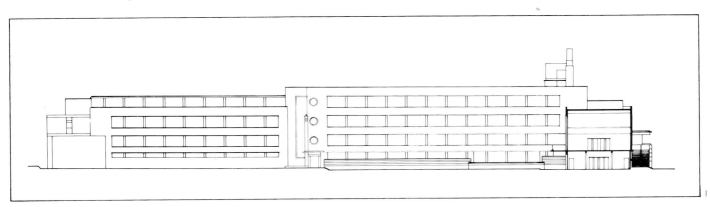

architects reverting to traditional detailing where proven detail sheets are available.[8]

In the aftermath of war the decline in the window must be viewed as a major technical problem. After 1918 the steel window frame and opening light were introduced: these were seen as an advance upon the earlier wooden or iron techniques although the georgian pane still represented the realisation of the enclosure. The long term problem with this material is that galvanising was not introduced until 1936 and ultimately those windows are having to be replaced as corrosion has distorted them: their

replacement currently is argued within the terms of the conservation of energy as their bowed shapes release too much expensively warmed air. After 1945 a wider range of unproven materials was rapidly developed to counter the acute shortage of traditional materials and the effects of these are still felt. The timber framed window wall was introduced as a cheap method of spanning between load bearing cross walls but a new approach to detailing was required and it was not universally successful as many horizontal surfaces were not weathered and the omission of positive drips led water back into vulnerable jointing. With the

standard of timber quality declining, due to lack of careful initial selection and insufficient time given for maturing after cutting, such detailed faults have proved very expensive as total replacement has been necessary with the onset of wet rot or dry rot.

New problems arose with the use of the window wall as architects had not experienced before the physical properties of superheated summer air in the sealed cavity between a glass spandrel and solid backup panel: with reinforced glass the coefficient of expansion of the reinforcing wire being higher than that of glass, and hot sunshine falling on to a

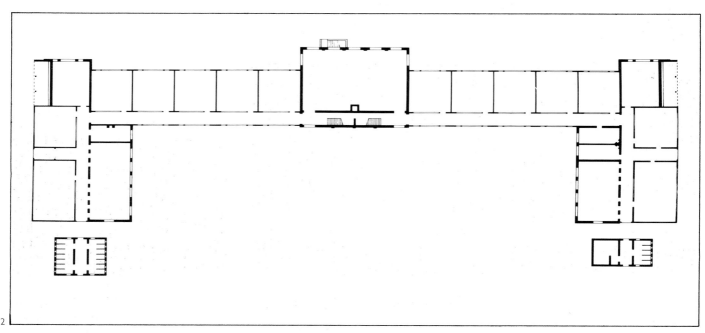

2

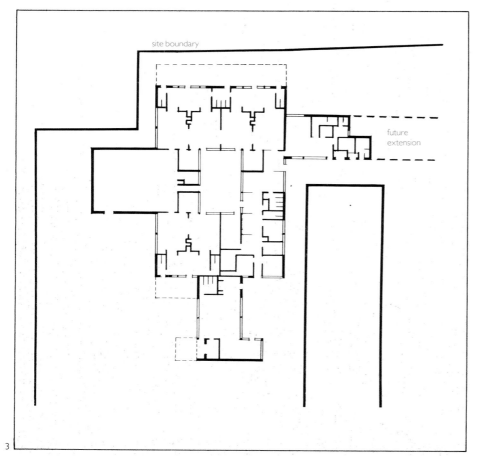

3

2 The elementary school of the 1920's and 1930's had a simple, single storey plan. A pitched roof is a formal response to this as it must be supported at its periphery and thus describes and contains the form beneath.
3 After 1945 the general adoption of the flat roof liberated the school plan. The primary school layout developed articulation as a response to educational requirements and, sometimes, the tightness of the inner London site.

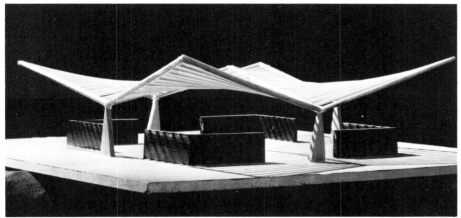

4 A hyperbolic paraboloid concrete roof covering an assembly hall with house rooms around the perimeter.

5 A model of the structure for a teachers' training college which was built in the early 1960's: here the structure is steelwork.

6 Steel framed windows seemed an advance in the 1920's upon their predecessors but they were ungalvanised. This led in due course to excessive corrosion creating bowing and distortion.

7 This is a predominantly single storey school, built in 1956, where it has been necessary to renew all of the external timber curtain walling and doors. It was decided to install a metal cladding system with stove enamelled panels which will need less maintenance and will require no redecoration. Specialist cladding contractors' tenders were based upon a performance specification.

8

dark painted back-up panel, provided a sufficiently high temperature to shatter the tightly framed glass. In the pursuit of economy patent glazing was extensively used and it has suited the architectural pursuit of raw technology: it has been over used in roof-lighting and sometimes in sidelighting producing not only unacceptable air loss through the open jointing but allowing build up of solar radiation, particularly in the extremely hot summer of 1976. A very cheap expedient for opening lights was the use of simple glass louvres – they also had the benefit of being architecturally neutral – but these have proved very expensive in terms of lost heat and admittance of unacceptable draughts as well as requiring intensive maintenance for continuous operation: they have also proved to be a favourite point for unauthorised entry.

In the 1960's the aluminium window became widely available but its cost could not be contained within the limits required by the DES: costing exercises were carried out continuously to check whether softwood windows painted could compare with hardwood windows or whether aluminium sections could be afforded over standard steel. The cheapest in capital cost was always selected and future maintenance costs will reflect this false economy.

A continuing problem was the propensity for children to hurt themselves upon outward opening casement windows: many expedients were tried, which included heavily planted shrubbery, to try to provide a tangible barrier but accidents still occurred and now all windows opening outwards have to be placed 6'0'' (1.80 m) above ground level.

Cost limitations have been the preoccupation of target setters and arbitrary programme makers without

reference to quality or value for money: the objective of capital limitation is a matter of national economy but the school building programme has narrowed the vision solely to basic needs – square metres of area provided per sterling pound or numbers of children catered for irrespective of the cost of maintaining the fabric. The national economy would have been better served by providing schools of larger area, better servicing and much better quality building materials and methods. What started, in 1949, as a laudable exercise to cut out unnecessary space and wasteful expenditure has produced an 'impossible struggle to produce good buildings with inadequate resources'.[9]

In the drive for building economy standards of construction and finish have undoubtedly suffered in London but there have been other consequences of capital cost limitations: in the Standards for School Premises Regulations, DES, minimum teaching areas are listed but vital supporting services are not. Thus, whilst for example, lavatory accommodation for secondary girls is mandatory, cloakrooms and restrooms are not and although these are invariably included in original schedules of accommodation they are almost as invariably omitted finally to effect savings in cost with the direct consequence that the girls use the lavatories as social areas with lavatory basins as seats producing a high level of damage. Again, recognisably necessary services, such as positively ventilating sports halls mechanically for use for examinations or social events, have been prohibited in the name of economy only to be added later at greater cost with enormous disruption. Whilst the value of external covered work areas immediately available to primary teaching spaces has been recognised and included

in briefs since 1966 very few have materialised as they represent an easily identified saving to meet cost limits. In 1876 the School Board decided to increase their building budget by 5% to provide 'architectural pretensions' over plain building: in 1976 such an addition would have increased a building's value for money many times.[10]

Over the years the ILEA has been aware of the inhibiting results of capital cost famine until the austere and utility nature of some buildings was so apparent that, in conjunction with tight and arbitrary programmes, it could be paraphrased that the inner London architect designed schools and colleges on a shoestring against the clock. The longest lasting problem for future generations of maintenance surveyors will be from the progressive reduction in specification standards as clay bricks were replaced by sand lime bricks and the cheapest steel windows flimsily substituted for solid, seasoned, selected timber whilst internal blockwork remained unplastered and floor finishes

8 *This single storey school was built in 1957 and by 1979 the external timber curtain walling was in urgent need of repair. It was decided to pursue a different solution from that shown in Fig 7 by installing a proprietary cladding system with patent gaskets which facilitate reglazing. Although it would cost slightly more than the solution used in Fig 7 it had the advantages that it avoided the need to prepare detailed design drawings and that development problems had already been solved by the manufacturer. In the event, after examining closely several systems this one was selected for its first application to a school building: this is hardly surprising since its cost would not be acceptable upon a new school subject to cost limits.*

9

9 *By 1970 utilitarian buildings became the norm in inner London due to the constriction of cost limits. The buildings may still be superbly planned but materials and detailing had to be tailored to suit capital costs not revenue requirements. Here is the widespread use of standard patent glazing to clad a new college with glass louvres at high level for ventilation: both have proved to be too cheap initially for reasonable running costs as both leak too much air. The rooflights cover a sports hall and gymnasium: both have had to have artificial ventilation added at a later date – it was proscribed by the cost limits during the design and construction stages – causing great disruption to the college's teaching.*

10 Plan of Building
In the late 1960's primary schools were designed with external covered work areas immediately accessible from teaching areas as recommended in the Plowden Report, 1967. Very few were built, however, as the covered area represented easily identified cost savings in an era of ever tightening cost limits. This building was designed with the covered areas as part of the architecture and their omission leaves not only a teaching requirement unfulfilled.

11 Plan
Some form of external covered work space has been provided latterly by the use of standard portal frames with roofs oversailing the school's main outside walls.

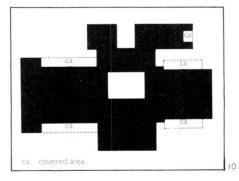

ca covered area

10

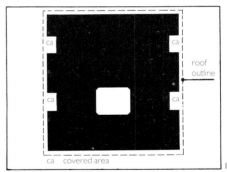

roof outline

ca covered area

11

slimmed away. Despite the gradual loss of quality a recent report[11] finds that nationally 'more failures occurred in design or execution than through faulty materials'.

Institutions such as schools have no apparent owners to care immediately and individually for their fabric. General maintenance can cope with obvious wear or damage but without simple everyday caring casual damage or even heavy wearing offer an uncared for, unkempt appearance and buildings rapidly degenerate. Whilst it can be assumed that individual classrooms reflect the interest of the teacher involved in working there it is staircases and corridors that suffer from lack of obvious ownership. Paradoxically these are the areas which do not receive the finishes necessary to give good service for their robust use because they are the

first in line for economies when savings have to be made to permit a project to proceed.

Circulation spaces have been the prime areas for dimensional reduction to the barest minimum allowed by building regulations for means of escape, and their finishes have also been reduced, typically, to paint and the cheapest linoleum floor cover often with skirting omitted too. ILEA buildings are not alone in this respect with provincial schools contemplating one way circulation systems.[12] There was a time when the Victorian institutional building with its wide, high corridor paved with terrazzo or oak block, having glazed brick dadoes to 1.20 m on walls with painted brick or plaster above, caused general repulsion and derision among architects imbued with clean, clear, ideal visions of architecture and behaviour but it has lasted well and continues to serve with the modicum of care. Circulation systems must be civilized providing positive social spaces, for 'corridors are our streets, the entrance hall and stairs our piazzas',[13] and not areas too rapidly reduced to shabbiness.

Since 1945 the flush door, symptomatic of efficiency in the use of materials and systematised production methods, has been in general use in London schools. As its manufacturers progressively managed to reduce its cost so did its quality reduce equally: they were responding to normal market pressures and cost limitation stringency steadily expected cheaper doors. Cheap doors in schools, however, are a poor economy and the early flush versions having hardboard faces, cardboard spacers and timber trimming to the two long sides, sometimes hardly survived the building contract's final account despite triumphantly meeting the needs of cost limits. In 1971 came the re-invigorated Fire Precautions Act and, although not yet applicable to school building, the ILEA has insisted upon the general upgrading of means of escape in its buildings since 1972: existing doors needed extra protective non-flammable panels added and ordinary glazed panels had to conform to the London Buildings Acts' requirements being of reinforced glass and of limited area only. This also acted as an incentive to regularise the standard of flush doors and for some years now only solid laminated timber doors are used anywhere in ILEA buildings: robustness has been restored and with it the omission of unecessary lower glazing to doors and side panels.

Specification of glass has been widely varied over the years and the incidence of accidents and their potential severity has been recognised by the current requirement to use laminated safety glass only, except where the London Building Acts specifically require reinforced glass in fire-resistant screens.

Since 1967 there has been an increasing educational requirement for room flexibility, initially for primary schools but later for secondary also: see Chapter 3 demonstrating the development of open-planning in primary schools – Prior Weston, John Evelyn and Hungerford continued to the present in Chapter 8 and Chapter 5 comparing two Secondary schools – Pimlico and Waterfield. The educational need has been for a day to day easily re-arranged teaching space with cost limitation inhibiting any sophistication. There has been no use of re-locatable partitioning systems but a mix of permanent spaces[14] with modular furniture (see Chapter 14) enables adaptation to changing needs within the existing framework of solid brick or block partitions.[15] The ILEA policy has been to provide 'initial variety' in order to offer a range of ready flexibility. It has been said that the quality most admired in the future will be the schools' 'susceptibility to alteration, adapation, transmutation ... meeting the changing demands of the

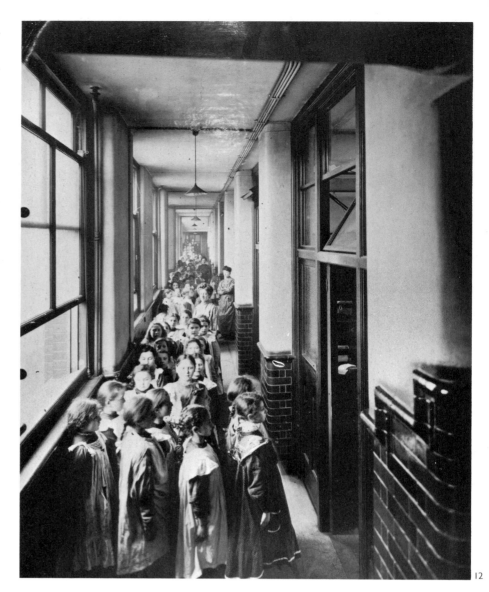

12

people who occupy them'.[16]

London's temperate climate and the 'Standards for School Premises Regulations, DES, have conspired to induce architects to design large windows to all teaching rooms: permanent supplementary artificial lighting installations (PSALI) were advocated by the DES in Bulletin 33, 1967, as an alternative to the high daylight factor required by the Regulations but these were not regarded as economic and have been used in one deep plan building only, Waterfield School (see Chapter 5). The consequential summer discomfort in rooms facing south-east to south-west has been compounded in some buildings by the increase of traffic noise and the torrid heat of 1976 finally caused some relatively new schools and colleges to need vigorous action to ameliorate unacceptable environmental conditions. Due to the economic need to double bank corridors and the developing stringencies of fire precautions, classrooms have not been cross-ventilated to provide the relief of air movement in summer. Solar film was used in some instances as a temporary expedient but methods of positive solar shading have been necessary. At Eaglesfield School, the exposed teaching block has had an

12 This view contains several interesting elements: a) the sheer hard wearing surfaces used in Victorian buildings – terrazzo flooring to corridors, glazed brickwork dadoes to 4' 0" (1.20 m) high on walls with hard plaster above requiring periodic painting only. Where glazed bricks are used the corners are rounded as are the plaster arrises above, b) single banked corridors allowed borrowed light from the corridor side into classrooms and cross-ventilation of the classrooms through fanlights, c) service pipes and conduits (the latter possibly added after the building was completed) are exposed but disciplined.

13

13

13 *The application of the 2% daylight factor to all working surfaces in all teaching rooms produced the popular vision of the modern school – large, high continuous windows. Since the end of cheap energy these represent elements of high heat cost in winter and when the summer sky is clear an unacceptable solar radiation gain. The latter can be more easily and cheaply solved than the former by the use of lightweight aluminium louvres giving shade in summer with the sun at its zenith and allowing low angle winter sunshine in the building. The supporting structure for the louvres permits easy access to windows for cleaning and maintenance.*

external horizontal light-weight aluminium louvre system added to provide positive window shading from May to September. The London Road Building of the Polytechnic of the South Bank suffered from excessive solar radiation due to the building's glazing profile, and experiments, using known computer programmes, were carried out to ascertain the optimal geometry of external louvre angles to allow normal window cleaning and maintenance whilst providing 100% shading from 9.30 am in May to September without enclosing the rooms in a continuous aluminium

carapace thus giving views to the outside. After using the summer of 1979 as a test period for various pilot schemes the installation was completed in January 1980. A pilot scheme monitored by thermograph in a room facing south-west showed that in August, 1979, with an outside temperature of 70 degrees Farenheit (21 degrees Centigrade) the room temperature reached a maximum of 75 degrees Farenheit (24 degrees Centigrade) at 4.00 pm whereas an unshaded room recorded 84 degrees Farenheit (29 degrees Centigrade). The external louvres had to be carried upon the existing patent glazing bars and live and dead loading were reduced to a minimum: a movable louvre screen operated by electric motors and controlled by electric photocells and mnemometers would have worked equally well but at twice the initial cost. Schools and colleges in inner London are now assumed to have a potential problem with solar radiation and rooms are positively treated to counteract it: if having to face south-east to south-west, windows are reduced to a minimum and shaded by overhanging eaves with the main light coming from the north, possibly using clerestorey lighting and cross ventilation – John Roan School

section demonstrates the current approach.

Until the late 1960's the majority of schools in inner London had coke-fired boilers with the need for voluminous storage and stoking: the coke shortage at that time caused the ILEA to replace these boilers with oil or gas-fired systems but conversion to oil was abandoned after the 1973 oil crisis. The increasing cost of energy since 1973 has had to be recognised in the fabric of school buildings. In 1972 the DES published 'Guidelines on Environmental Design in Educational Buildings'. It is significant that the title of Design Note No 17, 1979, is 'Guidelines for Environmental Design and Fuel Conservation in Educational Buildings'. This recognises the possible need for deeper planned spaces to meet educational requirements for the proximity of related activities and the consequent reduction of natural daylight levels from 2%. All elements of the building (new or remodelled) are to be considered with the intention of reducing electrical and heating input to within a recommended value of total energy consumption described in watts per hour using a primary energy unit factor, depending mainly upon heating fuel, to give a kWh/m² PEU.[17] Cost is also considered as measures taken to conserve energy should be self-financing in the long term, the total annual cost expressed in pence per metre square per annum: p/m² pa. The first two designs affected were Olga and Bellenden Primary Schools – see Chapter 8 – but it can be seen from the layouts how the tight site shape controls the aspect ratio (relation of building length to width) of the plan producing quite different architectural expressions with reduced window areas and higher levels of insulation.[18] Existing buildings are being more heavily insulated and windows are being checked for air leakage – bad examples are being replaced – but the major input into fuel conservation remains with different standards of expectation, better control systems and good daily housekeeping.

As building technology has developed countrywide since 1950 upon an unconsolidated foundation[19] due largely to a lack of full research budgets[20] – leaving a costly remedial trail emanating from high alumina cement, concrete additives, flammable plastics, inadequate adhesives and ill-digested building physics – so the need for supporting scientific investigation has grown.[21,22] The majority of ILEA building design and consultancy is carried out in-house and many of the questionable materials have not been used due to the weight of opinion against untried methods with the consequence that the majority of highly publicised building failures have not been experienced by the Authority. Investigative support is, however, always available from in-house scientists and materials specialists when problems have arisen and this has led to a large volume of reference and direction with proven details and specifications.

14

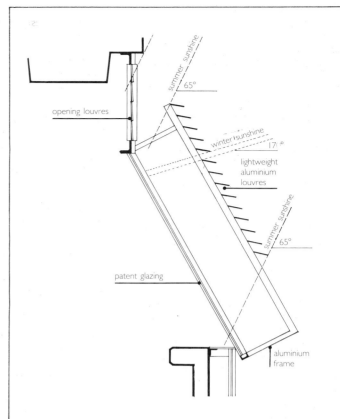

15

16

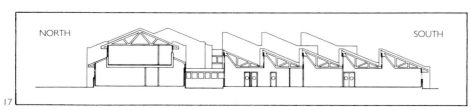

17

Within figure 15:

opening louvres

summer sunshine

65°

winter sunshine

17(°

lightweight aluminium louvres

summer sunshine

65°

patent glazing

aluminium frame

Within figure 17:

NORTH

SOUTH

14, 16 Upon a tight urban site surrounded by busy roads ordinary educational cost limits expose a building's users to unacceptable environmental conditions. In Fig 14 the original utilitarian nature of this college is revealed with areas of cheap — in capital terms — patent glazing cladding. Fig 16 shows the lightweight aluminium solar shading carried on the patent glazing bars. This section of the building was also recorded as receiving internally 66 dB(A) from the noisy adjoining main traffic route: double glazing was also fitted reducing the sound to 46dB(A) whilst more exposed rooms have had attenuated fans fitted for air supply/exhaust.

15 Lightweight aluminium louvres are carried on the patent glazing structure by means of an aluminium frame. This arrangement allows low angle winter sunshine to enter whilst precluding high angle summer sunshine except for one narrow band at high level. When standing, room users can see between the louvres and when sitting have an unobstructed view below them. A pilot scheme was used to determine the optimum spacing off the patent glazing face for cleaning and maintenance purposes.

17 John Roan School, Section
To counteract excessive solar radiation positive guidelines are followed at the design stage. Minimum windows only are oriented towards the South with overhanging eaves providing shade: main daylighting comes from the North with the possibility of cross-ventilation. See Chapter 7 for the layout of this deep planned school.

Chapter 10: References

1 Architects Journal, 27 January 1982, p 32: *relates that 'in the post-war period a whole series of coincidences and constraints . . . gave birth to new building methods'.*

2 Architectural Review, October 1972.

3 Ransom W H, Building Failures: Diagnosis and Avoidance, Spon, 1981, p 1.

4 What's New in Building, November 1981, p 97.

5 Allsopp B, A Modern Theory of Architecture, Routledge & Kegan Paul, 1977, p 35.

6 Architects Journal, 6 September 1972.

7 BRS Digest 144 HMSO states that mastic asphalt, properly designed and laid, should prove capable of lasting 50–60 years'.

8 Holmes R, and others, Maintenance Costs of Flat Roofs (Current Paper) BRE 1981 p 18, *concludes by regression analysis that upon school buildings lightweight flat roofs are consistently more expensive to maintain than heavyweight roofs (over a range of 4–35 years) and on p 6 states that, on domestic buildings, in the first thirty years after construction, at constant prices, flat roofs are estimated to have cost on average about four times as much to maintain as pitched roofs: in the sample used, flat roofs cost 30% more to build.*

9 MacEwan M, Crisis in Architecture, RIBA, 1974, p 22.

10 Service A (ed), Edwardian Architecture and Its Origins, Architectural Press, 1975, p 93.

11 Building Research Advisory Service (93), 1975.

12 Municipal Journal, 14 August 1981, p 652, comments upon Fallibroome School, Cheshire, noting the sheer quality but minimum size.

13 Arena (journal of the Architectural Association) November 1966, Attitudes to Architecture; Howell, Killick, Partridge and Amis, p 95–122, comparing minimal circulation with featureless bye-law streets.

14 Architects Journal, 7 January 1981, p 22.

15 Architect, January 1978, p 35.

16 Ward C (ed), British School Buildings, Designs and Appraisals, 1964–74. Architectural Press, 1976, Introduction (xiv).

17 Guidelines for Environmental Design and Fuel Conservation in Educational Buildings, Design Note 17, HMSO, 1979, p 15.

18 Building, 3 April 1981, p. 10, *reports the publication of an energy code by the Chartered Institute of Building Services (CIBS, Building Energy Code, Part 2) setting comprehensive target standards for energy consumption for a building's 'shape, thermal insulation, solar heat gain and the installations of heating, hot water, ventilation and lighting'.*

19 Ward C (ed), British School Buildings, Designs and Appraisals, 1964–1974, Architectural Press, 1976, Introduction (X): *School Architects 'to meet prescribed cost limits, have been obliged to welcome every new material or method which promises to reduce initial costs'. See Appendix C also.*

20 Building, 3 April 1981, p 11, *reports the continued neglect of proper research and development originally required in order to identify 'potential hazards likely to be of national significance'. As the BRE has been continuously starved of money and staff so brave governmental slogans increased attempting to disguise the long term effect of progressive cutbacks.*

21 Building, 12 February, 1982, p 29: *a prize-winning essay (Innovation of Failure) by Ted Happold sets out the rigid hierarchy of the building professions as being inimical to positive, competitive innovation.*

22 Construction News, 18 February 1982, p 5, *quotes a confidential report which aims to promote an independent national body to co-ordinate and fund construction research. Funding would be provided jointly by government and the building industry; using mandatory insurance as a means of generation funds to improve technical performance.*

Chapter 11
Maintenance

All buildings, like most other artifacts, begin to deteriorate as soon as they are completed: even if they are never used or occupied the climate alters chemical and physical properties and the decline, however gentle, begins. If a building is neglected its value and use are diminished and premature, accelerating deterioration will require heavy expenditure to achieve restoration. Maintenance is not an easily defined description but while there are as many opinions as there are building users and owners, most would accept that the aim should be to keep their buildings in a recognisably good state of repair.[1] Maintenance work covers a range of approaches, from the long planned maintenance set down over the years to replace worn and defective materials and components to the everyday minor work urgently required to keep a building, or a service, in use affording security and certainty to the users.

Until quite recently every year saw the number of ILEA buildings increase: the school and college populations were growing and required either more accommodation or the replacement of obsolete buildings with new. In inner London there are not many school buildings which predate 1870 but since then there has been continual expansion regulated by social development. The first period up until 1914 provided one third of the school buildings still in use today – seven hundred out of two thousand premises and seventeen million square feet out of a total of forty eight million. Suburban expansion between the wars gave three hundred new premises and eight million square feet. Since 1945 twenty three million square feet have accumulated from one thousand further premises. Premises do

not equal schools however and there are 880 primary and 210 secondary schools in Inner London (number of schools in use at August 1981). Additionally there are nurseries, colleges of further education, specialist colleges, day and residential schools for special education and five polytechnics all of which, except for the polytechnics, are maintained by the same organisation which provided them initially. These may appear to be a set of cold figures, mere statistics, but they represent buildings where a large number of people spend their working lives and the vast majority of inner London's children are formally educated and for the purposes of overall maintenance proper provision can only be made with well laid plans based upon known quantities. New education buildings may be firmly held in the embrace of cost limits but the cost is recognised and met – maintaining those same buildings is subject only to the scrutiny of the ILEA and the level of maintenance is a matter for the Authority's decision, this decision being based upon available information.

With such a large number of buildings in one ownership and used for similar purposes there are great advantages to be gained in cost and service from an established partnership between user, owner, designer and maintainer. The user may state a requirement, the owner sets levels of expenditure and general policy, the designer assesses previous building performance whilst the maintainer provides care of the fabric and service installations based upon continuing familiarity with the buildings. Knowledge of a particular building, or building type, is invaluable for maintenance and this explains how service is approached for the ILEA. Two

thousand buildings require large sums of money for proper maintenance – nationally it is estimated that the ideal amount spent on the maintenance of buildings should be the equivalent of between 1.5% and 2% of their replacement value and the ILEA is only marginally below this band.[2,3] Each year 90,000 separate maintenance jobs are carried out ranging from adjusting lavatory cisterns to complete re-roofing and the sheer size of the figures quoted – buildings and items – indicate the necessity for decentralisation just in order to cope with the flood of requests. By decentralising the maintenance organisation – four regions for inner London – into regional offices, which match the ILEA's own decentralised organisation, the local building user is brought into close contact with the local maintenance officers who carry out normal maintenance and regular inspections and become known and knowledgeable. In this way the scale of numbers and areas – mere statistics – are transformed into informal and mutual trust.

Due to the decline in the school population the picture has changed. Windows are still broken and roofs develop leaks and these are normal everyday occurrences which are dealt with promptly to reduce the likelihood of a more general deterioration leading to dereliction. With the reduction in the amount of floor area required or buildings necessary a more positive

1   Decentralisation of Maintenance
This map illustrates the relationship of the four maintenance regions and the location of their offices. In this way those responsible for maintenance became known to the building user to their mutual benefit.

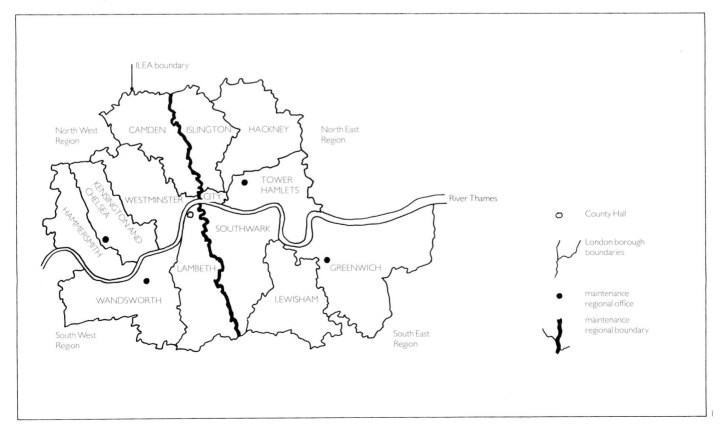

2

3

4

5

6

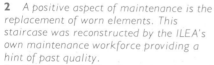

2 A positive aspect of maintenance is the replacement of worn elements. This staircase was reconstructed by the ILEA's own maintenance workforce providing a hint of past quality.

3 The design for this School Board for London building was used more than once in making elementary educational provision but it requires a coloured photograph to do justice to the mellow stock brickwork and cream coloured stone which were revealed when accumulated grime was cleaned off. With fresh collar and cuffs provided by gleaming white paint to the woodwork this educational facility has a new life ahead.

4 Sometimes it is necessary for the building designer to think positively about maintenance problems: here a simple material – patent glazing – offers an intractable problem through lack of access.

5, 6 Urinal slabs are a continuing problem due to the lack of a complete vertical waterproof membrane, such as asphalt, which will prevent the spread of noxious fluids into the building fabric. The slab and trough alone are insufficient and many are being replaced in planned maintenance programmes with stainless steel bowl urinals.

7 Flat roofs have generally cost more to maintain than pitched roofs although they were at one time cheaper to construct. Here differential movement without a slip joint exposes the false economy of incomplete detailing.

7

attitude grows, recognising the future needs of the ILEA: the premises which will represent the future building stock must be identified by the owner so that the fuller, planned maintenance service which is available additionally to the day to day care, can be used to its best advantage. As a consequence the proportionate amount of money spent annually upon daily maintenance over the last five years has declined and planned maintenance has increased: the third element of maintenance, redecoration, has remained constant as ILEA buildings are repainted externally on average every six years and kitchens every three years. As described in Chapter 4 the changing attitudes towards re-use of good quality older schools are reinforced by planned maintenance for when a school is positively identified as worth rehabilitation for its future role a new roof, complete electrical rewiring and replacement of the boiler installation may be good investments in radically altering and improving the building for its extended life. Where brick and stone cleaning are timed to coincide with rehabilitation and repainting the neighbourhood is offered a splendid new resource, aesthetic and educational, for the coming generations.

One major advantage of having the care of building in the same organisation as the production of buildings is the immediacy of feedback. When a particular material or detail can be demonstrated as deficient – or excellent – in use then the architect has every incentive to pursue the advantage of such information. He is made instantly aware of any problems arising from finished work, when his maintenance colleagues in the regions and in regular contact with the building users draw his attention to a detail or a specification. In this way the technical problems mentioned in Chapter 10 are exposed and solutions are sought jointly to everyone's advantage. More positive is the availability of the surveyor, who will maintain the finished building, during the detailed design process when decisions as to the use of alternative materials or arrangements must be made. Thus the flat roof, casement window and ironmongery can be discussed in the light of the surveyor's view of their longevity in the robust use of a school – see Chapter 10 also. These opinions are not based upon prejudice but upon observed conditions and their making: they are also reinforced by the general gathering of information from a huge sample.[4] The very size of the sample requires immense logical capacity and the computer, as a storage, comparative and retrieval resource, is welcomed. By the steady feeding in of quantitative information concerning the 90,000 separate annual maintenance jobs, it is possible to draw a profile of a building's likely cost in use. By careful programming the computer can give information as to the cost in use of various elements and materials as a

8 The most innocent detailing omission can serve to mar the appearance of a building – here algae has grown on a wall because the standard aluminium coping joint opened and allows a small amount of rainwater to drip on to the projecting brick panel below.

9 Ever since large areas of glass have been technically possible maintenance surveyors have requested the use of glass sizes which can be easily replaced without the use of scaffolding or cranes. Equally necessary in order to maintain the quality of appearance is the use of materials which can be expected to remain available: in their absence normal maintenance confers a patchwork effect upon a well-looked after building.

10 The desirable maintenance of a building in our climate requires the positive shedding of rainwater to keep its appearance. Flush detailing was a symbol of the international school of modern architecture but experience does not meet the ideal. With nothing to throw the water clear of the wall face at parapet level and at window sills maintaining the designers' original aims become impossible.

11, 12, 13 Flush detailing in joinery is not merely impossible to maintain in appearance – it requires constant work in gradual replacement until water is properly cast off the face of the building.

general guide, so that the architect can make use of feed forward based upon feedback. Here then, is the 'framework and methodology for assessing the effect of future costs in relation to initial construction costs and this enables choices of design solutions with differing first and future costs to be compared' as argued by all building economists.[5]

With a large building stock being used for similar purposes, budgeting becomes an essential tool and, based over many years experience, expenditure per square foot can be forecast with reasonable accuracy. Maintenance expenditure showed an increase in real terms of 30% from 1975 to 1979 but this reflected an overall average. Because each building is treated as a separate concern and is cared for individually, much information becomes available and, inevitably, is compared with similar buildings locally. Significant costs of day to day maintenance catch the eye. Why does school A have five times as much per square metre expended upon it as school B? How is it that school A has expended in locally determined every-day repairs sixty times as much as school B? The buildings are not necessarily identical in construction and finish but is it coincidental that A is a boys' secondary school and B is a girls' secondary school? School management has a positive role and is required to explain the reasons for abnormal maintenance costs and propose methods of reducing them.

Do boys habitually open all school doors with their feet? The casual study of pupil behaviour can do much to reduce the amount of repairs required in school building, particularly in secondary schools. Damage mainly emanates from sheer heavy use by careless teenagers and some from specific vandalism and it is a positive and highly successful ILEA maintenance policy to repair damage from any cause promptly – broken glass in an internal screen is not only a security risk but unsightly, dangerous and it encourages further damage or vandalism if not repaired immediately.[6] School management can do much to reduce mainten-ance expenditure – the heavy wear upon circulation areas, for instance, could be greatly reduced by the environment that the school sets out to achieve – and sympathetic design combined with essential measures can restrict damage (and vandalism).

A new word came into currency recently: terotechnology. It was being pressed by various government agencies as a key word in the quest for quality in construction, the proper use of scarce capital to produce buildings which would have low costs in use.[7] It assumes that architects designing schools are free agents in using allocated money and that by paying due attention to the wearing quality of materials the nation's economy would be relieved of much of the burden of building maintenance in future years: it has been generally accepted that whilst two thirds of the

output of the building industry creates new capital assets one third of output is required to maintain buildings. There are two elements which prevent the application of terotechnology in school building. Firstly, the building industry has changed – partly because of material shortage – from a craft-based to a technological industry. The period of change over was abrupt and the con-sequent lack of proper development and implementation exposed the industry as greatly under-capitalised and unable to achieve a new balance of production: the 'clear loss of craft skills has not yet been replaced by the relatively fault-free product typical of the truly indus-trialised process'.[8] Secondly, successive governments since 1949[9] have used tight central control over costs of new buildings. As rising costs were never fully allowed for in building programmes it was often necessary, in order to reduce costs, to effect economies both in detailing and specification.[10] Thus, whilst it might be considered normal that as the age of buildings increases there is a steady growth in the amount of planned maintenance, which must be undertaken to keep the buildings in a good state of structural repair, it is paradoxical that many of the hundred

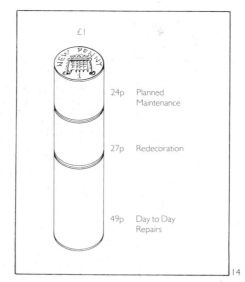
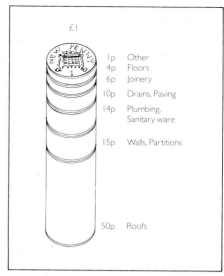

14   Total Maintenance Budget
This illustrates that just over half (51%) of the Budget is for planned maintenance or regular redecoration with the balance reserved for day to day repairs.
15   Planned Maintenance
For every £1.00 allocated for planned maintenance (see Fig 14 for overall Budget) this diagram shows how elements of building need to be catered for with heavy emphasis upon the needs of roofing which requires half of the expenditure.
16   *The older, traditional panelled door survived even in gymnasia for many years but the impact of the ubiquitous 5-a-side football tested some to destruction: only 1 hour, solid core doors are now specified in schools to reduce maintenance costs.*
17   *Double action hinges are often opened beyond the jamb opening straining the fixings and splintering joinery: this improved detail comes from maintenance experience and is now employed generally in remedial work to reduce leverage upon the screws leading to continuous replacement.*

18   *When school building design followed rationalised modular systems some elements became over-extended: here a 3'6" × 7'6" door (to suit the then current module) demonstrates that joint sizes may require future reinforcement through bracing rods as the bottom members cannot support the load of such a large heavy door. The maintenance of a building infers its serviceability and use: feedback from the maintainers limits similar over-sizing in future doors.*

19   *Doors of all ages in schools receive stresses well beyond their original designers' imaginations and instant repair is required to prevent further deterioration both to the doors and their general location. Here a door with a typically over-strained jamb receives immediate action because it has been demonstrated that prompt repairs reduce the likelihood of further damage.*

year old, solidly-built, robustly specified leviathans compare very favourably in maintenance costs with the more rapid deterioration recorded in some post war school buildings. Even with good, positive, swiftly reactive and far-sighted planning of maintenance work, the ILEA is only too aware of the results of restrictive capital cost limits, imposed by a centralised agency of government accounting, as the maintenance revenue costs inexorably mount due to building too cheaply and over which the DES expresses no opinion.

In the annual battle for funding capital spending programmes the Ministry of Education, succeeded by the DES, have proved singularly unsuccessful in obtaining sufficient money from the Treasury to permit the construction of schools of good quality. Comparisons both in area per pupil and cost per square metre show British educational budgets providing smaller and more cheaply constructed buildings than other European countries.[11,12,13,14,15] This parsimony may serve the national economy in the short term but centra-lised scrimping upon capital expenditure leaves the education authorities with the maintenance consequences of building too cheaply: the economist would say that 'the economic building is not necessarily the cheapest building but the one that provides the best value for

money'[16] The medium and long term consequences are continual disruption in teaching as defects are remedied, lack of flexibility in use, enhanced damage to vulnerable areas and tense relationships between teachers and providers. Even so, official government statements belie the facts: a Chancellor of the Exchequer can quite happily lecture architects and surveyors with 'Building economically does not mean building on the cheap. Money can be saved in the short term with cheap materials, but the life-cycle costs are often greater. A proper attitude to a project's economics could include using materials appropriate to the life of the building.'[17]

As the cost limits were too tight nationally – witnessed by many edu-cation authorities declaring their inability to provide long term economic buildings – they were grossly inadequate for inner London due to the much higher building costs in the capital and quite different sets of problems. Small sites, poor access, noisy roads, low-flying aircraft and competition with an energetic private sector intent mainly upon office block construction: all served to demand a higher capital allocation which was not forthcoming and have bequeathed a legacy of low cost building with consequential exponen-tially rising maintenance requirements.

Chapter 11: References

1 GLC Architects Review 2, Academy Editions, 1976, p 64.

2 Building Maintenance Cost Information Service – a continuous index from independent source.

3 Building Design, 22 January 1981, p 11, commenting upon a LAMSAC report Terotechnology and the maintenance of local authority buildings finds that maintenance spending for 1980–81 was of the order of 1% of the value of all schools, homes, day centres, libraries, civic centres, etc; housing was not included.

4 Ransom W H, Building Failures: Diagnosis and Avoidance, Spon, 1981; p 1: *calls for a 'system of information retrieval, better procedure for its dissemination and most important, the realisation that such an information search is desirable.'*

5 Stone P A, Building Design Evaluation: Costs-in-Use, Spon, 1980, Appendix A, p 185.

6 Lee R, Building Maintenance Management (2nd edition), Granada, 1981, p 1: *'The condition and quality of buildings reflect public pride or indifference . . . social values and behaviour'.*

7 Building, 8 January 1981, p 7, defines terotechnology as 'the application of managerial, financial and technical skills to buildings in pursuit of economic life-cycle costs'.

8 Ministry of Education, Circular, 209, 1949, introduced the concept of centrally controlled cost limits for education building.

9 Ransom W H, Building Failures: Diagnosis and Avoidance, Spon, 1981, p 151.

10 Service A (ed), Edwardian Architecture and Its Origins, Architectural Press, 1975, p 93: *E. Robson discovered in 1876 that 5% was the additional cost of 'a building of some architectural pretensions over the barest piece of mere construction'. The London School Board decided that it must be prepared to pay extra cost.*

11 The Times, 11 April 1975, which showed that in England £700 was spent in building each school place (unidentified) and in West Germany £1,416: *this recognised that the cost of construction per square metre in Germany was, at the time, 25% higher than the UK.*

12 Berliner Bauwirtschaft, Hefte 3 and 4, 1973.

13 Stone P A, Building Economy (2nd edition), Pergamon, 1976, p 18: *the problem is not confined to education buildings for the table illustrates the gross fixed capital formation as a percentage of the gross national product. The UK construction industry represents the lowest percentage in Europe and the USA: government policy has an important effect on the industry as it is responsible for half of the money spent on new buildings.*

14 A Study of School Building, DES, 1977, Annexe 2, paragraph 45, describes alarming deficiencies in the primary school building stock and a table indicates that at 2.20 m sq the teaching area per pupil (3.62 m sq gross) England and Wales provide the lowest area standards in Western Europe. See Appendix C also.

15 Bennet P H Mitchell's Architectural Practice and Procedure, Batchford Academic and Educational, 1981, however finds that 'building in the United Kingdom is significantly slower than anywhere else in the advanced worlds and as far as comparisons are practical, considerably more expensive'. This is unsurprising, reflecting an industry which is capital starved and, consequently, labour intensive.

16 Stone P A, Building Economy (2nd edition), Pergamon, 1976 Preface (xi).

17 Architects Journal, 5 November 1980, p 875, reports Sir Geoffrey Howe's address to the Association of Consultant Architects.

Chapter 12
The Aesthetic Challenge

Architecture is an inescapable and intrinsic part of the aesthetics of everyday life and the successive educational authorities of inner London, the School Board for Education, the LCC and now the ILEA, and their architects have been responsible for the inclusion of over 2000 buildings into the urban fabric. The school cannot be seen as an exercise in pure design any more than other urban buildings and its impact, is therefore, important. Rightly, as ordinary buildings offering service mainly in ordinary residential streets, their conception is dependent and relative. Upon rare occasions only are the buildings expected to be more than elements enclosing a street boundary and then a positive expression, either to maintain an important street's quality or to provide a criterion for future development, is the direct and desired outcome. In an inner city core with close proximity of buildings experienced by the passer-by, the connection of the building to the street and the promise of occasional longer perspective make the boundary edges and entrances vital ingredients in setting a sense of place and identifying the building's use.

The Victorians offered an exuberant, confident proliferation of styles, the architect having freedom to pursue the beautiful, and from 1870 their schools began to dominate their localities in London. Sites were small, closely enmeshed in the disciplined street network of housing, and the building volumes were large as each school was originally designated to accommodate between 800 and 1700 children. Such dense population and the use of town gas for lighting and, sometimes, heating required classrooms of large volume, the ceilings being over four metres high, to provide sufficient ventilation. As the massing of the school buildings grew so did their architectural importance in the city:[1] even now, after the deluge of towers of flats and office blocks the Victorian schools still stand out as urban landmarks, – 'brick islands in a lead coloured sea'[2] – with their contemporaries the corner pub and the church spire, in areas of two storeyed domestic terraces. In current planning terminology these schools would be 'out of keeping' because of their scale, their quite anarchic use of materials, colours and outlines and yet they became local images, centres of the community, focal points in an otherwise calm sea of domestic imperturbability for between 1890–1910 the Arts and Crafts Movement produced a blossoming in British architecture.[3] On other counts, mainly quantitative based planning, they would be unacceptable today for their small sites hardly contain their buildings: this presents teaching staff with problems as contemporary education requires increased use of external work areas and the playgrounds are often too small for the numbers of children at school. This crowding of a school on to a tight urban site, however, has enhanced the visual quality of the urban fabric for

in its setting it provides interest and rich comparisons of scale, the impact of which would be lost if these behemoths were to be seen in greater sanitised space rather than experienced close to. They are accepted as familiar elements of the urban scene and their scale and mass make them significant forms in a way that can experienced close to. They are accepted as familiar elements of the urban scene and their scale and mass make them significant forms in a way that can rarely be approached by today's low key schools where only occasionally a conception such as Pimlico (see Chapter 5) can capture the observer's sensibilities, – the sheer perversity of the architectural problem (a small, sunken site surrounded by older, larger buildings) has extruded a 'glinting facetted form' complementary to the larger buildings and 'a sufficient complexity' in its own right.[4] When a Victorian building has become obsolete and has been replaced by, for example, a hygienic, well-serviced, single storey block set back to a revised building line, there is an immediate sense of physical loss and the neighbourhood is architecturally diminished as tension and vitality are lost.

Is it possible by looking back over the last hundred years to see distinct phases of educational philosophy and its architectural consequences? The repetitive Victorian aesthetic exercises mirrored the authoritarian stance of the providers. The economically stagnant design exercises in school building between the two World Wars could not match the teacher's growing concern with a mutually acceptable teaching method. The great burst of individuality after 1945 reflected the progressive, liberal education policies current, showing the architectural response with a healthy and positive plurality – buildings reflecting the close influence of Le Corbusier, Mies van der Rohe, Tecton,[5] Stirling and, recently, Foster – and the house styles from Robson until 1939 were shattered. Now there is reassessment, of and reaction against, that progressive train – indeed the Modern Movement has been pronounced dead, rather like the report of Mark Twain's early demise[6] – which is beginning to be matched by a new architectural eclecticism and didactic revisionism which pose a generally recognisable and acceptable image[7] in an attempt to reassure the community[8] even if this requires the re-emergence of 'catalogued styles'.[9] Revered practitioners, just like Norman Shaw before them, have lost confidence in their own abilities and are reverting to academic canons of form.[10] Obsolete words are revived: 'aedicule' and 'elision'[11] are advertised as part of the current hunt-a-style historicism and a replica of Medusa's face transforms a wooden hut with 'explicit imagery meant to cue the perception of implicit meaning' or the equation of imagination with memory.[12] These factors demonstrate that there is no real correlation between educational

ideology and the aesthetic consequences of school building, for the architect here shows that he is largely a reflector of broader informed public attitudes and tastes, even of the present ambivalence: the built form has not determined the ideology. Modern architecture is evolving into a richer experience[13] than we have known over the last thirty years and, despite the academic slogans, schools will remain in the mainstream out of necessity. Schools present a recognisable image but sentimentality is no solution to the present impasse.[14]

Designers of inner London's schools and colleges have not generally pursued scientific aesthetic systems whether Fibonacci's algebraic series, Fechner's rectangles or Witmer's proportional preferences.[15] In eschewing formal correctness and symmetry for symmetry's sake they have also assumed that sublimity has little place in their buildings. One hundred years ago function required the massing of a Victorian school and from that sprang wholeness, proportion and clarity. Since then function has changed with the expectations of succeeding generations and the educational building has reflected its society chiming in time and firmness. Whereas Robson and Bailey adopted distinct styles of building for the Board and early LCC schools, their elevation principles pursued the needs of the street and not of the school building: the wide use of the Queen Anne style by Robson could be vindicated during the battle with Gothic by arguments which are again current.[16] From 1914 the needs of ventilation, daylighting and heating determined the school layout and orientation. The rise of the Modern Movement relaxed any sense of aesthetic purpose in the pursuit of functionalism – form was eschewed without content: 'purity, asceticism, anonymity, sobriety'[17] were the truths sought.[18] Now there is a movement towards architecture as art rather than being the 'self-referential dead end of technique'.[19] with this reversion going so far that 'rational thought is regarded as incompatible with intuition, scientific progress as inimical to art.[20] Nevertheless, it should not be forgotten that the Modern Movement is not a style but a rational approach to the design of useful buildings[21] and criticism from building users is immediate when this is forgotten.[22]

High brick walls or stout brick piers with decorative high wrought iron railings delineated the site at the rear edge of the pavement and one was aware of the mass of the perhaps unseen building from the scale and density of the very boundary. Traditional building techniques lent weight to the mass required to stabilise the top of a free standing pier or protect the top of a wall and these elements provide the close up, small quality of a Victorian or Edwardian city street which is universally recognised.

When the LCC developed its suburban housing estates, such as

203

1, 2   Two quite different architectural expressions presenting boundaries of similar quality to the adjoining streets. Entrances are celebrated by either a slender iron gate in a very solid brick wall (note how stoutly the gate was hung with the main load carried on a floor ring and the top hinge set into a large stone block) or a triumphal archway in decorated brickwork set into decorative iron railings.

3   It was recognised that the tops of walls needed protection against the weather and that brick or stone piers required added mass on their tops to stabilise them and in this illustration and Figs 1 and 2 structural necessity was transmitted into delight.

4   Small Victorian sites often produced overwhelming buildings but the scale of enclosure at street level remains human.

5   Athelney Elementary School, Site Plan

In the 1920's and 1930's the elementary school built on the LCC housing estates were a recognisable public element of the development without being disruptive. This was effected by having a building line similar to the adjacent houses, low development (usually single storey) and the use of similar materials to the houses in the neighbourhood.

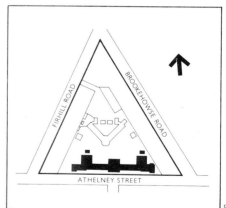

Bellingham, in the 1920's the school was provided with a larger, more fitting site in the expansive setting and was often given an important, focal position acting symmetrically as the closer along an avenue of mature trees as at Athelney, see Chapter 1. These schools were not set back from the normal building line and, as their scale was little more than the surrounding cottages, they were instantly a recognisable element in the street without being disruptive. They were redolent of continuity and appropriateness of function with an essence of rightness of place.

There was no straining intellectual effort to maintain and present a mathematical or metaphysical system – simply the right mass and materials. They were expected and accepted and the detailing of their boundaries demonstrates a simple but reserved use of materials with sturdy protective wooden fences backed by evergreen shrubs such as laurel or cotoneaster. This approach to detailing was in keeping with the neighbourhood whilst at the same time marking the school as a different site. The secondary schools of the time (see Red Lion, Eltham Hill, Chapter 1) were deliberately set apart educationally and architecturally, pursuing a debased classical style and managing to appear pompous but select.

The new post 1940 primary school, built in an area of existing older housing, can prove visually disruptive due to the needs of demolition which may interrupt a section of terraced housing or remove a pair of villas from a sequence. Replacement to a new building line some way behind the existing exacerbates the intrusion, and the scale of the new

school is unlikely to be sympathetic to the buildings already there. On economic grounds many such schools delineate their sites with 1.20 m high chain link wire fences as DES cost limits are not to be exceeded and the external works are usually reduced to gain financial approval. This form of control has had to be relieved in specific cases where the local borough, which is the planning authority in inner London, has insisted upon higher standards of site enclosure and the DES has allowed an increased cost under the heading of abnormals. At Ashmead Primary School (see Chapter 3) two large derelict houses were demolished to provide a site and Lewisham Borough Council required a screen wall to repair the visual damage and to provide an architectural link between the remaining houses. When a playspace was extended at Reay Primary School the Lambeth Borough Council refused to accept the standard chain link enclosure and a stronger, more elegant and, in the longer term, more economical fence resulted. These decisions were not pursued within the context of aesthetics as such but as the need for correct quality which, however humble the artifacts, maintains the rightness of purpose.

Without attempting to match the scale or size of its neighbours, Crawford Infants' School has improved the quality of the streets which surround it and demonstrates the easing of a building into its locality.[23] An alien intrusion would have been too easy without the overall humanitarian pursuit and demonstration of function. The surrounding three storey Victorian terraces with heavy bay windows and party walls

extruded above the roof line and their newer neighbouring four storey flats have, at first floor level and above, been given a length of perspective across the school site and the sheer interest of a modern building with all the business of a thriving primary school. But it is the street user who has gained more from the careful connection of the school boundaries to the back edge of the pavement, for here the external life of the school carefully unravels. The pedestrian is presented with a series of snapshots as the stout enclosing wall – articulated in plan to give greater unbuttressed strength – gives way periodically to steel fencing allowing glimpses of youthful endeavour and activity whilst offering the children security and protection. The pedestrian entrances are recessed to slow down decently those leaving school excitedly each day, and the quality of the urban finish is reflected in the neat brick paviors leading into the school. Crawford is another instance that primary schools are 'the main success of post-war British architecture'.[24] This was because they were concerned not with the sterility of spurious functionalism paraded as a style but with the perceived needs of the users: simple, humane and unsentimental architecture was the result. Being subdued it is more enduring and satisfying.

In order to avoid the total disruption of an existing Victorian street of neat repetitive facades some primary schools have been able to reinforce the perspective damaged by the demolition necessary for their site. The modern primary school could not easily sit on the existing building line due to the

6 Athelney Primary School
The garden at the main front has matured and evergreen shrubs proliferate: trees planted along the road are also full size. The original oak fence offered security and a clear distinction between school and street whilst admitting the school building, in materials and massing, as conterminous with the estate cottages.

7 Athelney Primary School
The oak fence has stood for fifty years and has gained a silver maturity. Necessary maintenance is achieved with the addition of zinc straps to reinforce the original nails as they have corroded.

8 Ashmead Primary School
When a row of three storeyed Victorian houses in a derelict condition were demolished to provide part of a site for a new primary school the local planning authority insisted upon a screen wall to link the remaining buildings instead of the normal chain link fence. Trees were retained and a better quality steel fence was allowed as an 'abnormal cost' to meet planning requirements.

9 Ashmead Primary School
When finished in 1972 the wall, with its punctuating but blind doorways matching the original and remaining, was seen as a somewhat whimsical requirement. By 1980 it would have qualified as full-blooded Post-Modern.

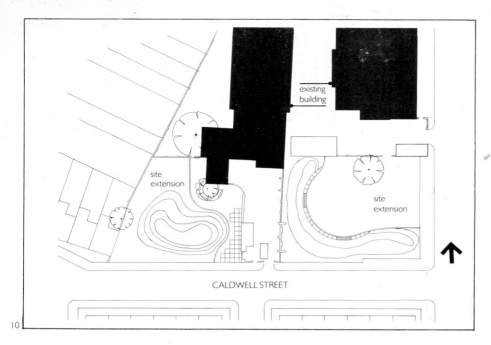

10 Reay Primary School, Site Extension
Typical of many old urban schools Reay was built upon a very small site and when the opportunity arose to provide better amenities than a few square metres of tarmacadam the ILEA took it.

The design shows how the rigid additional areas were landscaped with grass, paving and built-in seating to introduce a measure of delight into an otherwise shabby environment.

11, 12 Reay Primary School
The normal chain link wire mesh on slender steel angles is usually all that can be afforded in meeting cost limits for providing enclosure to school sites: when damaged it sags and attracts further damage. At this playspace extension a 3.00 metre high fence was required to keep balls within bounds and would-be intruders out. Lambeth Borough Council refuses to accept chain link fences upon planning grounds and this sturdy enclosure was designed with mild steel square section stanchions, angle rails and welded mesh for the panel infill: its additional cost will be repaid many times in lack of maintenance and sheer effectiveness without attempting to quantify its value to the street scene.

13, 14 Reay Primary School
In addition to a playspace extension the site of this school was extended to provide amenity in an otherwise deprived area. Old brick walls were retained and repointed, new accesses provided from the school and existing trees retained and protected. Retention to adjacent walls required higher ground levels and brick seats were introduced similar to those incorporated in the tree root enclosures.

15 Crawford Primary School
The addition of a new infants' and nursery wing upon a narrow sliver of land broke the original street enclosure but offered new perspectives to the adjacent houses. In the foreground is the nursery class and its external play area with granite setts used to provide both mounds and enclosures – the sand pit is protected by the wigwam. This school demonstrates the problem of scale between new single storey primary schools and neighbouring Victorian houses: upon an island site such as this the problem

is reduced but when a site is provided by the removal of a section from a similar terrace the physical loss is difficult to replace.
16 Crawford Primary School
The boundary assumes a greater importance with a low, small scaled building and the pedestrian is invited to have a passing interest in the local school. Boundary detailing demonstrates all of the points to be considered with reference to the street: structural stability, security from intruders, security for those infants

wishing to race home at the end of the day and the use of materials to signify quality and continuity.
17 Crawford Primary School
Apart from elevational appearance most inner London primary schools need careful consideration of the roof – the fifth elevation – due to overlooking. The deep building required for flexibility and open planning usually requires roof lights and these show a particular elegance contrasting with the heavy bay windows on all sides.

educational requirements of the brief, but it is still possible to contribute to the neighbourhood by its setting. At Nightingale Primary School (see Chapter 8) an awkward falling site has been carefully integrated into the street by bold cascades of brick boundary walls, which stand at the back of the pavement and undulate like large bay windows to signal entrances and their immediate protection. Existing trees are preserved, in fact, some schools have been designed around them as at Brooklands (see Chapter 2), and supplemented by new stock. New vistas open across and into school sites and the locality gains. The caring continuity as generations succeed communicates the unity of mankind and is expressed as contemplation or satisfaction.

Many of the ILEA's schools for educating the handicapped are either in suburban London or out in the country-side where large houses have been adapted for a new residential use. But inner London still has the need for day special schools, particularly for the physically handicapped or for the educationally sub-normal and both of these types of schools need to offer security and obvious protection to their users. Consequently they seek to exclude the street with its interruptions and over-interested pedestrians with high walls providing the necessary separation. In ordinary residential streets the potential bleakness of unrelieved walls at the back edge of the pavement would be unwelcome, perhaps even inviting local hostility, and at Bromley Hall School for physically handicapped children (see Chapter 13) the architect has expressed the building form with tall sweeping roof shapes which provide interest and variety in an otherwise unattractive environment. These roofs serve a specific, skylighting purpose but they also represent an exercise in high style and individual expressiveness.[25] Whilst the Bromley Hall roofs convey an impression of an ordered hierarchical society 'through a consistent architectural vocabulary'.[26] reflecting a tight, ordered plan, a similar problem at Queen Elizabeth II Jubilee School for educationally sub-normal children (see Chapter 13) was solved with a rambling plan, which allows the completeness of each entity and this is expressed spatially by the individual roofs conveying the feeling of a small village as they congregate in an apparently random fashion. Both provide a special resource to the community and each presents its own positive contribution to urbanity with the external walls and roofs framing and expressing their spatial and stylistic concepts.

Although the new primary school or special school is usually built in a residential area and finds a fitting scale for its size and sympathy for its use, as a local resource, the ILEA's larger buildings for further and higher education are often placed along major traffic routes and are distinctly major elements in the hard, urban landscape. Their scale

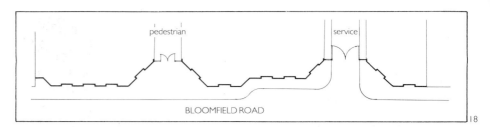

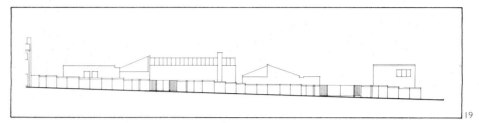

BLOOMFIELD ROAD

208

23

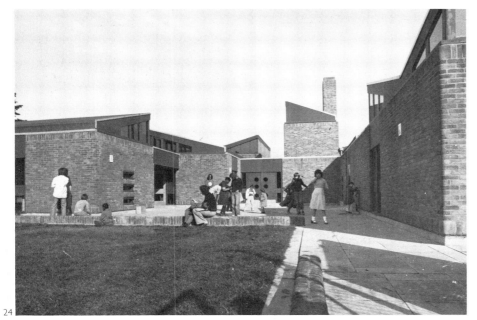

24

registers importance and they have a larger physical presence than education alone might imply. The Polytechnic of Central London's College of Architecture (see Chapter 15) holds a vital place in Marylebone Road providing 'highly successful street architecture'.[27] There is a danger of the blocks on the south side of the road becoming a series of blind boxes, without countervailing perspective, compared with the north side which has the dark trees and elegant terraces of Regent's Park, always drawing the eye to relief and lushness away from the aridity of the harder, less lively south. The college presents a clear picture of all the heroic principles of the modern movement, with its clean structural lines emphasising the elegant engineering, the bold emphatic forms of the high level studios cantilevering out over the pavement, the sculptured staircases at the end of the teaching block offering interest and modelling and above all the ingenuity of diverse use with a limited palette of materials – white concrete, silver aluminium, coloured curtains – emphasising the planes and cubes and structural inter-penetration.[28] The teaching block is part of, and in scale with, its neighbours in Marylebone and yet it offers more to the Road, for over the paved podium, one metre above the adjoining pave-ment, its cool, classical, suspended lines frame trees and planting and vistas into a nearby park. Its contribution to town-scape is as great again as its educational offering as architecture is demonstrated as a formal art whilst not pursuing an intellectual ideal.

By comparison with Marylebone Road, The Polytechnic of the South Bank's London Road Building (see Chapter 15) inhabits a harsh environment at the Elephant and Castle. The area is still desolate forty years after it was heavily bombed in World War II and large new buildings stand in isolation from the pattern of narrow old streets. There is no proper context or point of reference for a new building in London Road and so the architects had to provide their own on the longest site boundary along that road. As a consequence the whole site was developed as a single, unified block four storeys high but standing half a floor down at the original basement level. The building is compact and its periphery is extended to retain the whole site providing a built wall to all surrounding pavements whilst giving an assured identity. The major elevation confronts the heavily trafficked London Road and this has been given a bland blank wall of hard, red, self-cleansing tiles, relieved only by a single row of cantilevered, sloped windows to offices spanning between staircase and service pylons which mark the main entrance. The building has identity: it demon-strates integrity and thoroughness and there is a response to systematic logical apprehension with a completeness shown in the fact that no cladding tile required to be cut, thus meeting Perret's stated ideal. With its insistent

18 Nightingale Primary School, Main Entrance Plan
Primary schools cannot easily complement either in volume or adjacent space the remainder of a residential street however small the houses. In this instance a stout boundary wall was articulated (functionally, to produce strength without buttressing) in plan to produce smaller scale brickwork panels with the entrances treated as large bays to signal access and provide shelter.
19 Nightingale Primary School, Elevated View of Wall
20 Brooklands, West Elevation
Where large specimen trees, such as cedars of Lebanon as shown here, are already available on sites great care is taken to incorporate them as dynamic design catalysts: see Chapter 2 for the plans of this school. On inner London school sites great care is taken to preserve almost any mature stock and then supplement it with new planting.
21, 22 Bromley Hall
In a mixed and generally unattractive

neighbourhood the school provides a complete environment within the protective boundary walls. Roof lighting is essential and this is provided through tall sweeping shapes with skylights at the apex and these are vigorously expressed to the benefit of the locality.
23 Queen Elizabeth II Jubilee School
Schools for the educationally sub-normal need to offer security and enclosure for the handicapped child and this is demonstrated in the resulting architecture. Pavilions contain classrooms for differing age groups in association with external courts for playspace: main lighting comes from clerestorey windows with slots in the walls for outside viewing. The educational needs provide the aesthetics of the grouped pavilions.
24 Queen Elizabeth II Jubilee School
Although not reflecting the strict hierarchical plan of Bromley Hall – see Figs 21, 22 – the pavilions of Queen Elizabeth build up into a village of buildings with a recognisable centre as they rotate in plan.

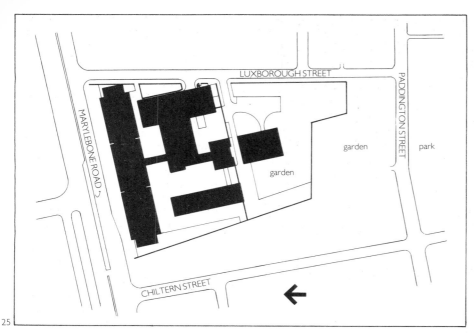

25

26

25 Polytechnic of Central London, Site Plan
Although this is a large, important development in Marylebone Road it allows visual relief from the hard, urban landscape by allowing glimpses and long vistas under the main teaching block and past the other individual buildings to gardens and parks with trees.

26, 27 Polytechnic of Central London
The large teaching block is articulated along Marylebone Road by vertical service shafts demonstrating elegant engineering, bold, emphatic forms and integrity of detailing.

28 Polytechnic of the South Bank
The integrity of the design is demonstrated by the expression of the 750 mm module upon which the structural system of the building is based being taken through the elevations with the limited vocabulary of patent glazing, dark red tiles and tubular steel handrail.

29 Polytechnic of the South Bank
The building presents a spare discipline and point of reference in an otherwise decaying area with its clear, crisp planning expressed as solid geometry.

27

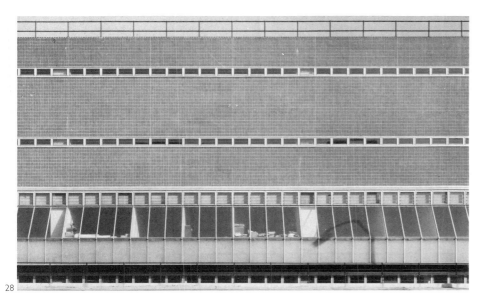

28

29

interest and interplay. With four storeys progressively stepping back and the mass of the block broken at three points to clarify access to its day centre, main school and social services suite, it has matched and continued the scale of the existing buildings in the road. Then the section of the building relaxes in a series of terraces southwards towards the park with its dark, lush trees. It has become a genuine symbol of local expression through its function and its placement and massing affirm this.

Education buildings cannot be appreciated independently of their utility. It is possible to view isolated examples purely as sculpture but this presupposes that one can judge the beauty of a thing in the abstract. Schools by their size and location constitute important features of their own environment just as their own environment is an important feature of them. Generally, in inner London, school buildings have accorded with the sense of place and are unique in their setting – the exceptions being some small post-1960 primary schools and those constructed from systems (see Chapter 3) which cannot meet the existing local scale successfully. Even this should be viewed as significant modesty.

The aesthetic problem of school building is that associated with the appreciation of novelty – the shock of the new: whether in 1873 when Robson started to build unusual shapes and masses very rapidly or after 1945 when a novel form – low flat roofs, wide plate glass windows, unusual materials like concrete and steel and the introduction of bright colour – was accepted into the London scene and even now curved steel carapaces smooth their way into settled neighbourhoods. Fortunately the appreciation of aesthetics continually changes and develops with the absorption of experience:[30] 'meaning is not an attribute of form, but a belief about form'.[31] It was only in the post-1918 suburban setting that the school was part of the same palette of the local housing and sank back into its neighbourhood. Architecture as the art of the ensemble is demonstrated at Hampton Court Palace, colleges at Oxford and Cambridge and the gothic cathedrals: they demonstrate that harmony is more than stylistic unity and now the brick buildings of 1873 are bearing adaptations and extensions in glass, concrete and sheet steel which currently may appear not to harmonise but are part of today's conception of the totality of the schools.

In school architecture the pursuit of aesthetics is peripheral to the art of building[32] – it is not fundamental and a successful school will not necessarily emerge from a generalised system of aesthetics – where the main aim is to be straightforward, honest, approachable, unselfconscious and relevant to purpose, for the school is essentially a public object: the expression of function in a utilitarian building becomes architectural homage to a non-spiritual objective.[33]

750 mm module taken rigorously through the elevations, with the limited materials of patent glazing, dark red tiles and tubular steel handrail, London Road has been offered a spare discipline, a spartan order and, although to some it seems an over-formal expression, a proper sense of place in the environment is the result and should offer a reference for all development along this blasted strip.[29]

Most new secondary schools have little immediate positive architectural bearing upon their locality as, even on the restricted inner city site, they usually break the original street building mass needing to be set back to afford service access and full exploitation of the space around them. Then they become remote from the street user who is aware of the fence and planting and gates and, distantly, a building alien in its form and position. When George Green's Centre (see Chapter 9) was designed for the Isle of Dogs to replace an old grammar school the architect had several options. Directly across the River Thames is Wren's Royal Hospital, now the Royal Naval College, with its powerful symmetry reflecting Inigo Jones' Queens's House immediately to

the south. It would have been possible to continue this baroque symmetry across the river on to the school site but this would have required a large gesture to be meaningful with the school building piled up beyond all educational function to provide a sufficiently scaled mass. On the shore line of the Isle of Dogs is a park with a large number of full size mature trees and it would have been necessary to master these also with the school to provide a continuing axis. Much more to the point is the fact that the school serves the local community with a particularly strong sense of its own needs and character and the school is therefore placed immediately on the pavement line heralding availability to all. Rather than obeying the distant grandeur of Greenwich, the building fulfills a local townscaping need as it guides a slow bend in Manchester Road, marking the apex of the curve with its thrusting theatre/gymnasium block in close collusion with the adjoining spire of the Church of Christ and St. John. Having achieved the smooth transition of the road curve, the building relaxes with undemonstrative expression, for its detailing is simple blockwork with steel windows, relying on its proportions for

211

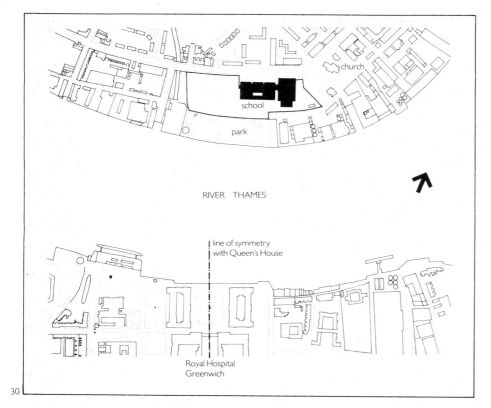

RIVER THAMES

line of symmetry
with Queen's House

Royal Hospital
Greenwich

30

30 George Green's Centre, Site Plan
Although, to the South, Greenwhich exerts a powerful symmetrical pull the Centre's main function is to serve the local community and an architectural response to Wren and Inigo Jones would have produced a building which could not fulfil its main requirement.

31 George Green's School
The design was developed so as not to participate in the axial symmetry of Greenwich to the south across the Thames. It is part of the local street and this is emphasised by its role in marking the bend of Manchester Road with its projecting theatre/recreational block in conjunction with the adjoining spire of the church of Christ and St John. Mannerism is achieved for an honest aesthetic of human scale and approachability.

32 George Green's School
The street front progresses in section to the informal teaching layout as the building steps down to the south with terraces overlooking a Thameside park. The simple building material of concrete block is moulded providing massing to delineate the parts of the building with the crisp, taut staircases acting as articulators and separators of function.

33 George Green's School
The park side of the building shows the movement from formal street front to relaxed recreation complete: in addition to the informal massing as the terraces descend, the detailed simplicity of the parts further reduce the apparent size of a large building.

34 Montem Elementary School
When Robson started producing school buildings they were Gothic in spirit but rapidly matured into the Queen Anne style then currently in favour. Bailey followed Robson and Classical detailing began to be expressed.

All of these exercises were novel in the London scene both in scale and appearance although built from the prevalent technology.

35 Langdon Park
Even as the large Victorian school represented novelty in the London streets so the present extensions in steel, aluminium, plate glass and concrete offer a contemporary use of available technology in the total conception of the campus now.

31

32

33

34

35

Chapter 12: References

1 Service A (ed), Edwardian Architecture and Its Origins, Architectural Press, 1945, p 93: *points out that in 1876 the School Board decided to pay the 5% additional cost for buildings of architectural pretensions 'over that for mere construction'.*

2 Girouard M, Sweetness and Light: the Queen Anne Movement, 1860–1900, Architectural Press, 1977, p 64.

3 Architects Journal, 12 November 1980, p 916: *review by Service A, of Arts and Crafts Architecture: 'The search for earthly paradise'. Davey P, Architectural Press, 1980.*

4 Architectural Design, April 1966, p 177.

5 Frampton K, Modern Architecture; A Critical History, Thames and Hudson 1980, p 253: *traces Lubetkin's powerful influence in the LCC example of his 'extended facadism' and it is possible to trace this same approach to the large secondary school of the mid-50's – see Chapter 2, Garratt Green and William Penn Schools.*

6 Watkin D, The Rise of Architectural History, Architectural Press, 1980: *is happy to state in the Preface (xi) 'now that the Modern Movement is over . . .' However, in the New Statesman, 3 April 1981, p 19, Burford W, says that it is a fashionable gesture to declare the end because the perceived end is obviously providing so many with so much employment. It may be more profitable to view the Movement not as a path leading to a finite destination but as a journey towards a prospect – see Reference 12.*

7 Girouard M, The Outside Story, Times Literary Supplement, 23 February 1973: *argues for a return to a more acceptable – possibly classical architecture. The parallel with classical dogma is the prefabricated industrialised system: both are based upon misguided utopian morality and both insist that function is subordinate to dogma narrowing the range of options within very strict conventions – see Chapter 3 for the bondage imposed by system building.*

8 New Statesman, 3 April 1981, p 19, Buford W: *says that 'Modern Art has always assumed the values of originality: that the noteworthy will be found in the new'. In school design this may have been the case after 1945 (see Chapter 2) as the new educational buildings were the standard bearers for the functional approach to the brief and its expression. Over the intervening years Wordsworth's reflection of*

*'. . . craving for the marvellous gives way
To strengthening love for things that we have seen,
When sober truth and steady sympathies,
Offered to notice by less daring pens,
Take firmer hold of us . . .'*

may have grown in strength both in architects and the general public but without a general desire to return to an antique form of building. Alvar Aalto also noted that 'Repetition and use make everything acceptable'.

9 Lethaby W R, in a speech at the Architectural Association, 1915, was concerned to defend 'English free building' against 'catalogued styles'.

10 Scott G, The Architecture of Humanism, Constable, 1947, p 200: *recommended the use of academic form (i.e. classical) whereby 'even the uninspired architect could secure at least a measure of distinction'. The danger of this approach is that, deprived of fresh circulation, it might lead to a hardening of the categories. A further problem is that the theoretical basis of classical aesthetics (based upon the beliefs of the fifteenth century) cannot be re-established upon the basis of modern physics; even when almost any building appears to be able to be included in Free Style Classicism (AD 52, 1/2, 1982).*

11 Architectural Design, May/June 1980, Post-Modern Classicism, p 12.

12 Hobbes T, Leviathan, 1651, part I, chapter VI: 'Imagination and Memory are but one thing'.

13 Architectural Record, January 1981, p 72 and Architectural Design 51, 1/2 1981, p 9. *Ada Louise Huxtable sets out an optimistic answer to those who proclaim the death of the Modern Movement placing it and Post Modernism, Post Classicism, Abstract Formalism into context.*

14 Architects Journal, 19 March 1980, McKean J M, 'The Images of School' p 578.

15 Rowe C, The Mathematics of the Ideal Villa, MIT Press, 1976, compares and contrasts: *proportional systems used upon well-known buildings (eg Corbusier's Villa Garches and Palladio's Villa Malcontenta) but such intellectual rigour was not generally pursued in London's school buildings.*

16 Builder, 1874, pp 539–540, Stevenson J J, – a founder of the Queen Anne style described it as 'the common vernacular style'.

17 Architectural Design, November/December 1980, Supplement, The Counter Reformation.

18 Progressive Architecture, May 1974, p 74: *in reaction to the Modern Movement's dogma of 'ornament is crime' came Robert Stern's new slogan 'contextual, allusive and ornamental'. The reissue of Robert Venturi's 'Complexity and Contradiction in Architecture' in 1977 (originally published by the Museum of Modern Art, New York in 1966) by the Architectural Press gave the new eclecticism a new handbook.*

19 Architectural Review, February 1981, p 75.

20 Cantacuzino S, Howell, Killick, Partridge, Annis: architecture, Lund Humphries, 1981, p 43.

21 Architects Journal, 23 September 1981, p 605.

22 Building Design, 12 March 1982, p 6: *the general administrator of the newly opened Barbican Centre is quoted as saying 'Many architects want to see the form triumph over the function of a building'.*

23 GLC Architects Review, 1974, Academy, pp 36–37.

24 MacEwan M, Crisis in Architecture, RIBA, p 16.

25 Architects Journal, 27 August 1969, pp 505–522.

26 Architects Journal, 20 August 1969, p 433.

27 Architects Journal, 2 June 1971, p 1255.

28 Architectural Review, January 1971, pp 833–846.

29 Architects Journal, 28 April 1976, pp 833–846.

30 Scruton R, The Aesthetics of Architecture, Methuen, 1979, p 84.

31 Bonta J P, Architecture and Its Interpretation, Lund Humphries, 1979, p 12.

32 Seaborne M and Lowe R, The English School, Its Architecture and Organisation, Vol II, 1870–1970, Routledge & Kegan Paul, 1977, pp 152–153.

33 Allsopp B, A Modern Theory of Architecture, Routledge & Kegan Paul, 1981, p 9.

Chapter 13
Special Education

Before 1939 in inner London it was possible to discover discreet, modest, neat timber constructions known as open air schools. They were formed from individual classrooms, approximately 20'0'' (6.00 m) square, raised from the ground on stout brick piers and they had pyramidal pitched roofs. Their sides were only half enclosed, the remainder being open and they were for the delicate children of the neighbourhood: occasionally a local elementary school had an isolated classroom of this description enabling the delicate child to attend what was ostensibly an ordinary school. There was also a duty for the local education authority to provide special education for blind, deaf, physically handicapped, epileptic and mentally retarded children. The history of this provision is long. In 1872 the London School Board began to provide education for the deaf and the blind long before legislation requiring this was made. They were educated in special centres attached to ordinary schools, fourteen for the deaf and twenty-three for the blind where some blind teachers worked also. By 1896 there were twenty-four special schools for the physically and mentally handicapped.

The education authority's duties were extended to ten categories by the Education Act 1944 with the addition of the partially sighted, partially hearing, educationally subnormal, maladjusted, delicate and those with speech defects. The types of handicaps have changed considerably since 1944: poliomyelitis and tuberculosis have virtually disappeared and the number of blind and delicate pupils has declined sharply whereas those suffering from spina bifida, multiple handicaps, educational subnormality and maladjustment have increased. Until 1971 mental health committees had catered for the severely subnormal categorised as 'unsuitable for education' but these then became the responsibility of the education authority. See Appendix D for provision and expenditure pattern 1947–74.

Inner London is a sufficiently large area with a large enough population to need to provide special buildings for the specific education of the handicapped, catering for their varied disabilities in detail. Because of the particular nature of handicaps and the provision of specialised education, over 50% of places at some ILEA school are filled by children from other education authorities. Many of the disabilities require boarding education and the majority of these schools are located in the countryside around London where, typically, a large existing country house or mansion has been adapted and extended to provide a suitable home and school for the handicapped: however, many purpose built special schools have had to be built in inner London to cater for local needs.

What these schools seek to do is to reinforce the child's impaired ability in order that the child may be assimilated into the community upon becoming adult: in order to provide continuity of education the schools offer education to the 5–16 age range. By careful, detailed design the architect can offer the school building and its environment as a direct aid for the disabled: the partially sighted are given very high levels of lighting, artificial and natural: the partially hearing have very quiet buildings with electronic acoustic enhancement: the physically handicapped are offered every conceivable physical aid, including a large physiotherapy pool in which limbs can be relaxed, manipulated and taught. The very handicaps and their reduction provide architectural form through the specific function that they provide.

The Warnock Report, 1978, The Education of Handicapped Children and Young People, did not specifically recommend the integration of handicapped pupils into ordinary schools but reinforced the principle that handicapped and non-handicapped should be educated in a common setting so far as possible. Categories of handicap will be ended under future legislation (White Paper, 1980) and requirements will be based on the concept that certain children have a special educational need'. The 1981 Education Act new approach means that instead of 2% of children being in need of special provision 20% of the total will need some special education at some time in their school lives.[1] This represents a move away from what the handicapped cannot do to an appreciation of what they can achieve given assistance and opportunity: they will benefit socially from being taught with their non-handicapped peers and academically from their access to a greater range of specialists and facilities. In common with the ordinary ILEA primary and secondary school the special school is now beginning to be equipped with computers and their effect, with the integration of the handicapped, will be far reaching in the need for special buildings. A modified curriculum programme is available for children with language, behavioural and sensory-motor difficulties and the individual needs of those whose difficulties reflect a wide spectrum of learning and study problems: this will assist the attendance and integration of handicapped children into ordinary schools perhaps rendering the special school obsolete.

Shawcroft School

The first fully residential school for maladjusted children was built at St. Mary Cray, Bromley, for fifty boys aged 10 to 16 years.[2] The building is set in the old kitchen garden of Kevington Manor and the garden's original walls are incorporated into the design firmly enclosing[3] the two connected L-shaped blocks around a courtyard.[4] On three sides of the courtyard there is a covered walk and the grouping provides domesticity[5] and shelter as the site is bordered to the south and north by open agricultural land. The school was designed in 1970 and finished in 1974.

Teaching accommodation is contained in the single storey east wing with a gymnasium and communal facilities to the south. On the north side is the staff residential accommodation of flats and bedsitters with child care facilities. Above this there is accommodation for the boys, a mixture of dormitories and single bedrooms: child care experts have flats at this level also.

The form is a deliberate attempt to convey a sense of unity, restfulness,[6] shelter and security[7] and the courtyard is the key to this environment with areas for sitting and quiet activities affording easy access to the communal rooms via the covered ways: internal corridors are reduced to a minimum.

Load bearing walls for the ground floor support a concrete slab in order to allow a quite different room layout on the first floor with special trusses carrying the pitched roof to the external walls. The roofs are low-pitched with wide overhangs and unify the different

1 Site Plan
The school building completes the shelter offered by the original kitchen garden walls with an enclosed courtyard layout.

2 Ground Floor Plan
The teaching wing is to the East and shows a full range of educational activities with a different scale and organisation than usual, the rooms tending to be self-contained yet informal in character. Staff accommodation to the North consists of flats and bed-sitters with child care facilities. Communal activities are located on the South side of the quiet, sheltered courtyard.

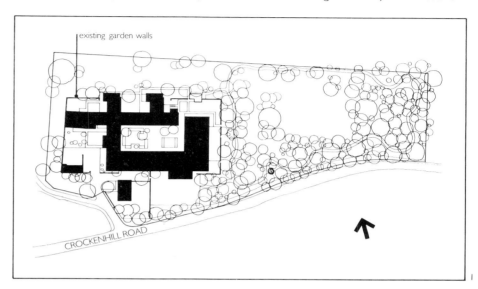

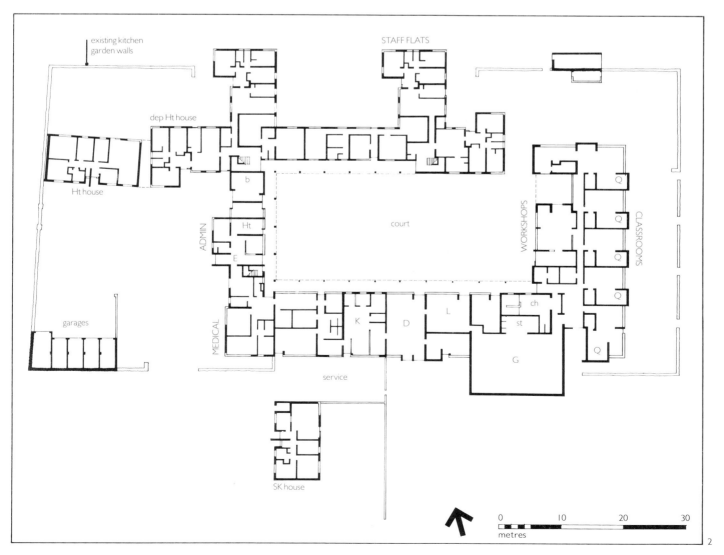

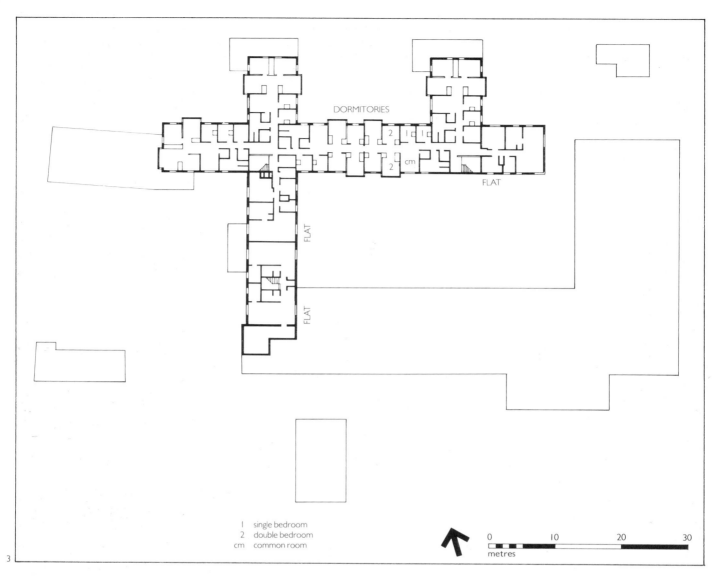

DORMITORIES

FLAT

FLAT

FLAT

1   single bedroom
2   double bedroom
cm   common room

0   10   20   30
metres

3

4

218

blocks with deep eaves: the roof line's continuous ridge is occasionally interrupted by roof windows which identify different parts of the building.

Brickwork was selected and designed to extend the mode of the existing garden walls and the roofs are clad in a complementary brown grey concrete slate.[8,9,10] The rural character of the area has been retained by careful tree felling and positioning of games areas in the spaces beyond the garden walls.[11]

3 First Floor Plan
There is a mixture of dormitories and single bedrooms for the boys with shared common rooms. Expert child care is available also.
4 *The enclosed courtyard offers quite a different environment from the surrounding woods and agricultural land. A calm, ordered but informal space has been created with few materials and simple forms.*
5 *The low, horizontal sweep of the eaves echoes the top of the enclosing garden wall*

with rooflights identifying different parts of the building. In the foreground are classrooms with quiet bays expressed as solid brickwork with lay lights in the roof: the larger rooflights illuminate the deep general teaching areas. The larger building to the left is the gymnasium.
6 *View from the south with the staff flats in the background and the medical suite to the right.*
7 *View of the classroom wing from the south.*

5

7

6

Frank Barnes School

When the original brief for this primary school to accommodate eighty deaf children was developed it contained a requirement for twelve equal size teaching rooms to form teaching groups according to the age ranges. After lengthy discussion between the ILEA inspector, a head teacher and the job architect this was varied to provide two home bases for eight children each,[12] and a small quiet room grouped around a large practical area shared by all sixteen: this was a movement towards the current thinking on ordinary primary schools but with the elimination of the normal call for flexibility and movable partitions as these are incompatible with the needs of deaf children.

Briefing produced three necessary environmental conditions; reduction of sound penetration and internal reverberation, elimination of amplified sound overspill and good lighting to facilitate lip reading. An ambient noise level of 40 dB (A) and a reverberation time of 0.4 seconds in teaching areas was agreed with the DES to meet the first. The site is on a very busy road junction at Swiss Cottage and a noise survey showed a peak of 75 dB (A): the building form initially became dominated by the need to exclude traffic noise. A sound barrier wall was constructed on the boundary and the school was built at the

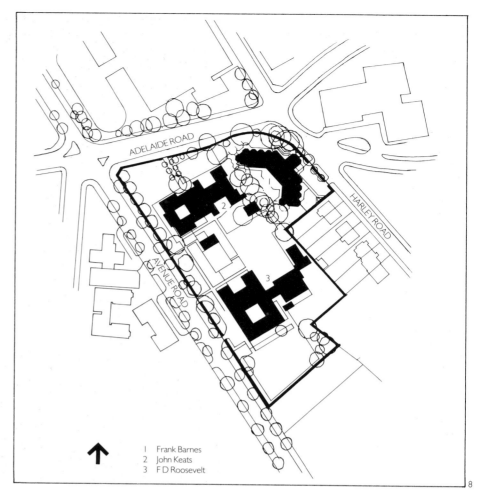

1 Frank Barnes
2 John Keats
3 F D Roosevelt

8

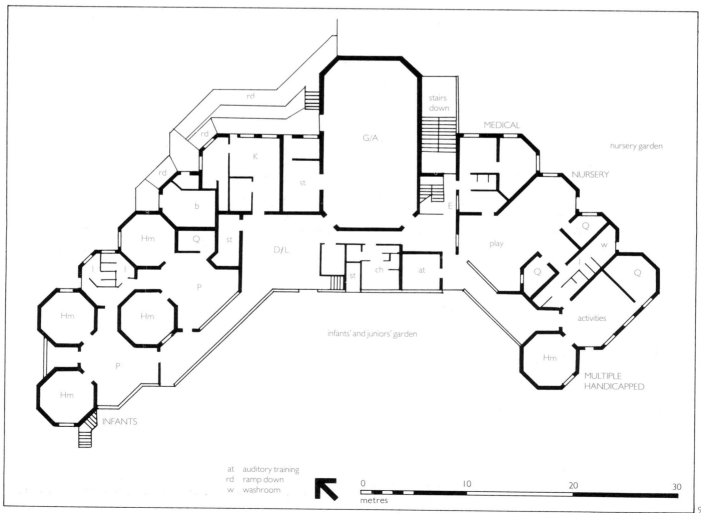

at auditory training
rd ramp down
w   washroom

0   10   20   30
metres

9

8 Site Plan
The proximity of the available site to the very busy adjacent roads produced a form built to exclude traffic noise. Also sharing the site are two other special schools (John Keats and Franklin Delano Roosevelt) designed in 1955, see Chapter 2.

9 Ground Floor Plan
Individual elements attest to the problems of external noise and internal sound. The use of a heavy structure is reinforced by small windows facing North whilst the South facing elements are opened over a treed garden. The usually open nature of primary schools is not possible here due to the technical needs of enclosure: children are normally taught at special desks set out in a horse shoe arrangement and the octagon is the nearest and most economical shape for containment.

10 First Floor Plan
A very similar arrangement is followed for the juniors as for the infants on the Ground Floor. Teaching rooms with audio-induction loops are staggered vertically to prevent feedback.

11 *To preserve internal quietude the building presents an unyielding protective wall to the main roads – the traffic noise source. Air-conditioning is necessary as the School is sealed from the outside: in the centre is the cooling tower above a plant room.*

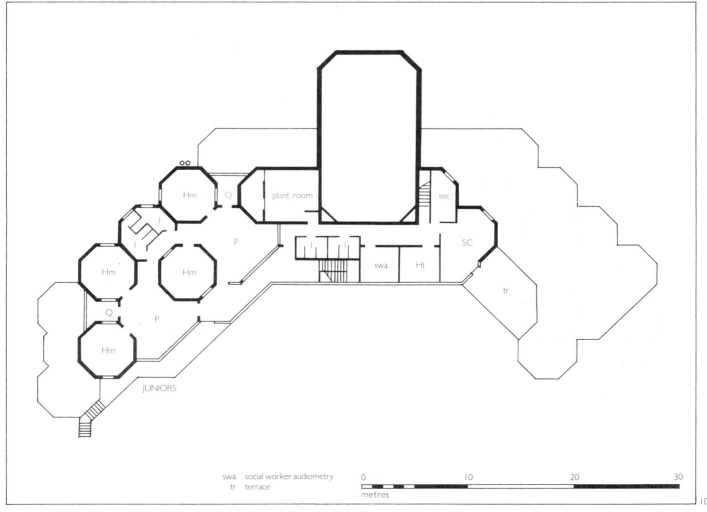

swa social worker audiometry
tr   terrace

0   10   20   30
metres

original garden level 1.80 m below pavement level, thus providing an acoustic shadow. The plan form shows a wrap around shape protecting the teaching areas with a heavy-weight structure for floors and roof with dense masonry walls: very few windows pierce this sound barrier. The main entrance is protected from the noisy street junction, and inside circulation and communal spaces provide a series of enclosed sound lobbies before the teaching areas are reached. Solid, unyielding protection on the north side gives way to a fully glazed curtain wall to the quiet south overlooking a shared garden with mature trees. Chapter 2 shows adjacent schools, John Keats and

Franklin Delano Roosevelt, sharing the same garden outlook. The design was started in 1973 and construction was completed in 1978.

Audio induction loops are used in floor screeds to give greater individual amplification to hearing aids and, to avoid overspill of amplified sound, teaching areas needed to be spaced out:[13] on a tight urban site (0.75 acres, 0.30 hectare) two storeys were necessary and teaching rooms with loops had to be staggered to avoid feedback. Groups of eight children are taught together and special desks with built-in amplification equipment are normally set out in a horse shoe arrangement: the nearest architectural shape and the most

economical form to contain this layout was the octagon and this shape then defined the character of the plan form. The polygonal form helps to diffuse sound, breaking up confusing echoes and the walls are lined with pin-up board backed with mineral wool for acoustic attenuation. Floors are carpeted or have foam backed vinyl sheet and there are suspended acoustic ceilings everywhere except for areas of high humidity. Finally, to exclude any external interference the windows are sealed and the school is fully air-conditioned. Lighting levels are high to facilitate lip-reaching and muted colour schemes and materials are used to ease eye strain.

12, 13 *As the traffic noise diminishes the character of the building begins to change from a solid masonry barrier to an open garden outlook. The form of the building reflects the basic teaching arrangement based upon an octagon.*

14 *A typical classroom, octagonal in plan to contain the horseshoe arrangement of eight desks. This polygonal form also helps to break up confusing echoes and diffuse sound giving the quietest background possible for the teaching of deaf children. The floor and the ceiling contain induction loops to reinforce amplified sound to individual hearing aids.*

Bromley Hall School

This school for one hundred and fifty physically handicapped children between the ages of 5 to 16 years was completed in November 1968. There is a wide range of handicaps to cater for including muscular distrophy, spina bifida, heart disease, loss of limbs and deformities attributed to thalidomide.

Permanent access to the site is possible only from Bromley Hall Road as Leven Street will be closed when the surrounding area is redeveloped: the site (1.25 acres) is flat and all accommodation is developed upon ground floor level with no changes in level. All children are taken to and from school each day by a fleet of specially adapted buses: a large forecourt allows all the buses to arrive and unload simultaneously. Upon entering the school those children who require wheelchairs, walking frames, etc., can obtain these from the store adjacent to the entrance hall. Once inside the building the children do not need to return to the potentially dangerous vehicular area of the forecourt until the end of the school day.

Due to the large age differential two parallel sets of corridors provide separate circulation flanking the shared communal central area.[14] Circulation space is generous to allow unimpaired individual movement and the main routes are broken down into a series of wider lobbies which give direct access to the adjacent rooms: these lobbies have direct views into courtyards and provide extra space for group work or individual study.

Each of the six classrooms has its own enclosed courtyard which is designed to be an extension of the room only from which access is possible: this allows varied work, indoors and outdoors, to be easily supervised.[15] Each court is planted with evergreen species and each provides a view of the outside world whilst preserving the school's privacy. The large central court is the infants' play area. One long side of the library can be opened to the air and in the middle of the day it is used as a rest room for those with severe heart complaints: stores next to the assembly hall house beds and act as a sound baffle. A central medical suite provides not only routine treatment but urgent attention when necessary: the hydro-therapy pool was included in the original design but was not built until 1978 due to lack of funds.

As the site environment is unattractive an introverted design was developed with the building providing its own outlook very largely, with the boundary walls forming the final enclosure against the street. The loss of direct daylight due to the domestic height of the eaves is compensated by rooflights[16] which give an even distribution of soft, reflected light to each individual room.

Externally the tall, sweeping forms of the individual roofs relieve the bleakness of the boundary walls: these pyramidal roofs are constructed with laminated timber hip members, rising from a laminated timber tension ring at the eaves to a laminated timber compression ring at the top.[17] Only vertical dead loads are imposed on the walls. The roofs are covered with dark grey artificial slates and this is the only material used for all hips, valleys, ridges and sweeps.

The structure is of load bearing walls with smooth brown engineering bricks used generally as cladding, externally as well as internally, giving 'a consistent architectural vocabulary'.[18] Floors of the main rooms incorporate hot water heating coils with lino tile finish. The nursery class, constructed in the same idiom as the original building, was completed in 1979.

15 Ground Floor Plan
A tight, urban site with unattractive surroundings produced an introverted design with all rooms facing on to internal courtyards which also light the parallel corridors: these corridors progress the age ranges around the central shared provision. The main load bearing walls also provide the boundary to an adjacent street.

Since completion a hydrotherapy pool has been added as well as a nursery class: both follow the same modes of construction and materials.

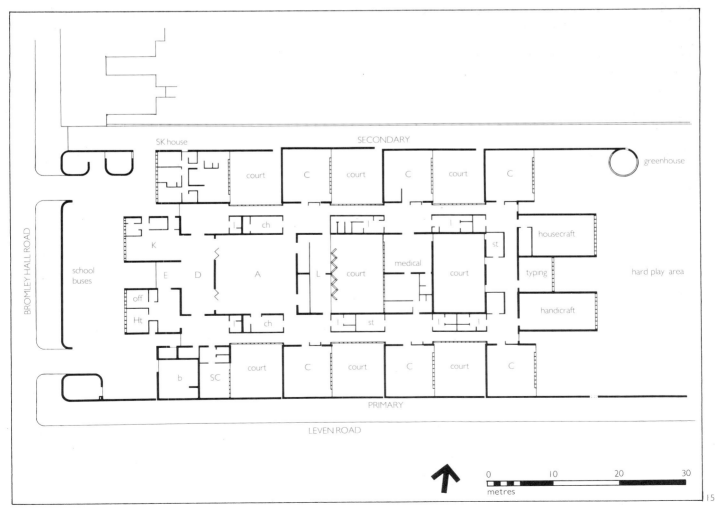

16 View from Leven Road. The surrounding area is composed of decaying terraced houses and blocks of flats. The school is a very private place behind its walls.
17 The library opens directly and fully into its adjacent court.
18 South corridor shows the consistent use of materials and simple forms of the building.
19 Each classroom has its own court which is planted with evergreen shrubs and trees.

20 *Classroom roof monitors face east to minimise solar gain. The large rooflight, right, provides a changing light pattern to the assembly hall.*
21 *The greenhouse.*
22 *General view of the school from the play area.*

20

21

22

Richard Cloudesley School

Like Bromley Hall this is a decidedly urban building surrounded by high flats and busy roads. It was completed in 1972 and was designed to provide not only the facilities necessary for one hundred and sixty physically handicapped children but also to provide warm yet stimulating spaces with views out on to enclosed courtyards.[19]

The children are aged from 5 to 16 years and as these children will probably spend most of their school life in the one building the plan was developed to provide a feeling of progress through the age groups from nursery to secondary.

Vehicular access is from Golden Lane allowing the special buses to approach the raised platform for loading and unloading the handicapped: a store for walking aids is immediately available and one wide central corridor gives easy circulation.

To give a measure of privacy in an otherwise overlooked building, boundary walls enclose the school, with some rooms having their own planted courtyards. Primary classrooms are open planned whilst the secondary rooms cater for general lessons as well as specialist subjects such as art, needlework, science, typewriting, commerce, wood and metalwork and housecraft.

Ancillary accommodation includes areas for diagnosis and treatment of various handicaps. This includes a medical inspection room, speech and audiology rooms, a remedial exercise room with a hydrotherapy pool including showers and changing rooms. All lavatory and changing accommodation is designed to facilitate the use of wheelchairs: all taps are either hospital longarm or toggle pattern, easily used by handicapped children. As at Bromley Hall School handrails in corridors and special door fittings are only some of the provisions made to help the children overcome their handicaps and operate independently. 'Spaces are meticulously designed and finishes specified with the

greatest care, their colour and richness lending visual richness everywhere'.[20]

Construction is of load bearing brickwork with a flat timber roof relieved by very large monitors giving clerestory lighting to each teaching area.[21] Ground conditions necessitated a reinforced concrete ground slab. Walls are generally lined with pin-up board with a suspended acoustic tiled ceiling throughout. Heating is by ducted warm air except in the primary classrooms and therapy rooms which have underfloor heating.

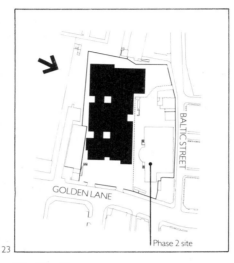

23   Site Plan
The site is tightly surrounded by busy roads and high blocks of flats. The main building was built as phase I upon a very small area: the second phase has not yet been included in the site.

24   Ground Floor Plan
The plan is developed to allow children to progress from nursery to secondary education by a recognisable sequence. Circulation space and lavatory accommodation is generous to allow wheelchair passage and handrails and special fittings are used to induce independence. Due to the bleak surroundings there are few windows in external walls but planted courtyards provide attractive and stimulating views. Daylighting is by means of large roof monitors with clerestorey windows.
25, 26   *A totally different range of fixtures and fittings are required for the physically handicapped.*
27   *Top lighting provides even illumination and leaves wall space clear for pin up.*
28   *The hydrotherapy pool has distinctly marked stepped levels to provide a range of options.*
29   *Roof lighting monitors reduce the feeling inside the school of encroachment by the taller, closely adjacent blocks of flats.*

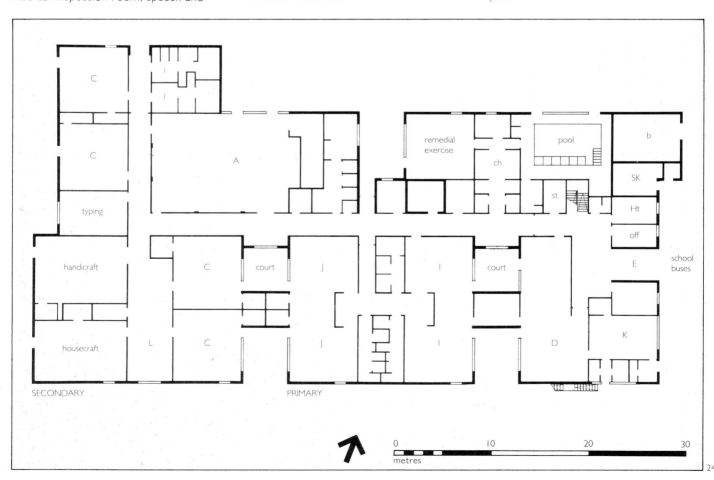

25

26

27

28

29

Clapham Park School

Two existing schools for partially sighted children were amalgamated to form Clapham Park which provides one hundred and five places for children aged 5 to 16 years. It was completed in 1969.

Heavy traffic is carried by two of the roads which flank the flat site but the other two are relatively quiet. Children travel to and from the school by special buses which use a lay-by made in Park Hill. The surrounding buildings vary from large, early nineteenth century houses along King's Road to modern two storeyed flats elsewhere, but the site's crowning natural glory is the fifty or more large mature trees. Most of these are around the perimeter of the site forming a natural barrier and screen which has been augmented by new planting including low shrubs.

Special consideration was given to orientation and the required level of daylight which has given the school its form.[22] In order to achieve a high intensity of natural lighting inside the building split pitched roofs are used to throw an even wash of light through clerestoreys over the main ceilings and large vertical windows supplement this, allowing good vision out and offering a good level of spectator interest in the passing scene. Artificial lighting is designed to give a high level of lighting and the building positively glows with colour. The walls are load-bearing faced with warm dark Wealdon Stock bricks externally, dark stained cedar fascias and dark blue asbestos slates accentuated by bright red doors to help locate entrances and exits. The school is a cluster of linked blocks arranged around a

pyramidal hall and enclosed courtyard.

Quieter classrooms and the school-keeper's house face the quieter roads whilst the pottery and woodwork areas and service spaces face the noisier environment. Although the infant classrooms are cellular rather than open plan the general design is informal and relaxed. To provide as normal an experience as possible a certain number of natural hazards, for example steps, changes in level and a variety of ground surface textures have been deliberately included.

30   Site Plan
The site is flat in a residential area with a variety of house and flat types. The peripheral mature trees were all retained and added to in order to provide a screen against the surrounding roads.
31   Ground and First Floor Plans
Noise from two adjacent roads is diminished by placing teaching rooms near the quieter boundaries, Park Hill and Clarence Avenue. Admission of daylight is a high priority and large windows are supplemented by clerestorey windows and a high level of artificial illumination.

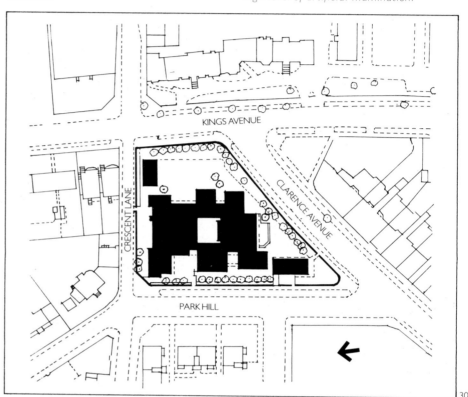

30

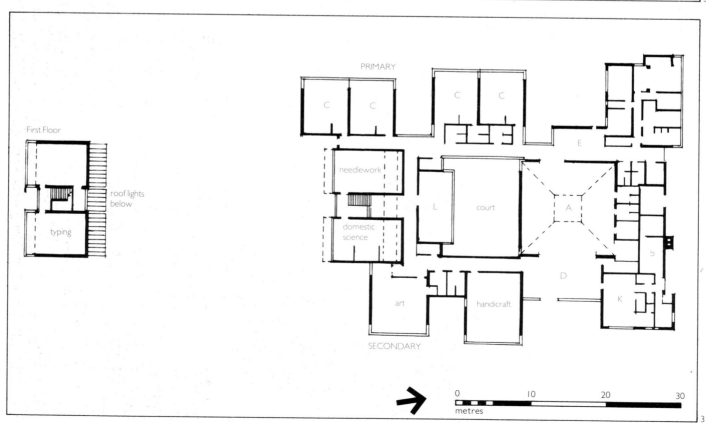

31

32 The monopitch roof form springs from the need to provide a very high level of daylight as the far side of these two classrooms (art, craft and pottery to the left: woodwork and metalwork to the right) has a tall clerestorey supplementing the light from the ordinary windows.

33 From the south the upper rooms (typing and a classroom) appear to overshadow the needlework and domestic science rooms but the lower rooms have rooflights across the rear. Rooms generally have cedar ceilings following the roof pitch and have a very high level of artificial illumination in addition to daylighting.

34 In the centre is a single storey classroom showing the clerestorey additional to the ordinary windows. Changes of levels and a variety of ground surface textures have been used deliberately to provide experience.

Queen Elizabeth II Jubilee School

From 1971 it became the responsibility of education authorities to provide education for severely sub-normal children and since then the ILEA has provided such schools: this particular school replaces two older special care units.

Special buses are used to transport children to and from the school and because of the high percentage of disabled pupils a raised loading platform is provided giving direct access to the wide corridors. Altogether there are one hundred places aged 3 to 16 years with a special care unit for twenty children. The school is planned to progress through the age and ability range with each section having a largely enclosed, hard paved courtyard directly accessible to the teaching spaces: immediately adjoining the paved areas are lawns with trees providing another element of enclosure. All teaching areas have a covered play/work space leading on to the paving. The form of the building is a series of pavilions with butterfly roofs linked by a generally flat roof: this evolved through the need to provide separation between the different teaching spaces and the external enclosures form the solution, articulating the different elements of the layout.[23] The classrooms are virtually enclosed brick boxes with small windows and low level viewing slots: a high level of natural light and ventilation is provided through the clerestory windows of the butterfly roofs.

Construction is traditional with load bearing brick walls with timber roofs. In addition to the ordinary gas fired low pressure hot water heating, supplementary heating is provided to the special care unit. Designed in 1974 the school was completed in 1977.

35 Site Plan
The building is set back from the southern boundary to protect the line of a proposed service road for redevelopment along that side.

36 Ground Floor Plan
Like other special schools this is designed to allow children to progress according to age and ability. Each grouping has its own largely enclosed, hard paved courtyard directly accessible to the teaching spaces. Separation of the groups has provided the architectural expression with a series of pavilions articulating the plan. The classrooms are virtually enclosed brick boxes with high level daylighting via clerestory windows below butterfly roofs.

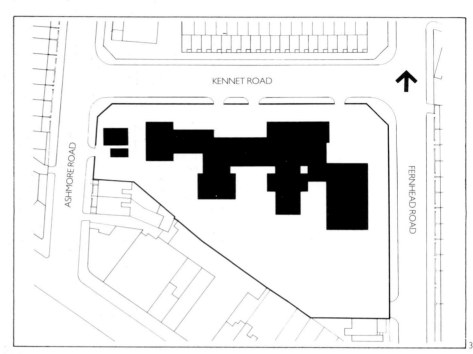

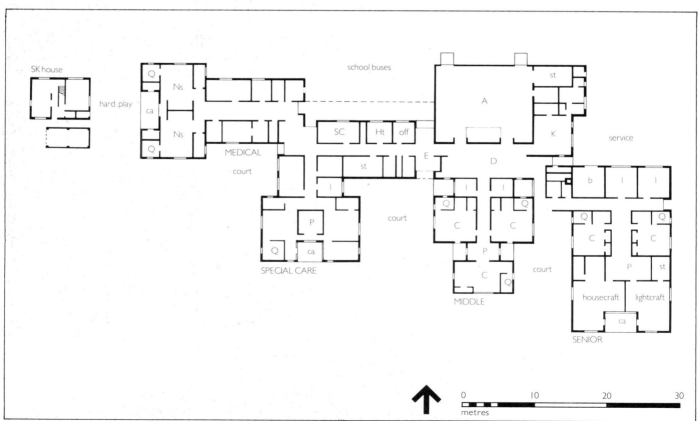

37 The nursery unit from the south-west showing the high level of daylighting provided by clerestorey windows under the butterfly roofs and the low level viewing slots. The covered play area is shared by both classes.

38 Middle courtyard from the south with the buildings skirting a mature tree. On the right are the middle classrooms. Teaching areas are on the south of the building with non-teaching areas to the north adjacent to Kennet Road.

39 Senior courtyard looking west at the middle classrooms. The design of a series of pavilions with butterfly roofs creates an apparent village of development offering privacy and small scale enclosure with warm brown brickwork.

Chapter 13: References

1 The Times Educational Supplement, 18 June 1982, p 1.

2 Building Design, 21 February 1975, p 22.

3 Surveyor 28 February 1975, p 12–13, Shawcroft School is something special.

4 Concrete Quarterly July/September 1976, p 10–11.

5 RIBA Journal July/August 1979, p 19.

6 GLC Architects Review 1974, Academy p 34–35.

7 Building Design, 1 August 1974, p 4.

8 Bauwelt, 22 August 1975, p 91–93.

9 Arkitekten (Copenhagen), 23 September 1975, p 338–339.

10 Building, 9 January 1976, p 51–58.

11 Built Environment, September 1975, p 91–93.

12 Architects Journal, 15 November 1978, p 929–944.

13 Building Design, 24 February 1978, p 16–17.

14 Interbuild, June 1966, p 12–15.

15 Architects Journal, 27 August 1969, p 505–522.

16 Architects Journal, 20 August 1969, p 433 is a detail sheet showing the design of the pyramidal roof structures.

17 Wood, April 1970, p 6–10.

18 Architects Journal, 20 August 1969.

19 Architecture and Urbanism, February 1974, p 131–134.

20 Architects Journal, 12 June 1974, p 1323–1341.

21 Bauen und Wohnen, July/August 1975, p 317–319.

22 Architects Journal, 29 March 1972, p 652.

23 Building Design, 7 March 1980: *the controversial HMI Report upon the ILEA published in November 1980 singled this school out as a model of special school provision.*

Key to drawings

A	assembly hall
AEI	adult education institute
AH	activities hall
C	classroom
CR	common room
D	dining
Dr	drama
DW	dining/work
E	entrance
G	gymnasium
H	houseroom
Hm	home bay
Ht	head or principal
I	infants
J	juniors
K	kitchen
L	library
Lt	lecture
M	music
Ns	nursery
P	practical area
PC	play centre
Q	quiet area
S	secretary
Sc	science
SC	staff common room
SH	sports hall
SK	schoolkeeper
Sw	swimming pool
W	waiting
YS	youth service
b	boiler
ca	covered area
ch	changing
cl	cloakroom
l	lavatories
s	servery
st	store

Chapter 14
Furniture & Design

Although school buildings demonstrate physically what their designers considered to be the most important aspects of their being, it is the use of the rooms provided which illuminate the attitude of the educators. Further, it is the furnishing of the teaching areas which reflects the education offered.

When the School Board for London buildings were originally constructed there were few precedents for furniture and equipment and instructions for their use had to be included for those using the schools as the Board took great care to provide the correct items. The intention was that schools should be 'Healthful, Pleasant, Attractive, Stimulative, Instructive, Useful, Influential'.[1] Whilst the buildings have stood, and will continue to stand, educational philosophy has developed and expanded and this development and expansion has taken place within the walls, being fed and fostered physically by varying the furniture and fittings available. Many of inner London's schools have stood for over one hundred years serving their local communities and a large proportion of them still have a long and profitable life ahead of them – see Chapter 4. In that time various teaching emphases have grown and then dwindled away to be replaced by others and the classrooms are photographically recorded to show them. By casual inspection of the records it can be concluded that for nearly eighty years the actual furniture in use hardly varied, for right up until 1950 the general pattern of provision remained constant.

That which might be perceived as rigid Victorian authority is reflected by the ubiquitous use of cast iron framing to desks: these usually seated two pupils upon a hinged solid bench with the desk top sloping towards the bench. The desk top was of solid oak and was hinged to allow easy access. Two inkwells were let into the top with a single groove for holding pens and pencils. A shelf, again of solid oak, ran below the desk top to take extra books. This standard piece of furniture was known to generations of London schoolchildren and its very longevity testifies to its sturdiness as the carved initials of occupants relentlessly ate into the desk top. What is also very apparent is the hardwearing nature of the classroom with solid deal floors, glazed brick wall bricks to shoulder height, leaving only the upper part of the room to be periodically painted. Perhaps this robust provision reflects the practical realisation of the destructive nature of children – or is it to withstand the onslaught of the universal boot worn by all pupils? The desks were progressively stepped upwards through the room to give both better views of the blackboards at the front of the class and better supervision over pupils at the back – there were up to sixty in a class.

The classroom then was perceived as a vehicle for instilling information with learning by rote without distraction and the remainder of the furnishing supports this principle. At the front of the classroom was a simple table-desk on a dais for the teacher with a box lectern on top acting as a drawer. On the front wall were fixed blackboards with easel blackboards available as auxiliary supports. The blackboard was the main instrument of instruction, supplemented by large coloured maps and diagrams. Exercise books were used mainly for the development of meticulous handwriting, considered important for future office workers. Other written work was done with slate pencils on slates kept in a slot in the desk front. For the instillation of

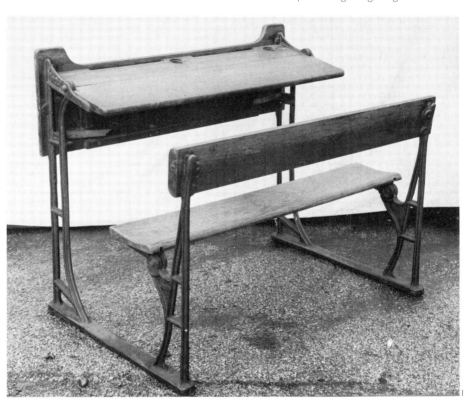

1 *The standard desk with its cast iron frame known to generations of London schoolchildren from 1870 to 1950. The hinged desk top and bench seat were made from solid oak.*

2 Albion Street School, 1908
The solid nature of Victorian and Edwardian classrooms is conveyed in this view of a botany lesson. The desks are progressively higher towards the rear being mounted on a stepped floor. The high volume of the room is evident and was partly necessary to provide sufficient ventilation for town gas lighting.

numeracy a large abacus stood in a frame and an oak framed clock with roman numerals was used for education as well as time keeping. There are few teaching aids and these were contained in a small wall cupboard behind the teacher's dais. This pattern of provision was universal, the only difference being that infant boys and girls were mixed in the room arrangement but elementary pupils were rigorously separated, with the girls occupying the front benches and the boys seated behind them. Secondary schools were not mixed at all, having single sex admission only.

What is generally noticeable is, despite the discipline imposed upon the apparently decorous and almost uniformly clad pupils in the stark severity of the Victorian and Edwardian classrooms, the general shabbiness of the rooms brought about by the badly composed and ill-designed rooms themselves. The structure of the floor above obtrudes very crudely. Gas lighting pipes march haphazardly across ceilings to feed the mantles of lights suspended upon long rods from the ceilings. The hardwearing lower surfaces of the walls appear harsh and can be overpowering when stepped to follow the galleried seating platforms. Air inlet and exhaust boxes overpower corners only to stop at arbitrary heights and the internal windows to corridors break up the enclosure of the rooms. When pictures are hung they follow no particular pattern because the Board School rooms had no particular pattern being mere working spaces in buildings with handsome external proportions and balance.

Specialist rooms show more care and interest than the general classroom with the calm elegance of an art room or the busy simplicity of a woodwork shop. A drawing lesson shows a disciplined approach to art which has quite ignored the coming (and going) of the Impressionists, Post-Impressionists, Symbolists and the untameable Fauvists. Science benching had reached a stage which remained constant and inflexible well beyond 1950 whilst fume cupboards were glazed boxes with a simple zinc flue. Modelling in clay was carried out on special tilted stands and housewifery

3   The abacus was used for the teaching of basic arithmetic.
4   Putney Secondary School, 1910
The elegance of the girls matches the handsome appointments of the room. The standard plaster casts used for drawing are in keeping with the smock and bow of the art teacher. Electric light was installed in this room.
5   Bellenden Road Elementary School, 1908
Woodworking practice changes very slowly and many tools now are similar to those seventy years ago. The rooms used, then and now, are workshops and the close lighting and heating arrangement reflect their semi-industrial nature.
6   Alma Elementary School, 1908
The name of the lesson was 'Object Drawing' and shows that elementary boys were faced with quite different tasks from secondary girls (see Fig 4). Boys stand, girls sit. Boys are marshalled, girls dispose themselves. Blinds at the windows provide a general soft lighting, reducing harsh shadows upon the object.
7   Addison Gardens Elementary School, 1908
Science was one subject where boys and girls shared lessons. Many items in this room (benches, shelving storage and fume cupboards) remained standard for fifty or sixty years.

reflected the very solid, simple domestic arrangements with very few utensils available. No special provision was made for physical education but stern drill would be carried out by boys under a ferocious eye in the playground[2] whilst girls practised more decorous but equally disciplined movements in the school hall.

Under the notice 'The KITCHEN is the INSTITUTE of the NATION' girls were taught cookery under basic conditions whilst young infants were expected to lie down and sleep in the afternoon.

Many of the Victorian iron framed desks survived until 1950 but some of the suburban estate schools built in the 1920's began to introduce simple sturdy wooden tables seating two with individual wooden chairs. Even with the greater relaxation of the time, however, no attempt was made to present the general classroom as anything other than the most basic provision and the result is unassimilated clutter. By the late 1930's a general range of furniture[3] was available and at the same time the scope of activities widened each year with an enlarging curriculum. Large classrooms were proposed allowing re-arrangement by furniture into small groupings.[4]

After 1945, when the LCC had to repair and replace thousands of items of furniture destroyed in the war, the break was made with the original cast-iron framed desk with integral bench as these were no longer available. Utility was the post-war euphemism for austerity and simple wooden tables and chairs were substituted under the aegis of the 'General Specification for Utility Furniture' published by the Board of Trade in 1948: under this, traditional jointing with mortise and tenon was relaxed in favour of plugged dowel joints and tubular steel was recognised generally for structural frames, whilst the search for scarce suitable materials – paralleled in building construction (see Chapter 2) – went beyond plywood to plywood substitutes, in essence hardboard.

But school building designers in the late 1940's were fired with the same urgency and pursuit of principle which manifested itself originally in E Robson's 'School Architecture', 1874, when the architect to the School Board for London concerned himself with every detail of the new buildings, including the pupils' use of furniture. Furniture and equipment, however sparse by current standards, were devised for the Board with the same care as applied to the design of schools. In this book, Robson gave directions for building and equipment use: 'At the word "Desks" the flap should be raised quickly but without noise' and 'At the word "Stand" the scholars should rise smartly with arms straight by their sides.' This utopianism was reflected by a new generation of architects who were willingly forced by social demands to project a new view of educational process fostered by the 1944 Education Act. By 1950 a general dissatisfaction was expressed at the paucity of available furniture and the Festival of Britain, 1951, demonstrated new departures with lightweight steel frames and ergonomically designed seats. In 1952 a general survey upon school furniture was instituted to discover the range and need for equipment. The survey justified the design of inter-related furniture and the specific design of items to a recognised standard. From then onwards furniture and industrial designers worked closely with LCC, and later ILEA, architects in making a comprehensive provision for education buildings. Further impetus was provided by the Ministry of Education Building Bulletins concerning the design and use of school furnishing and the application of colour.

Throughout the 1950's the range of furniture was reviewed and new designs were implemented to replace those available which were not considered suitable. Great use was made of laminated timber for basic structures and this is exemplified by the single locker desk, 1955, which has a solid beech top with a deep tray underneath for books and bent laminated mahogany legs: the chairs were made from laminated plywood. Earlier schools had acquired, over many years, several different types of cupboards for general storage – as this was progressively expanding with teaching aids – and as these were based upon no specific modules they lent a general air of unease to the corridors in

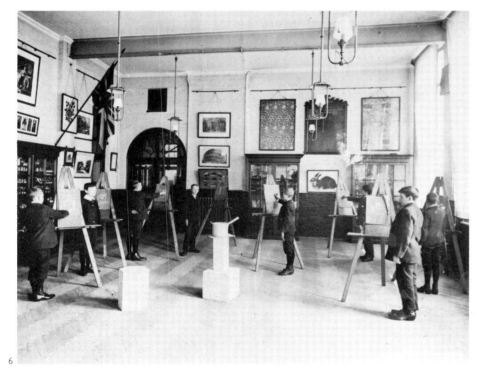

6

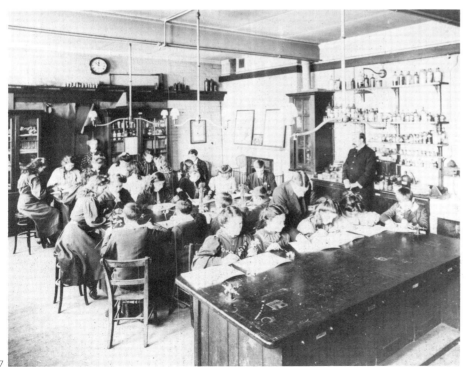

7

237

8 East Lane Domestic Economy Centre, 1930

The cookery room was a larger version of the cottage kitchen and did not change for half a century. Only the hair style and length of skirts prevent the date being 1880 or 1950. Gas lighting was still employed in 1930 in some schools.

9 Effra Elementary School, 1938

In the late thirties some schools were finding it necessary to recruit children younger than five years old in order to maintain numbers and retain teachers. One consequence was that these nursery age pupils required quite different resources.

10 Ballamore Road Elementary School, 1931

An infants' classroom showing a newer range of furniture from the ubiquitous desk (see Fig 1) with very solid wooden tables and individual chairs. This pattern could be found in the newer suburban schools.

11, 12 *In Robson's book, 1874, the architect gave directions for building and equipment use.*

8

9

(4)—" *Desks.*"

At the word "Desks," the flap should be raised quickly but without noise, and the hands dropped.

272.—"DESKS."

11

10

(5)—" *Stand.*"

At the word "Stand," the scholars should rise smartly with arms straight by their sides.

273.—"STAND."

12

which they invariably stood. In the 1950's, however, the storage became part of the teaching room and was integrated as part of the furniture being designed upon the preferred architectural 3'4" (one metre) module: carcasing was from solid hardwood, usually mahogany, and fully dovetailed jointing was employed. In keeping with the architectural finishes of the day, the doors were finished in sapele mahogany veneer which was the preferred main door finish also. Solid hardwoods were used for worktops and carcases because of the ease in refurbishment that this offered in the robust climate of a school. With the other normal classroom finishes of the time — a fibreboard false ceiling on battens; tungsten lighting with carefully calculated visual cut-off angles; an electric clock; a large, specially lighted, double, sliding blackboard; increasing pin-up areas; a smooth linoleum floor finish; loudspeaker system giving instant, school-wide communication — the standard LCC school furniture became an integral part of education.

Specialist furniture began to develop as subjects broadened and required more aids. By studying the basic needs of the pupil in a given subject the designer was able to provide bespoke furniture. A tubular steel frame was introduced as the base for the art table/easel as it gave greater span strength and flexibility in use than hardwood and could cope easily with additional items such as cantilevered paint trays and sliding supports for drawing boards. Heavy construction necessitated the use of solid beech throughout the geography/history dual table as this size proved most economical in space use with the study of large documents and maps. Typewriter tables were required to be heavy to maintain a rigid classroom layout: the necessity of enclosing the machines when not in use required their stands to fold away leaving a work top at normal desk height. As early as 1952 the science work benches had been under scrutiny and after many tests solid iroko tops

13 The new standard of classroom provided for secondary schools in the 1950's. The cast iron framed desk had gone being replaced with an individual desk with a fixed top and an open shelf below. Legs for desks and chairs were from laminated wood — an attempt to maximise materials in a time of shortage. Lighting is better and more specific, radio communication is available through loudspeakers, smooth linoleum flooring introduces colour and easier hygiene and a modular storage range is general.

14 The use of tubular steel, 1955, gives positional variety to art table/easels and the introduction of fluorescent lighting provides cool, shadowless illumination.

15 1955. Although steel tubing was now being used for furniture bases wider spans such as the geography/history dual table required solid beech: this size of table proved most economical in space use with the study of large documents and maps.

16

17

were used, and still are, in preference to the lighter laminated plastics available: again, when refurbishment is considered by the building owner those materials which initially seem cheaper and more hygienic cannot withstand the use that they must undergo and cannot be returned to their pristine condition without extensive replacement. Science stools were of solid wood. By the mid 1950's a fully integrated range of classroom storage furniture was available, known as the 600 range: its module was 3'4" (one metre).

Gradually the whole teaching spectrum was supplied with specially designed furniture and, as it was purpose made to a very high standard, other education authorities became customers, for the high volume of LCC require-

18

19

20

ments created economies of scale for wider provision. Modifications were incorporated as required by users and as school architects recognised the primary relationship between good products and their own buildings' use. In 1962 a book was published 'School Furniture, London County Council' and it demonstrated the full range available from infant school to polytechnic use based upon the decision to adopt a range of chair and table dimensions founded upon extensive anthropometric research.[5] It also was seen to be of interest and value to teachers, architects and administrators both in this country and abroad.

The primary school range included mobile storage units, made from solid agba, with pin-up surfaces on the back. Tubular steel frames were generally used for tables and chairs and blockboard was introduced for worktops with a laminated plastic surface and beech lipping. Juniors had individual locker desks and storage units were available. The secondary range had every possible teaching detail catered for, from glass storage racks in science rooms to internally illuminated display cases for geography and history, apart from the detailed fittings required for large, busy school libraries. Further education necessitated extending the range to include housecraft and a wider variety of science fittings and underpinning all, was the general storage furniture now updated to the 700 range. Based upon the 3'4" (one metre) module still, the units could be used singly or in banks and it was normal to see a continuous row in a science room under the main windows, with a solidly-built wall bench providing a continuous work top: the storage range was made from solid mahogany or mahogany veneered blockboard.

As education attitudes changed so did the buildings and furniture which sought to serve them. Until 1967 infants worked around tables seating eight and juniors had individual locker desks but in that year the acceptance of the recommendations of the Plowden Report, 'Children and Their Primary Schools', radically altered the traditional approach to primary teaching with new requirements 'covering anthropometric, educational and functional needs'.[6] With the introduction of larger groupings of children giving greater flexibility in

16, 17 *With the wider scope of secondary education offered in 1956 came more specialist resources. Typewriters became common and required security: the response offered a worktop too.*
18 *By 1955 the science work bench had been redesigned with solid iroko tops and this is still the standard provision. The modular storage range on the far wall demonstrates small enclosure and display elements. Compare with Fig 7.*
19, 20 *One of the high volume production units was the single locker desk with its sturdy beech frame and mahogany locker under a beech worktop/lid. The laminated chair was used throughout the 1950's and 1960's and well into the 1970's.*
21 *New secondary schools had large libraries included in their design in the 1950's and a general range of fittings was evolved based upon the 3' 4" (one metre) module. Angled display shelves were included among bookshelves for magazines and new acquisitions; reference cabinets for control and retrieval; and softer chairs than the normal laminated chairs were available.*

22 *With the rise in interest in hi-fi sound reproduction the original landspeaker units (see Fig 13) were found to be too insecure and a new cast alloy unit with secret fixings bolted to the main building structure was produced for general use in 1975.*

teaching – initially four groups of forty children which could be organised to give a range of group sizes to suit their teaching requirements – school buildings had to cope with a variety of arrangement, and furniture was required to be virtually redesigned. The flexibility afforded by furniture became so vital that a 'plan without furniture is a meaningless shell'.[7] Adaptable, flexible and mobile furniture resulted, with individuals' storage provided with a trolley containing interchangeable locker units: their tops corresponded to the working plane and could be used in conjunction with tables, draining boards, etc.[8] Book storage became mobile, screens were used as dividers and floor areas could be changed monthly, weekly, daily.

Some secondary schools were affected by the new open plan primary school (see Waterfield, Hydeburn and Blackheath Bluecoat Schools) but their furniture requirements were not as radically affected. A new storage range was becoming necessary. however, and was available from 1974 after stringent value analysis. It was called the 1000 range being based upon a one metre module and consisted of an interchangeable set of units providing teachers with 'a new kind of freedom'.[9]

Main storage was based upon steel vertical ladders with runners at 100 mm intervals.[10] Moulded trays are available in two depths and fill either one or two runner spaces: dividers are used in the trays to subdivide them as necessary for

the storage of miscellaneous small objects.[11] Large objects are more easily stored in deep wire mesh bins which are four runners deep. Trolleys form part of the system, being able to transport trays[12] holding complete sets of

23

24

25

26

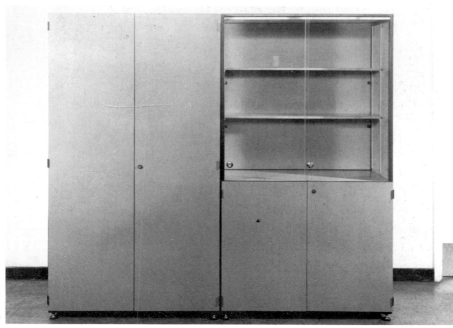
27

23, 24 The 1000 (one metre module) storage range
Constructed from cold rolled steel angle the sides are, effectively, vertical ladders formed from runners which carry a range of shallow trays, deep trays, shelves or wire mesh bins. Steelwork is painted dark brown and the trays are vivid green or scarlet.

25 *The 1000 range ladder system has a solid chipboard back and the addition of sides and doors provides an enclosed cupboard range also.*

26 *Trolleys form part of the 1000 range being able to carry complete sets of equipment in trays for a particular subject from storage to teaching area. The trolley can be open or enclosed with doors: in height it matches the lower cupboard in the range.*

27 *Enclosed with high density chipboard finished in semi-matt lacquer the 1000 includes a complete cupboard system.*

28 *The 1000 range in use at Hydeburn Secondary School, 1977*
The worktop is supported upon a cantilevered cast alloy leg frame permitting the storage units to be free-standing. In this view are moulded plywood stacking chairs temporarily substituting for polypropylene shells using the same steel undercarriages as the plastic models.

29 *Another high volume production unit widely used by many other education authorities is the ILEA polypropylene chair. It was designed in the late 1960's and comes in sizes ranging from nursery to polytechnic use. There is a range of colour and upholstery, if desired, and the steel undercarriage permits easy stacking. Shown here is a version having an upholstered moulded plywood seat instead of the original polypropylene shell: a plain version can be seen in Fig 28.*

30 *General stool for school and college use, found in laboratories and art rooms, having a steel undercarriage and polypropylene seat.*

equipment for use in specific areas. The units were constructed from cold rolled steel angle with doors available in chipboard with laminated plastic on both faces and enclosures of high density chipboard finished in semi-matt lacquer. Continuing development has modified the system with the steel frames being substituted by solid carcasing and this new range, the 100, is now being used in refurnishing. The system gives a very high density use for storage providing half as much again for floor area as previous and other available ranges. A cast alloy cantilevered leg frame provides support for continuous work benching with free-standing low units from the range. Periodic rearrangement by teaching staff provides the possibility for secondary school flexibility if required.

Development continues with research into new and improved materials. In the late 1960's one piece, injection-moulded, polypropylene seats for chairs were designed for use on steel undercarriages[13] and the sizes range from nursery to polytechnic needs with the sturdy tractor seat stool ubiquitous from art room to[14] science laboratory. The use of plastics produced unexpected problems as it became clear that the additional chemicals used to limit their flammability could produce toxic fumes when chairs did eventually burn. Much more research work has been necessary to cure the problem and, as an interim measure, a moulded plywood chair (see Fig 31) was developed to meet the annual demand for replacement. Education needs are continuously developing and special furniture is designed to meet specific circumstances.[15,16] Again, storage needs are being reviewed in the light of feedback from primary and secondary schools: replacing complete ranges of furniture in schools is, however, a long exercise as currently it is scheduled to last for thirty five years.

28

29

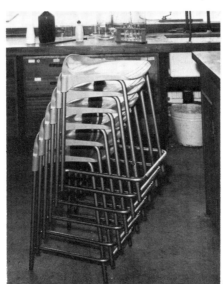
30

Chapter 14: References

1 Resolution of General Purposes Sub-Committee of the London School Board, 1872.

2 Education, 19 March 1982, p 208: Digest 'Teaching Physical Education' says that 'the intention was to instil discipline in the participants and for this reason schools which taught drill qualified for a sixpence per head grant'. The instructors were or had been soldiers.

3 Architects Journal, 28 May 1936, p 843–850, shows the general range of furniture then available for schools.

4 Builder, 2 September 1938, p 420–422, Tendencies in School Design by S E Urwin, the Cambridge County Architect, who deplored the continued use of the dual desk with the fixed seat.

5 Wood, September 1962, p 360–361.

6 Design, June 1967, p 29–36.

7 Official Architecture, September 1966, p 1284.

8 GLC Architecture, 1965–70, GLC, p 76–77.

9 Design, August 1977, p 40.

10 Design, October 1967, p 34.

11 Casabella, September 1976, p 58.

12 Airoldi, R., Innovazione Didattica e Spazi, ISEDI, 1977, p 92–101.

13 Design, October 1967, p 34.

14 The Designer, September, September 1971, p 11.

15 Design, February 1969, p 68 – showing special furniture designed to the requirements of Vittoria, a split-level experimental primary school.

16 The Designer, September 1971, p 12.

Polytechnic of the South Bank - London Road

In 1967 the ILEA decided to replace the leased accommodation of the City of Westminster College at Victoria with a new building of 1700 square metres on a 2.25 acre (0.90 hectare) site at the Elephant and Castle.[1] In 1972, whilst still under construction, the new building was incorporated into the recently designated Polytechnic of the South Bank: it was completed in 1975.

The brief was closely developed by the architects with the College, and latterly the Polytechnic, and required that shared facilities should be easily accessible to adjacent Polytechnic buildings: these facilities are the library, auditorium, sports hall and students' union accommodation and are approached at first floor level through a three-storey arcade which governs the overall plan. All accommodation is contained in a single, four-storey building which covers the whole site in order to retain the main street pattern: this form is based upon the development

of peripheral density and is most apt for this site.[2] The ground floor is at the original basements' level and the main entrance is half a storey above pavement at first-floor level. In essence, the building is a large working library with ranges of associated lecture theatres, teaching and seminar rooms. In organisation, the arcade slices across the building[3] to permit the communal areas to face the sunshine whilst the teaching areas are arranged around a series of internal courtyards in order, not only to provide every room with daylight and natural ventilation in a very deep planned building, to protect the rooms from the high traffic noise levels in London Road. The arcade is a natural centre, social mixing area, indoor street, the transition to all other elements in the building and it is a forerunner of the current interest and use of large scale internal malls.[4]

The planning geometry is neat, simple and orderly with the obvious future flexibility for teaching room rearrangement countered by the street bustle of the arcade and the transparent openness of the social spaces. The rationality of the layout is pursued in the construction with a wide span in-situ concrete frame and waffle slabs on a 750 mm module.

Solid external walls are clad in red clay tiles whilst anodised aluminium patent glazing for windows maintains the external expression of the module: the patent glazing is generally sloped, progressively setting back the profile of the building. Staircase towers and service pylons are treated as solid, tile clad columns which mark the entrances and articulate the form of the building.

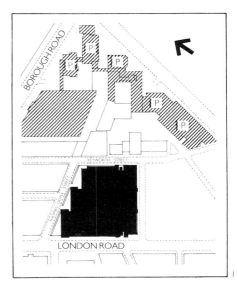

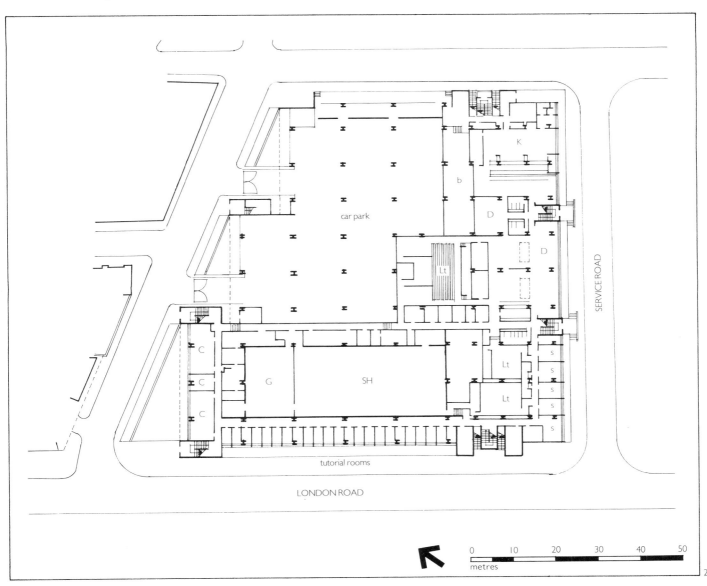

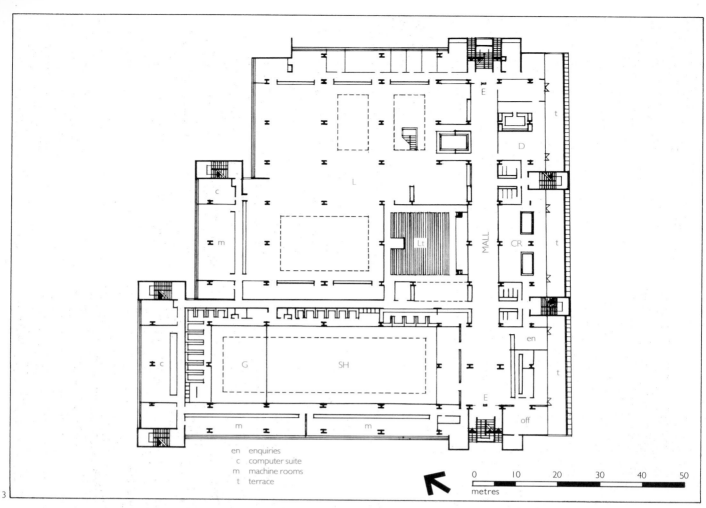

en   enquiries
c   computer suite
m   machine rooms
t   terrace

0   10   20   30   40   50
metres

3

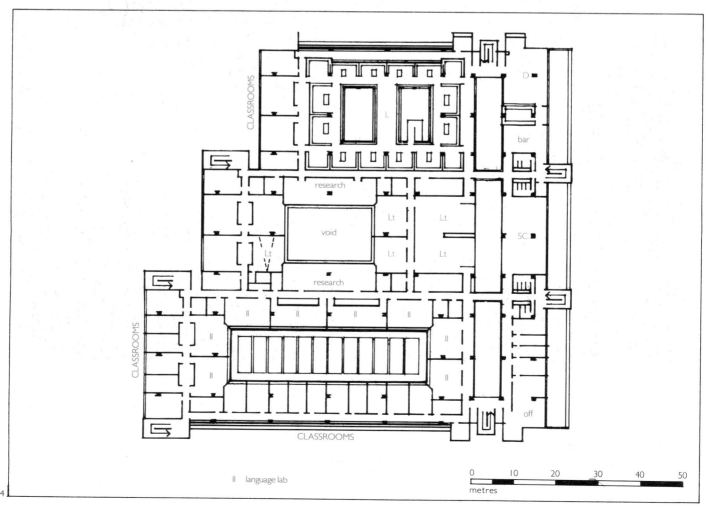

ll   language lab

0   10   20   30   40   50
metres

4

248

3 First Floor Plan
The mall differentiates the building into communal/administration to the South and working areas to the North. The essence of the building is shown by the area given over to the library with the main auditorium in the centre.

4 Second Floor Plan
By using the principle of dense development of the periphery it is possible to free large areas in the centre of a building. In this instance this was used to face as many rooms as possible away from the noisy roads and over internal glazed areas. The mall continues its separation of function through the whole height of the building. Window walls set back 750mm. at each floor level producing a cascade section.

5 Large internal volumes, such as the sports hall, are released by the development of peripheral density at the site boundaries. The space frame structure is painted scarlet.

6 The mall separates teaching areas on the left from communal spaces to the right.

7 The communal rooms on the south side of the mall have glazed partitions inviting activity and offering interest.

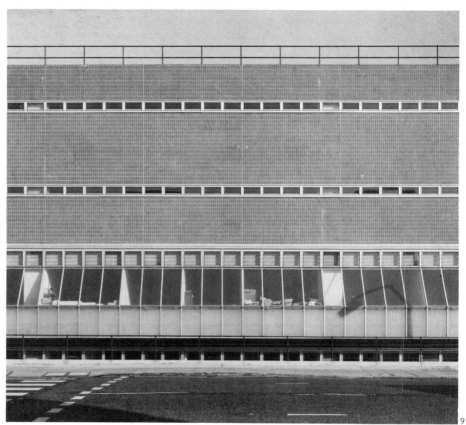

8

9

8 *Internal areas above the sports hall, gymnasium and library are fully glazed providing maximum daylight and natural ventilation in a deep-planned building.*

9 *Facing the noisy London Road the building presents a bland impregnable face of red clay tiles and aluminium framed patent glazing: the rooms just above pavement level were originally machine rooms but they are now tutorial and welfare accommodation with secondary glazing and mechanical ventilation to ameliorate traffic noise.*

10 *The stepped face of the building seen against one of the staircase towers facing south: there is a terrace behind the solid parapet leading from the common and dining rooms.*

10

The Polytechnic of Central London - Marylebone Road

In the 1960's the Polytechnic used up to twenty seven different premises as it had gradually expanded its objectives since becoming the Regent Street Polytechnic in 1881. In an attempt to integrate architecture, building, civil engineering, surveying and town planning studies with the addition of the school of management a 3.90 acre (1.56 hectare) site was developed on Marylebone Road.[5] It was to be a college for the whole of the building industry and the brief was drawn up in 1960 by the LCC, the Ministry of Education and the Polytechnic and the disciplines were to be interrelated. A hall of residence for 218 students was included and housing for 115 families as well as offices for the LCC District Surveyor. The complex was completed in 1971.

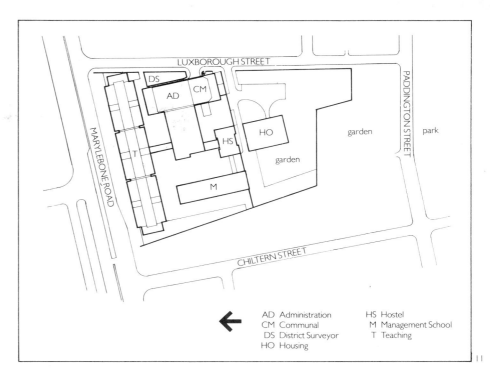

AD Administration
CM Communal
DS District Surveyor
HO Housing
HS Hostel
M   Management School
T   Teaching

11

11 Site Plan
To the North is the extremely busy and very noisy Marylebone Road whilst to the South is a quiet garden leading across Paddington Street to a small park. Adjacent roads are lined by tall Edwardian blocks of flats. The layout demonstrates

functional separation into teaching, administration, communal, residential, local authority housing and offices for the District Surveyor.
12 Ground Floor Plan
The general level is one metre above adjacent pavements and is a paved podium

over three storeys of underground laboratories, workshops, stores, car parking, etc. The housing block is placed among gardens three metres below podium level: see Fig 15 for section.

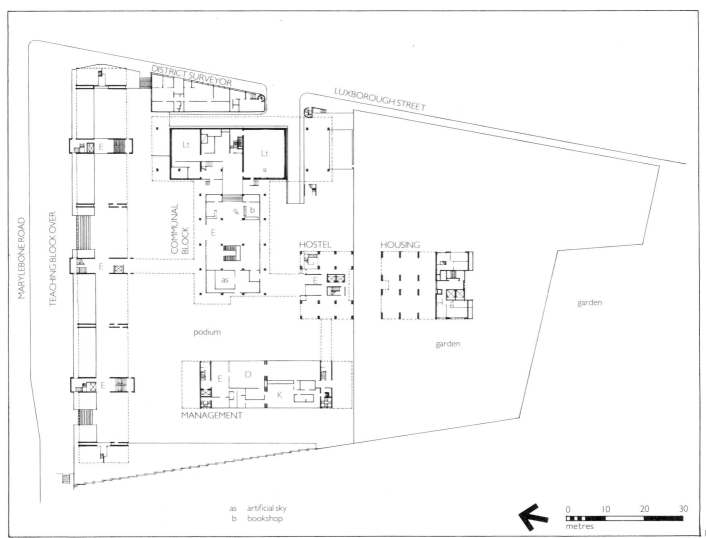

as artificial sky
b   bookshop

0 10 20 30
metres

12

251

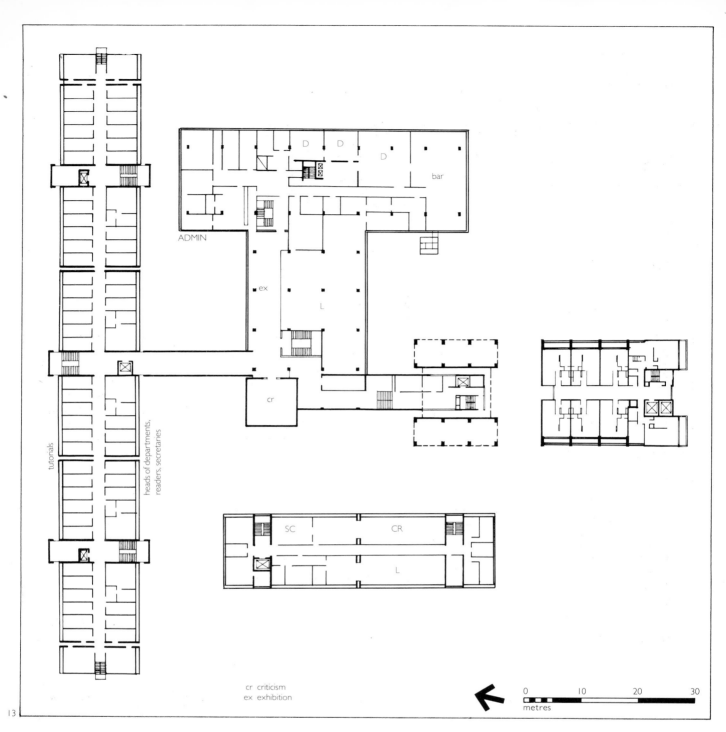

heads of departments, readers, secretaries

tutorials

ADMIN

ex

L

cr

D D

D

bar

SC   CR

L

cr criticism
ex exhibition

0   10   20   30
metres

13

The range of teaching accommodation is very wide with two huge construction halls with service road, laboratories, tutorial, teaching and seminar rooms and a complex of interrelated studios. With administrative, library and dining areas to be considered also the architects pursued the planning objective of functional grouping to resolve and distinguish the elements of the college.[6] Thus the teaching facilities are grouped along Marylebone Road in a seven storey block culminating in a massive hammerhead for the top two layers of studios. The construction halls and associated laboratories are buried deep underground with their roof forming a podium one metre above road level whilst the communal/administrative/library block is connected with an enclosed overhead walkway to the teaching block: the

podium one metre above road level whilst the communal/administrative/library block is connected with an enclosed overhead walkway to the teaching block: the communal block is connected in turn with the residential block. The school of management studies was required to be wholly separate, even to its kitchen accommodation. The elements are expressed in a clear geometry of white concrete and aluminium sliding windows.[7] The teaching block structure has white in-situ cores (containing staircases, lifts and lavatories) and twin cross walls (forming vertical ducts and expansion joints) at 15.00 m centres with end cantilevers up to 6.00 m giving clear floor areas of 200 square metres without vertical interruption: the structural edge beams are of polished precast concrete with Portland stone

aggregate.[8] The residential block (and closely associated housing block) is expressed as a twenty four storey tower with the construction largely of in-situ concrete and precast facing panels under windows.[9,10]

13 First Floor Plan
The teaching block structure allows wide clear areas with demountable partitions giving full flexibility within each 200m² space. The management school has the same type of construction including the end cantilevers. The library represents the central point in the general development. Housing takes the form of small flats at this level.

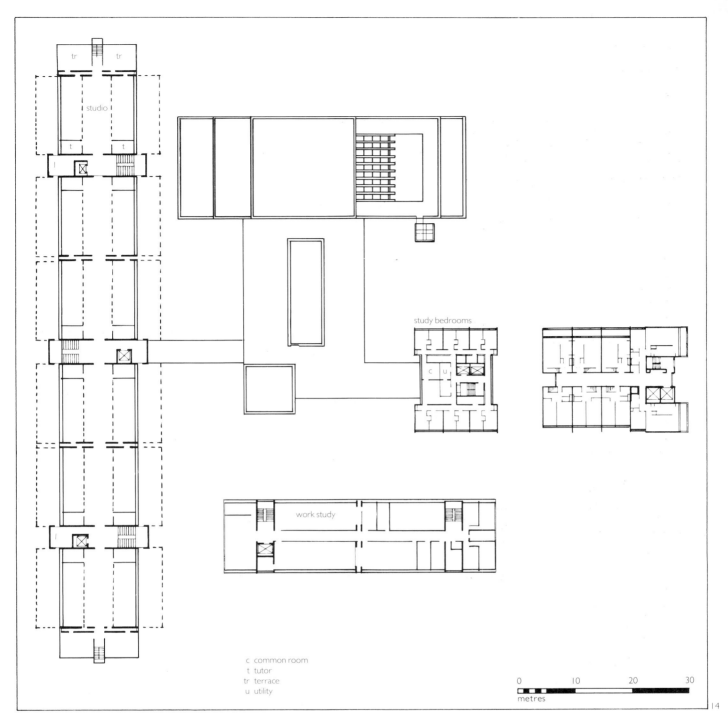

c common room
t tutor
tr terrace
u utility

0   10   20   30
metres

14

14 Fourth Floor Plan
*The three storeys of interlocked studios
begin at this level with the fifth floor
studios shown dotted. Residential
accommodation has twelve individual
student rooms to each floor with shared
bathrooms, utility rooms and sitting rooms.
Housing has maisonettes at this point.*
15 Section
*The section demonstrates the functional
separation of the different blocks again
describing their differing internal and
external scales according to use.*

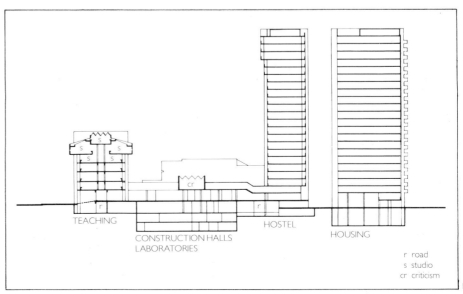

TEACHING

CONSTRUCTION HALLS
LABORATORIES

HOSTEL

HOUSING

r road
s studio
cr criticism

15

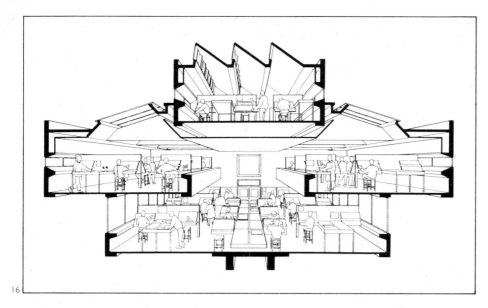

16

19

17

18

20

16 Original sketch of interlocking studio arrangement.

17 Massive engineering construction halls form the basement under the teaching block with full road access within the site for large low-loader and articulated lorries.

18 At the top of the teaching block the studios are contained in cantilevered elements. Internally they interconnect.

19 The studios cantilever out over Marylebone Road: all floors are of precast concrete ribs as expressed in the soffit.

20 With the teaching block on the right an enclosed bridge gives connection to the residential and communal blocks to the left.

21 Across the podium the teaching block faces south with the separate management accommodation to the left. Finishes are limited to white concrete, aluminium window frames with aluminium cladding to the cantilevered ends of the teaching block.

22 From Luxborough Street one sees the end of the teaching block, an access to the podium, the district surveyor's office immediately at street level with the communal block over. The residential blocks tower over all.

23 The teaching block continues the scale and urbanism of Marylebone Road whilst providing pedestrians views across the podium to gardens and trees.

24 An axonometric drawing of the complete development.

21

23

22

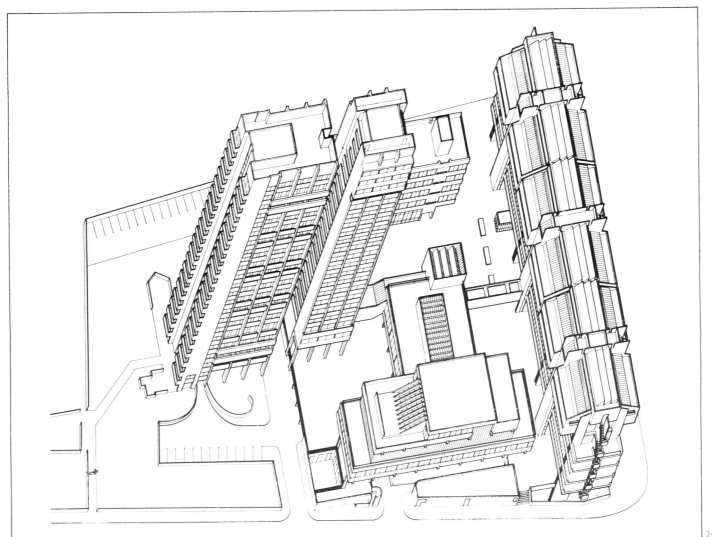

24

South East London Technical College—Breakspears Road

Since the construction of the original Tressilian building in 1929 (see Chapter 1) many annexes and leased buildings had been used to expand the College activities to meet local needs. The new building, containing 2457 square metres of accommodation, was built between 1973 and 1977 in order to provide better accommodation for the existing electrical, mechanical and catering departments which required more sophisticated servicing than that provided in the earlier building: moving these activities from Tressilian would allow the building to be remodelled to rehouse outlying departments. The Breakspears building also contains a large refectory, library and an examination and recreation hall.

The site is 5.45 acres (2.18 hectares) and is closely bounded by roads and large Victorian villas. When the building was being designed allowance had to be made for one of the proposed urban motorways (Ringway 1) which was being designed to pass within a few metres of the completed block. Due to the anticipated high noise levels from the motorway and the adjoining railway a sealed block was developed a provide an acceptable internal environment: this implied mechanical ventilation and an economical plan was devised with a low floor to external wall ratio to keep the building within cost limits. The eventual form is a square, fully air-conditioned block arranged on five floors. At a late stage the motorway was cancelled but the building proceeded as designed.

Each floor generally contains one department with the smaller, quieter rooms placed around the perimeter separated by a racetrack corridor, acting as an internal sound barrier, from the larger and usually noisier areas in the centre core. Circulation is direct and simple with four staircases located at each corridor change of direction. A large number of glazed screens are arranged in the corridor walls to

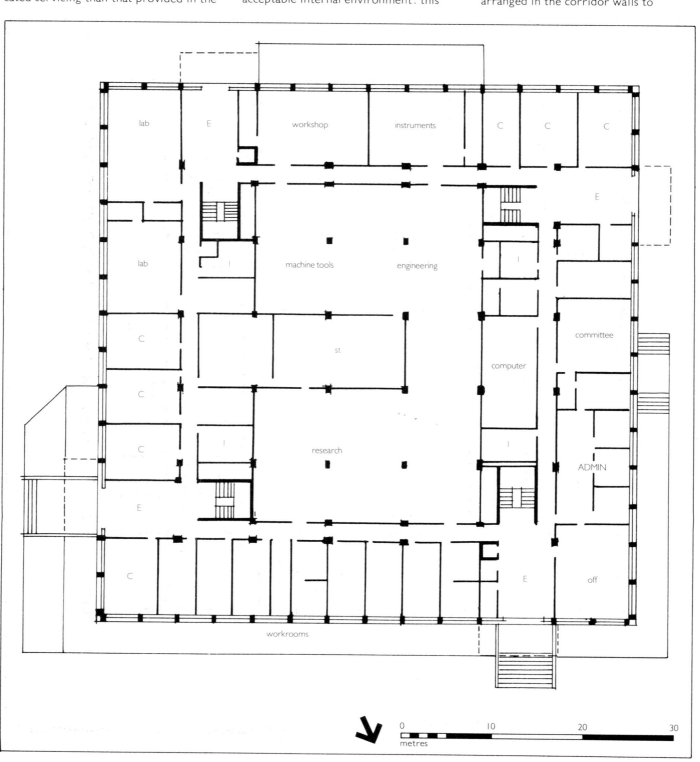

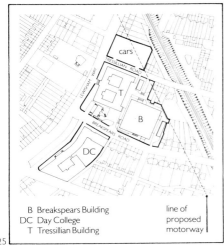

25 Site Plan

The original South East London Technical Institute (see Chapter 1), now known as the Tressillian Building, had expanded to include the South London Day College upon an adjoining site and had several annexes, some of which were several miles away.

The Breakspears Building was intended to make the South East London Technical College more centralised, reducing administrative and travelling costs. The line of the proposed motorway Ringway 1 indicates the proximity of high noise levels in conjunction with the railway line.

26, 27, 28 Plans, level 2, 4 & 5

The shape shows a deep building sealed against projected noise from a proposed closely adjacent motorway: once the building requires to be sealed and air-

conditioned these properties can be used to their maximum effect in the building function producing a square plan.

Level 2 is effectively a raised ground floor above plant rooms and heavy machine laboratories.

Level 4 and 5 show the arrangement of large central spaces with smaller peripheral teaching spaces: there are many internal glazed screens in corridor partitions to give outside views from the central core.

B Breakspears Building
DC Day College
T Tressillian Building

line of
proposed
motorway

25

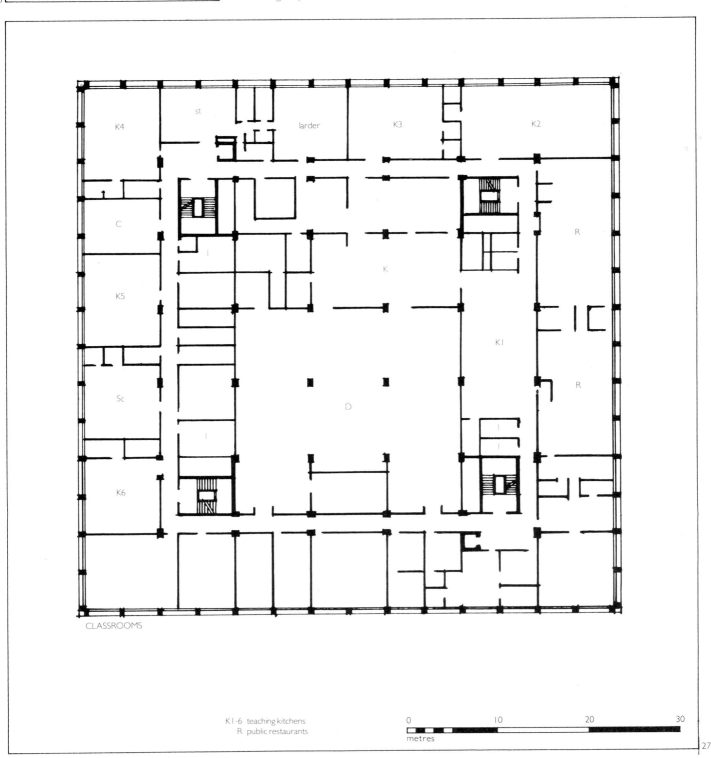

CLASSROOMS

K1-6 teaching kitchens
R public restaurants

0   10   20   30
metres

27

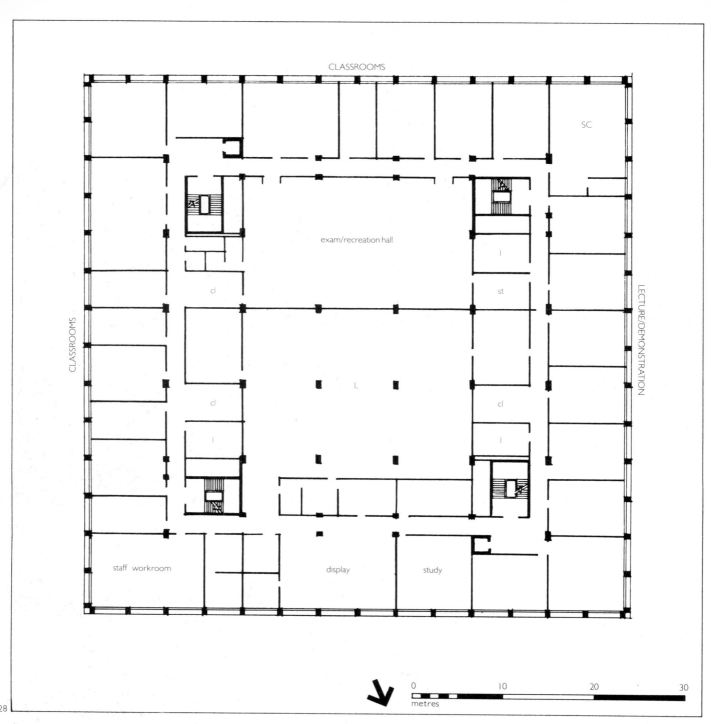

CLASSROOMS

SC

CLASSROOMS

LECTURE/DEMONSTRATION

exam/recreation hall

cl

st

l

cl

cl

L

l

l

staff workroom

display

study

0   10   20   30
metres

28

provide a visual link to the external environment.

The main structure is an in-situ reinforced concrete frame with columns at 8.40 m centres with floors designed to take 5KN/m2 over the entire area. Apart from the columns, staircases, ducts and lavatories are the only static elements on each floor providing a high level of future flexibility necessary for the type of courses offered by the College. External cladding is with exposed aggregate precast units with direct glazing: these units are heavily sculptured with deeply recessed windows to provide internal shade and avoid solar heat gain. Perimeter rooms have suspended ceilings containing air-conditioning trunking and terminal reheat boxes whilst this equipment in the central laboratories and workshops is exposed and painted.

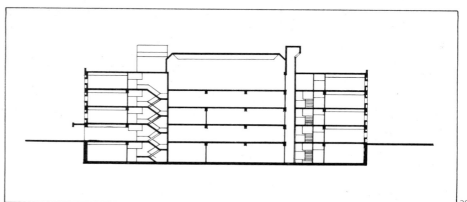

29

29 Section
The section shows the servicing arrangement, with the central areas having exposed air-conditioning trunking fed from the deep horizontal ducts above corridors, which also supply the teaching rooms *(which have suspended ceilings). The main vertical air ducts run alongside the four staircases. In the central core laboratories are progressively quieter as they rise, producing acceptable sound levels in dining and examination halls.*

30   View from the east.
31   External cladding is heavily modelled
to avoid solar gain in order to reduce load
on air-conditioning plant. Deeply recessed
windows are glazed direct with gaskets
into the concrete structure.
32   Detail of corner junction showing
jointing of precast structural frame.
33   A typical general classroom on the
perimeter of the building. The windows are
fixed and the suspended ceiling contains
air-conditioning ducts.

Thames Polytechnic

This Polytechnic was formed by the amalgamation of institutions as far apart as Woolwich and Hammersmith and by 1970 it was apparent that an ideal site could be identified at the proposed centre of Thamesmead for the development of a complete new campus of buildings. Although the area was clear of other buildings and was comparatively flat the sheer size of the undertaking spawned a complexity that only figures can convey initially. The four faculties of architecture, social science, science and engineering would provide 6,300 full time student places, requiring a total floor area of 99,750 square metres. Teaching and support staff would swell the number of people on the campus to 8,500 and residential accommodation for 750 students would be required.

The proposed site was 18.00 acres (7.20 hectares) with its southern boundary against a lake and its northern tip adjoining the main business/shopping centre of Thamesmead: a canal skirted the eastern edge and a main bus route crossed the top of the site whilst a playing field separated the western side from a potentially noisy primary traffic route. Total site development was programmed to progress in five consecutive construction stages starting in 1976 and finally completing in 1986. Against these requirements the architects set out with some deliberation towards a development plan using a method for arriving at conclusions which provided flexibility and a range of options to accommodate unforeseen change whilst providing a framework for decision. Roles of groups involved in the planning process were described, principles were recorded in developing the working method and a permanent record of decisions made with physical and policy alternatives for their implementation.

Site constraints (including the Thamesmead network of pedestrian routes, cycle ways and canal links) were put into context with environmental records, Faculty structures and needs were analysed with a breakdown into use specialised, activity specialised and use shared: from this options were identified giving a range of proposals based upon faculty interrelationships. Linear and nuclear growth were weighed against a centralised library, administration and services with the need to maintain pedestrian, vehicular and fire brigade access during all phases whilst extending the necessary underground services.

Studies of education building modules in relation to proposed use produced a basic construction grid of 7.20 m which translated easily into a band element of 14.40 m describing space use and structural alternatives: a system of planning grid choices evolved demonstrating the possibilities and consequences of briefing decisions − planning grids with solid and open

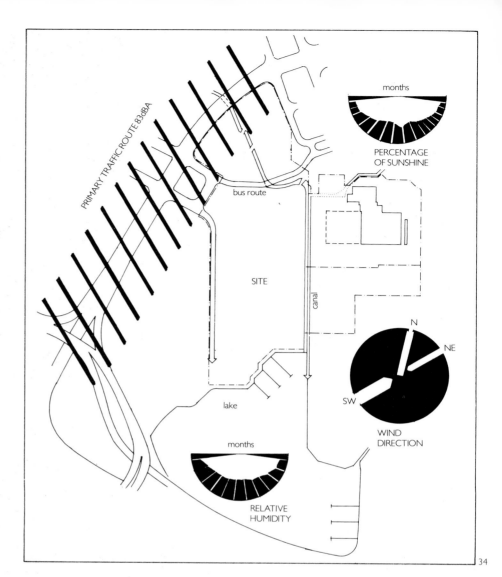

34

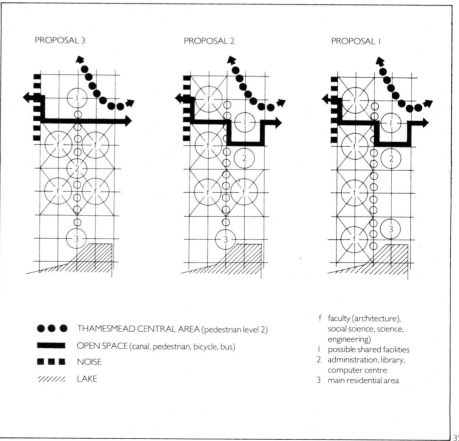

PROPOSAL 3   PROPOSAL 2   PROPOSAL 1

●●● THAMESMEAD CENTRAL AREA (pedestrian level 2)

▬▬ OPEN SPACE (canal, pedestrian, bicycle, bus)

■■■ NOISE

/////// LAKE

f faculty (architecture), social science, science, engineering)
1 possible shared facilities
2 administration, library, computer centre
3 main residential area

35

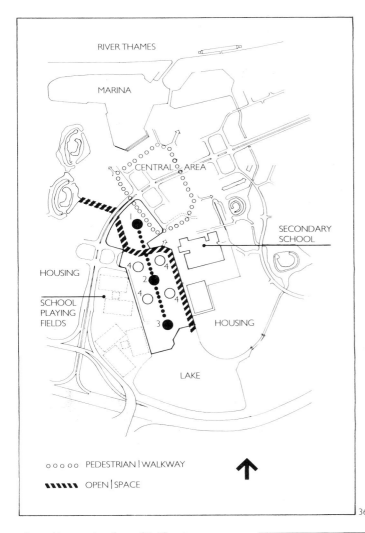

elements ranging from 21.60 m to
72.00 m portrayed an average building
height of 2.75 storeys rising to seven
storeys. The outcome was a proposal for
a generally four storey development
along and around courtyards with the
main spine an open street with banks,
shops and cafes marking the faculties and
leading from the Thamesmead Centre's
high level pedestrian shopping centre
down to the lake. At the northern, and
noisiest, end of the site were placed the
buildings – the sports centre, arts
centre, assembly hall, students' union,
communal catering and some student
housing – which also had a public
attraction with the Centre's associated
ecumenical, medical and law centres and
the main bus terminus. The teaching
accommodation would be arranged in an
indeterminate way allowing faculties to
expand and contract as demanded, for
the proposals worked in terms of overall
grids, with linkages and routes lines of
circulation produced a framework of
building spaces. Whatever was built
initially left many options for future
development, for a finite set of buildings
was not proposed but a system of
relationships within which were many
options.[11]

The national economy faltered in late
1973 and this Polytechnic development
plan was never realised physically. The
Polytechnic remains centred in
Woolwich with many leased premises
and annexes.

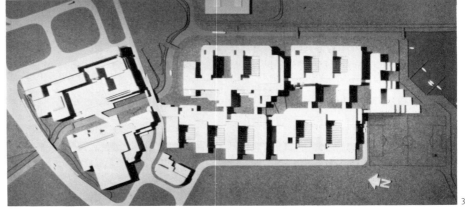

34   Environmental Constraints, 1972
*A large (18 acre) urban site provides many
environmental considerations ranging from
traffic noise from the primary traffic route
to the west to percentage and angles of
sunshine apart from other local
requirements such as – at Thamesmead –
canals, pedestrian and cycle routes,
permanently accessible service ways and
bus routes which may cross the site.*
35   Faculty Constraints, 1972
*A range of proposals based upon faculty
interrelationships emerged as optional
arrangements weighted against linear or
nuclear development.*
   *Proposal 3 was considered to provide the
optimum flexibility and this was pursued.*
36   Final Proposal, 1972
*The diagram shown in Fig 35 translated
into physical terms with the campus*

*adjoining the business centre in the North
and the lake to the South.*
37   *Photograph of the working model
shows all five stages constructed with the
areas for potentially sharing with the
community – sports centre, arts centre and
assembly hall – on the left adjacent to the
Thamesmead Central Area. At the top is
Waterfield Secondary School (see Chapter
6) across a canal and pedestrian/cycle
route.*
38   *View of the working model from the
north showing the general arrangement of
the faculties and the character of the
'street' leading down from Thamesmead
Central Area to the lake: the blocks
represent a framework of building spaces
based upon overall grids, services and
circulation routes.*

Merchant Navy College

In 1968 the College was formed by the amalgamation of the Incorporated Thames Nautical Training College (HMS Worcester) with part of the King Edward VII Nautical College and the inclusion of marine radio studies from South London College. The College now offers education and training in navigation and radio disciplines to young people and to practised mariners seeking to extend their expertise with the intention of producing fully integrated ship management team members.

The site is 37.00 acres (14.80 hectares) at Greenhithe, Kent and rises 30.00 m from the flat south bank of the Thames to the crest of the North Downs. On the flat, lower half of the site are extensive games facilities whilst the buildings are constructed on the rising ground. The site is bisected by a major lorry route in a cutting and two disused chalk pits leave a spur projecting from the hillside.

The administration and communal facilities are contained in a four storey block which forms the hub of the complex and crosses over the cutting:[12] as the College is fully self-contained a sick bay and laundry are additions to the normal facilities found in an establishment of this size. Dining is at the north end of this block having a two storey hall overlooking the river.[13] Above this block is the full size replica of a ship's bridge and this is backed up by a windowless radar cabin with scanners mounted on adjoining roofs and on the ship's mast which surmounts the complex. The main teaching rooms are in a single storey wing fronting the playing fields and running under the main block: these contain a planetarium, chart and instrument rooms. At the western end of the teaching accommodation is a games hall and swimming pool for survival training. Boatwork is centred around a boathouse, slipway and

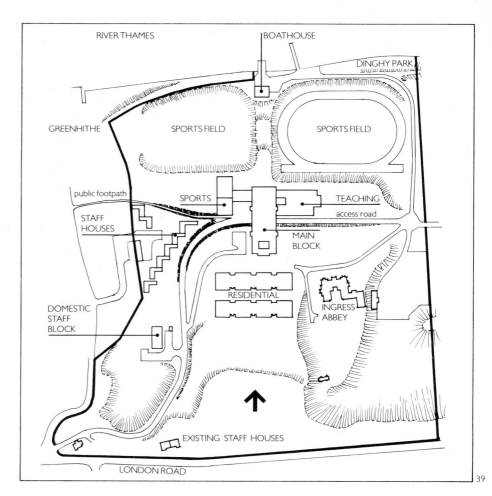

dinghy park which are astride the river wall.

Students' residential accommodation is in two separate blocks which step back and match the contours of the steep hillside.[14] There are 268 self-contained individual cabins with suites for resident instructors and a large recreation room. Staff accommodation is a block of nine stepped houses on the western boundary giving direct pedestrian access into Greenhithe. Domestic staff and the caretaker are

accommodated in a block by the main access road.[15]

The main building and teaching accommodation has an in-situ reinforced concrete frame with coffered floor and roof slabs.[16] Residential accommodation is of loadbearing white concrete blocks with in-situ concrete floor and roof slabs. Exposed concrete is white and window frames are stained pine with metal opening lights. The building was completed in 1975.

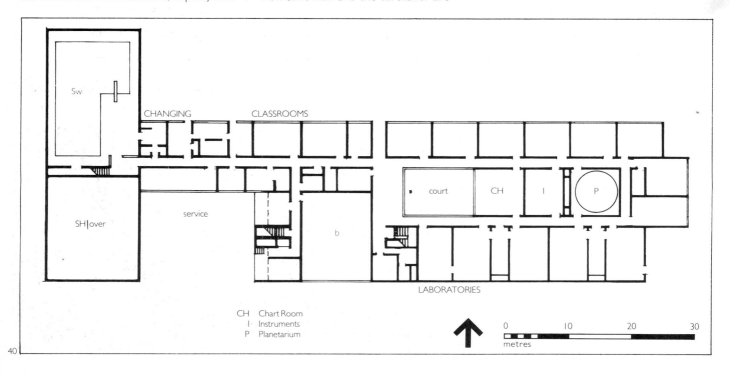

CH   Chart Room
I   Instruments
P   Planetarium

0   10   20   30
metres

39 Site Plan
*The main buildings are placed on the flat
riverside plateau below the crest of the
North Downs whilst the residential blocks
are constructed on rising ground. The site
is bisected by a major lorry route serving
industrial areas to the East.*

40 Ground Floor Plan
*A single storey teaching block passes under
the administration and communal block
linking with the swimming pool and games
hall.*

41 Second Floor Plan
*The main entrance level is raised to
provide headroom over the lorry route
which passes below the kitchen. The
southern end of the block is open giving
direct access to the residential blocks
through a courtyard.*

42 Third Floor Plan
*This level provides mainly staff rooms with
the double-height dining room overlooking
the Thames. Above the dining area, on the
roof, is a complete ship's bridge with full
working wheelhouse and radar systems.*

43 Residential Floor Plan
*The residential blocks are on three and
four levels and as they step back up the
slope the floor levels vary: this represents
the typical layout for the second level.*

44 *View from the west showing the main
administration/communal block straddling
a major lorry route to nearby industry. On
the left is the games hall and to the far
right is the residential area.*

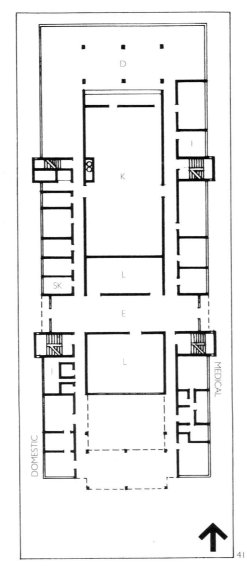

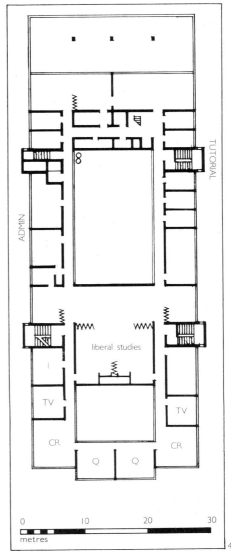

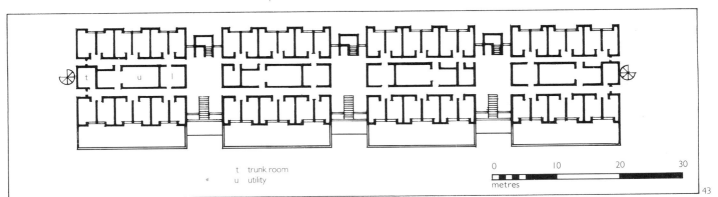

t trunk room
u utility

45

45 *General view from the north-east showing the four storey administration and communal block, surmounted by a replica of a ship's bridge, with the single storey teaching block running underneath. On the right is the swimming pool and games hall and the residential blocks rise up the hill behind the main block.*
46 *The dining hall commands the sweep of the river Thames. Main construction, of in-situ white concrete, is expressed and the windows have brilliant coloured curtains to full height.*
47 *On the roof of the main building is a working replica of a ship's bridge which commands the view of the river Thames. The bridge is fully equipped with radar, radio and other electronic aids.*
48 *Above the teaching and training elements of the College the residential blocks rise up the face of the North Downs. Each block steps up the contour face and contains individual cabins. Framed by the blocks is Ingress Abbey a listed building of historic interest.*

46

48

47

264

Hammersmith and West London College

This College was formed by the amalgamation of West London College, Hammersmith College for Further Education and Hammersmith College of Art and Building which between them formerly occupied nine separate buildings. The opportunity to rebuild arose with the purchase of the site of St Paul's School which had itself been rebuilt at Barnes. New housing occupies the northern half of the site and the College has the southern 6.00 acres (2.40 hectares) which adjoin a six lane major road giving high traffic noise.

In order to provide acceptable conditions for the 2,500 students the layout has been designed to shield the majority of teaching rooms from traffic noise.[17] Most of the teaching accommodation is in two crescent-shaped blocks of five and seven storeys which, effectively, turn their backs upon the nuisance using corridors and storage space as buffer areas. These two blocks contain a variety of teaching space from classrooms to seminar and tutorial rooms and they are linked at second floor by a ring of accommodation including common rooms, dining rooms and the main administration suite. The link between the blocks is substantiated by a large two storey library with its own wide, internal spiral staircase. As a further barrier against noise the communal block is placed to shield the western crescent. This block is virtually sealed containing a sports hall, gymnasium, a dance/drama centre, main kitchen and dining areas.

Held between the four blocks is an irregularly shaped piazza at first floor level which resulted from the requirement to allow a public, pedestrian concourse to traverse the site. In order to obtain pedestrian and internal service traffic separation the concourse is gradually raised by steps and interlocking ramps providing at the focus of the buildings the piazza[18] with its beds of flowers and shrubs and sculpture, a place to sit for the student or passer-by. A careers office opens off the concourse. The main entrance steps rise between planting boxes to the reception area at second floor level. It is from here that an internal promenade, with red quarry tiles, links all four blocks together.[19] Below the level of the piazza and other raised areas are a television studio, language laboratories and a youth club which caters for the neighbourhood.

Construction, which started in 1976, is an in-situ reinforced concrete frame with red engineering brick cladding which is prevalent inside in circulation and communal areas and providing a diamond cut, sparkling red building, 'smart and powerful'.[20] The piazza and all external works and walls are in the same red brick with the brick used for the adjoining housing used in panels. Windows are softwood stained black with a secure type of glass louvre for opening lights. The College was completed in 1980.

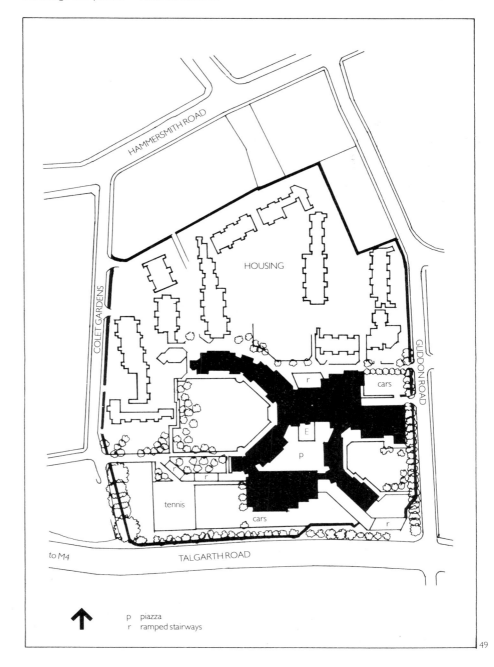

49 Site Plan
The site has a very busy feeder road to the M4 on the South, with new housing to the North shielded by the College from traffic noise. Public walkways run from Colet Gardens to Gliddon Road and from Hammersmith Road to Talgarth Road.

p piazza
r ramped stairways

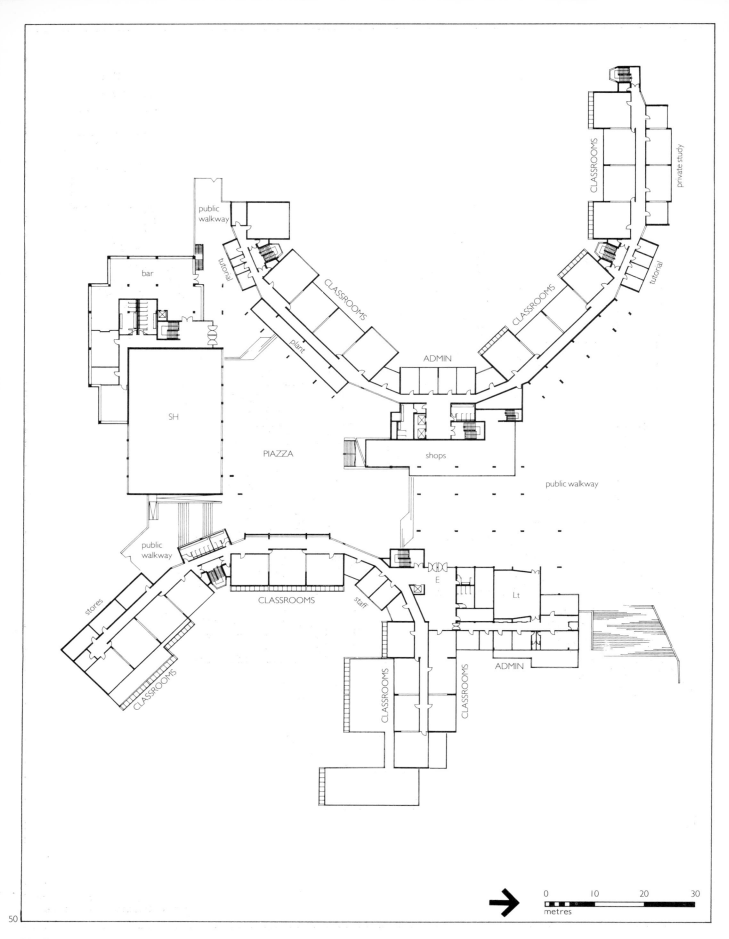

50 Plan Level 2
Three raised pedestrian routes meet in the piazza. Below this level are car parking, service roads, gymnasium, TV Studio, language laboratories, boiler room and peripheral classrooms.

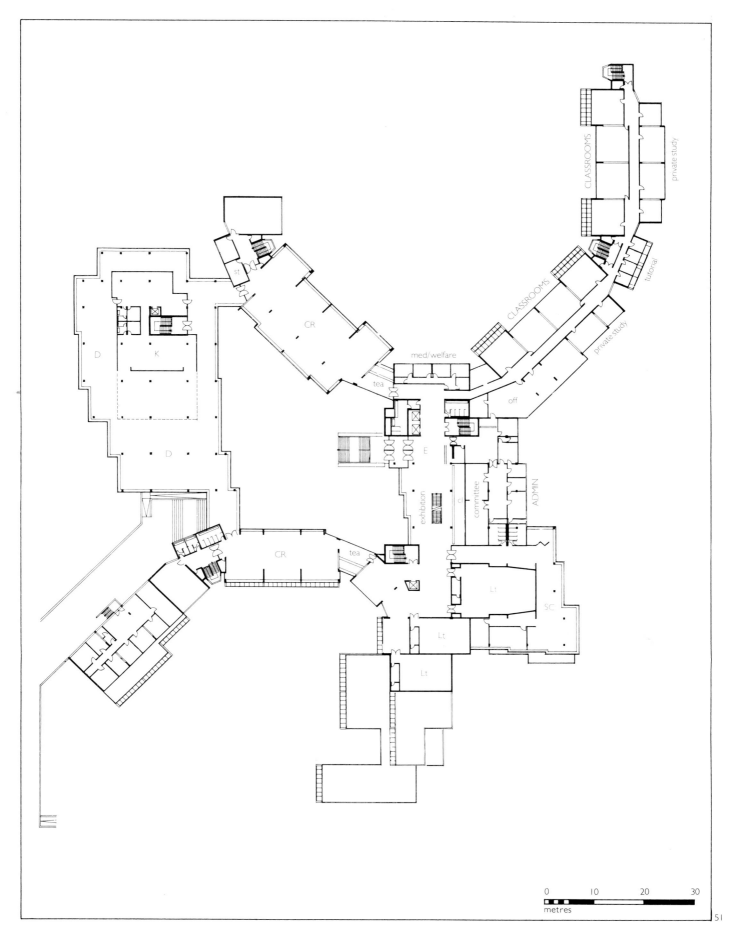

Plan labels: private study, CLASSROOMS, tutorial, private study, CLASSROOMS, med/welfare, off, tea, st, CR, E, exhibition, cl, committee, ADMIN, tea, CR, Lt, SC, Lt, Lt, D, K, D

0 10 20 30
metres

51 Plan Level 3
The main entrance is one storey above the piazza and the building form shows the teaching wings using corridors and storage areas in order to protect teaching areas from traffic noise.

51

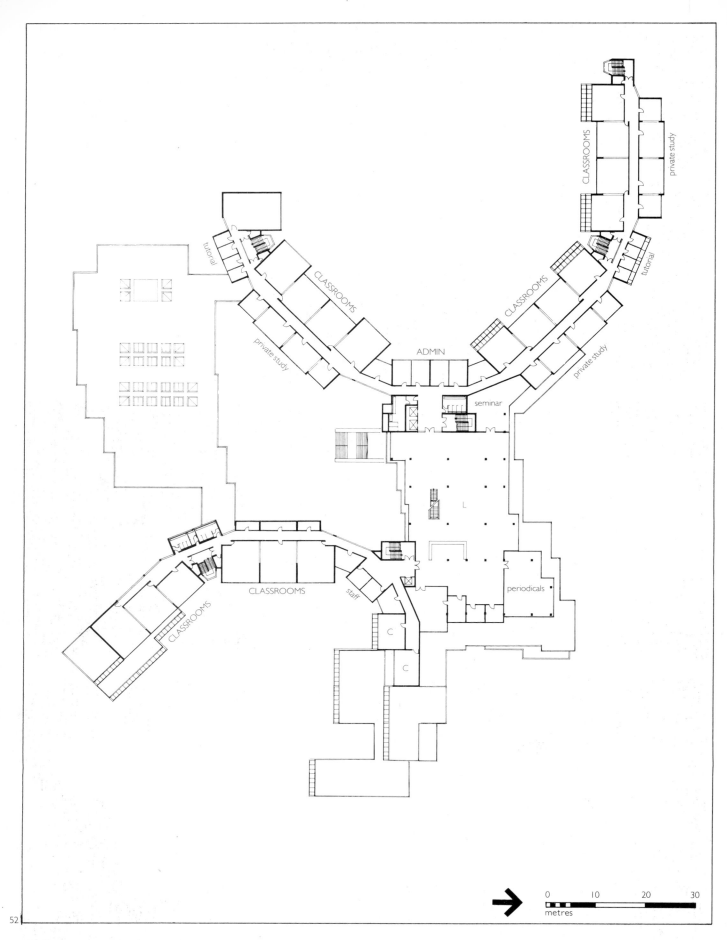

tutorial

CLASSROOMS

private study

CLASSROOMS

ADMIN

CLASSROOMS

tutorial

private study

private study

seminar

L

staff

CLASSROOMS

periodicals

CLASSROOMS

C

C

0   10   20   30
metres

52 Plan Level 4
*The library acts as the main link between
the two teaching wings. Classrooms
continue upward to level 7.*

53 The library is on two levels connected by a spiral stair.
54 The communal block is placed as a barrier against high traffic noise to protect the teaching wings.
55 Dining area faces south.
56 One of the fully-equipped lecture theatres: the consistent use of materials throughout the building provides unity.
57 The western teaching wing sweeps around a garden.

53

54

55

56

57

58

58 The eastern teaching block has its own small enclosure.
59 At first floor level the main entrance masters a piazza which is part of a public walkway bisecting the site. A service road runs beneath the piazza. Cladding is red engineering brick with black-stained window frames.
60 Spotlights illuminate the piazza and public walkway after dark. The library acts as a link between the two teaching wings.

59

60

270

City of London Polytechnic

In 1970 the Polytechnic was designated being an amalgamation of four colleges: the City of London College, the Sir John Cass School of Science and Technology, the Sir John Cass School of Art and the King Edward VII Nautical College. The colleges inhabited fourteen different sets of premises eleven of which were leasehold. The initial intention was to draw these institutions together with a new building complex in the Dockland area with an associated City Centre to maintain traditional business education links with the City. A combined total of 7,000 full time students was intended for 1981.

Due to high numbers of students pursuing sandwich, part time, block release and short time courses the 'student day' had first to be determined by analysing the range and volume of activities. From this a schedule of general teaching spaces was logically evolved from the complexity of inform-ation by the use of computer program-ming to maximise space utilisation. The Dockland building was to be centred upon the library as a learning resource centre which would feed the associated classrooms, seminar, tutorial and study areas. The library would not only be the teaching centre of the Polytechnic but the physical focus also.

Several Dockland sites were in-vestigated and in 1975 a proposal was published for using the abandoned London Dock to form the nucleus of a new building. This could not be realised, however, and another site of 6.00 acres (2.40 hectares) was purchased by the ILEA fronting the Thames and centred upon the Free Trade Wharf, built in 1795. The development plan shows a teaching wall against the traffic noise from the Highway breaking down into courts, roof decks and gardens towards the river where a public riverside walk can be entered through the Free Trade Wharf buildings which were to be developed as a piazza descending with shops. The Wharf blocks would have been rehabilitated as staff and student common rooms at the lower levels with squash courts, activities room, weight training area and games hall above being made available as a local community sports centre. The main entrances into the Polytechnic would have been from the piazza and the whole scheme would have been realised in five stages.

The national economy prevented the new building being included in any firm building programme and government legislation (The Local Government, Planning and Land Act, 1980) makes it unlikely that it will be realised.

61 *Among the early proposals for new buildings for the Polytechnic was one utilising the disused jetties and warehouses at the London Dock.*

The central jetty, which extends across the site was built to carry vehicles with pedestrian traffic at a different level. Around this nucleus would be built a range of teaching rooms upon six levels with the main library/resource centre above the vehicular access.

62 *Ground Floor Plan*
A listed building, The Free Trade Wharf, represents the centre and focal point of the development being the main link from the public road to the riverside walk. It also represents the major community interest in the building giving access to shops, meeting rooms and games facilities. The library learning resource centre is complete upon this level serving the associated classrooms, seminar, tutorial and study areas. The development would have been carried out in five separate phases. The basement level is given over entirely to car parking (337 places) and service areas: all unloading/collection is to be carried out from the main road through loading bays.

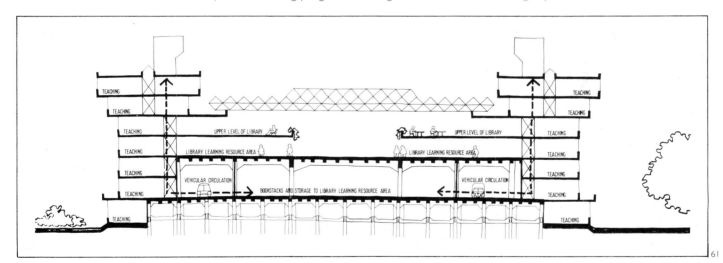

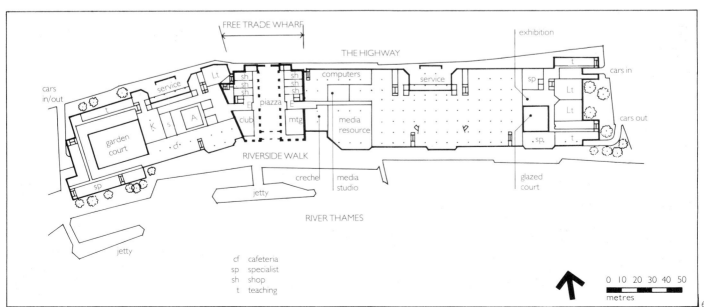

cf cafeteria
sp specialist
sh shop
t   teaching

0 10 20 30 40 50
metres

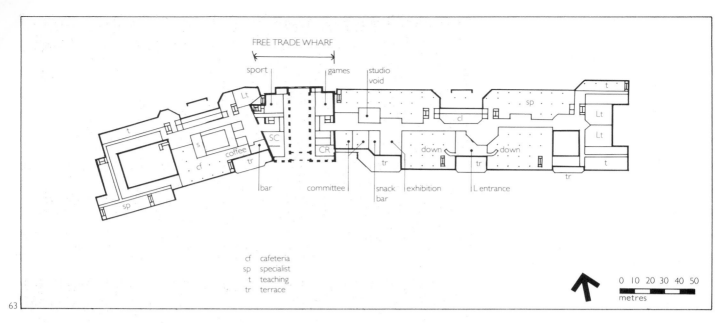

FREE TRADE WHARF

sport   games   studio
                  void

Lt
                              sp
t   Lt
          s   Lt
SC   cl
      coffee   t
cf   CR
          tr   down   down
sp   tr   tr
                                         tr

bar   committee   snack   exhibition   L entrance
                    bar

cf   cafeteria
sp   specialist
t   teaching
tr   terrace

0 10 20 30 40 50
metres

63

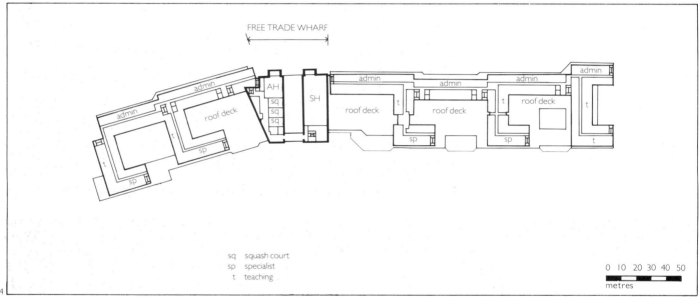

FREE TRADE WHARF

admin   admin   admin   admin   admin
                    AH
admin   SH
          roof deck   sq   roof deck   roof deck   t   roof deck
                       sq   t
          t   sq   t
                                              sp   sp
sp   sp   t
sp

sq   squash court
sp   specialist
t   teaching

0 10 20 30 40 50
metres

64

65

63 First Floor Plan

With the site shape demanding a long building, relief from long straight corridors is introduced by the articulation of the circulation providing casual places for exhibition, views over the Thames and access to the outside air.

64 Second Floor Plan

From this level upwards administrative areas provide a wall against traffic noise whilst the teaching/specialist areas enclose South facing courtyards overlooking the Thames.

65 View from the south of the development model showing the Free Trade Wharf only left on the site. This was to be the sports and communal centre for the Polytechnic forming a nucleus for the following stages of construction. The space between the two blocks would have been developed as a public piazza with shops and cafes descending from the Highway to the riverside walkway.

66 Development after three stages of construction.

67 The complete development with the building form showing a series of courts, roof decks and gardens descending towards the riverside walk from the tallest blocks fronting the Highway.

68 View of the Polytechnic model looking east along the Highway showing how a teaching wall was proposed against traffic noise and how the teaching wall stepped down to the main pedestrian access at the original Free Trade Wharf entrance. Practically the whole basement area would have been used for car parking with service access of the Highway in lay-bys under the building.

66

67

68

Chapter 15: References

1 Architects Journal, 14th May 1975, p 1021.

2 RIBA Journal, May 1967: *Leslie Martin's 'An Architect's Approach to Architecture' p 198, demonstrated the development of peripheral density as a means of freeing large central areas. The Polytechnic design uses this logic in providing an urban scale to the surrounding streets whilst releasing central space for sports hall and library.*

3 Architects Journal, 28 April 1976, pp 833–846.

4 Architectural Review, September 1980, pp 136–138, 144–153, 170–180.

5 Architectural Design, June 1964, pp 273–276.

6 Architectural Design, November 1970, pp 550–552.

7 Architectural Review, January 1971, pp 7–18.

8 Architects Journal, 2 June 1971, pp. 1245–1264.

9 Deutsche Bauzeitung, April 1973, pp 379–380.

10 Town and Country Planning, February 1974, pp 137–139.

11 RIBA Journal, May 1967: *Leslie Martin's 'An Architect's Approach to Architecture' p 193, demonstrated the options obtained through the use of indeterminate grids using linkages.*

12 Building, 13 January 1978, pp 47–54.

13 Building Design, 10 June 1977, p 24.

14 RIBA Journal, January 1977, p 24.

15 Architect, March 1977, p 55.

16 Concrete Quarterly, January/March 1977, pp 32–35.

17 Contract Journal, 10 March 1977, pp 26–27.

18 Architects Journal, 10 December 1980, pp 1137–1151.

19 Building Design, 5 September 1980, p 19.

20 Architects Journal, 10 December 1980, p 1137.

Key to drawings

A	assembly hall
AEI	adult education institute
AH	activities hall
C	classroom
CR	common room
D	dining
Dr	drama
DW	dining/work
E	entrance
G	gymnasium
H	houseroom
Hm	home bay
Ht	head or principal
I	infants
J	juniors
K	kitchen
L	library
Lt	lecture
M	music
Ns	nursery
P	practical area
PC	play centre
Q	quiet area
S	secretary
Sc	science
SC	staff common room
SH	sports hall
SK	schoolkeeper
Sw	swimming pool
W	waiting
YS	youth service
b	boiler
ca	covered area
ch	changing
cl	cloakroom
l	lavatories
s	servery
st	store

Appendix A New Primary & Secondary School places, 1947-74

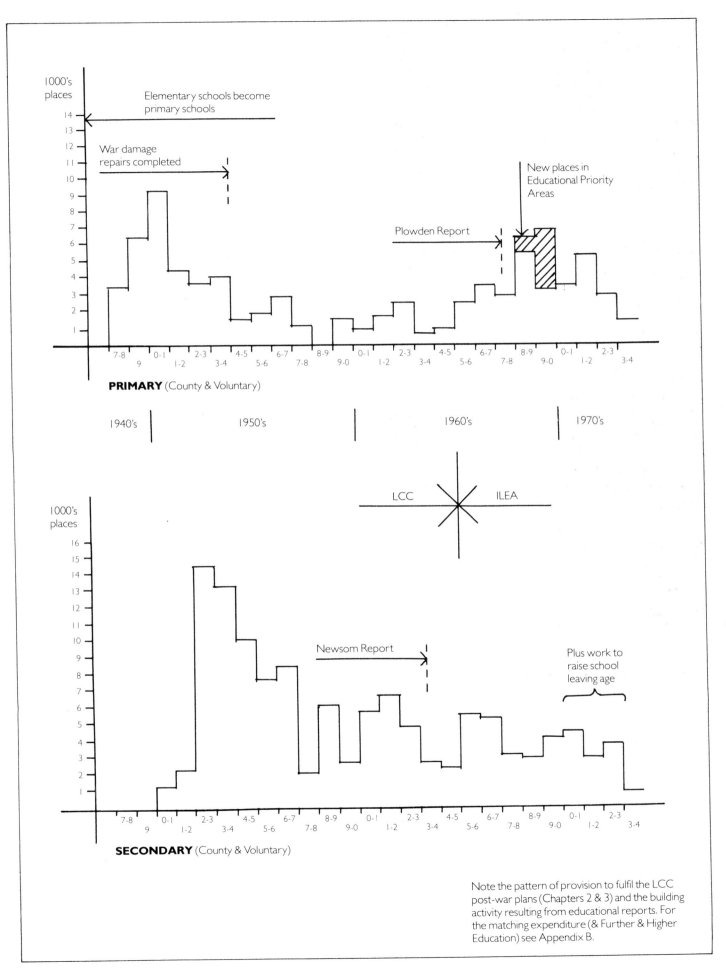

PRIMARY (County & Voluntary)

1940's | 1950's | 1960's | 1970's

LCC / ILEA

SECONDARY (County & Voluntary)

Note the pattern of provision to fulfil the LCC post-war plans (Chapters 2 & 3) and the building activity resulting from educational reports. For the matching expenditure (& Further & Higher Education) see Appendix B.

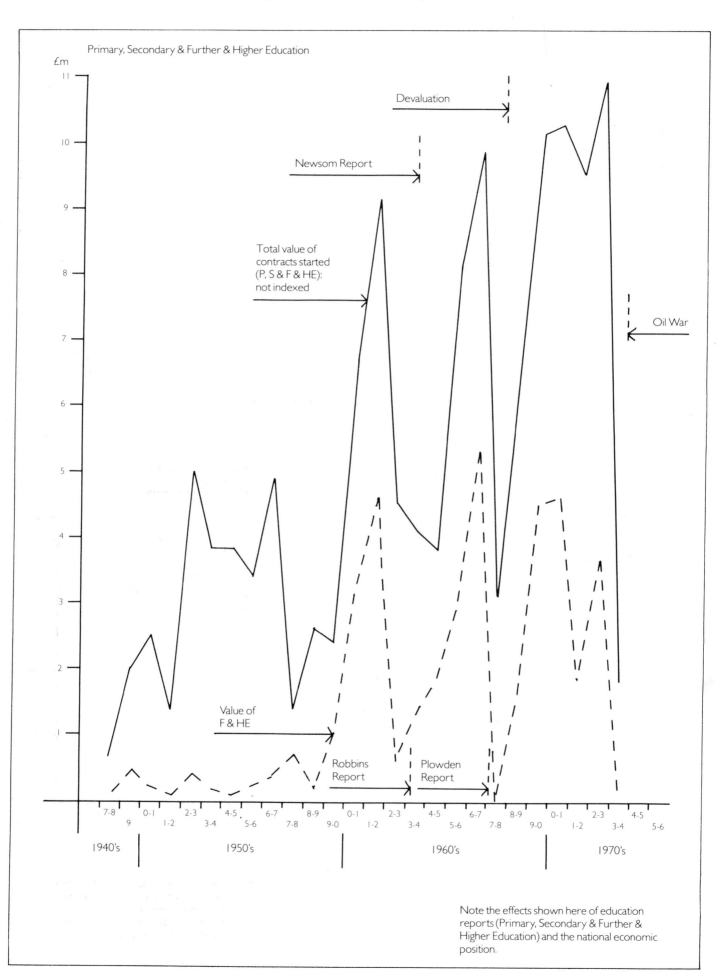

Primary, Secondary & Further & Higher Education

£m

Devaluation

Newsom Report

Total value of
contracts started
(P, S & F & HE):
not indexed

Oil War

Value of
F & HE

Robbins
Report

Plowden
Report

1940's   1950's   1960's   1970's

Note the effects shown here of education
reports (Primary, Secondary & Further &
Higher Education) and the national economic
position.

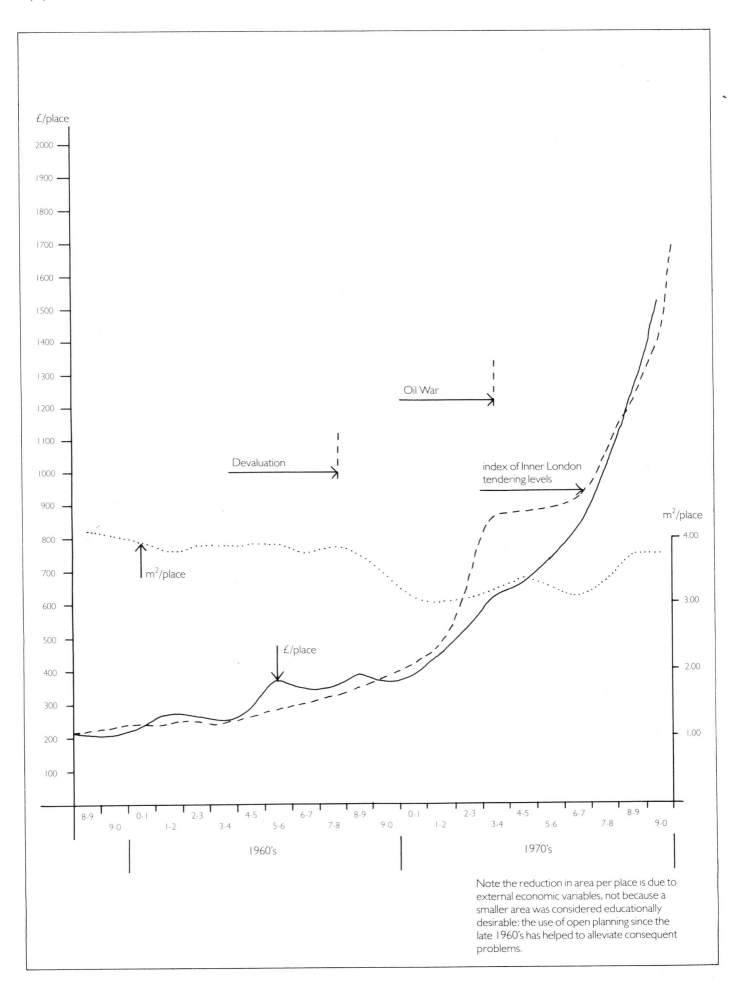

£/place

2000
1900
1800
1700
1600
1500
1400
1300
1200
1100
1000
900
800
700
600
500
400
300
200
100

Devaluation

Oil War

index of Inner London
tendering levels

m²/place

£/place

m²/place

4.00

3.00

2.00

1.00

8-9   9-0   0-1   1-2   2-3   3-4   4-5   5-6   6-7   7-8   8-9   9-0   0-1   1-2   2-3   3-4   4-5   5-6   6-7   7-8   8-9   9-0

1960's

1970's

Note the reduction in area per place is due to
external economic variables, not because a
smaller area was considered educationally
desirable: the use of open planning since the
late 1960's has helped to alleviate consequent
problems.

Appendix D *Special School provision and cost, 1947-74*

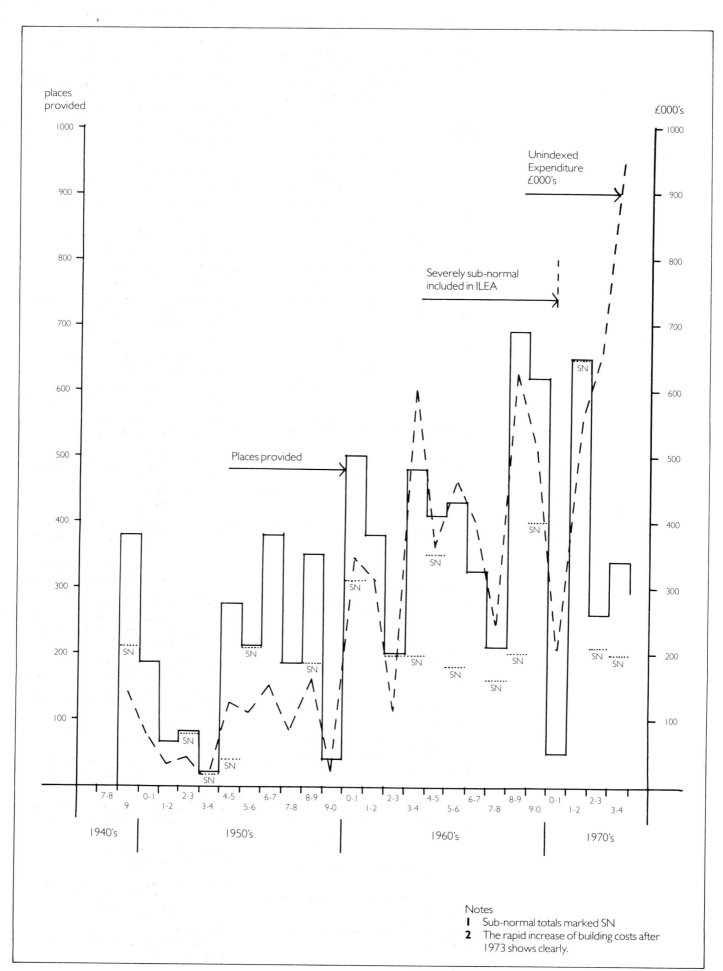

places provided

£000's

Unindexed
Expenditure
£000's

Severely sub-normal
included in ILEA

Places provided

SN

1940's | 1950's | 1960's | 1970's

Notes
1 Sub-normal totals marked SN
2 The rapid increase of building costs after
   1973 shows clearly.

278

Bibliography

Ader J, *Building Implications of the Multi-Option School*, OECD, 1976

Airoldi R, *Innovazione Didattica e Spazi*, Instituto Editoriale Internazionale, 1977.

A Study of School Building, Report of the DES Interdepartmental Group, HMSO, 1977.

Benn C, and Simon B, *Half Way There*. Report on the British comprehensive school reform McGraw-Hill, 1970.

Briault E, and Payling D, *London Comprehensive Schools 1966*, ILEA, 1967.

Brodner E, and Kroeker I, *Schulbauten*, Verlag Hermann Ring, Munich, 1951.

Building for School and Community, Volumes 1–3, OECD, 1978.

Clay F, Modern School Buildings (3rd edition), Batsford, HMSO, 1929.

Department of Education and Science *Building Bulletins*
Design Notes
Laboratories Investigation Unit Publications, HMSO.

Dent H C, *1870–1970: A Century of Growth in English Education*, Longmans, 1970.

Goldsmith B, *Design Data for Wheelchair Children*, Disabled Living Foundation, 1980.

Goldsmith S, *Designing for the Disabled*, (3rd edition), RIBA, 1976.

Kohl H R, *The Open Classroom*, Methuen, 1970.

Lawrence E, *The Origins and Growth of Modern Education*, Penguin, 1970.

Lowndes G A N, *The Silent Revolution*, OUP, 1937.

Maclure J S, *Educational Documents, England and Wales, 1816 to the present day (4th edition)*, Methuen, 1979.

Maclure J S, *One Hundred Years of London Education*, Allen Lane, 1970.

Marks P, *Principles of Planning*, Batsford, 1901.

Morrisseau J J, *Designing and Planning: The New Schools*, Van Norstrand Rheinhold Co, 1972.

Myles Wright H R, and Gardner M R, *The Design of Nursery & Elementary Schools*, Architectural Press, 1938.

Nursery School Association of Gt Britain, *The New Nursery School: An Appraisal of Current Design NSA*, 1962.

Nellist I, *Buildings for Handicapped Children*, Crosby Lockwood, 1970.

Newsom, J H, *The Child at School*, Penguin, 1950

Otto K, *School Buildings*, Volumes 1 & 2, Iliffe, 1963.

Pearson E, *Trends in School Design*, Macmillan, 1972.

Pedley R, *The Comprehensive School*, Penguin, 1969 (revised edition).

Plans and People: Secondary Education – The Brief and Buildings, Lancashire Education Authority 1973.

Price B, *Technical Colleges and Colleges of Further Education*, Batsford, 1959.

Primary Education in England, Survey by HM Inspectors of Schools, HMSO, 1978.

Robson E R, *School Architecture, 1874.* Leicester University Press, 1972.

Rodhe B, *Teachers and School Building*, OECD, 1976.

Rogers T, *School for the Community*, Routledge & Kegan Paul, 1971.

Roth A, *New School Building*, Thames & Hudson, 1966.

Royal Institute of British Architects, *Modern Schools*, RIBA 1939

Royal Institute of British Architects, *New School*, RIBA, 1948.

Rubinstein D, and Simon B, *The Evolution of the Comprehensive School, 1926–66*, Routledge & Kegan Paul, 1969.

Schools – For the New Needs, Architectural Record, F W Dodge Corporation, 1956.

Savage G, *The Planning & Equipment of School Science Blocks*, John Murray, 1964.

Seaborne M, *Primary School Design*, Routledge & Kegan Paul, 1971.

Seaborne M, and Lowe R, *The English School: Its Architecture and Organisation*
Volume 1, 1370–1870
Volume 2, 1870–1970
Routledge & Kegan Paul, 1977

Selleck R W, *The New Education, The English Background, 1870–1914*, Pitman, 1968.

Service A (ed), *Edwardian Architecture and Its Origins*, Architectural Press, 1975.

Sharp J, *Open School*, Dent, 1973.

Singh Sandhu J, and Hendriks Jansen H, *Environmental Design for Handicapped Children*, Saxon House, 1976.

Stillman C G, and Cleary R C, *The Modern School*, Architectural Press, 1949.

Stone P A, *Building Economy (2nd edition)*, Pergamon, 1976.

Stone P A, *Building Design Evaluation: Costs in Use*, Spon, 1980.

Taylor A, and Vlastos G, *School Zone, Learning Environments for Children*, Van Norstrand Rheinhold Co, 1975.

Taylor G and Saunders G B, *The Law of Education (8th edition)*, Butterworth, 1976.

Taylor J, *The Science Lecture Room*, Cambridge UP, 1967.

Ward C (ed), *British School Buildings; Designs and Appraisals, 1964–74*, Architectural Press, 1976.

Whitbread N, *The Evolution of the Nursery–Infant School*, Routledge & Kegan Paul, 1972.

Credits

Chief Architects to the School Board for London, the LCC and the GLC, 1879–1983

Chief architects to the School Board for London: when the LCC took over the responsibilities of the Board in 1904 Bailey was appointed as Architect to the Education Department until he retired in 1910.

E R Robson   1871–1884
T J Bailey   1884–1904

Architects to the London County Council

W E Riley   1904–1919
G Topham Forrest   1919–1935
E P Wheeler   1935–1939
F R Hiorns   1939–1941
J H Forshaw   1941–1946
Sir Robert Matthew   1946–1953
Sir Leslie Martin   1953–1956
Sir Hubert Bennett   1956–1965

Architects to the Greater London Council

Sir Hubert Bennett   1965–1970
Sir Roger Walters   1971–1978
F W Pooley   1978–1979

Director of Architecture, GLC/ILEA

P E Jones   1979–

Education Architects to the Inner London Education Authority

M C L Powell   1965–1971
C E Hartland   1971–1972
G H Wigglesworth   1972–1974
P E Jones   1974–1982
B E T Noble   1983–

Schools Architects to the LCC/ILEA

M C L Powell   1956–1965
C E Hartland   1965–1971
J J Pace   1971–1974

Produced in the Department of Architecture and Civic Design, Greater London Council.

Job Architects
All architects or designers of the buildings illustrated are named, where known, in the Index

Structural Engineering
Design work was normally carried out by the Structural Engineering Section or Division of the LCC or GLC, Department of Architecture and Civic Design.

Environmental Services
Design work was normally carried out and supervised by the Engineering Section of the LCC or GLC Department of Mechanical and Electrical Engineering.

Drawings
Produced by members of the Education Branch, Department of Architecture and Civic Design.

Photographs
LCC/GLC Photographic Unit or reproduced by courtesy of The Architectural Press.

Graphics and Book Design
John Beake and Joe Hale.

Editorial Control
Coralie Davies and David Atwell. Any enquiries regarding the contents of this book should be addressed to the Principal Information Officer, Department of Architecture and Civic Design.

Manuscript Typing
Laura Hughes and Vivien Bucke.

Index